I0483421

Car Shots

Because a picture's worth a bunch of words ☺

Copyright 2014
GTC Press
Indianapolis, IN USA
Ken O. Eldib

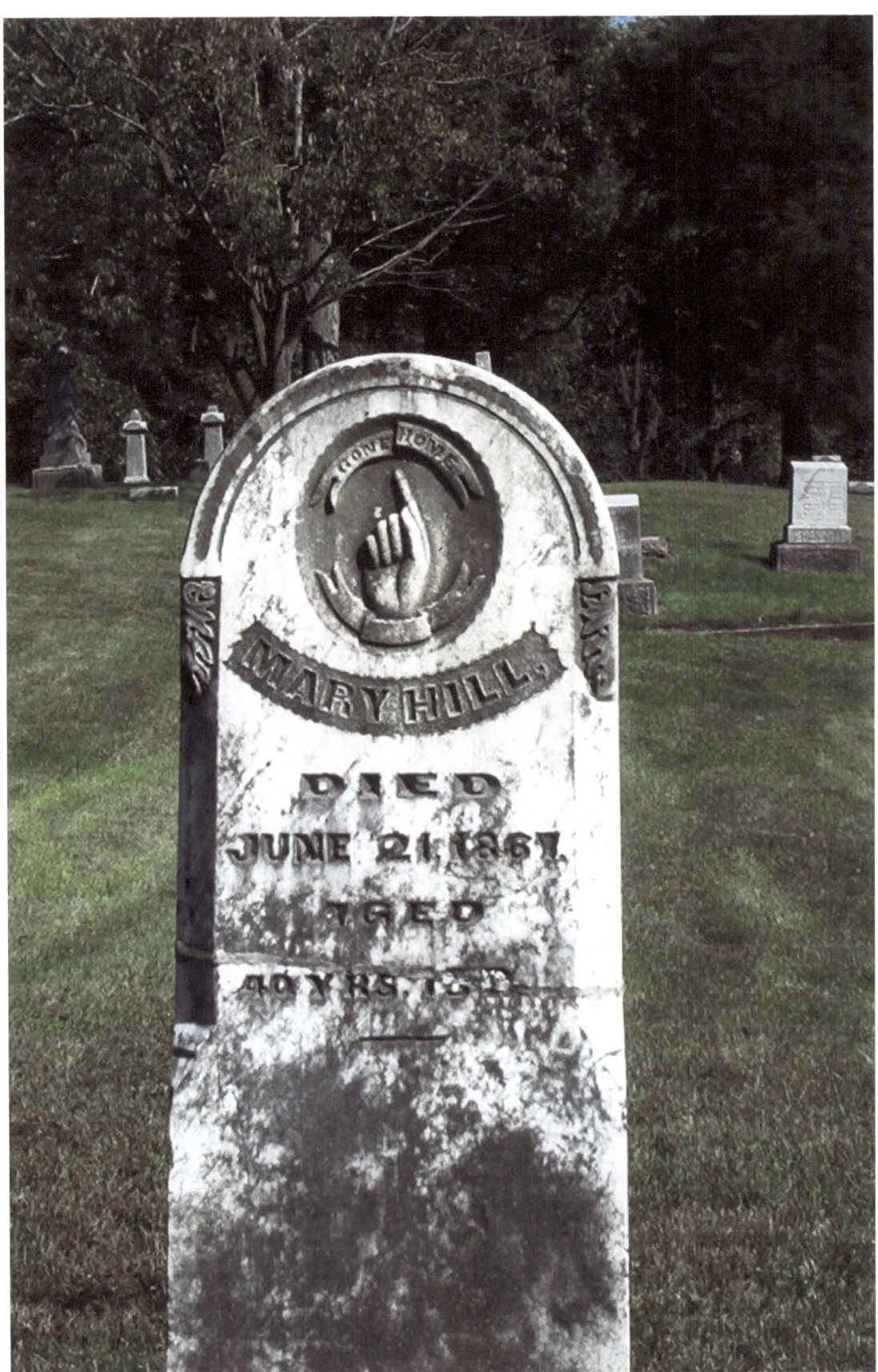

Indiana

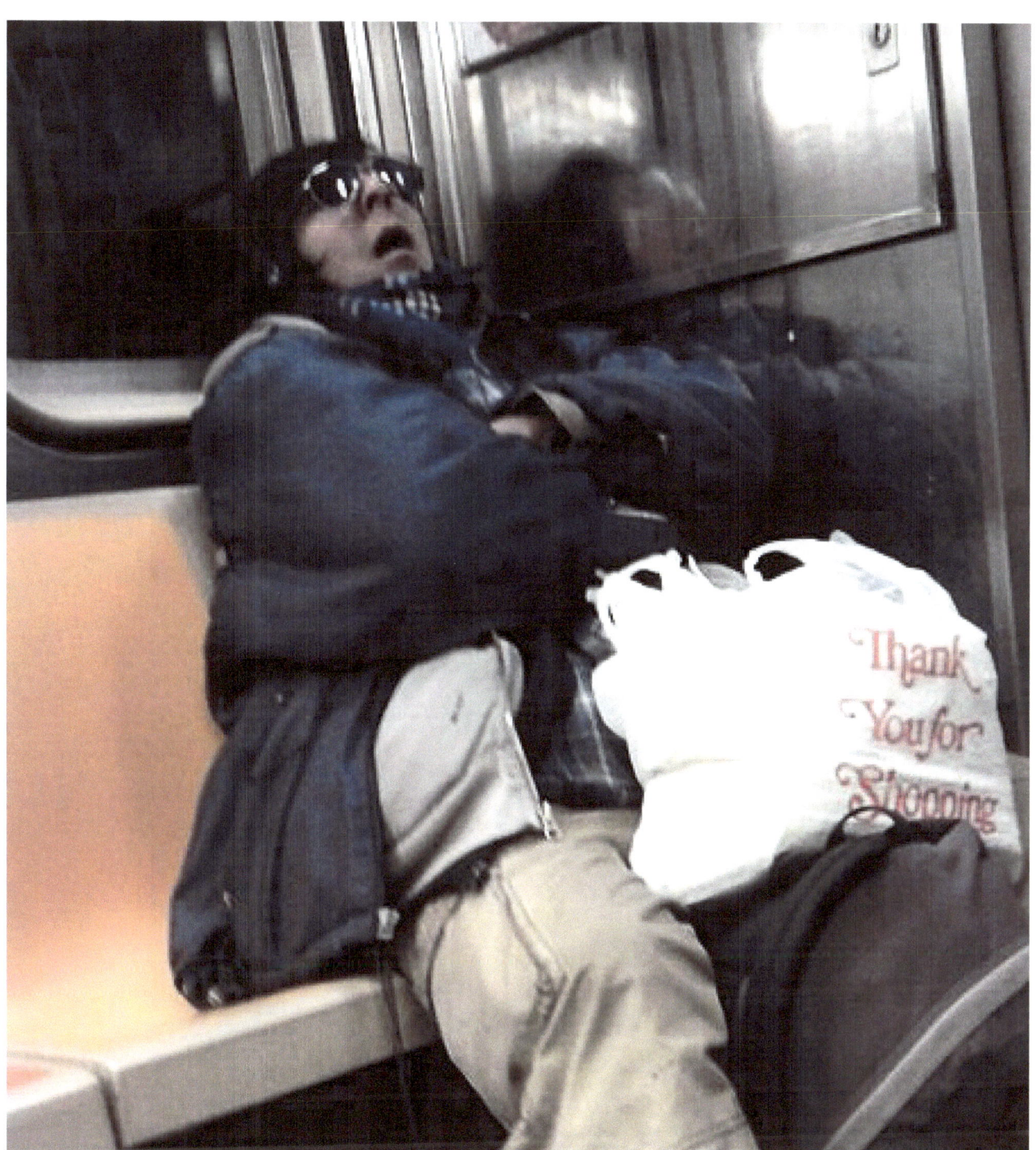

New York City

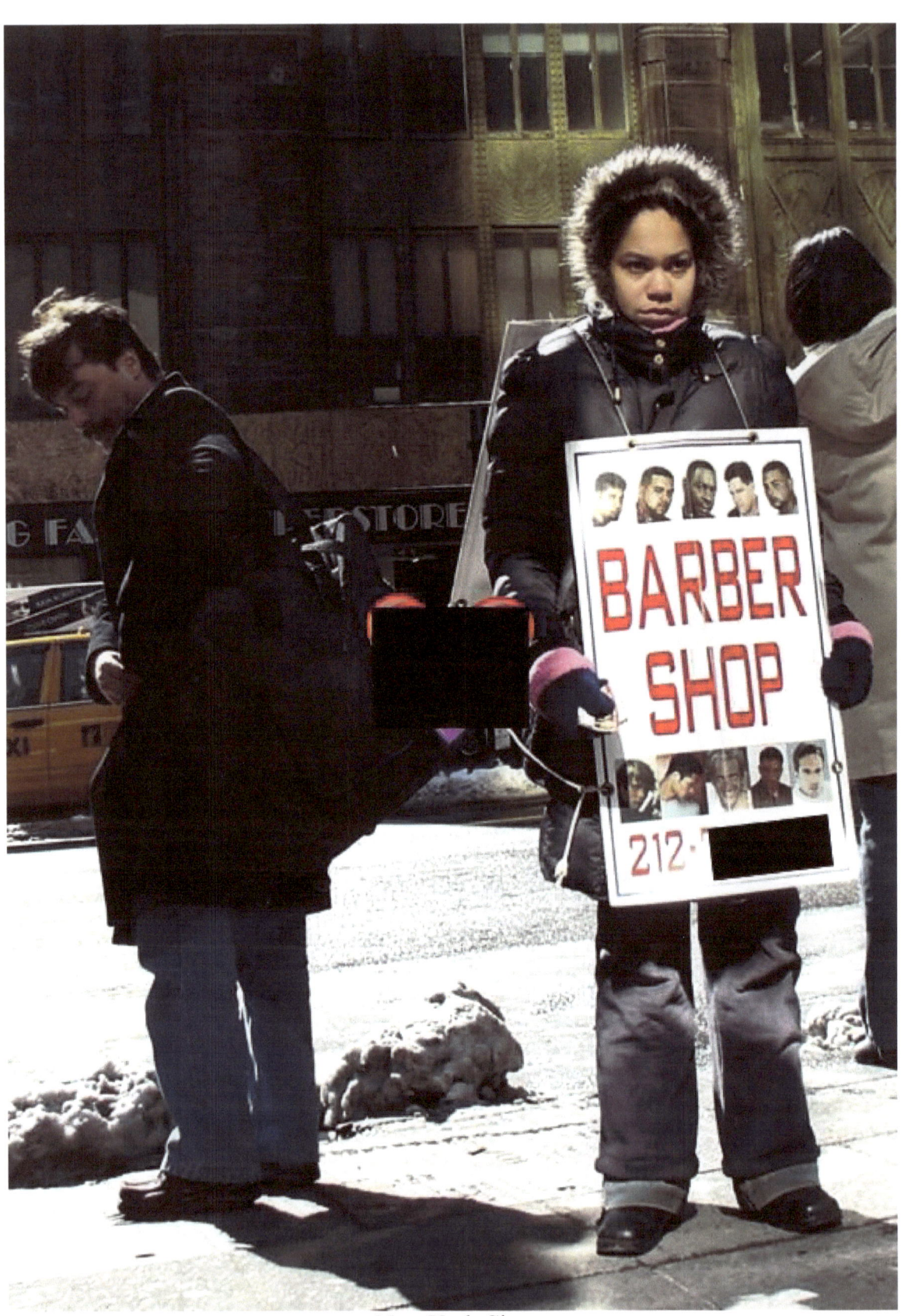

New York City

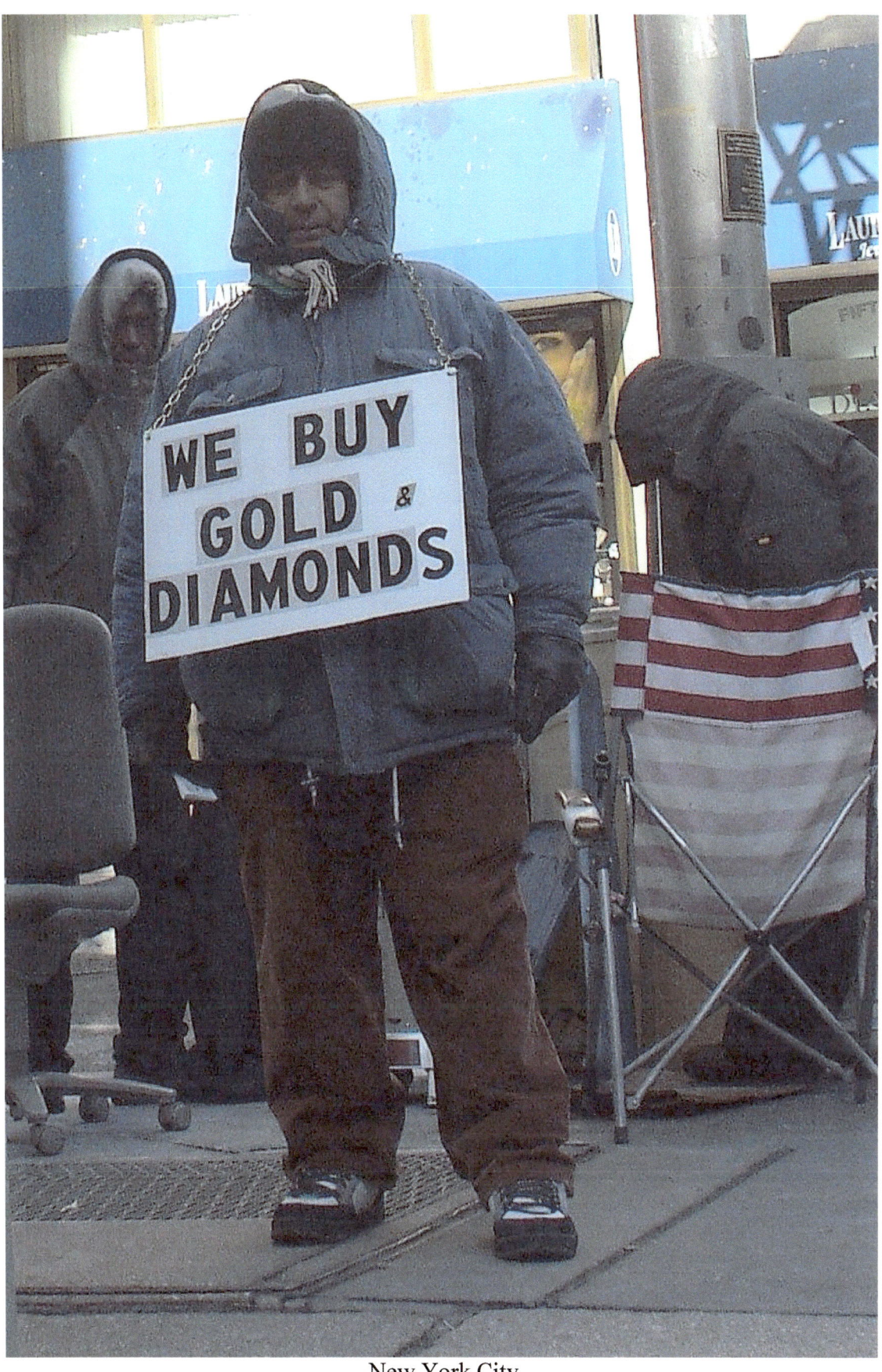

New York City

BAPTIST CHURCH

THOU SHALT HAVE NO OTHER GODS BEFORE ME

Indiana

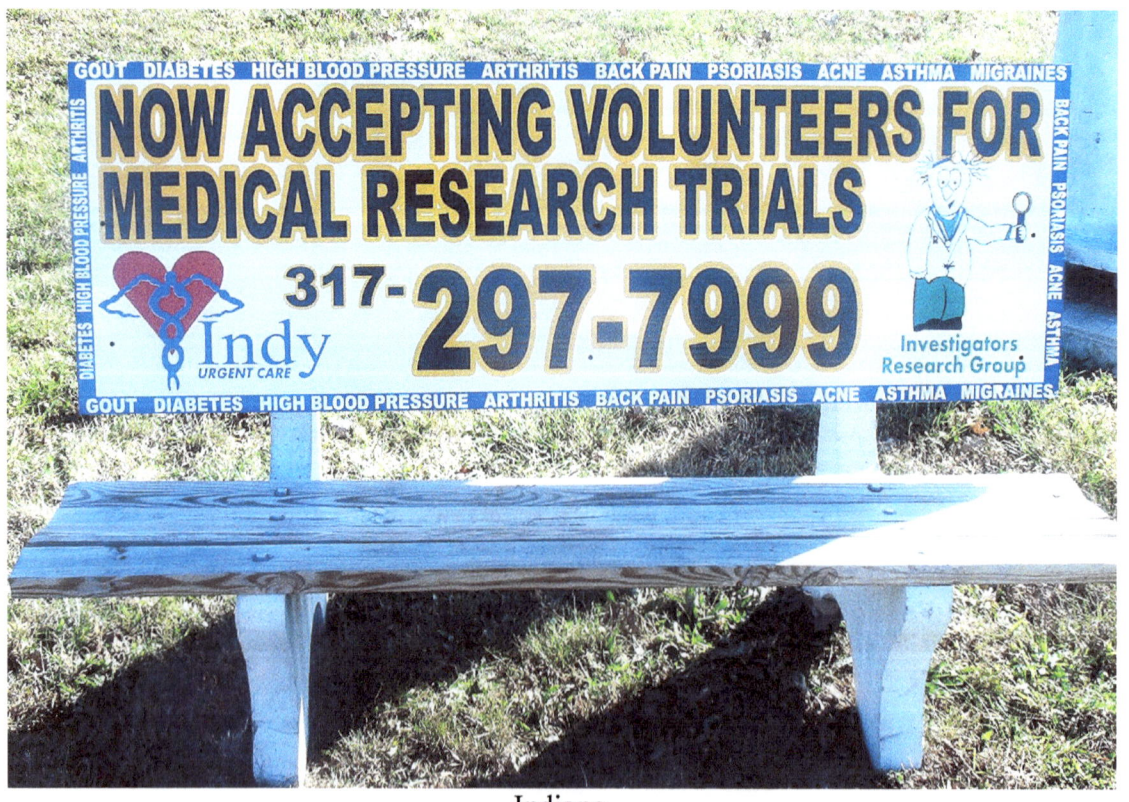

Indiana

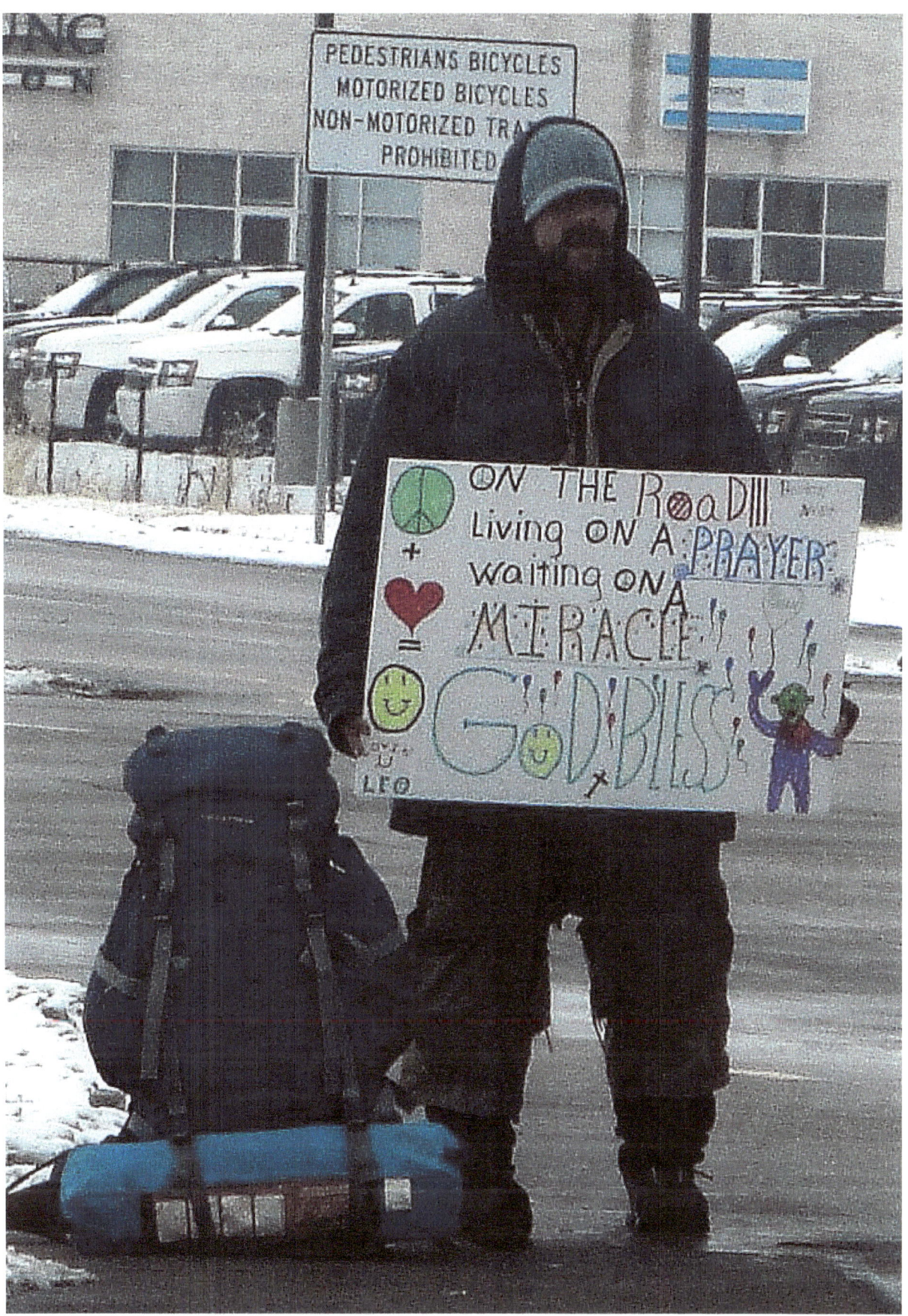

Indiana

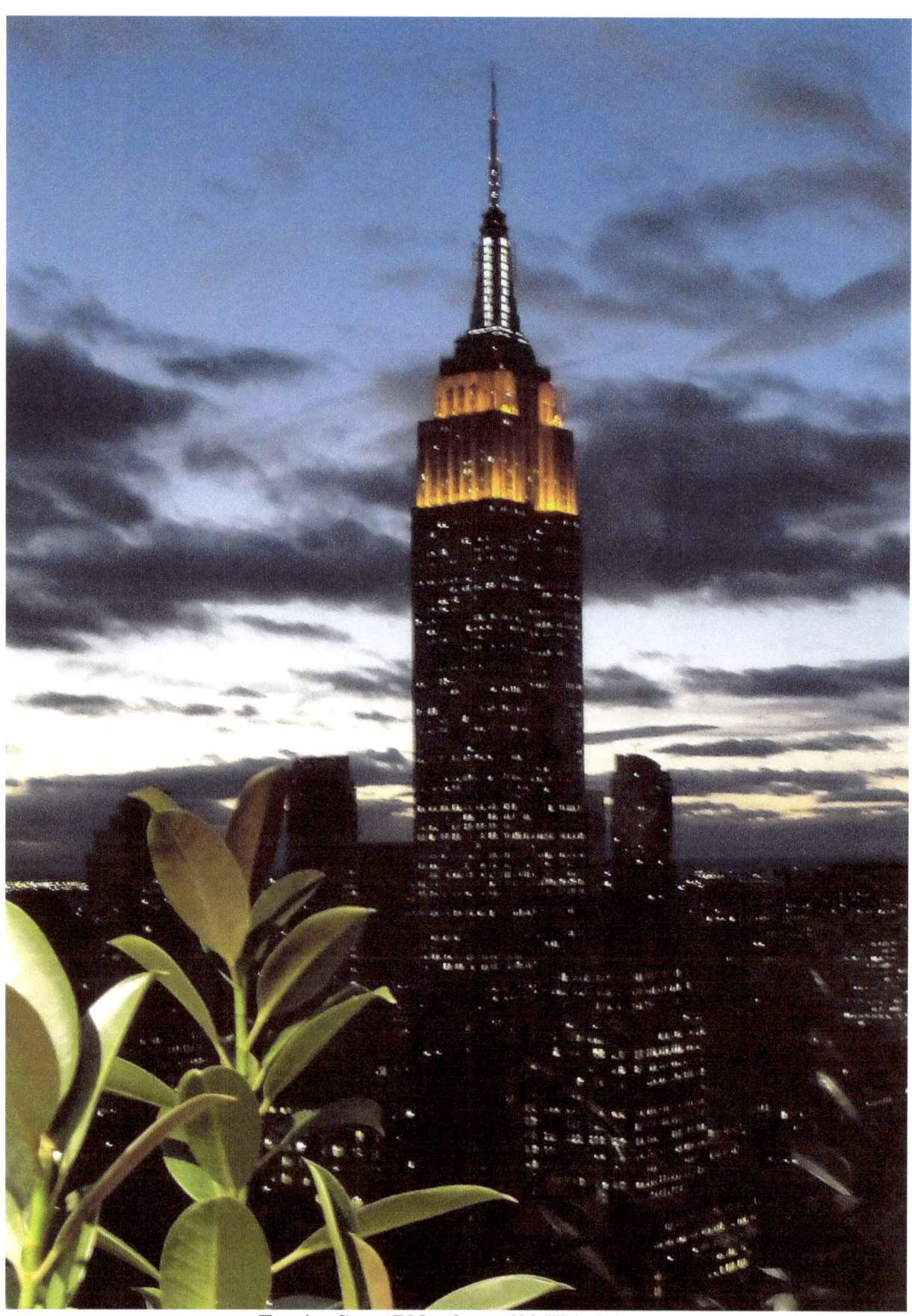

Empire State Bldg. from 600 Third Ave.

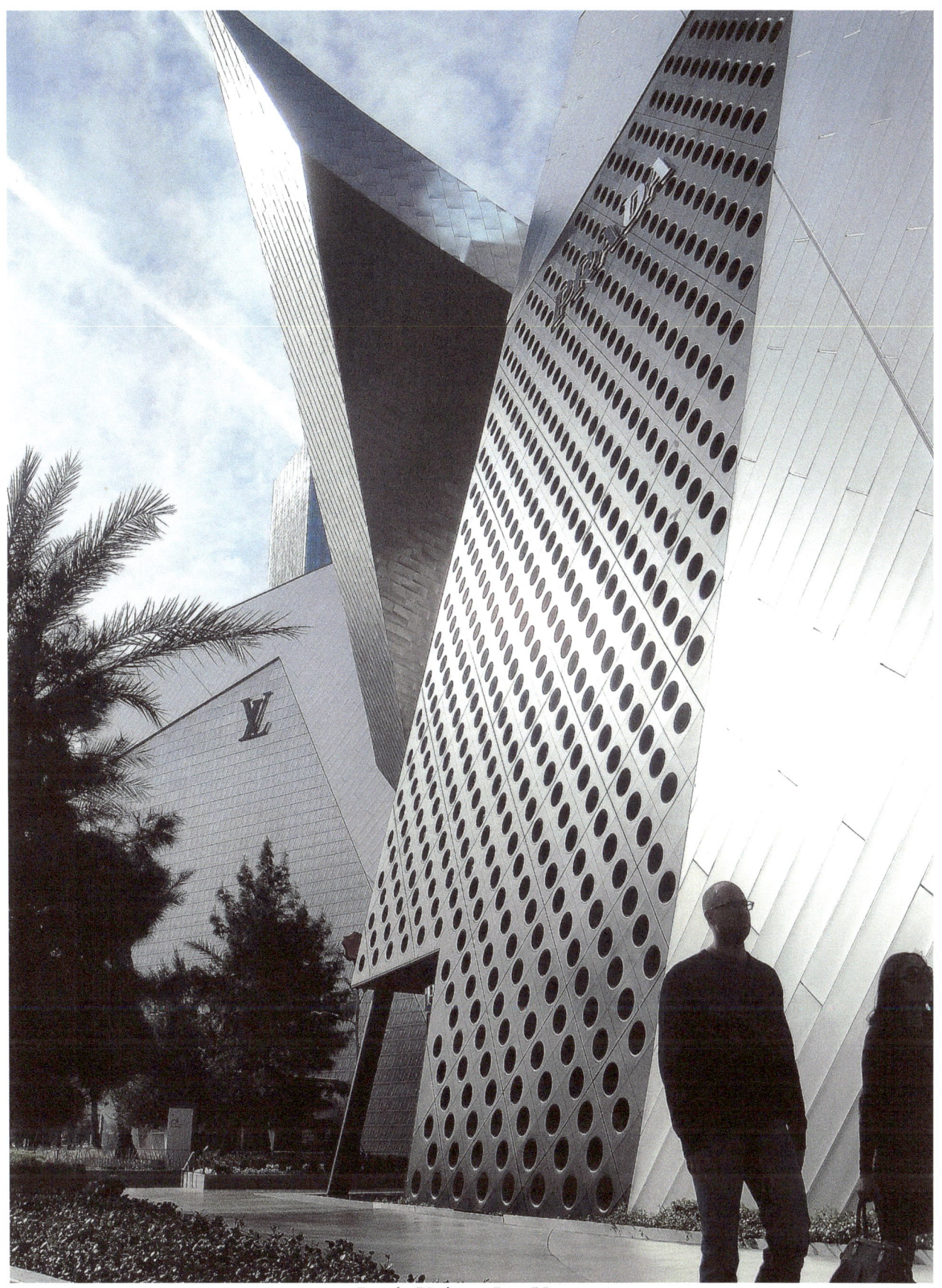

Louis Vuitton Las Vegas

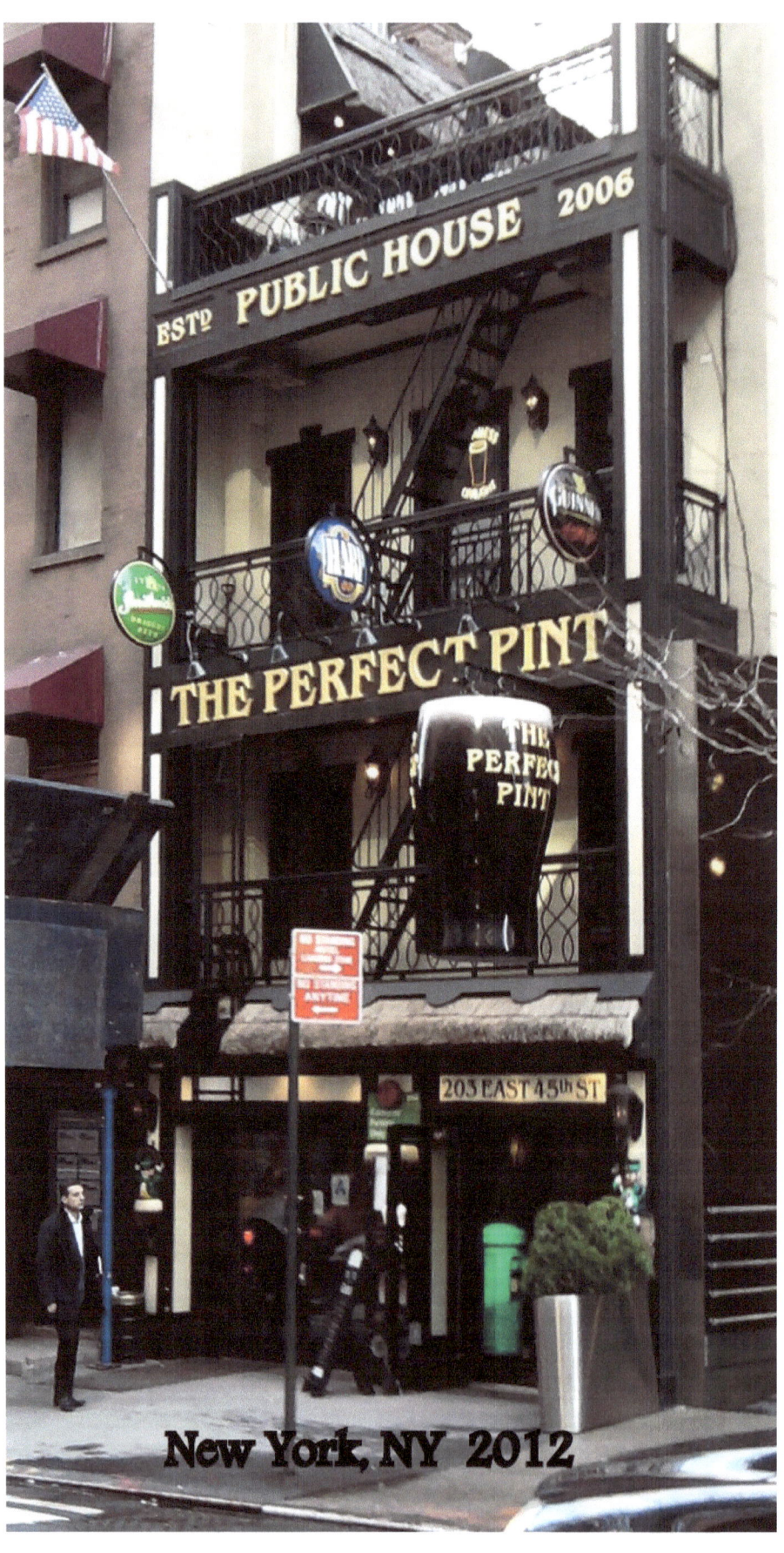

New York, NY 2012

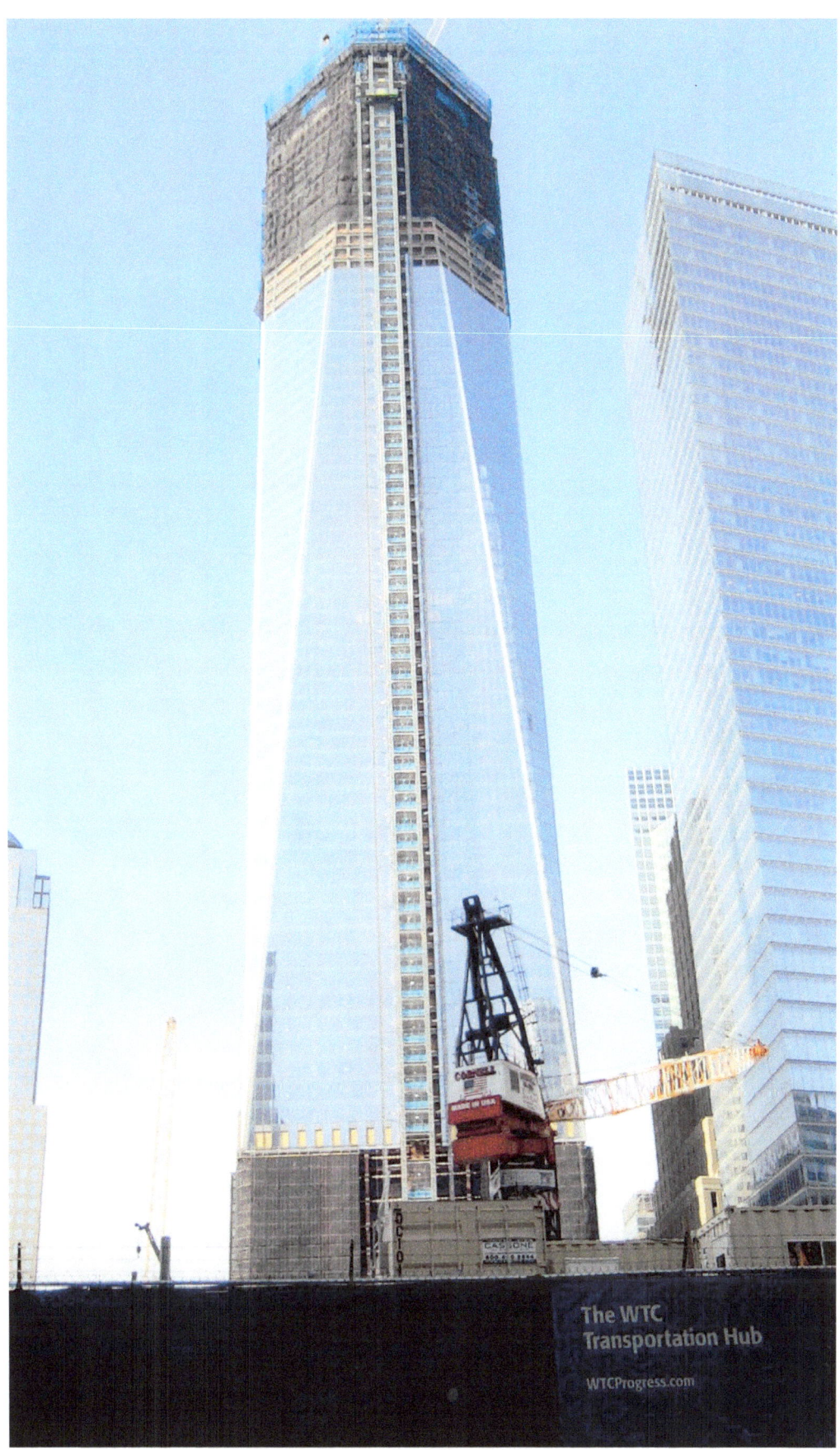

The WTC
Transportation Hub

WTCProgress.com

Tower One Jan. 2012

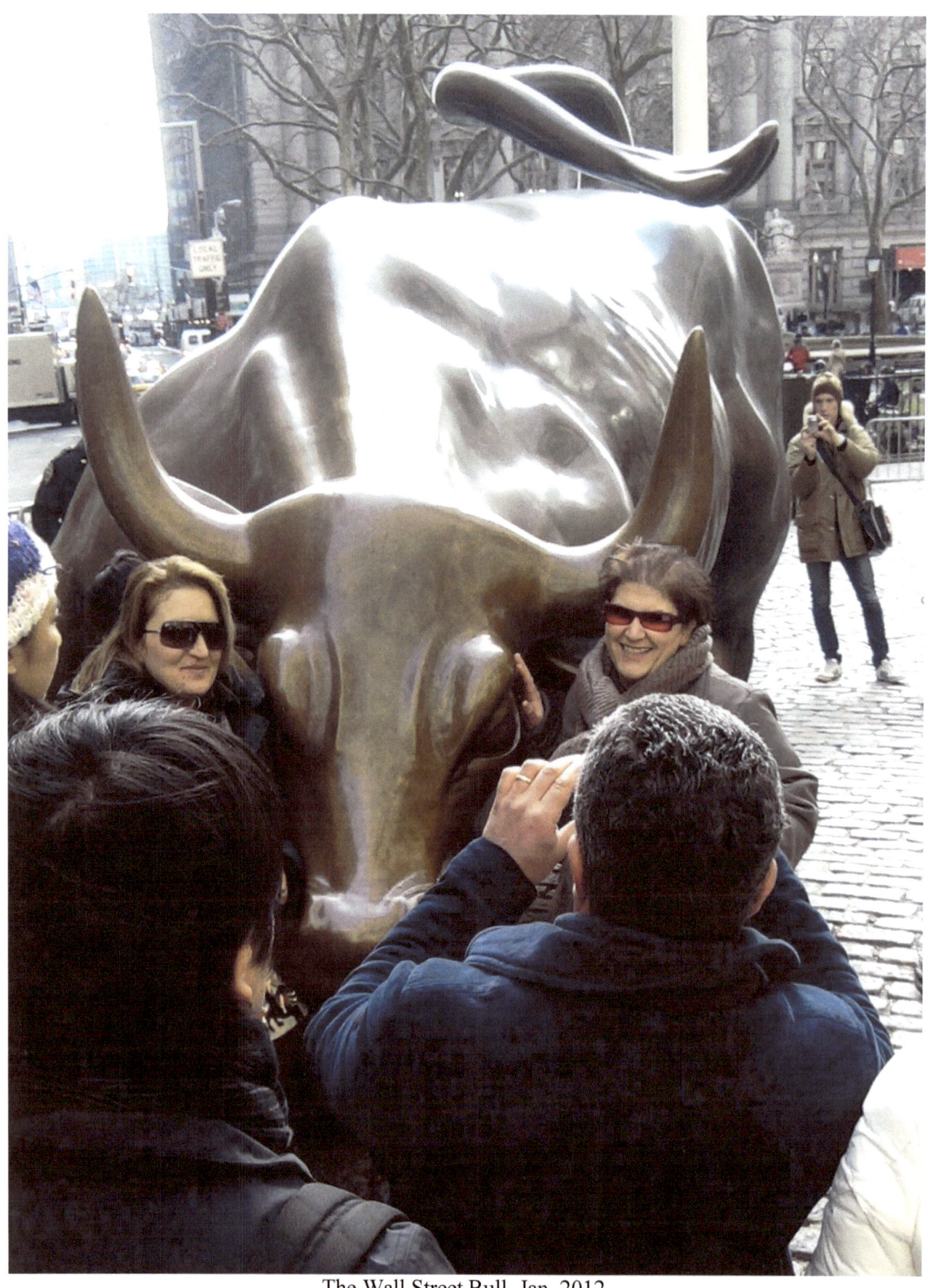

The Wall Street Bull, Jan. 2012

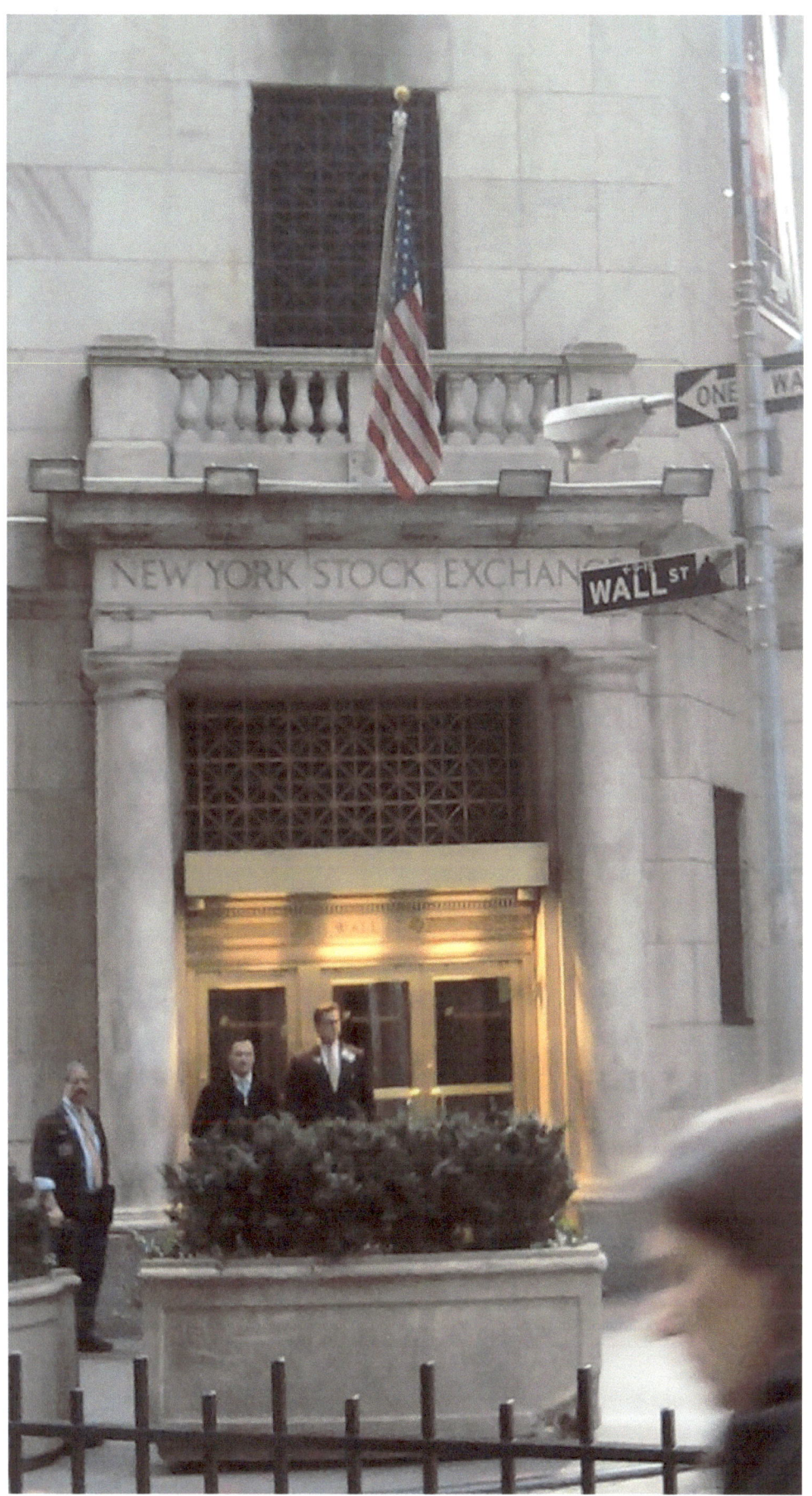

New York Stock Exchange Jan. 2012… watching our money

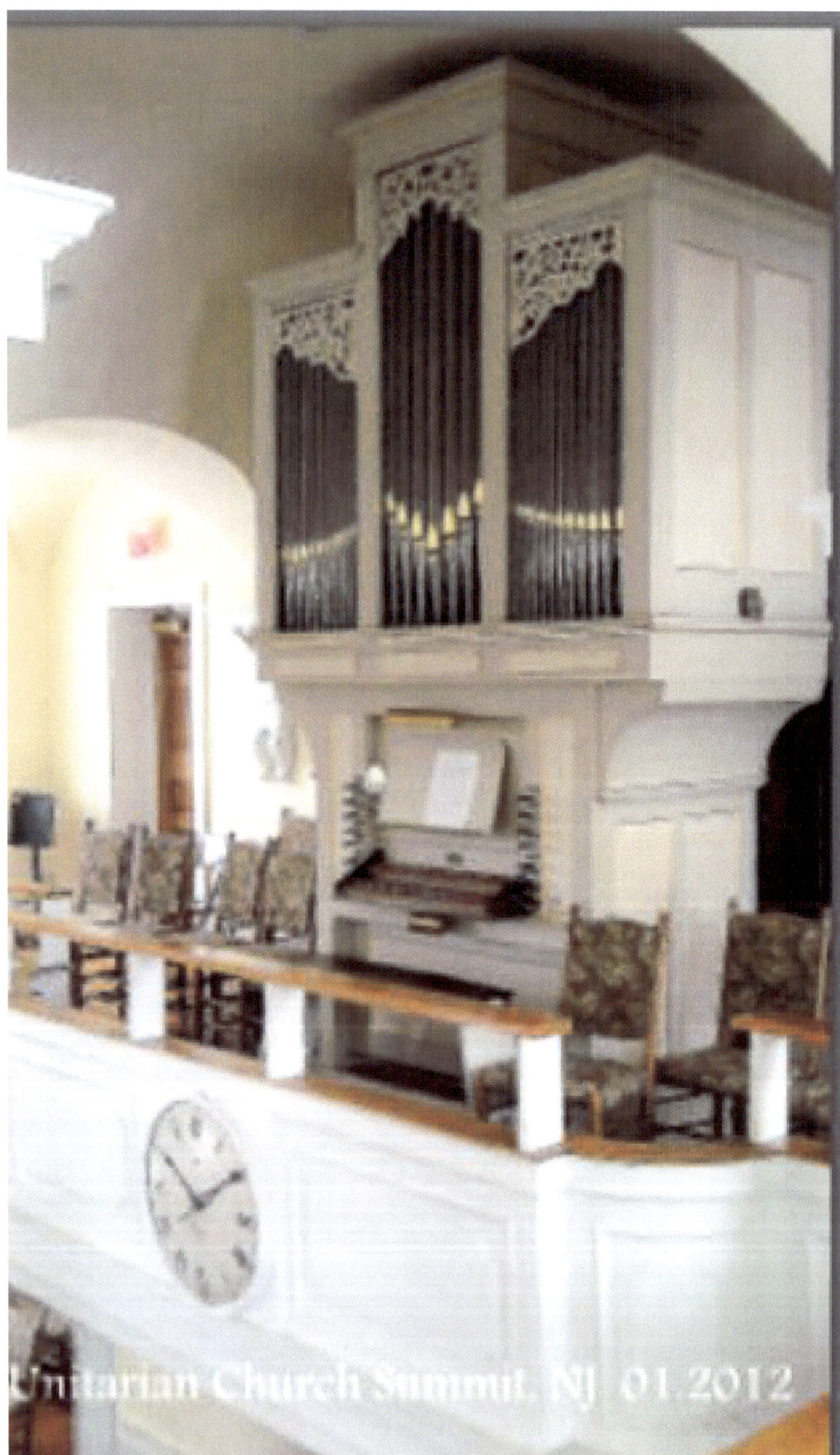
Unitarian Church Summit, NJ 01 2012

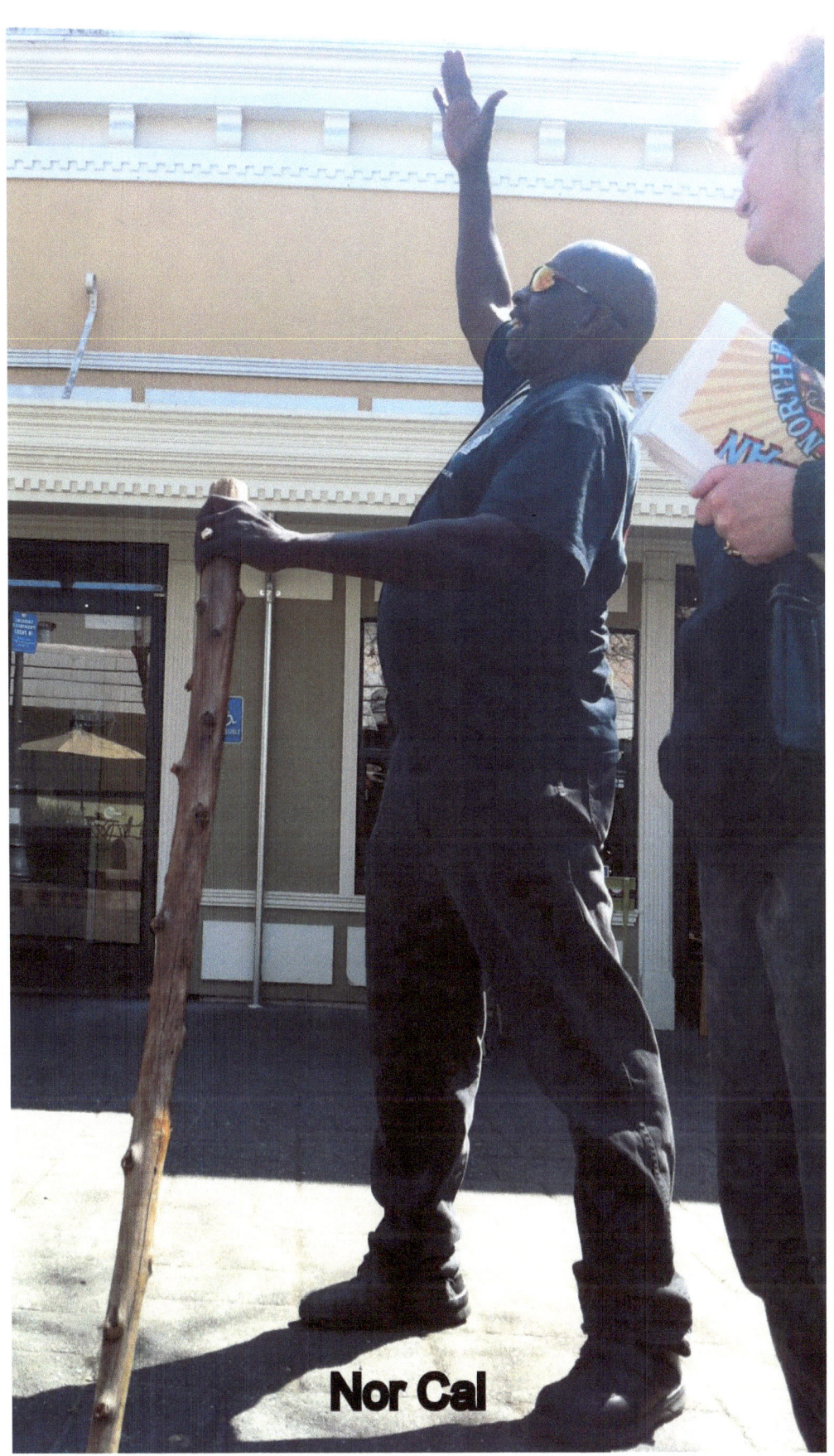

Nor Cal

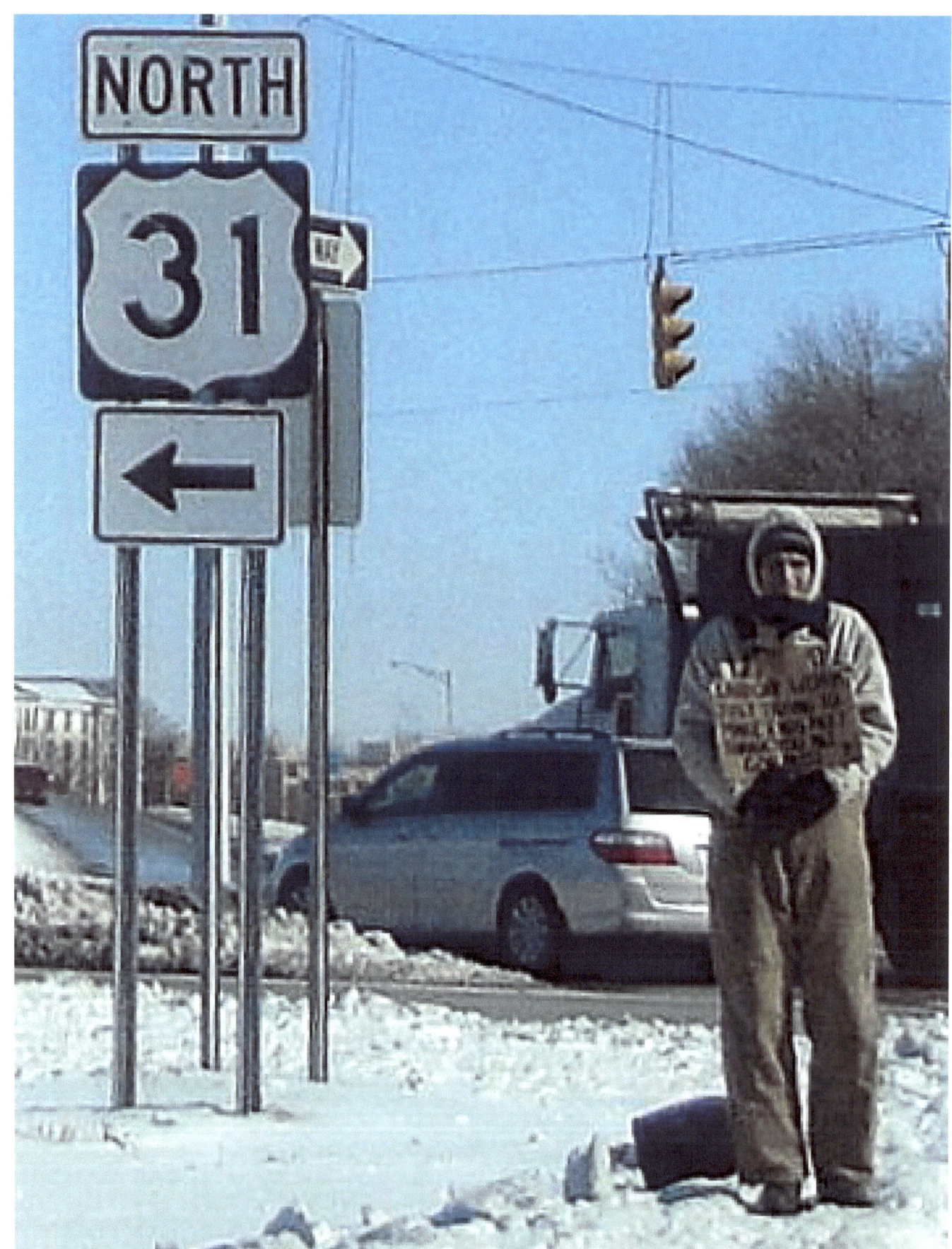

Indiana

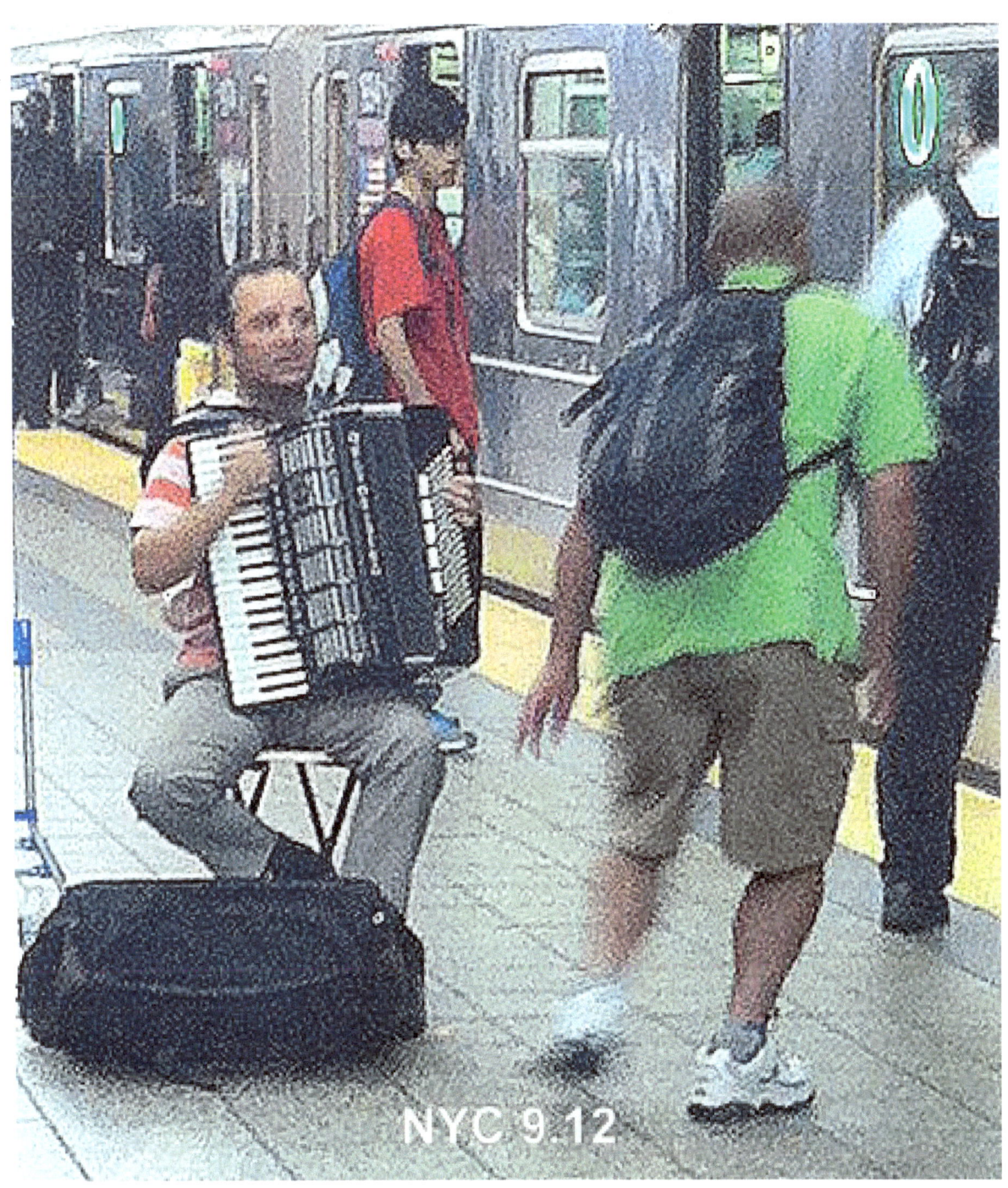

NYC 9.12

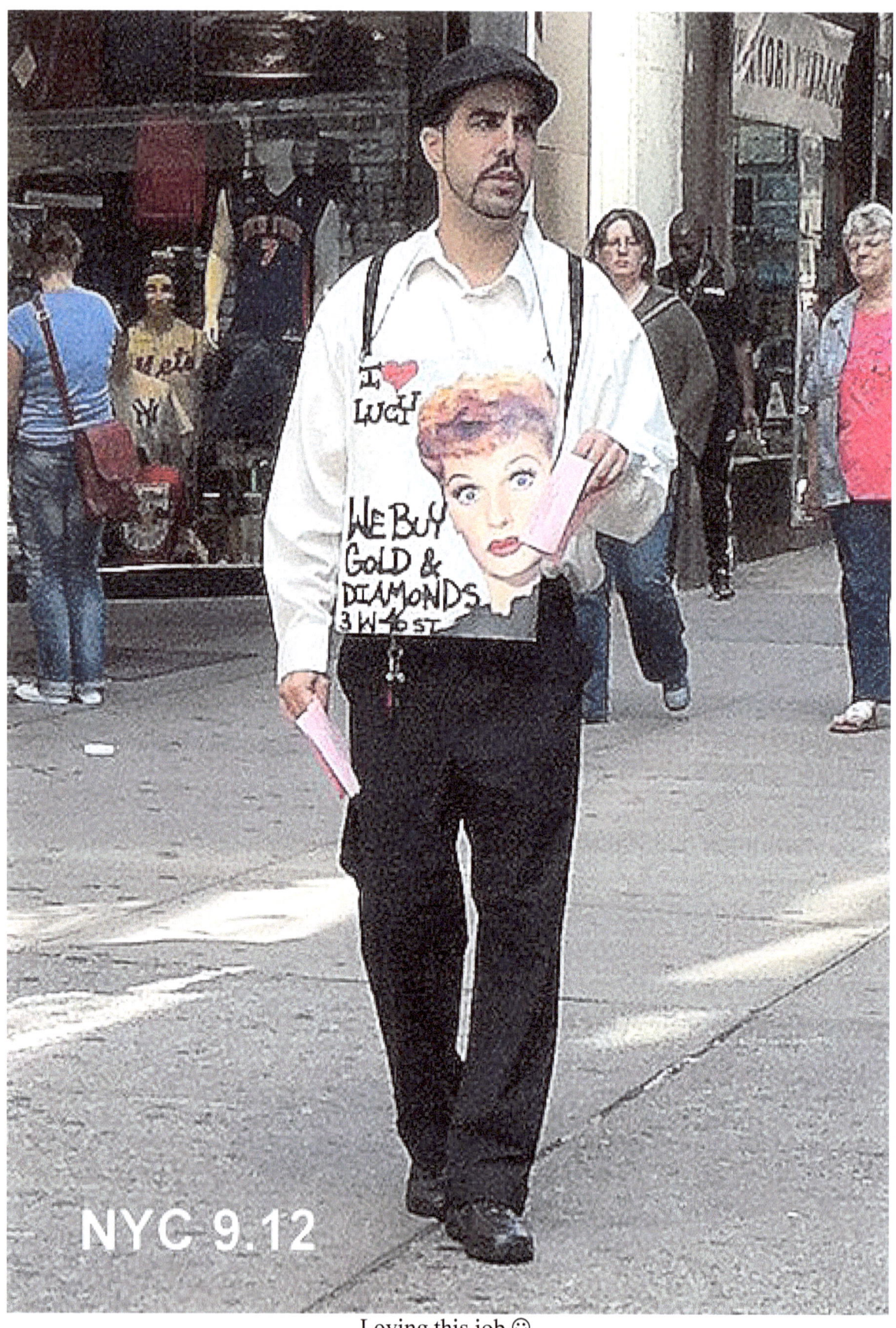

NYC 9.12

Loving this job ☺

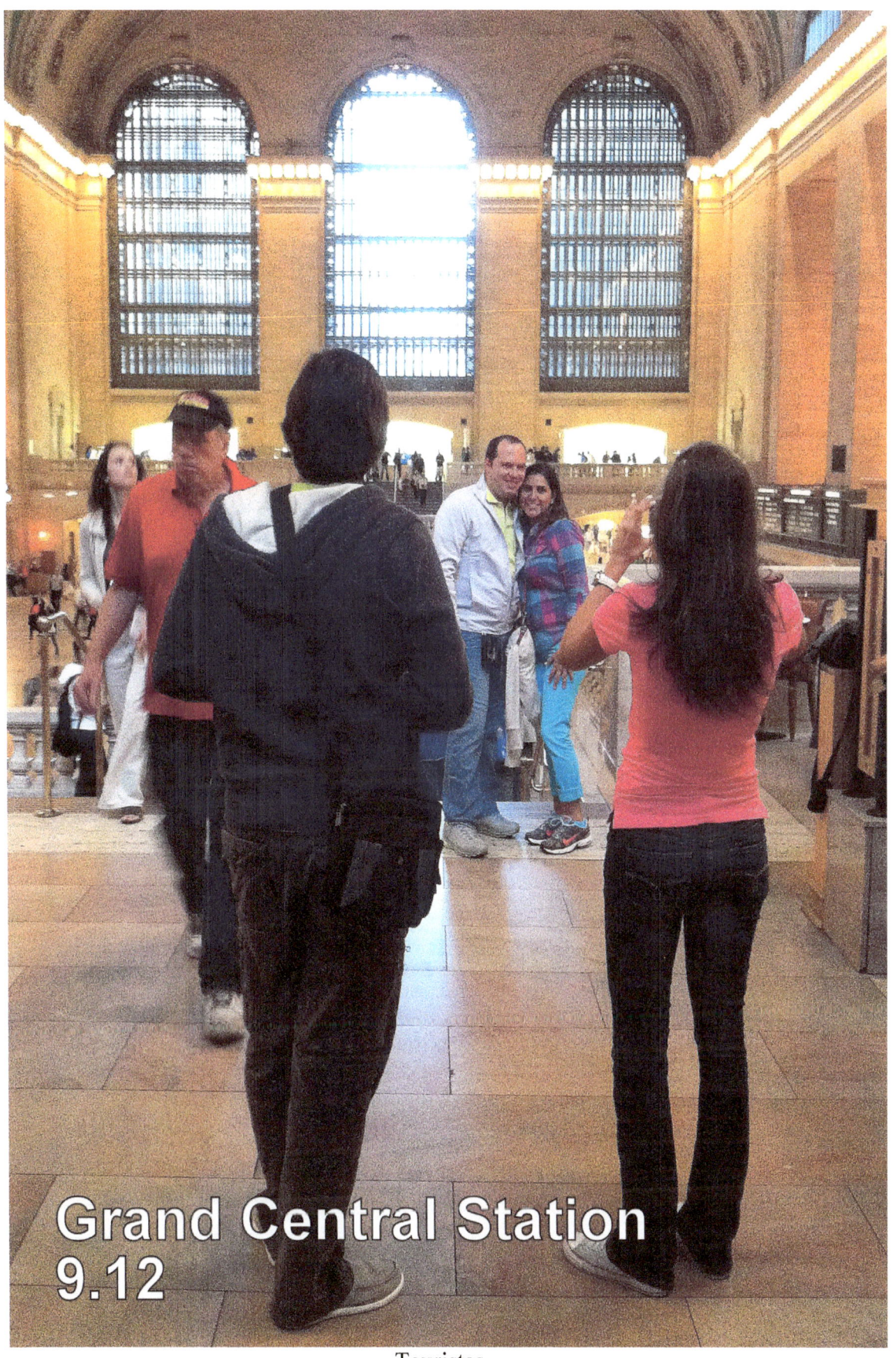

Grand Central Station
9.12

Touristas…

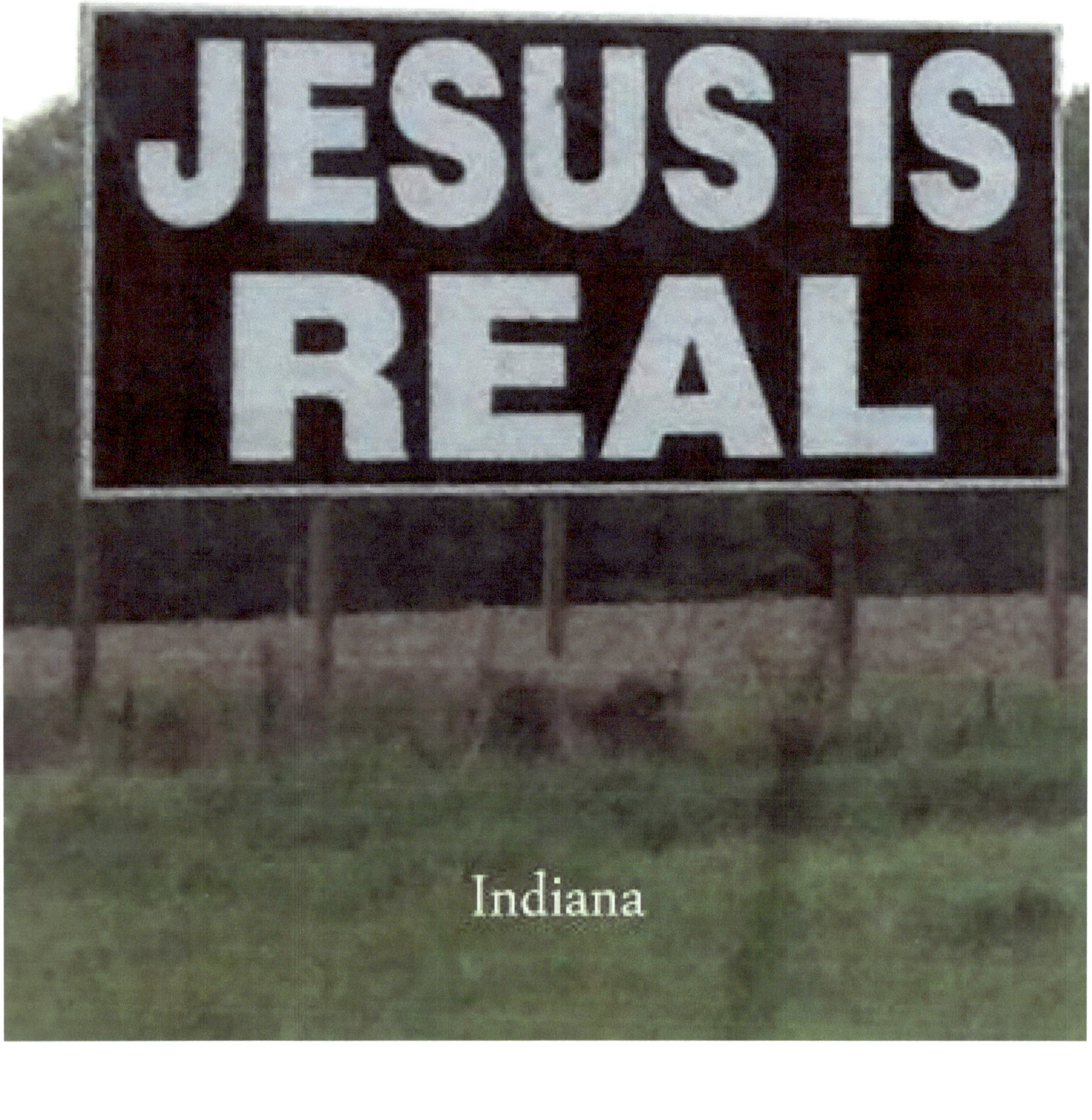

JESUS IS REAL

Indiana

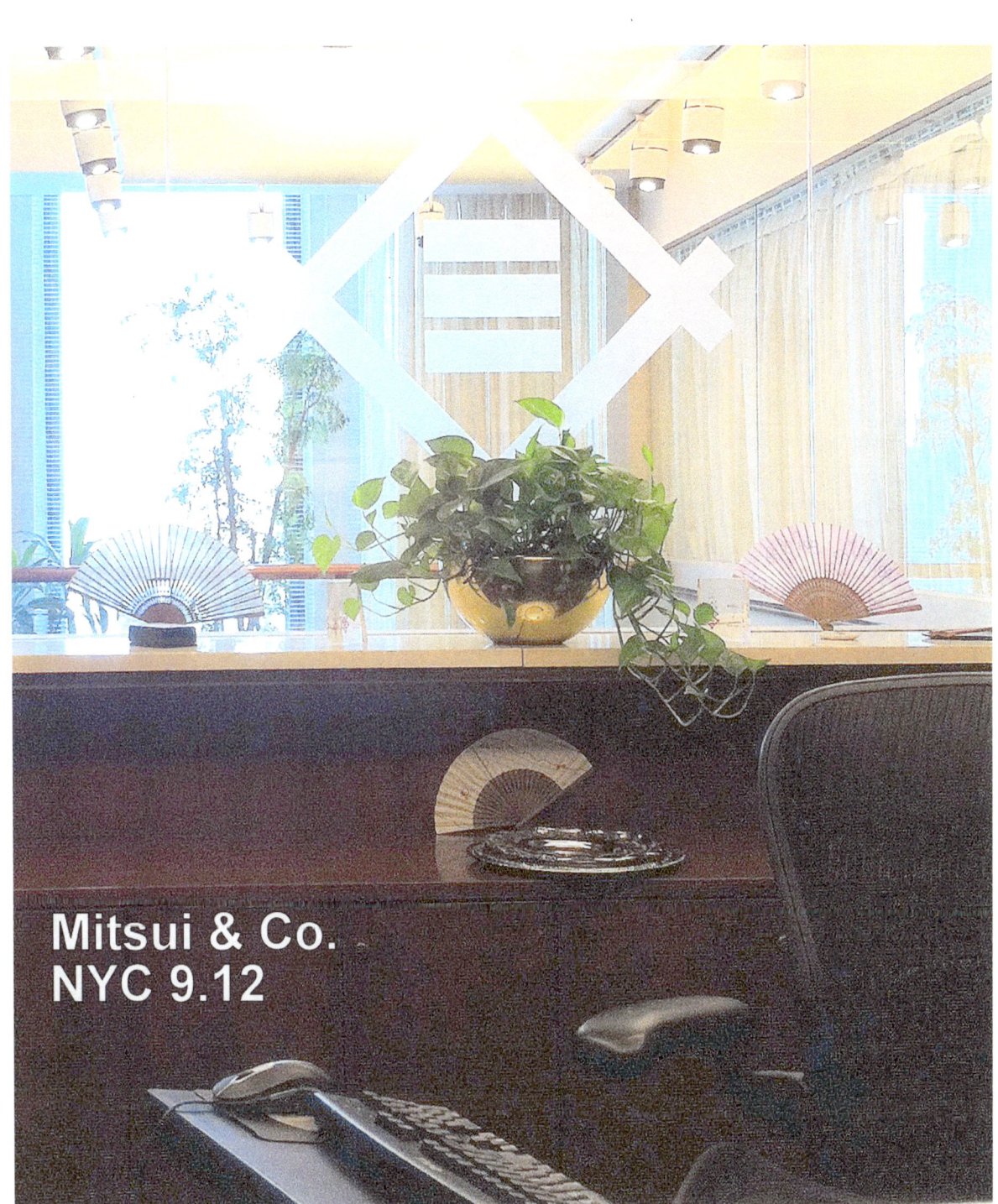

Mitsui & Co.
NYC 9.12

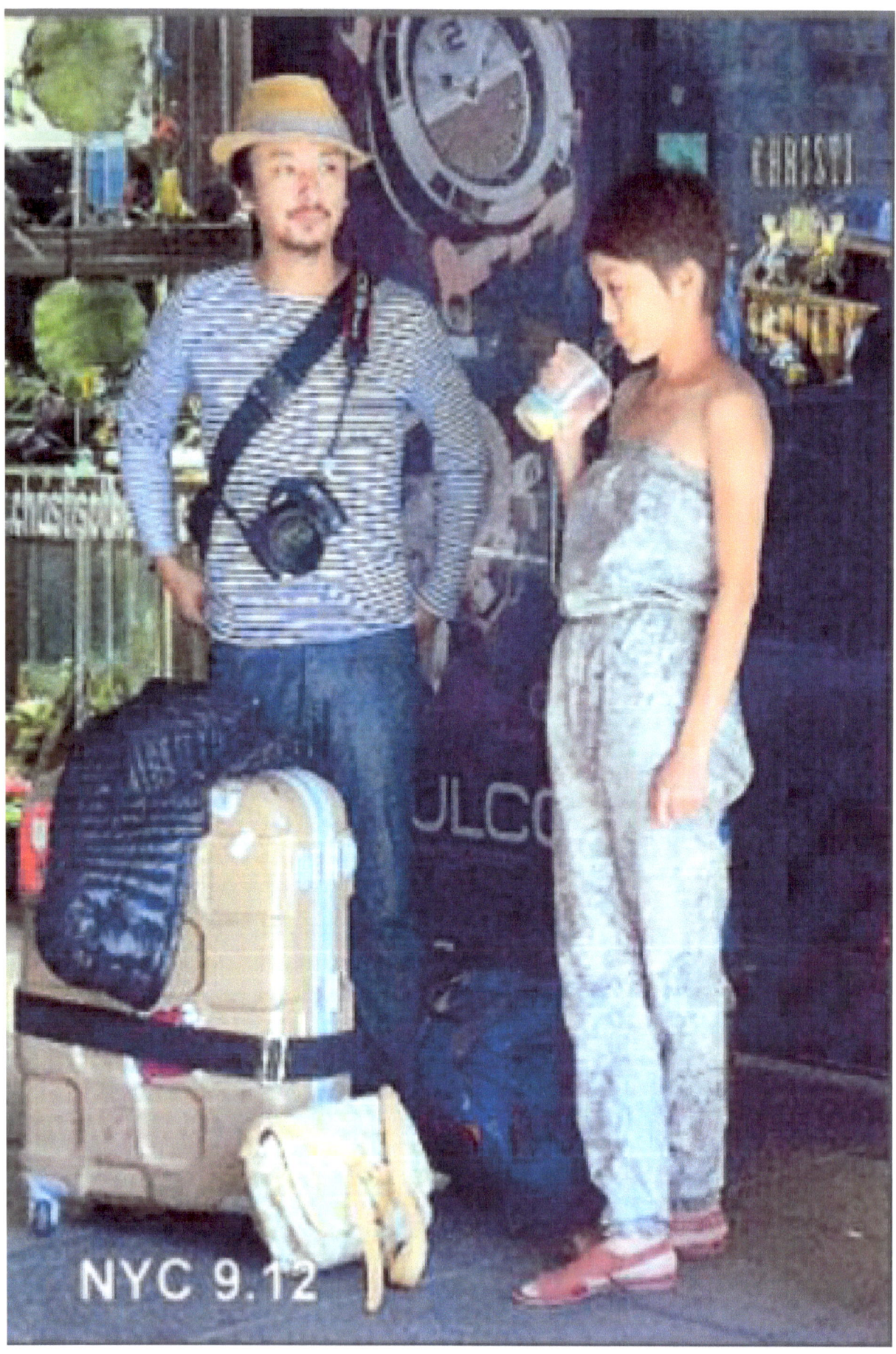

NYC 9.12

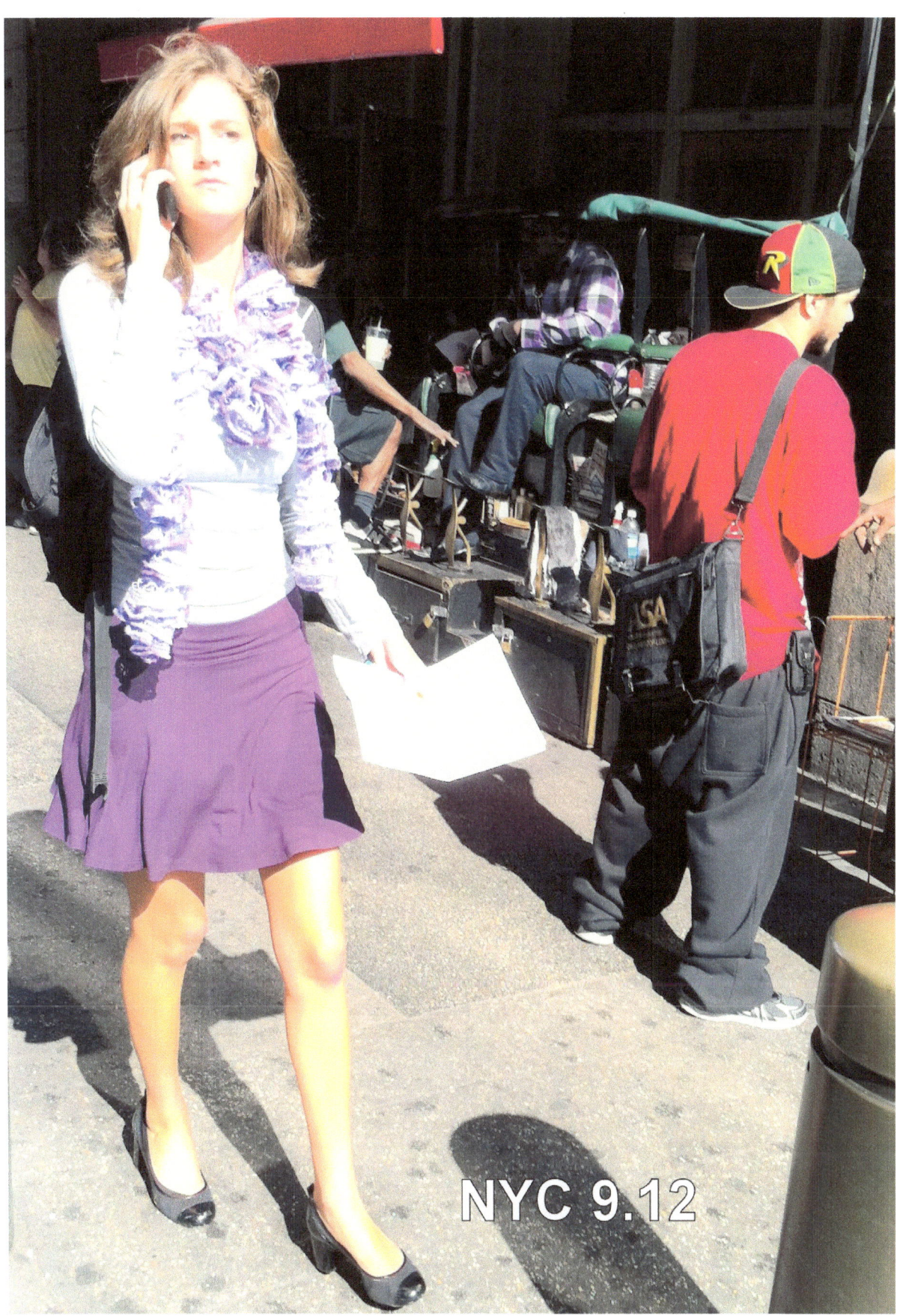

NYC 9.12

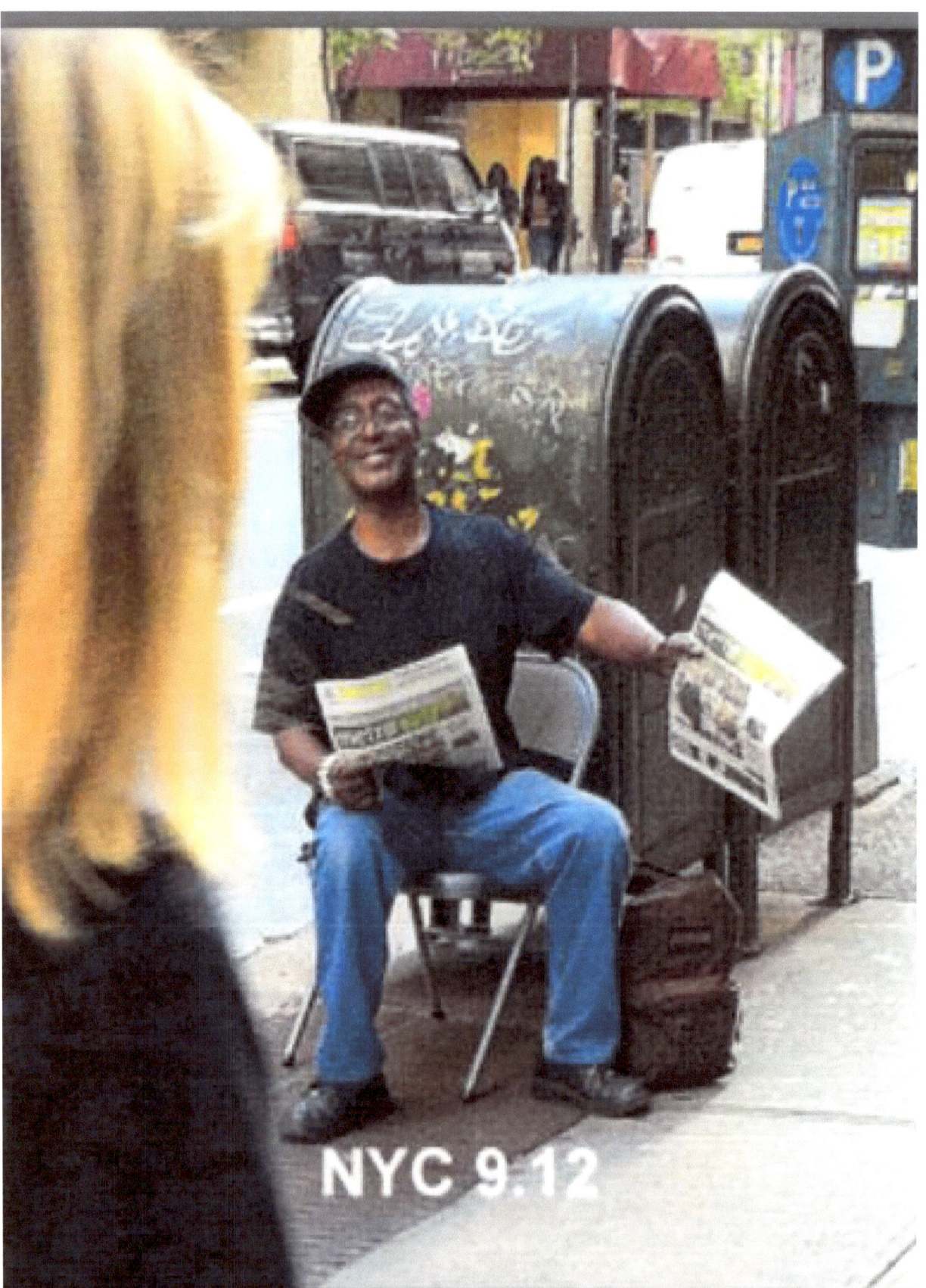

NYC 9.12

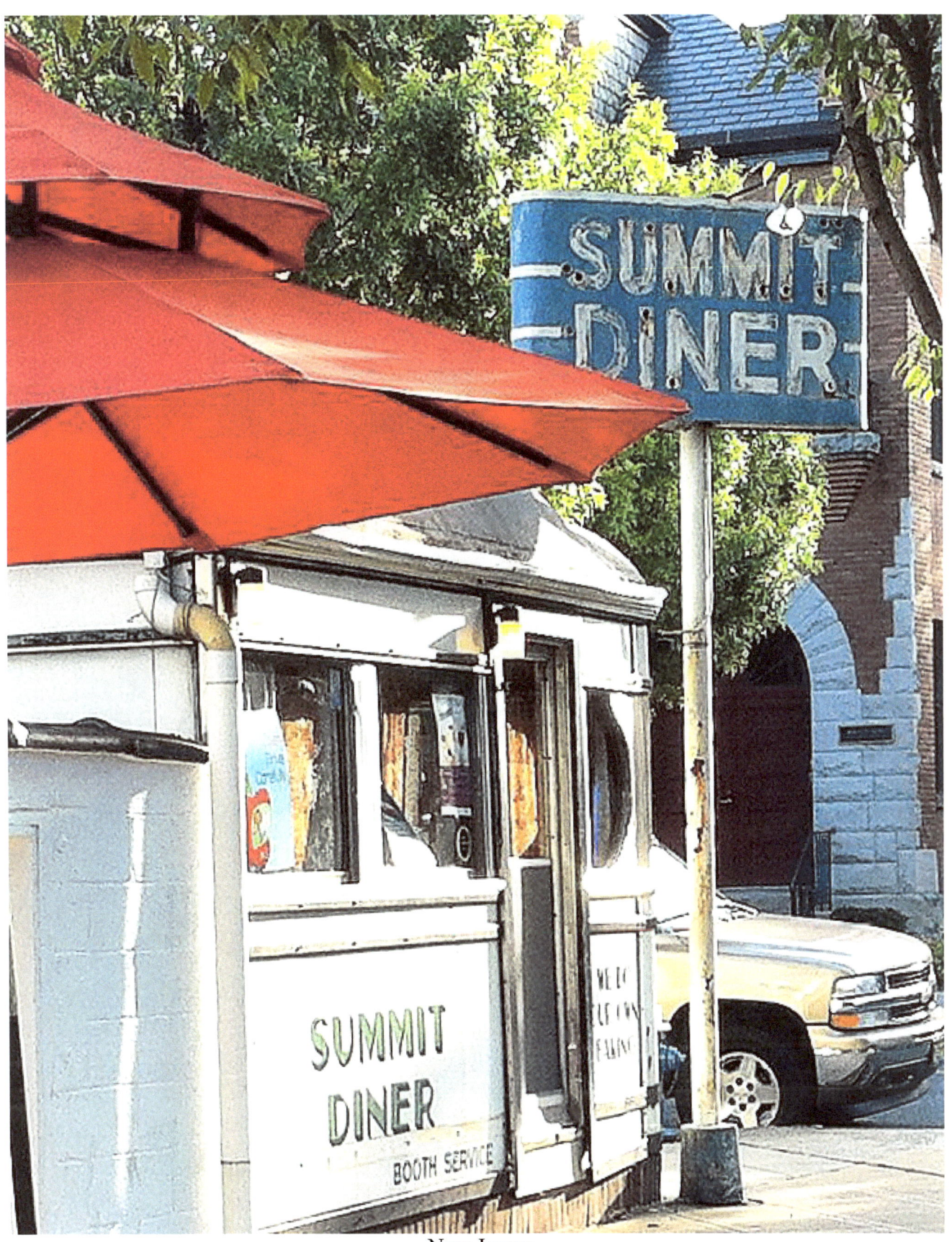

New Jersey

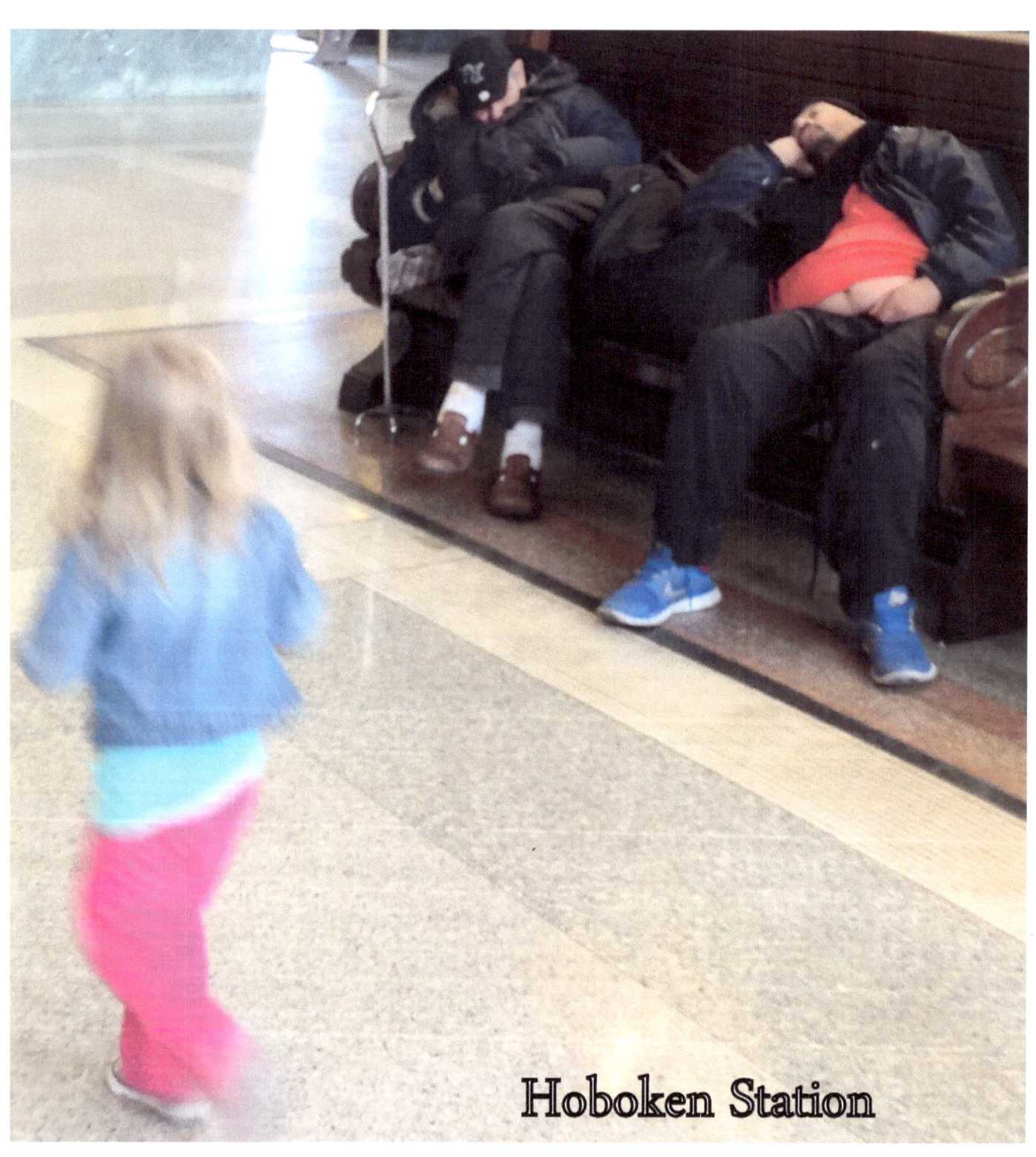

Hoboken Station

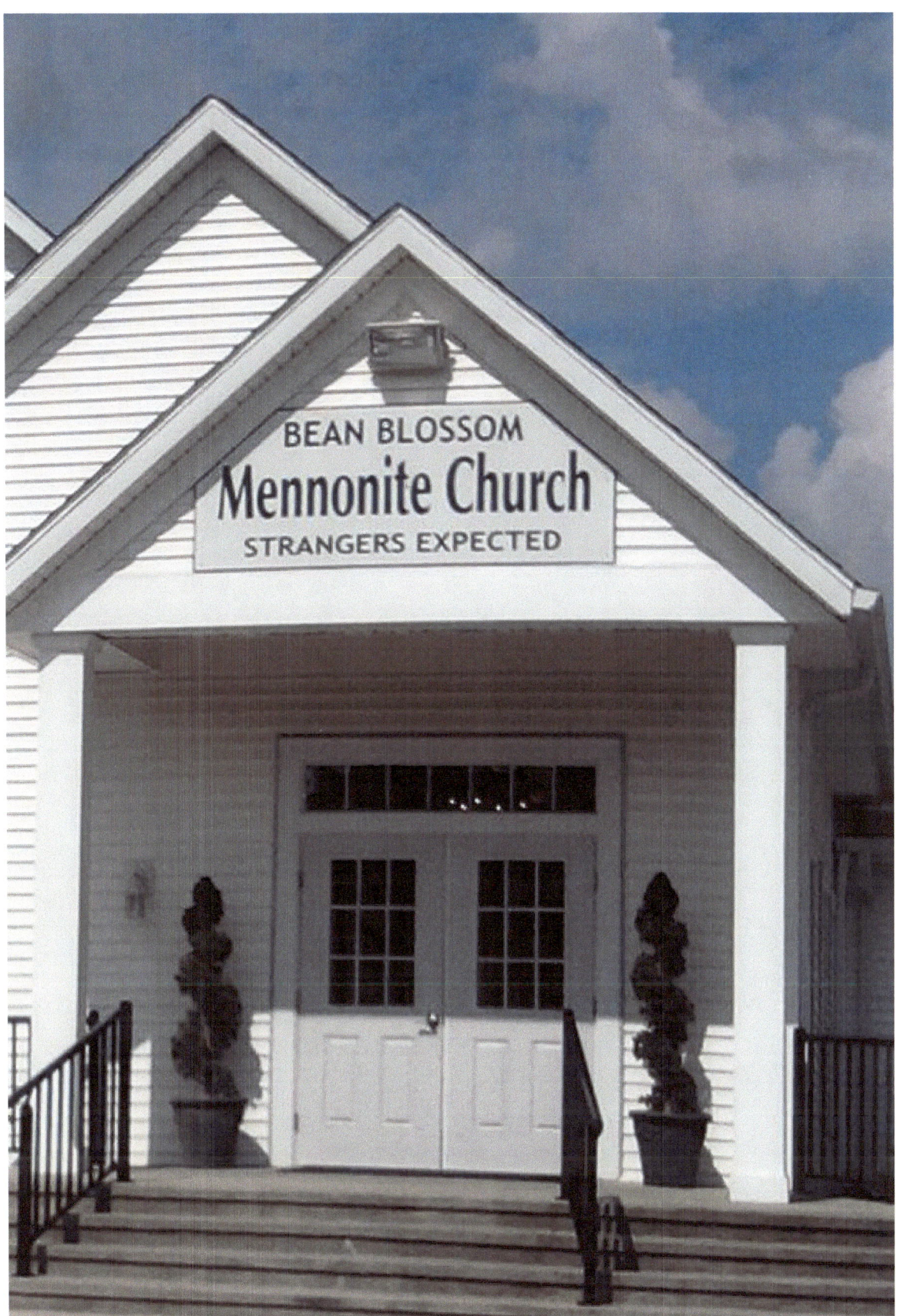

Indiana

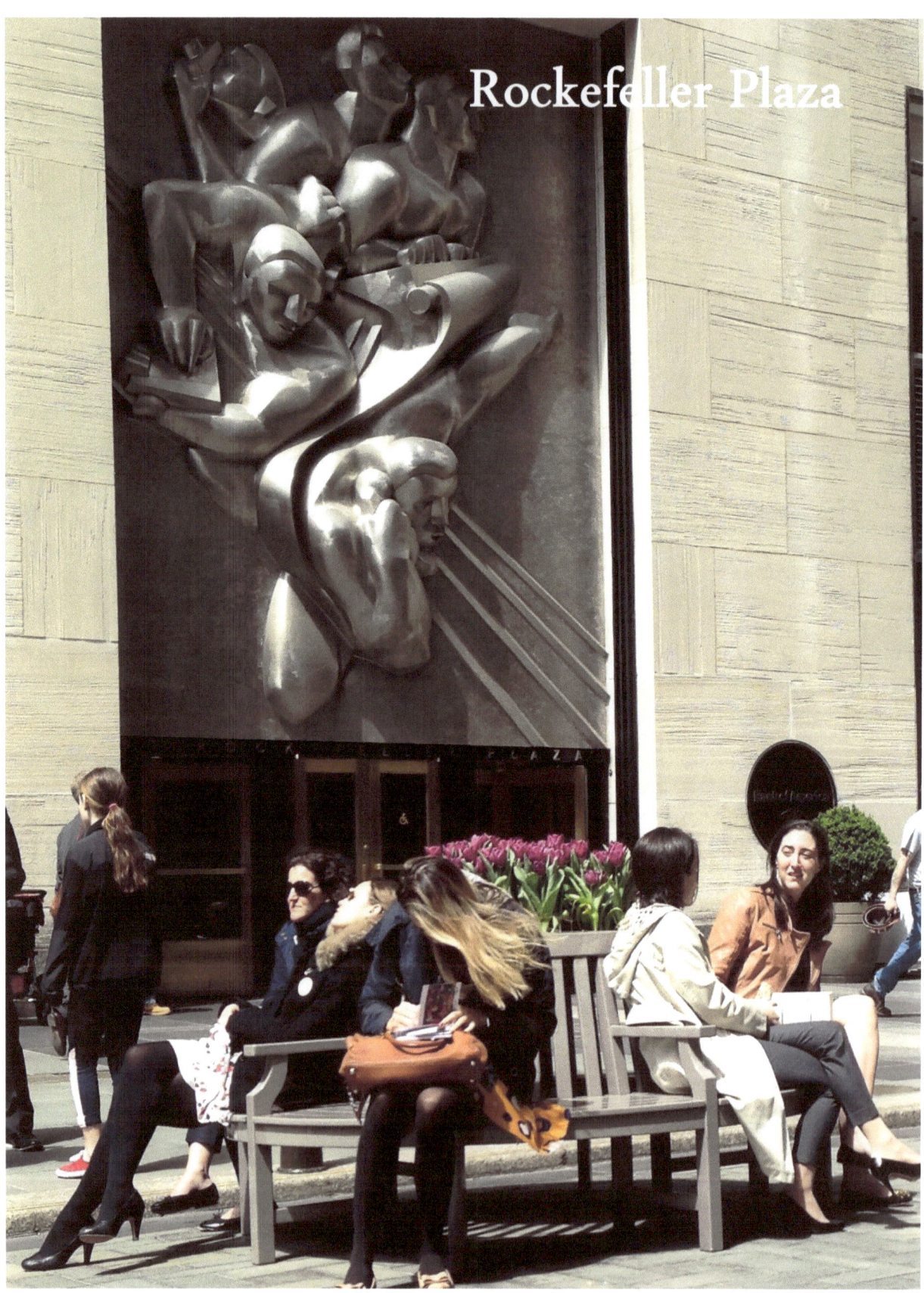

Rockefeller Plaza

New York City

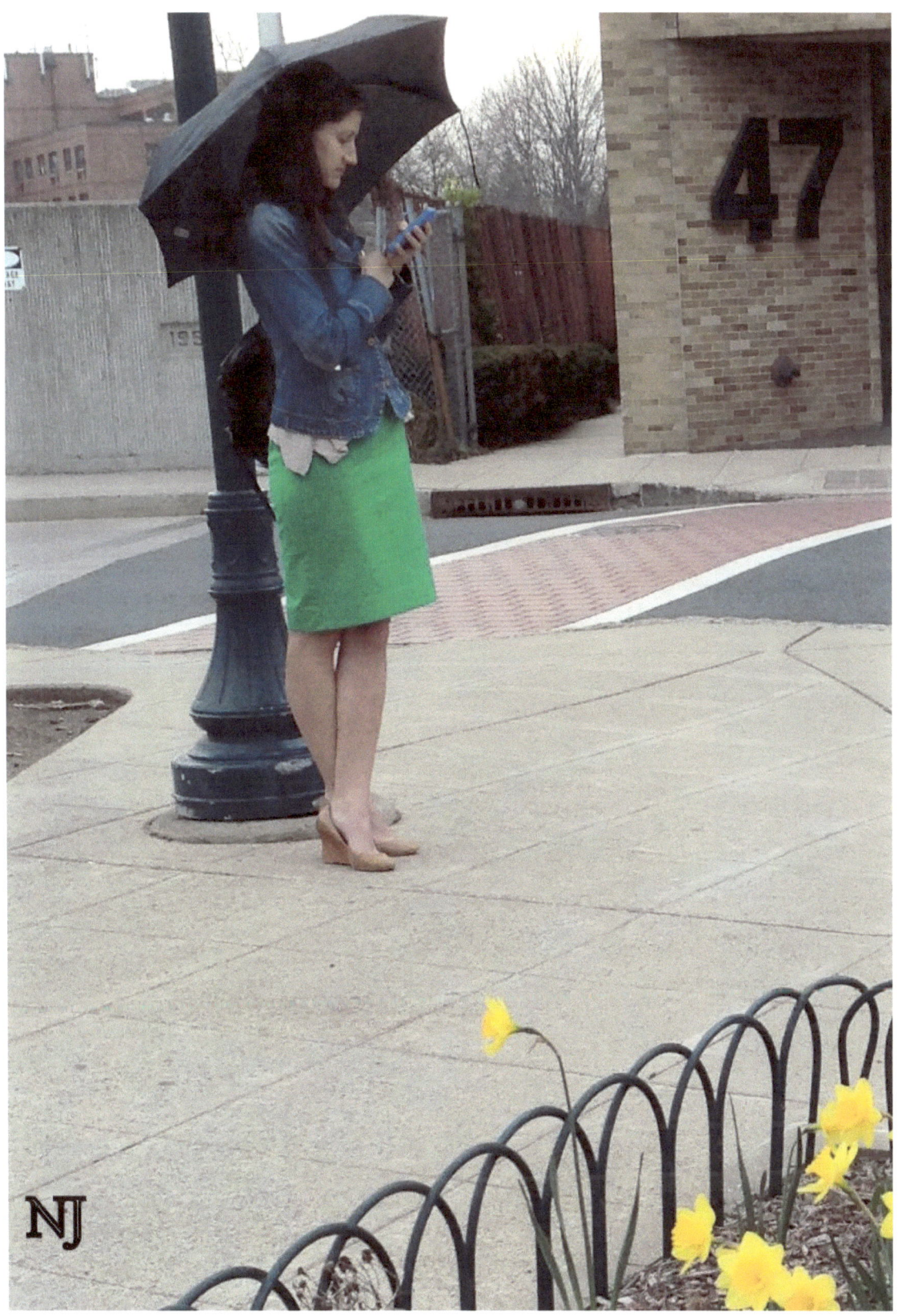

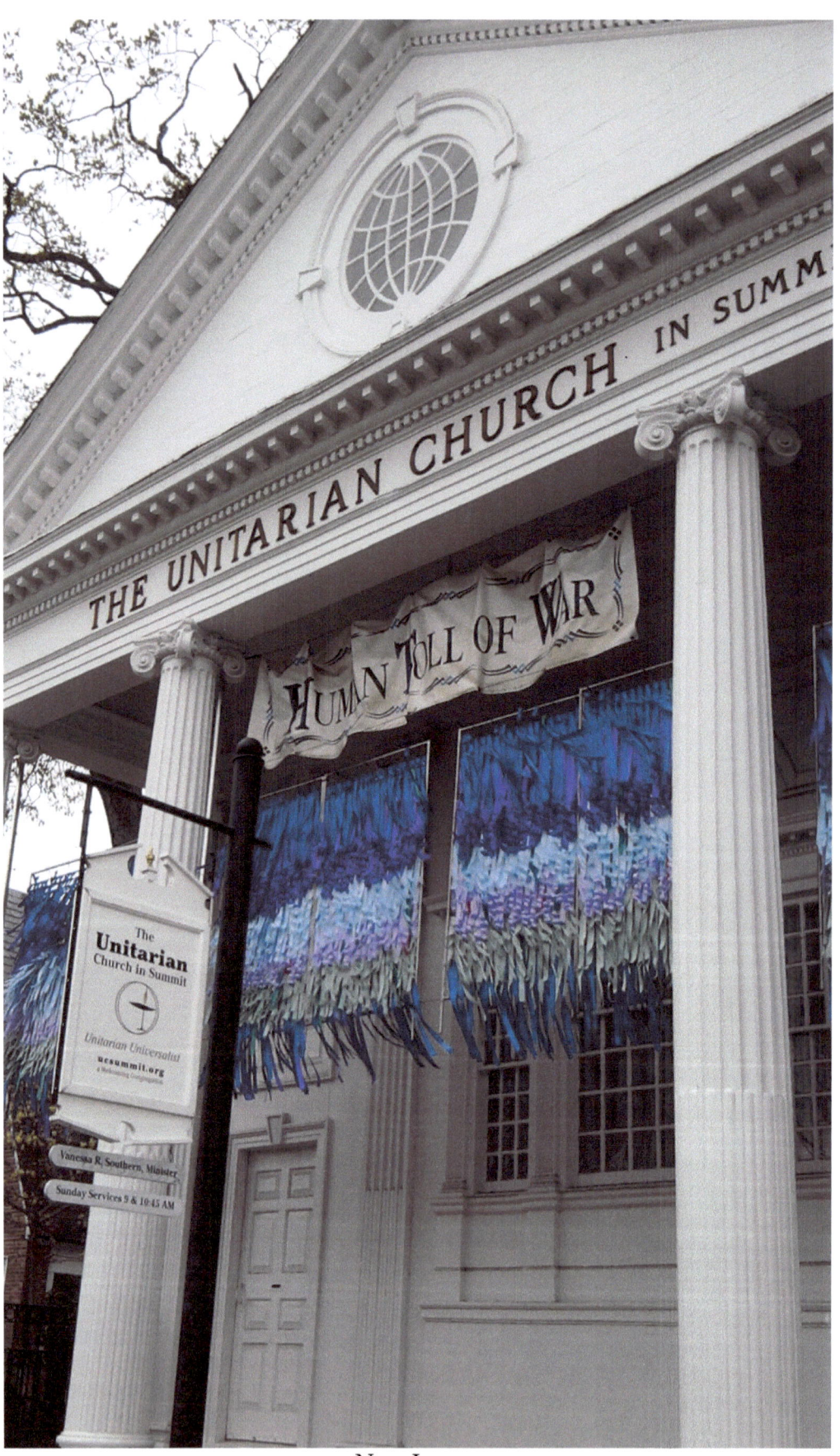

New Jersey

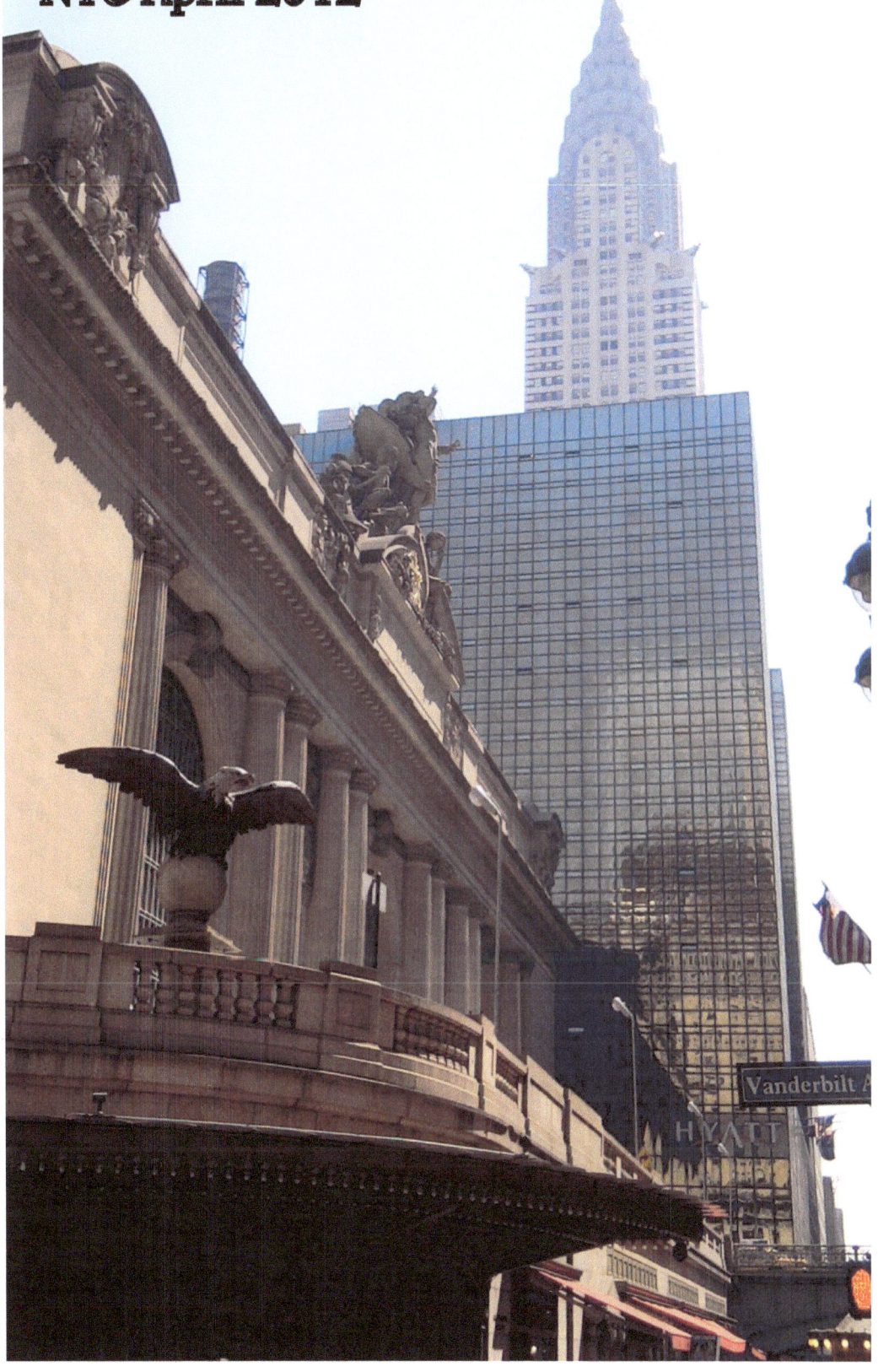

Grand Central & Chrysler Building
NYC April 2012

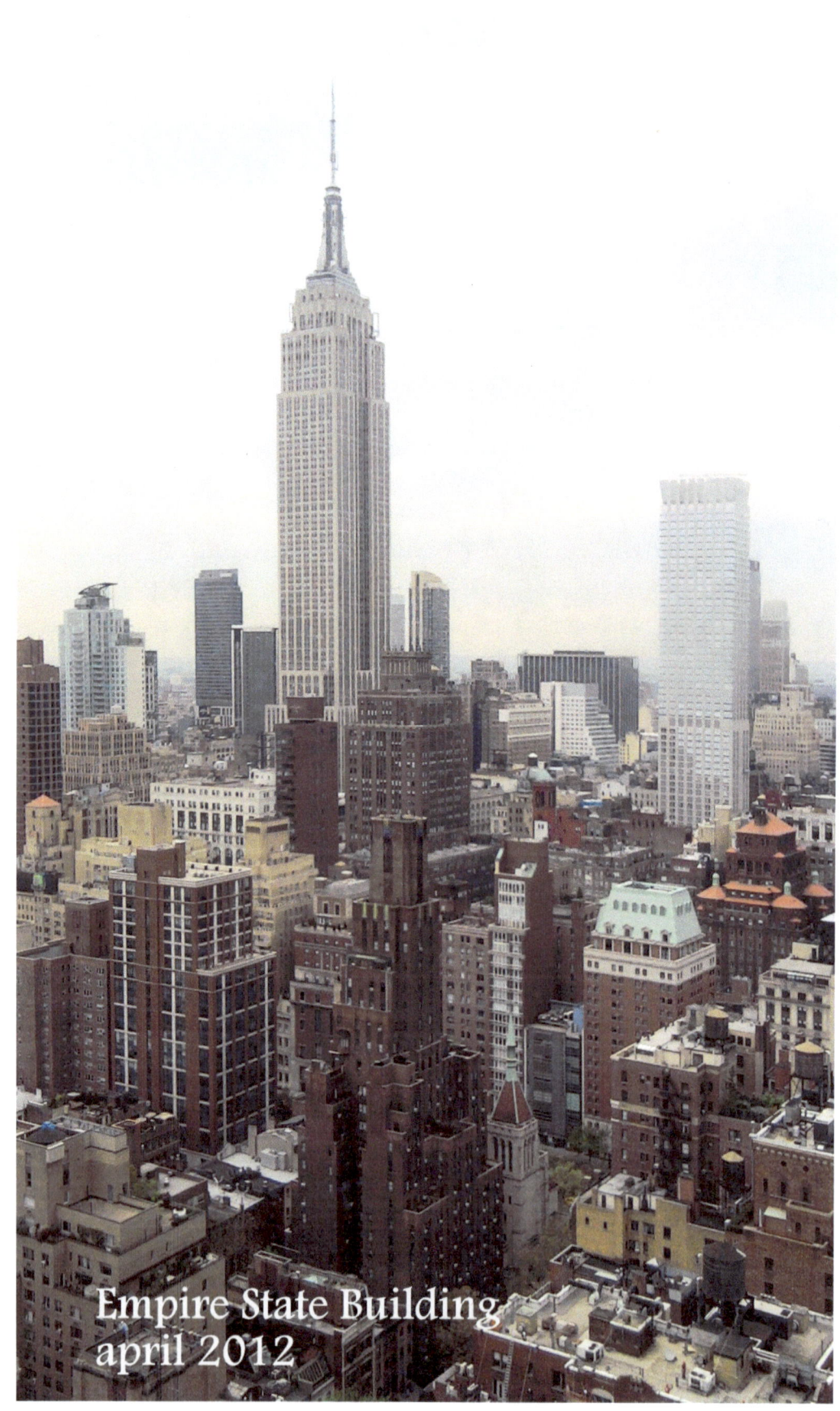
Empire State Building
april 2012

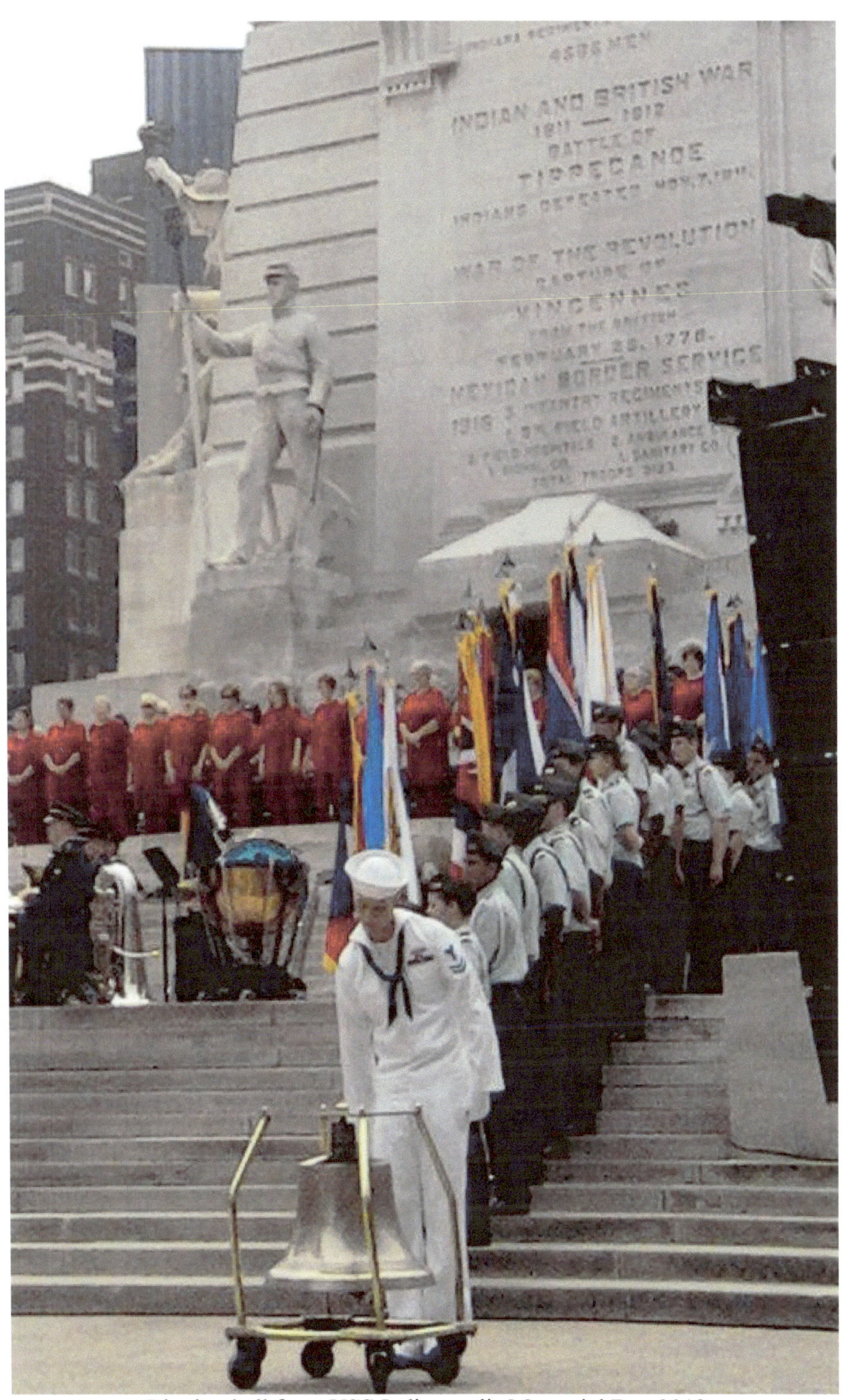

Ringing bell from USS Indianapolis Memorial Day 2012

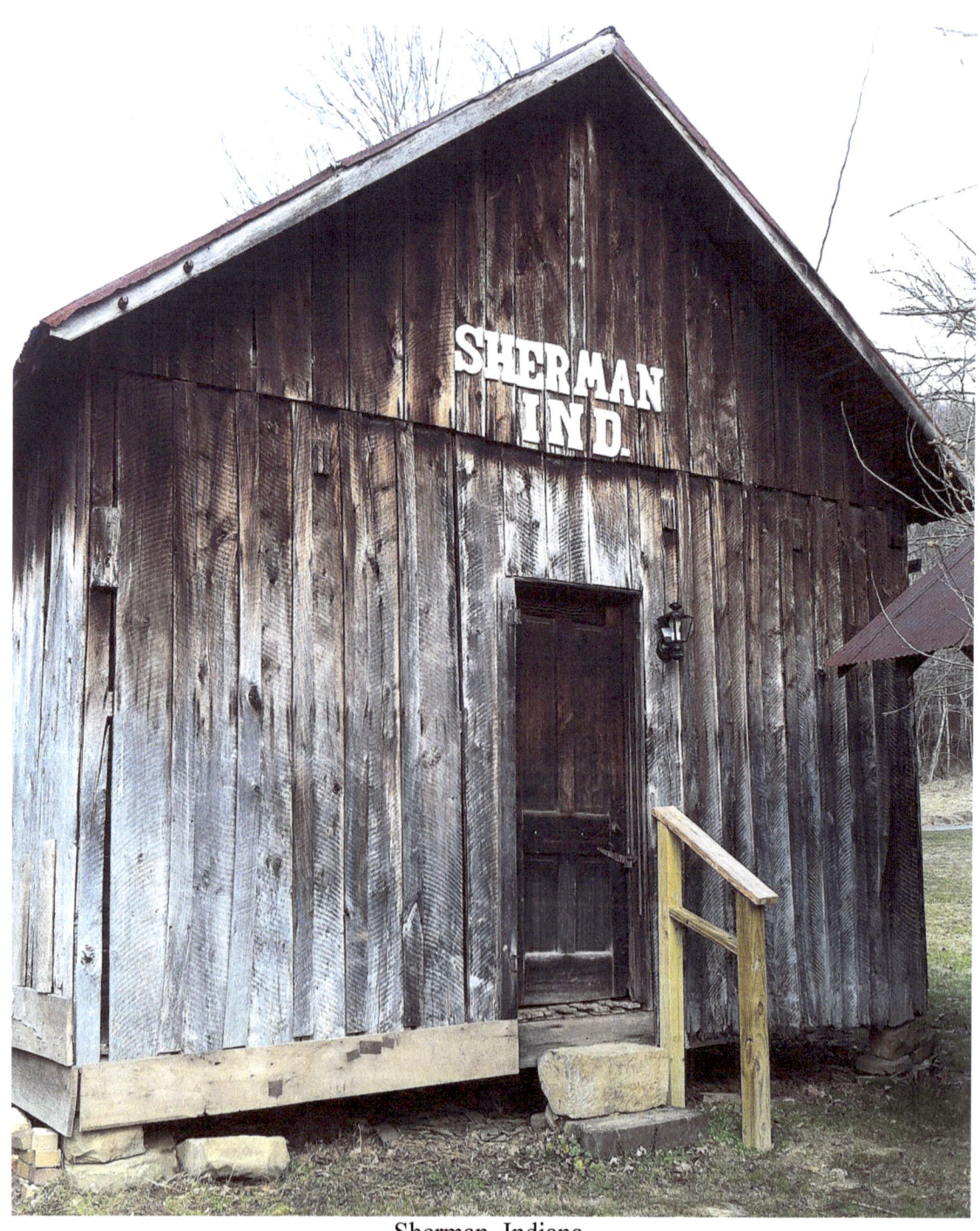

Sherman, Indiana

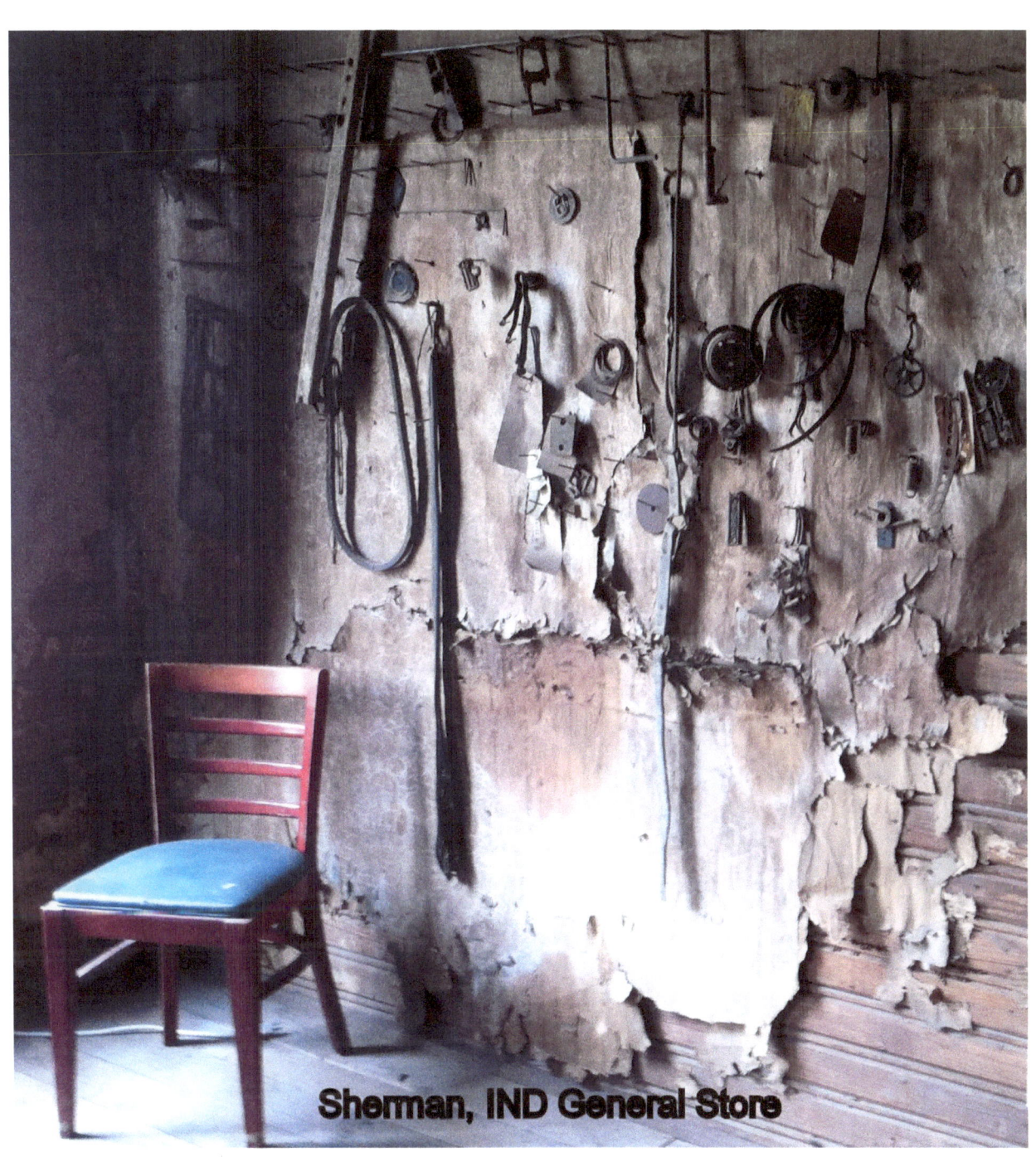

Sherman, IND General Store

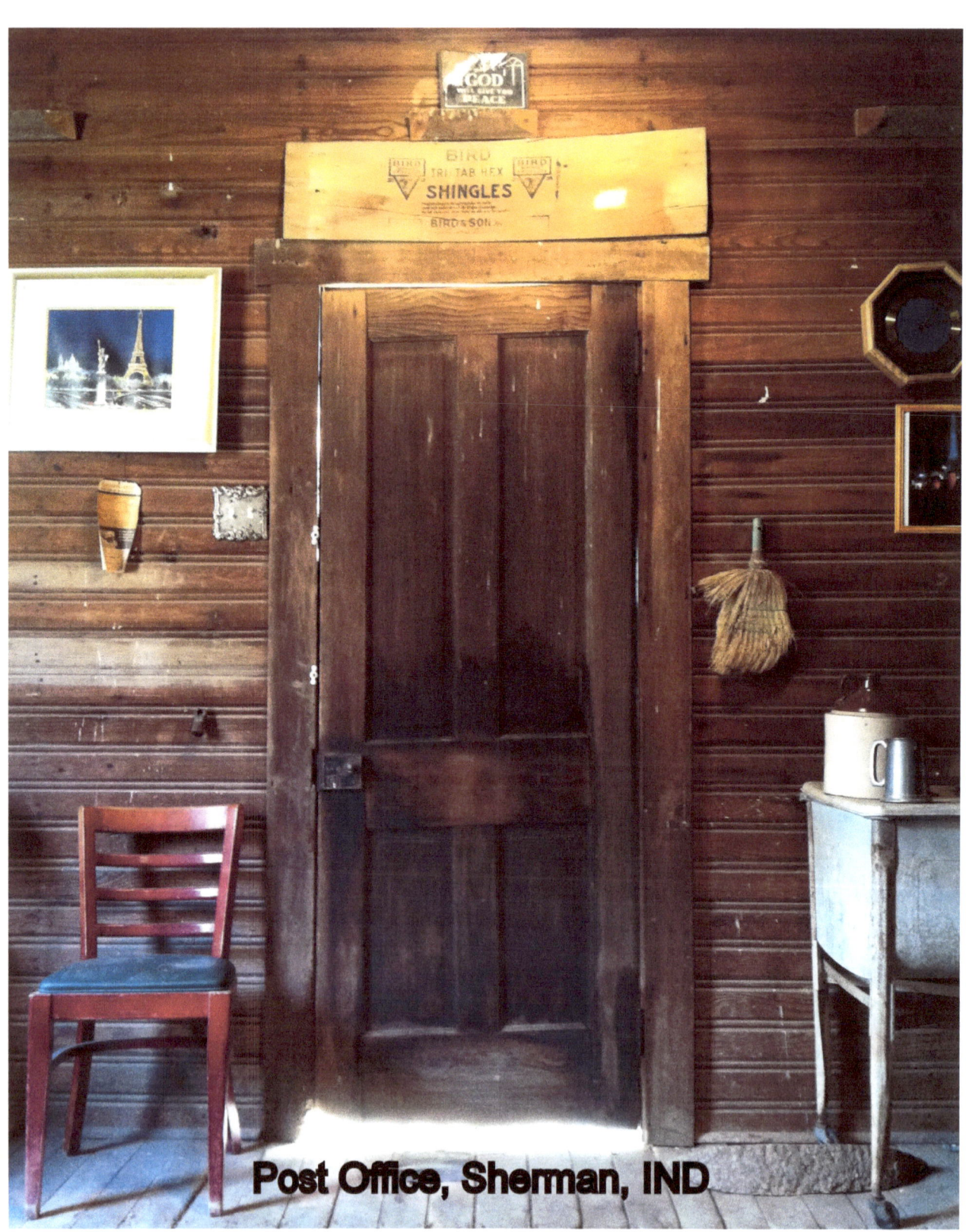

Post Office, Sherman, IND

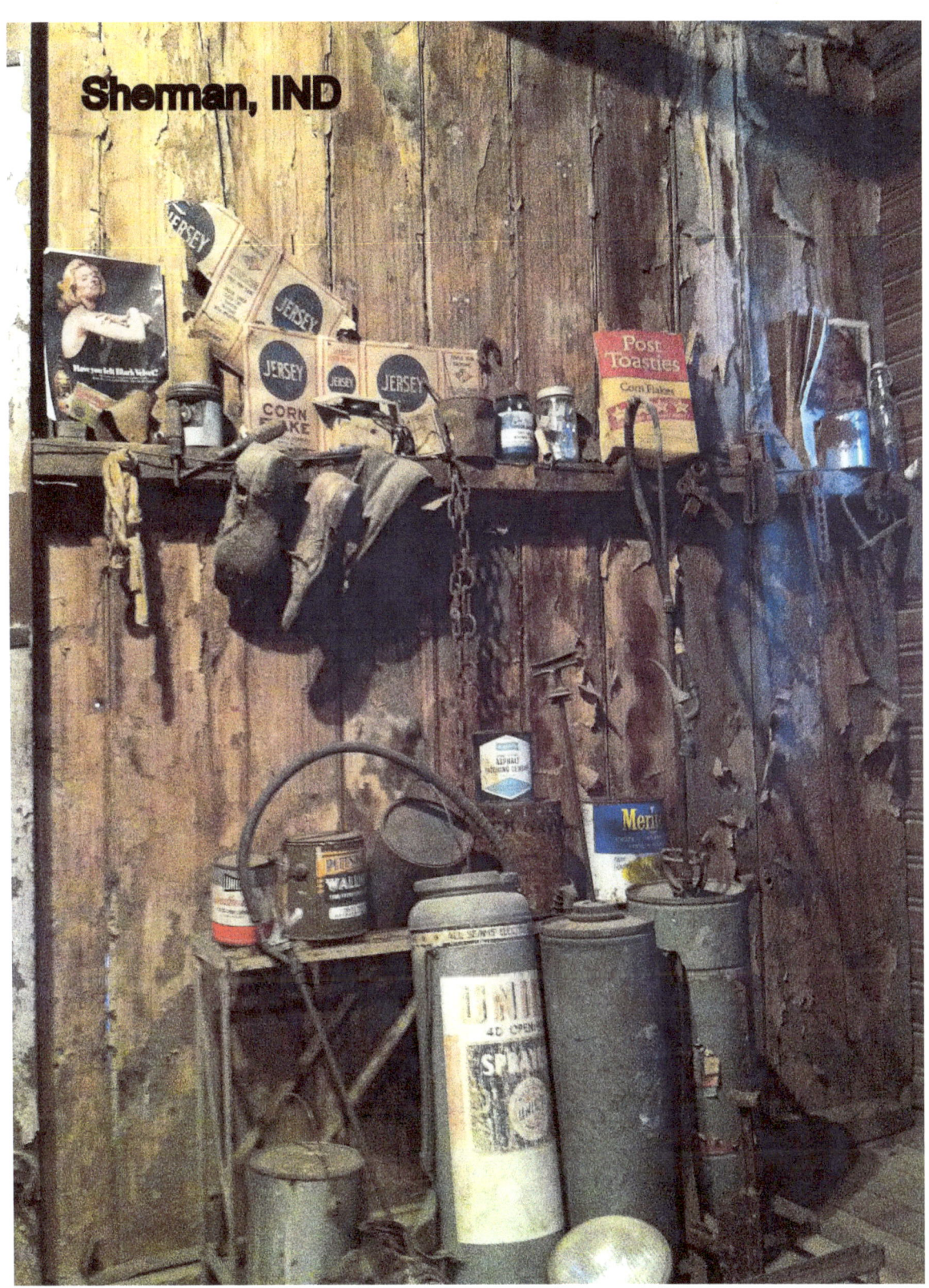

Sherman, IND

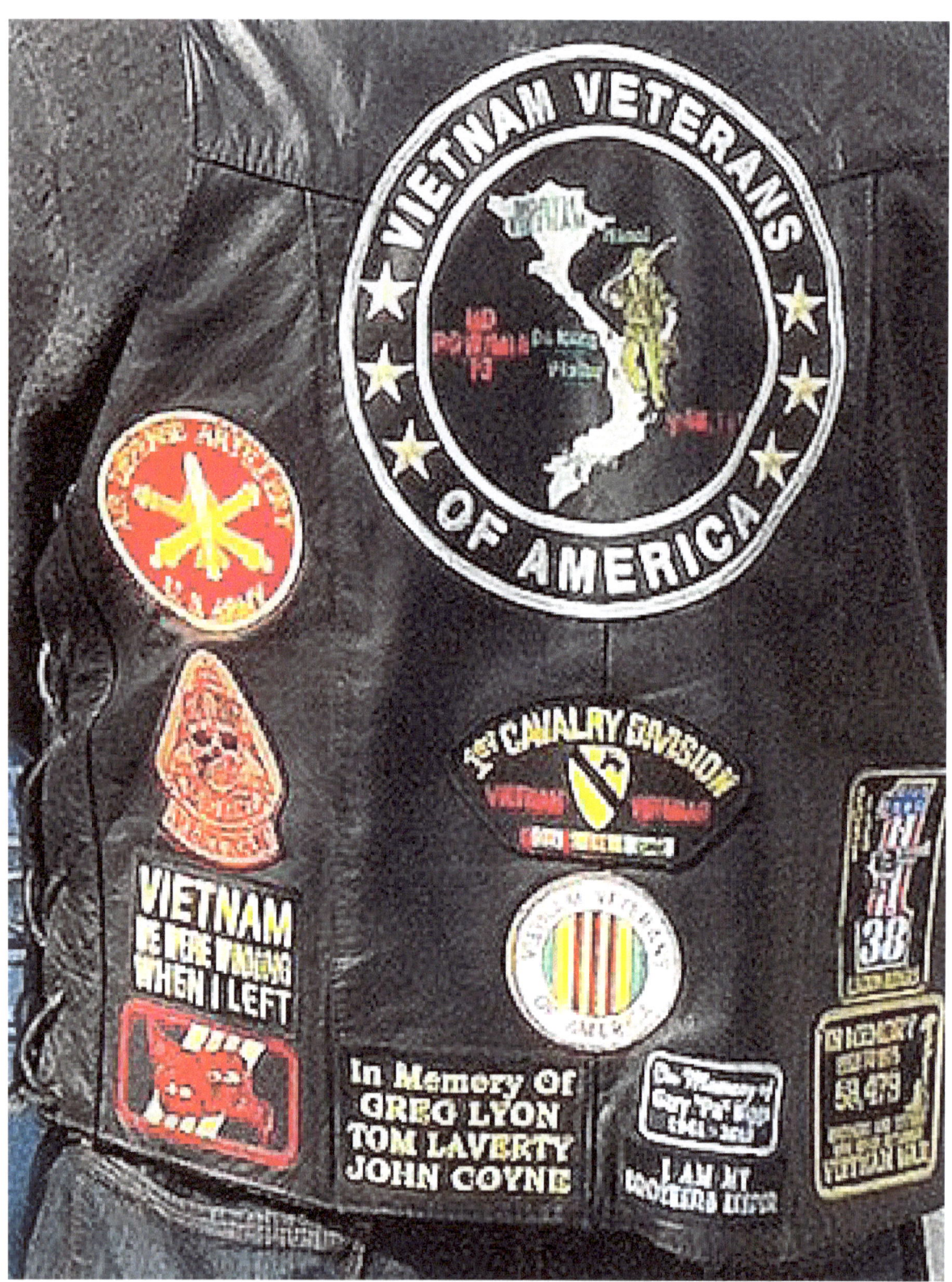

Indiana

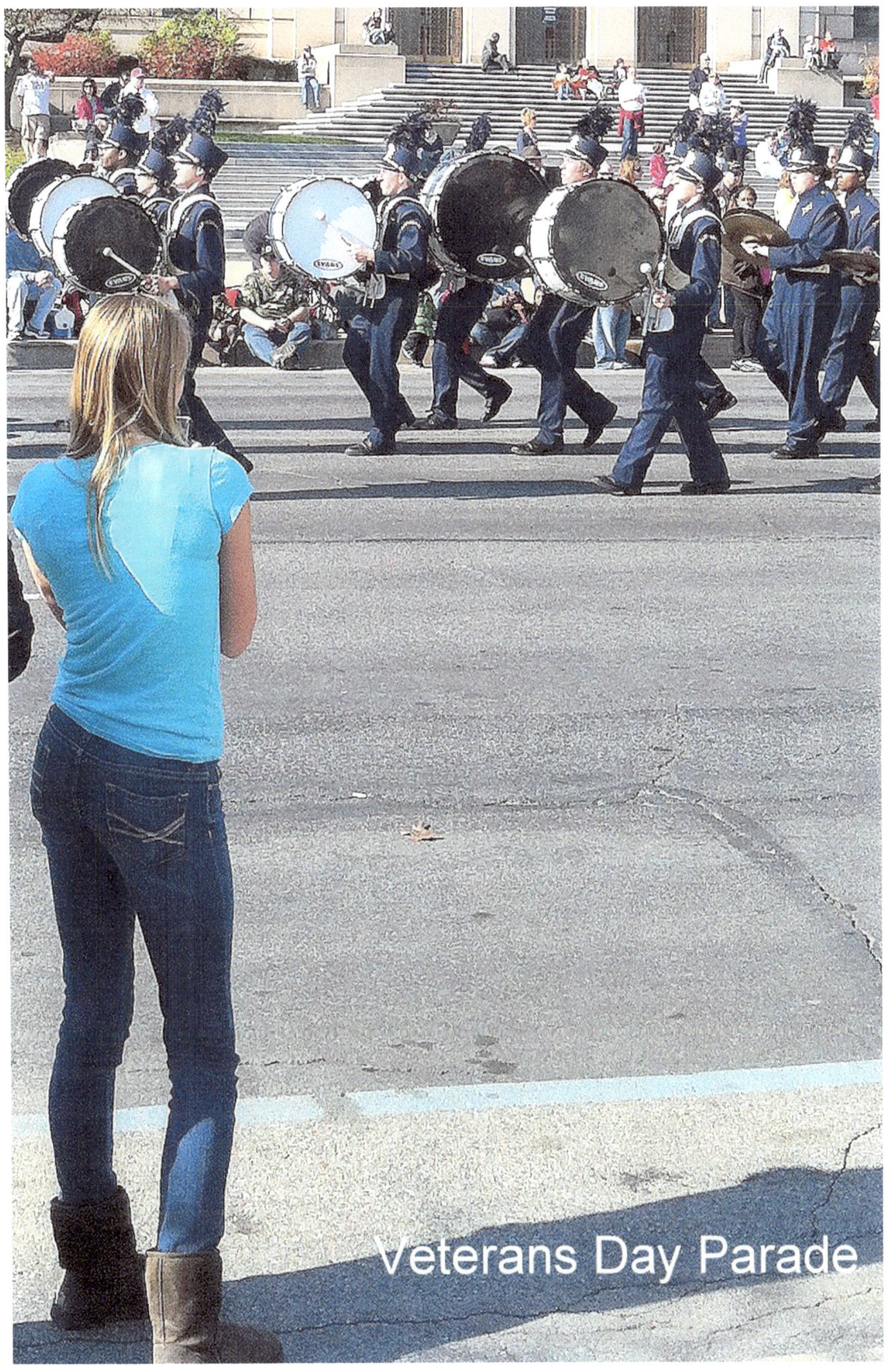

Veterans Day Parade

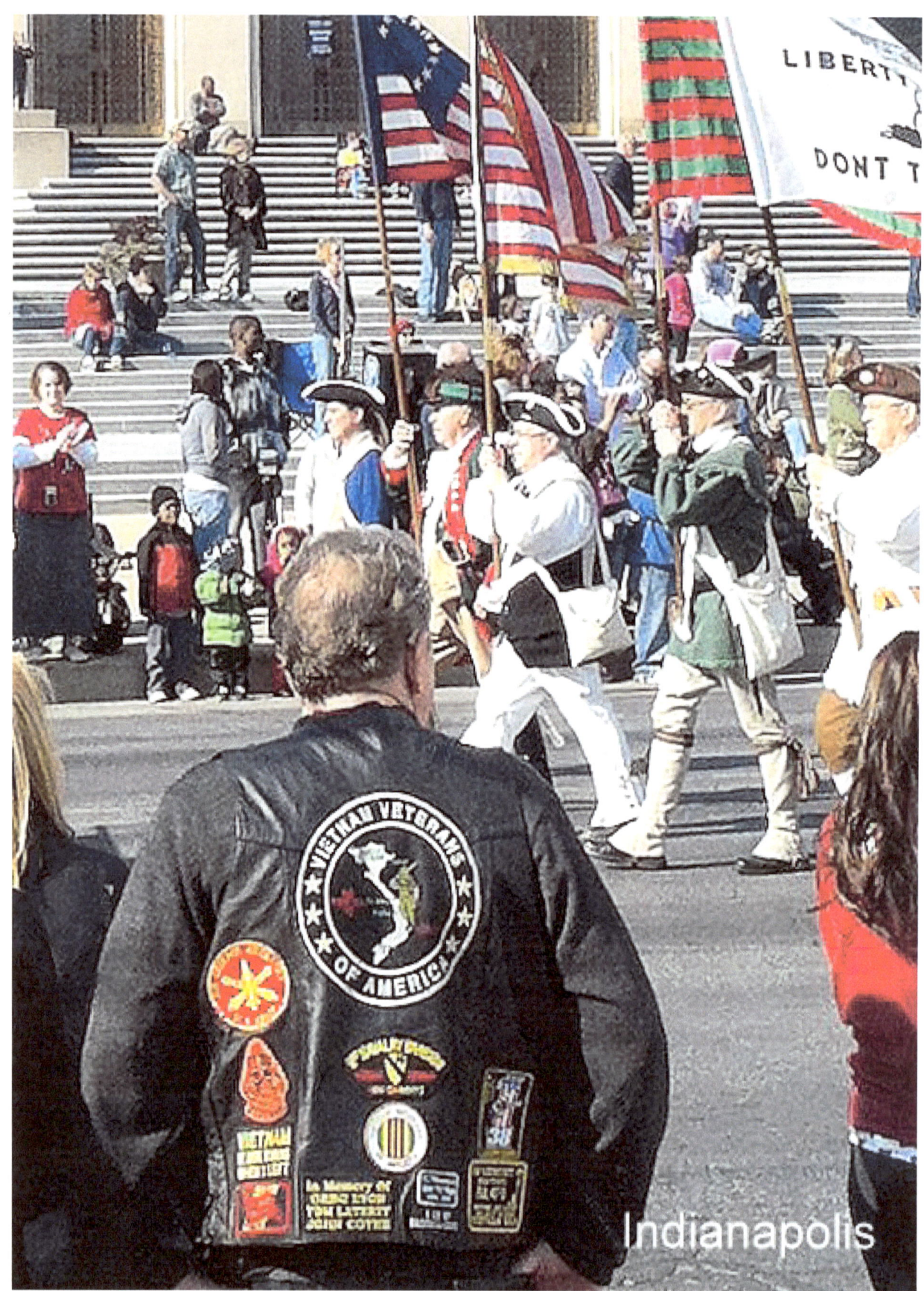

Indiana

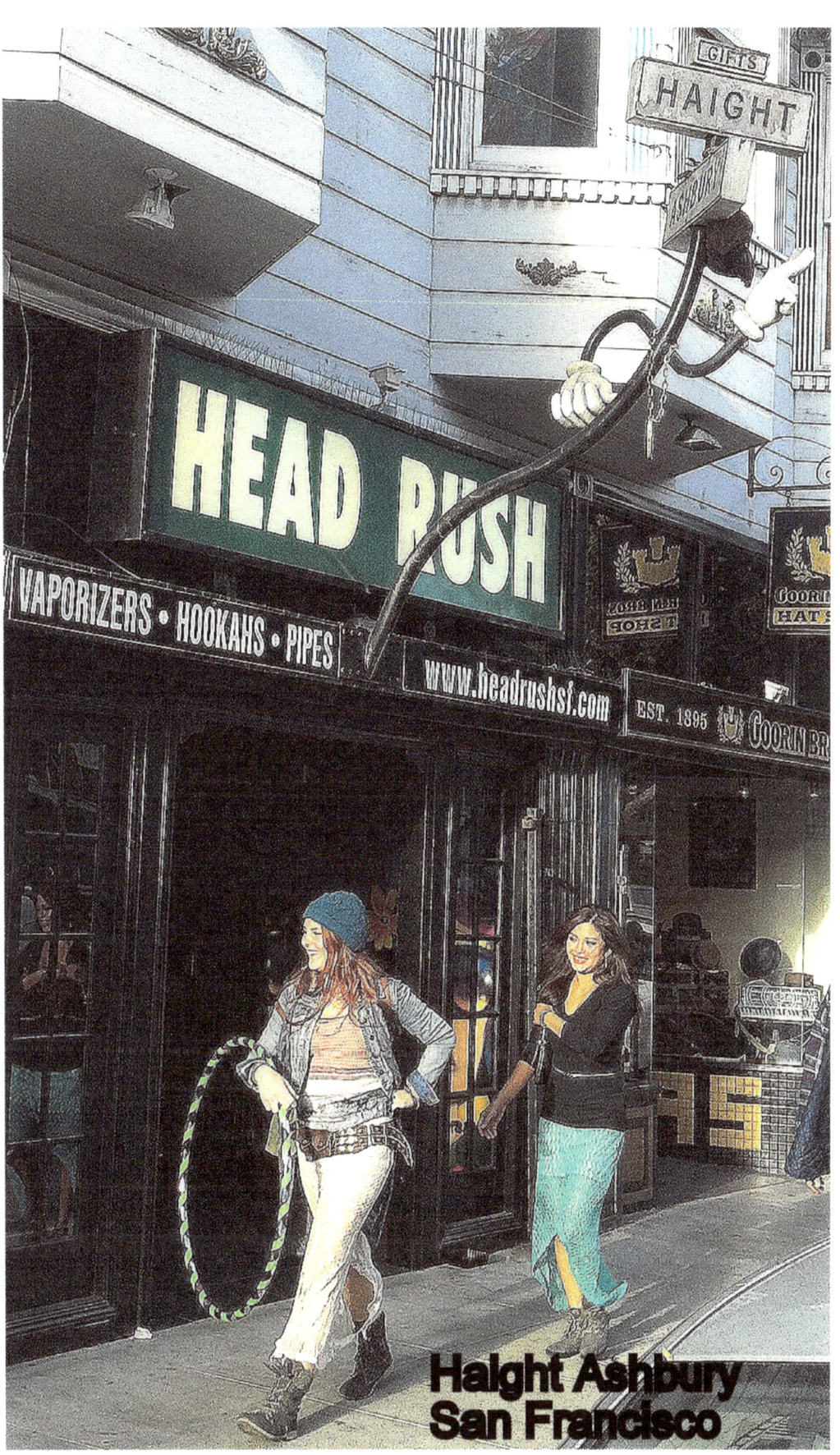

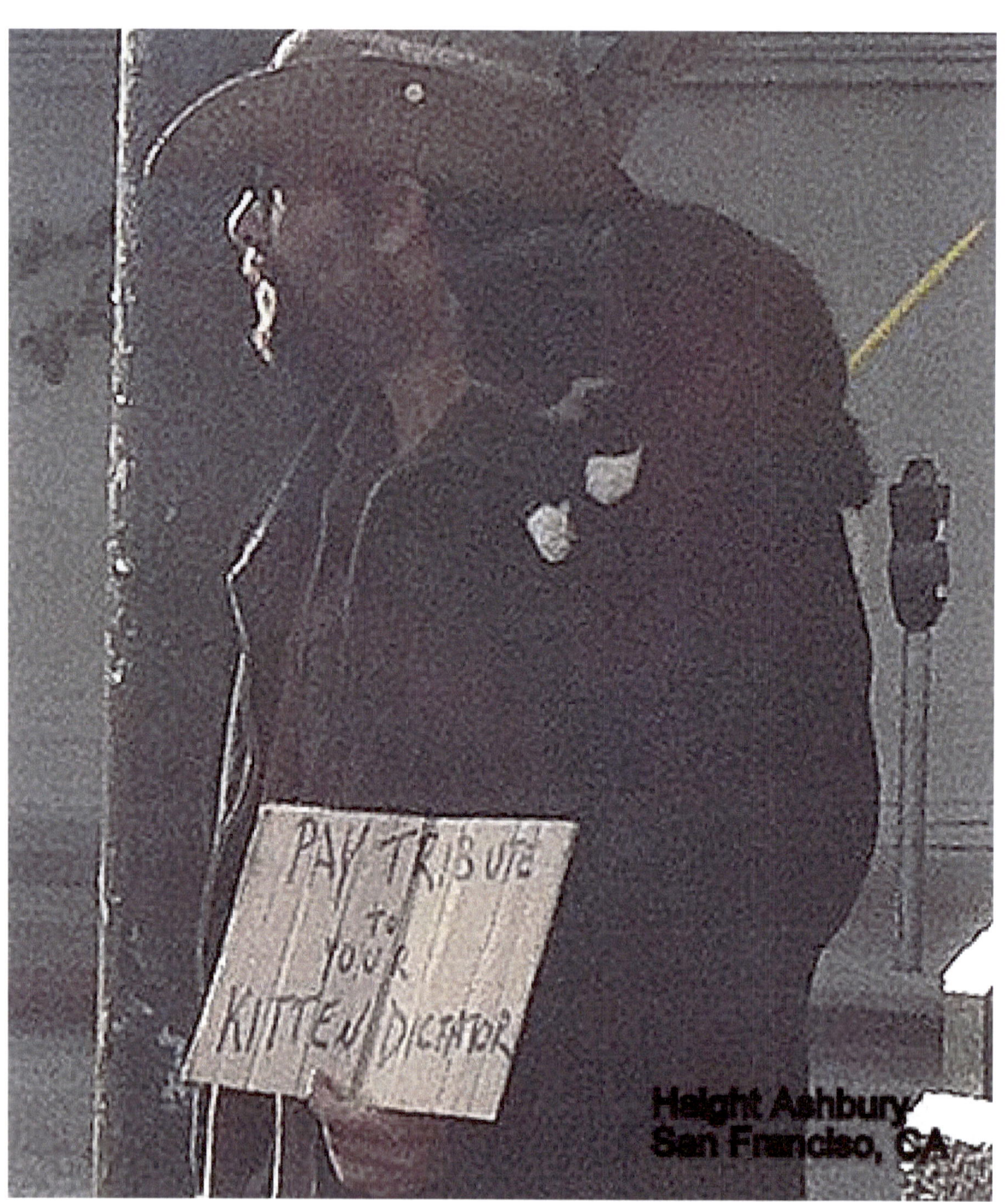

Height Ashbury
San Francisco, CA

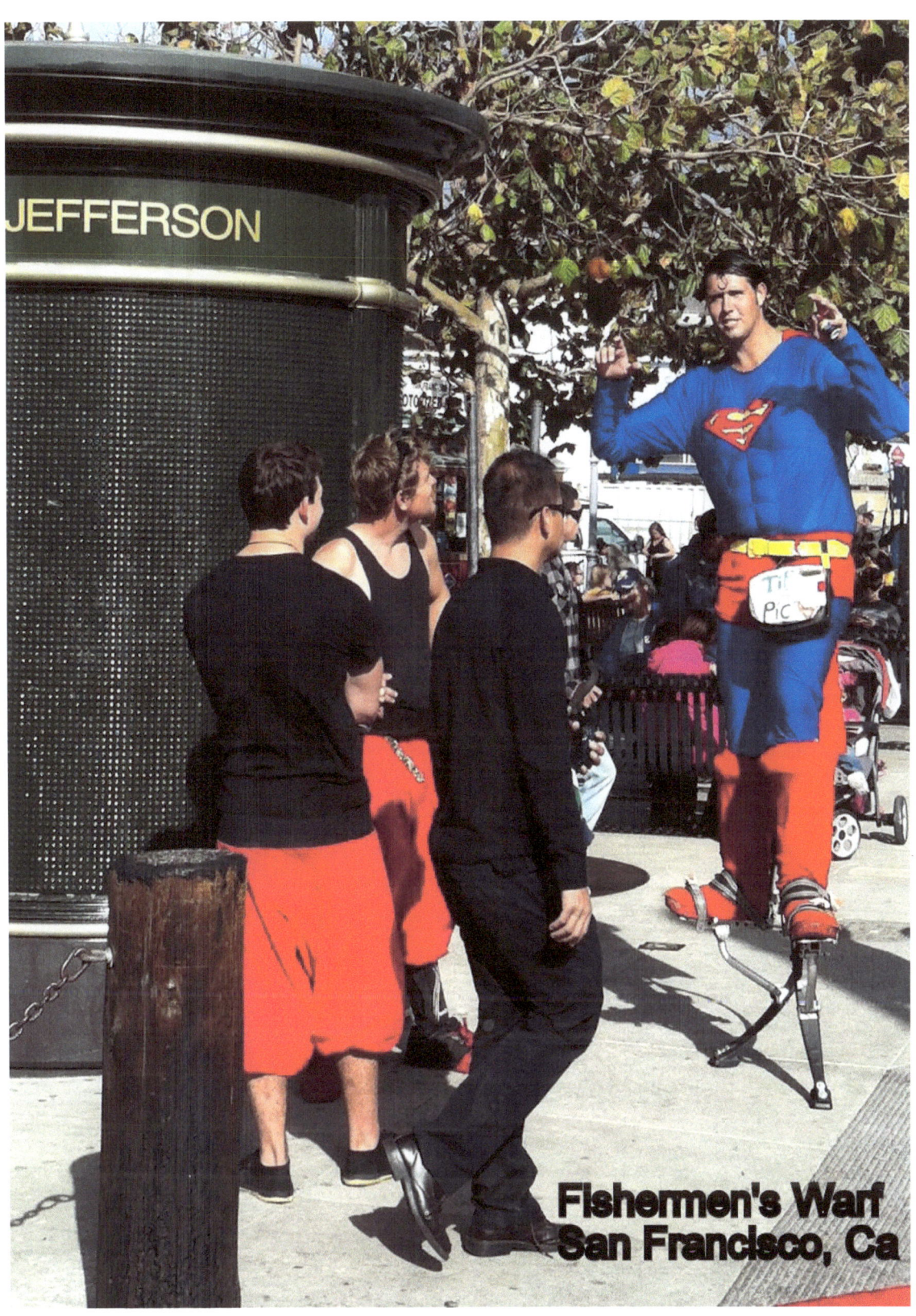

JEFFERSON

Fishermen's Warf
San Francisco, Ca

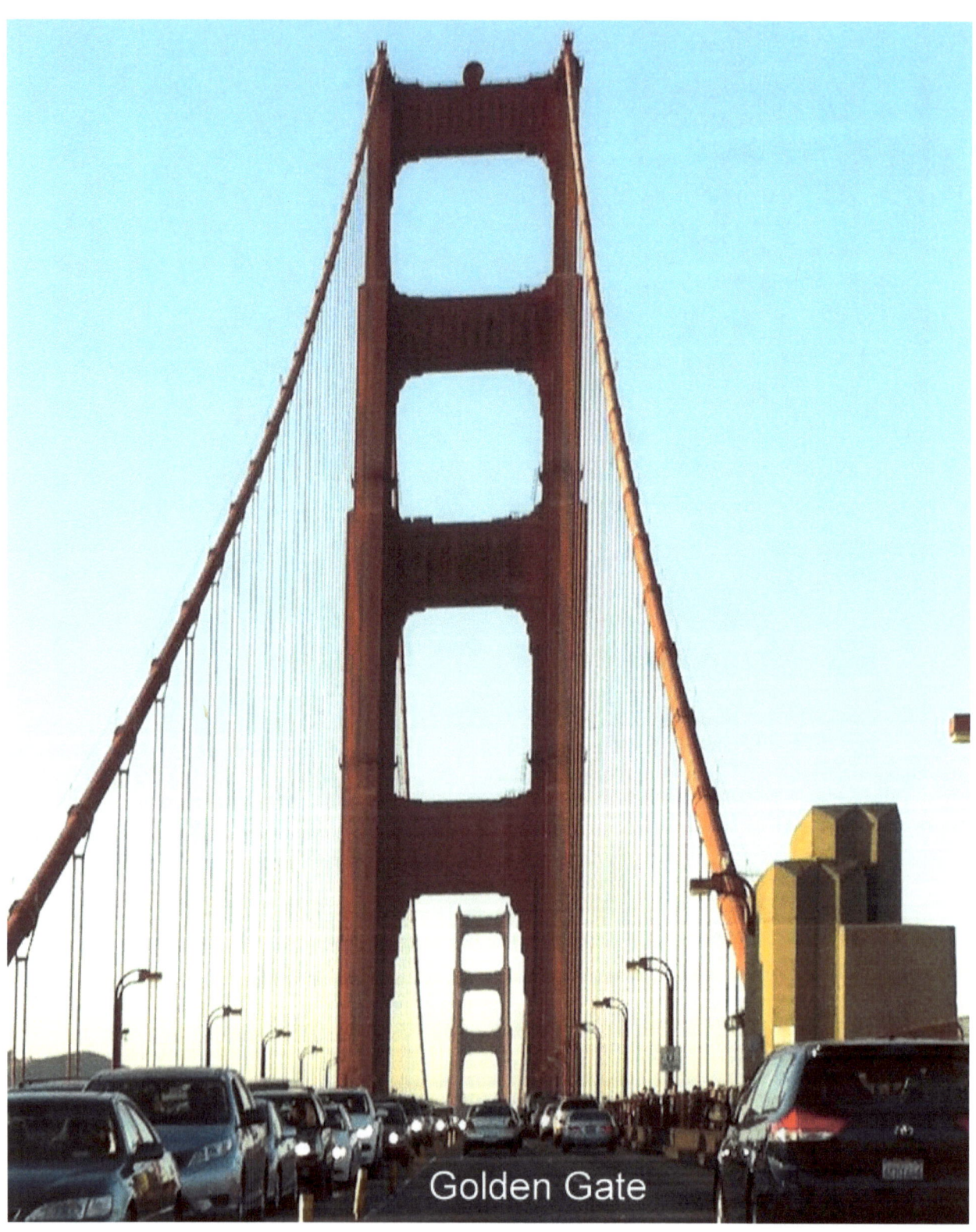

Golden Gate

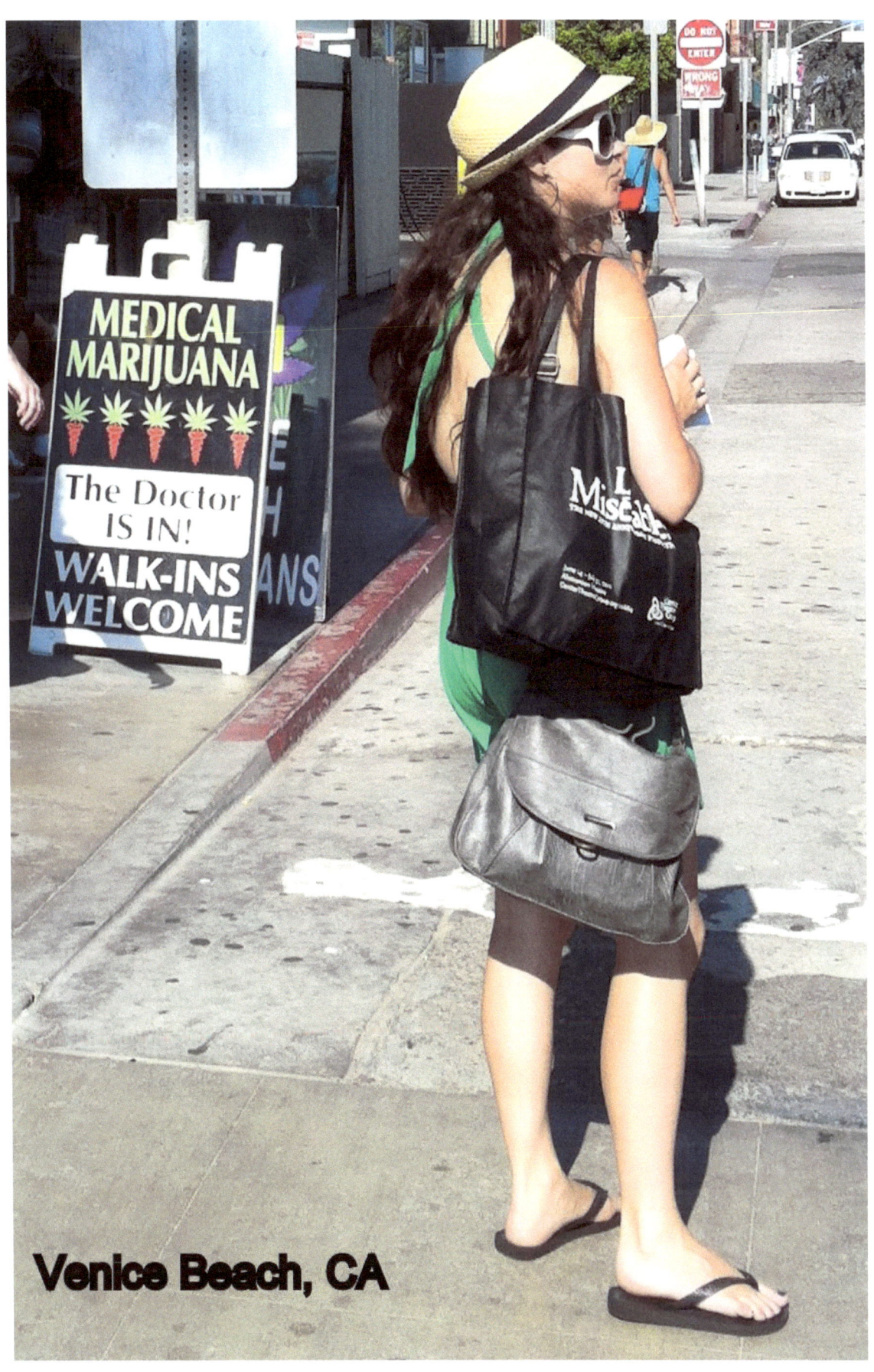

MEDICAL
MARIJUANA

The Doctor
IS IN!
WALK-INS
WELCOME

Venice Beach, CA

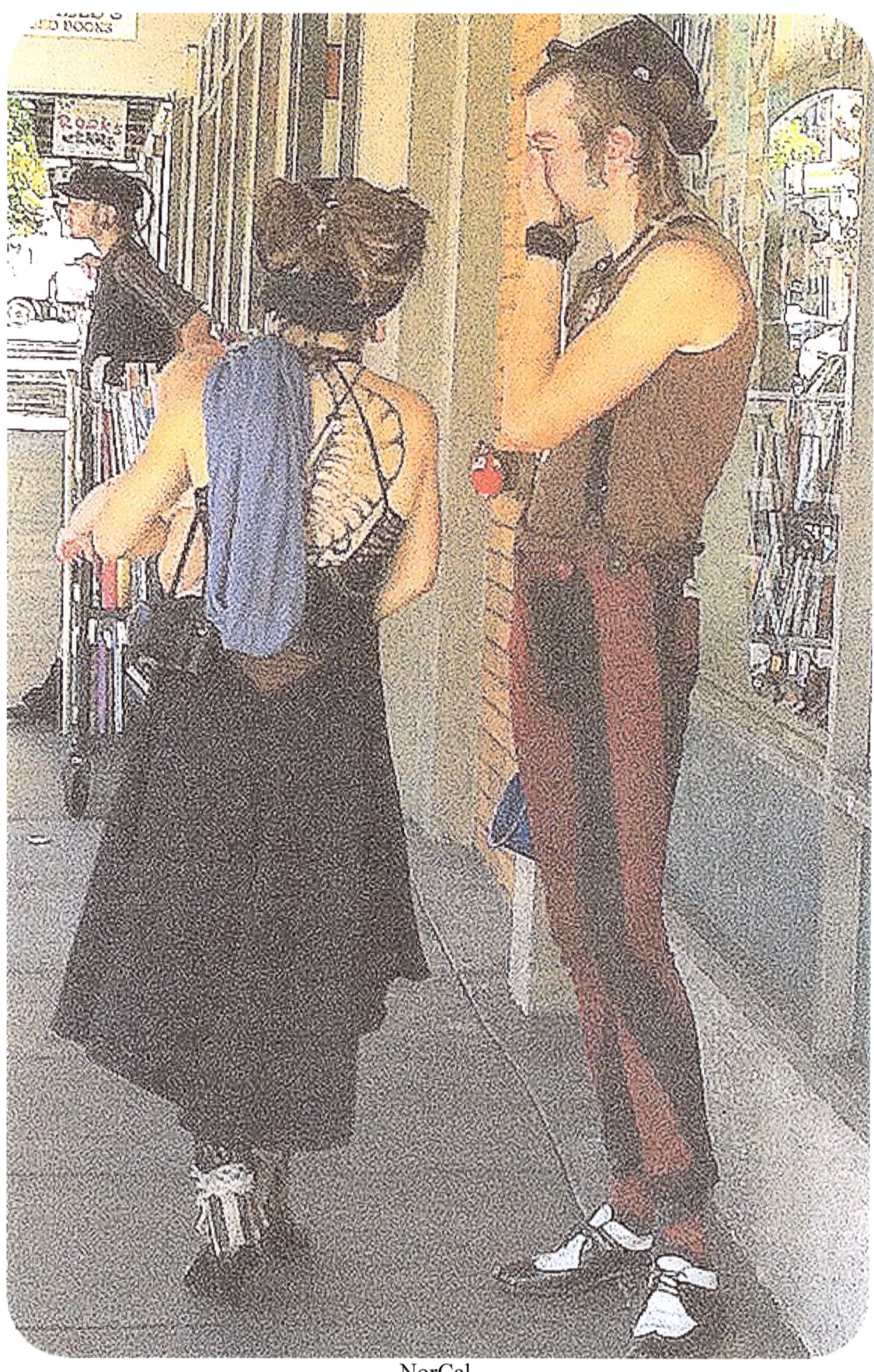

NorCal

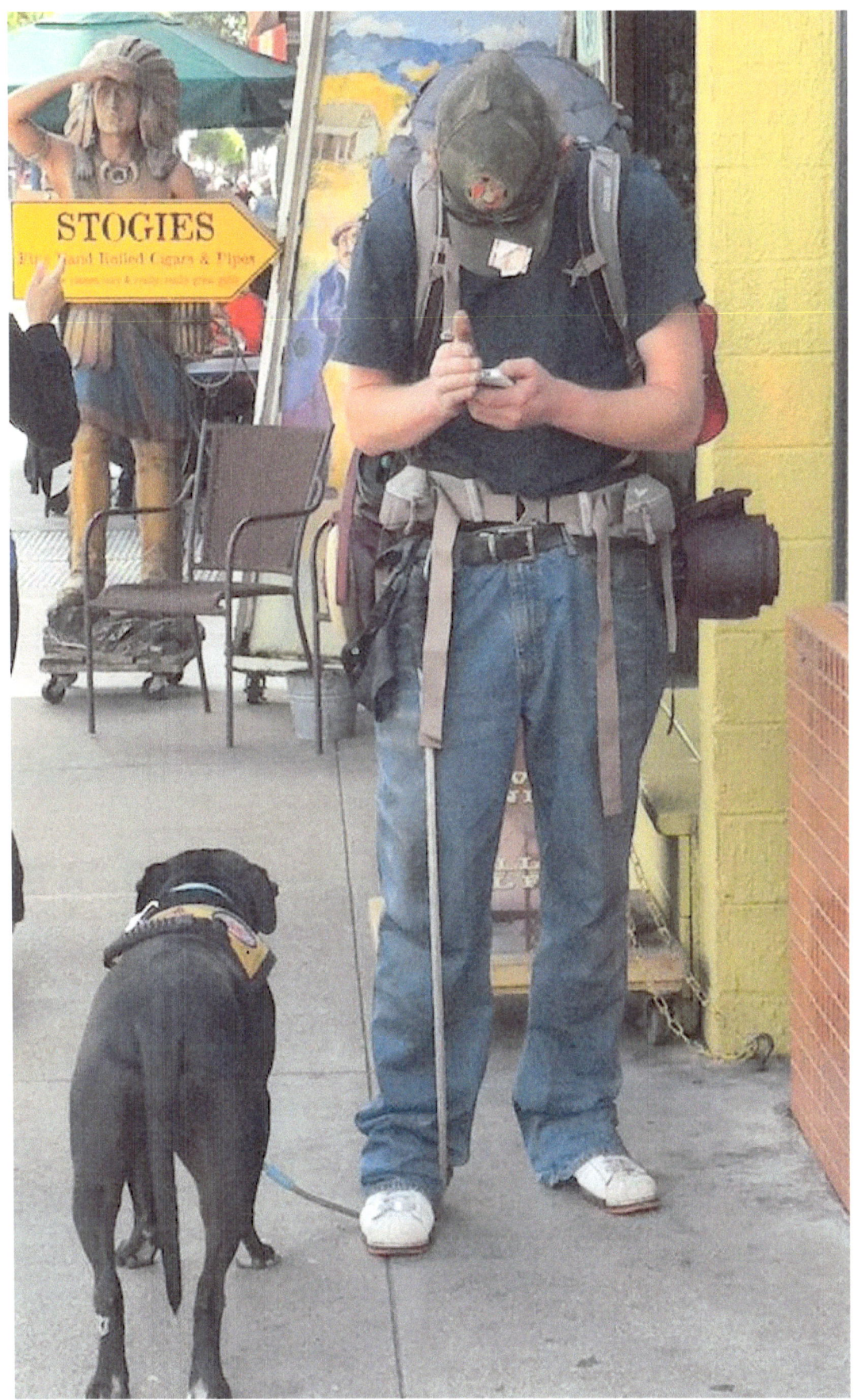

NorCal

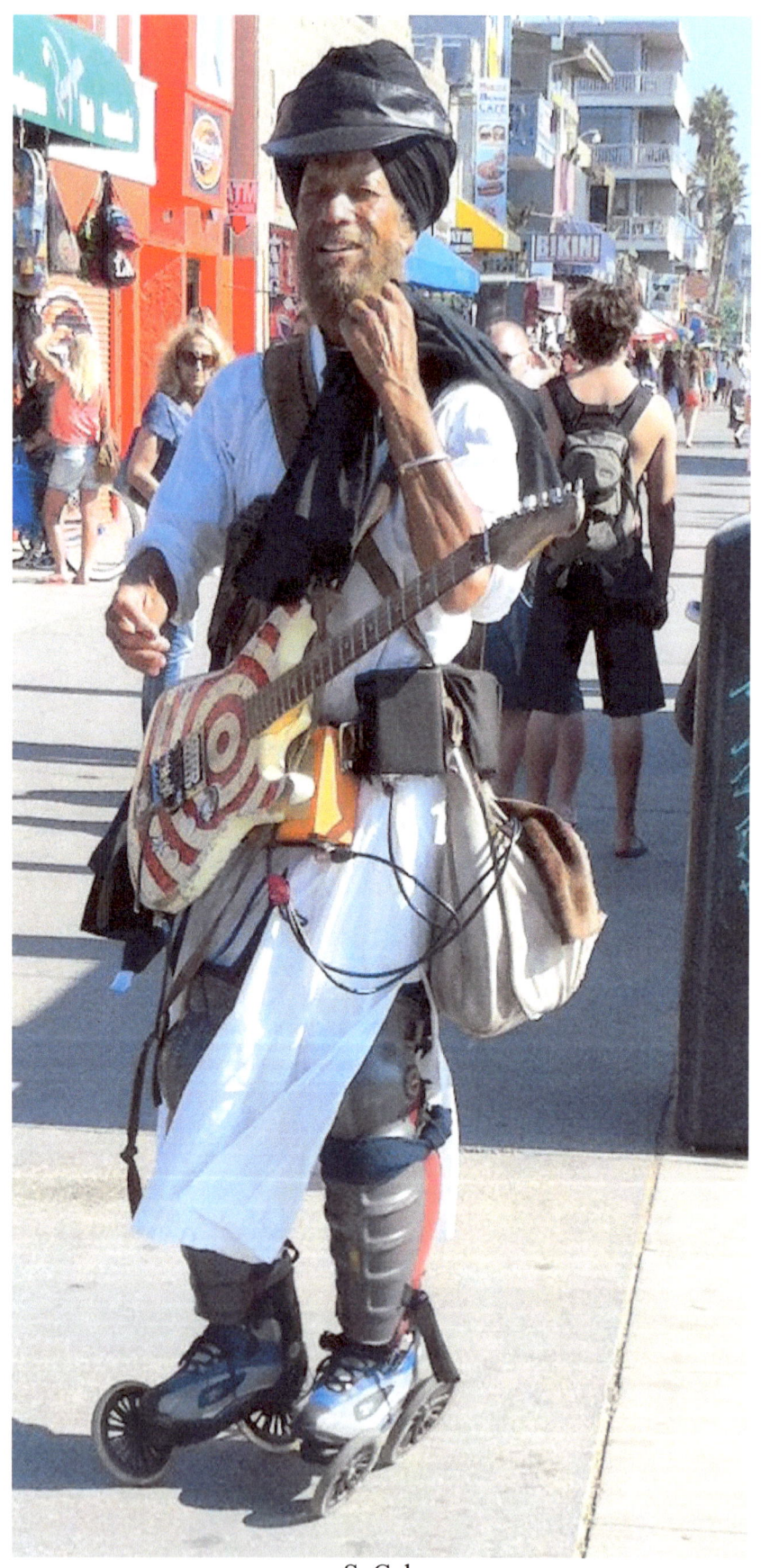

SoCal

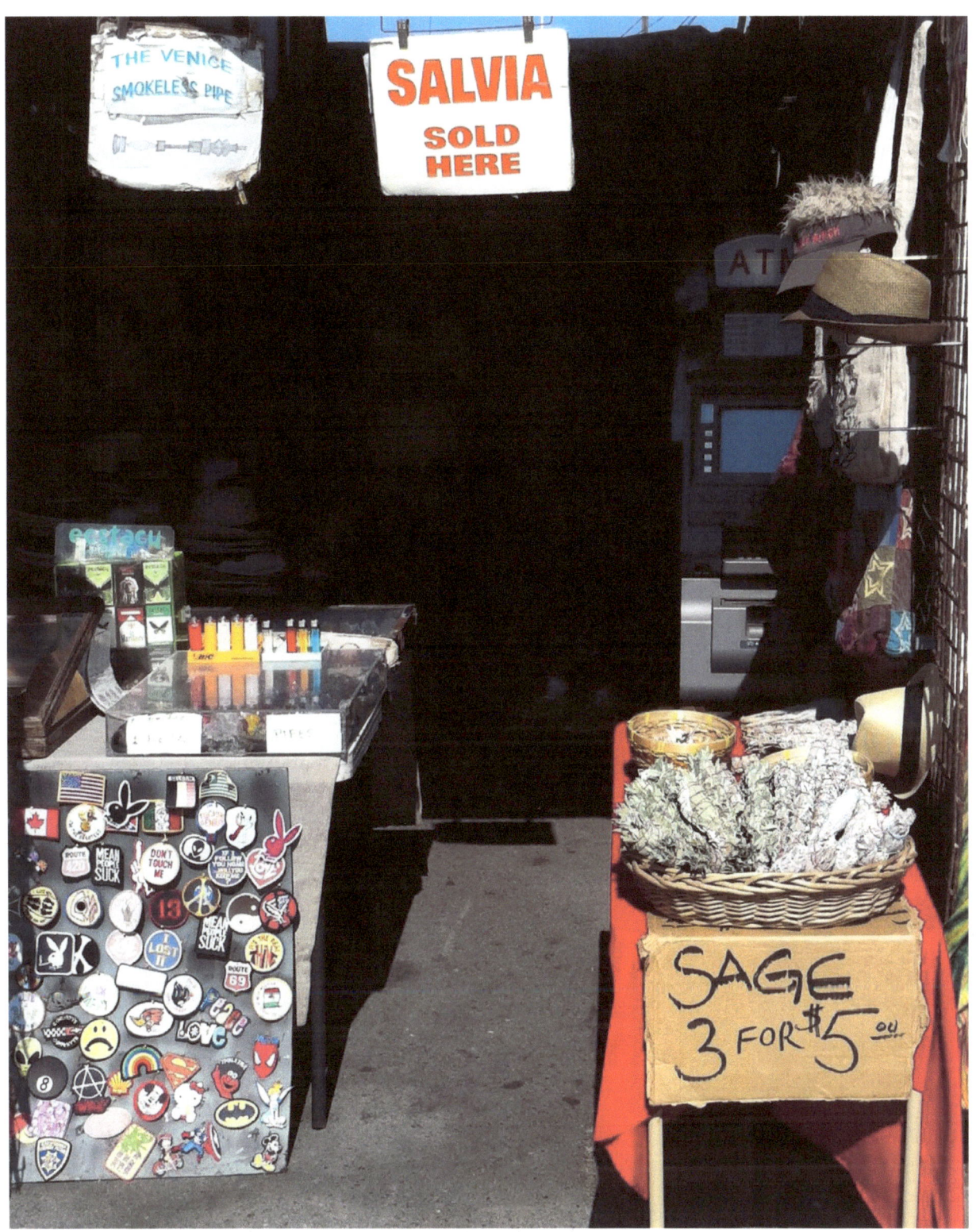

SoCal

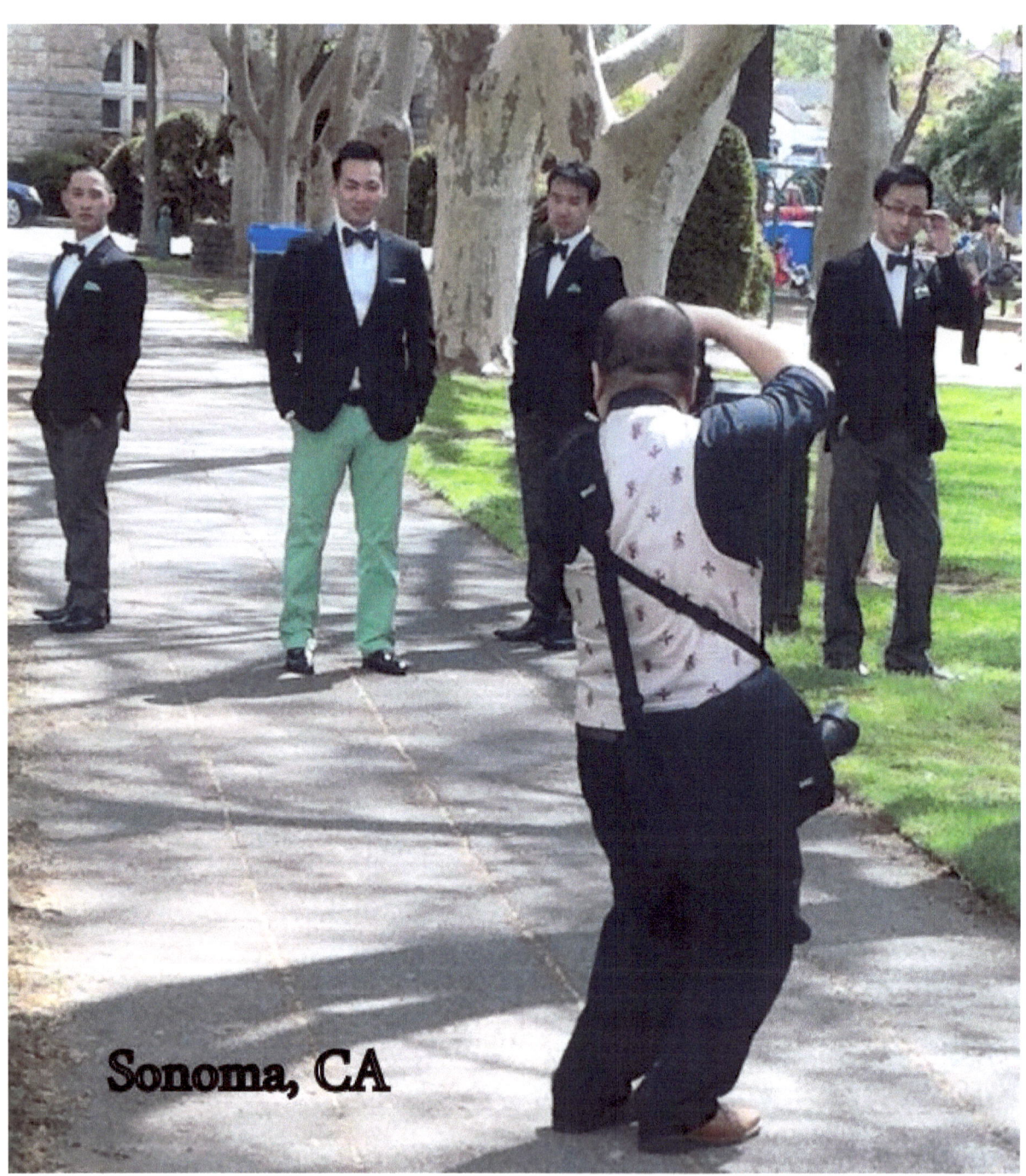

Sonoma, CA

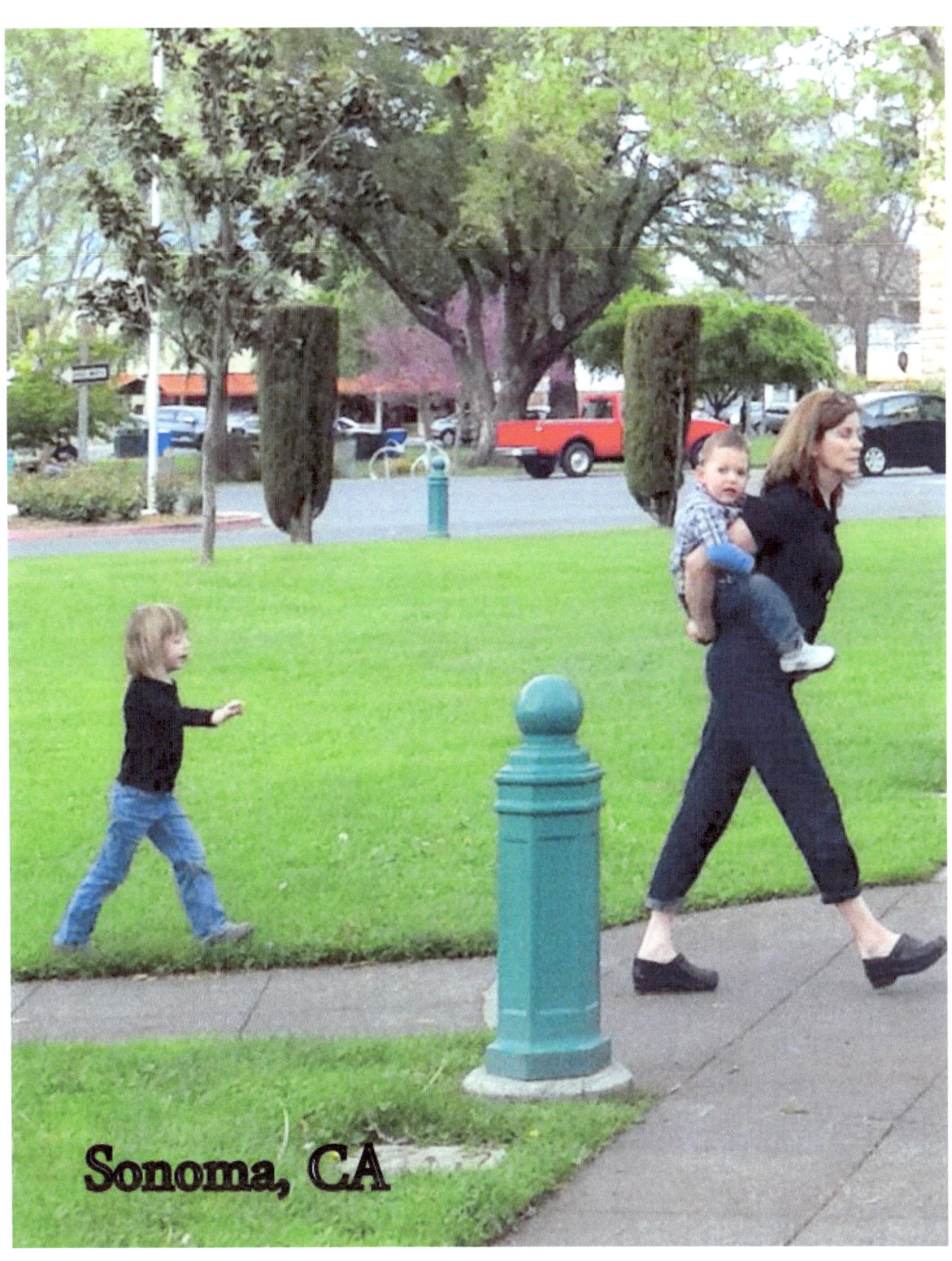

Sonoma, CA

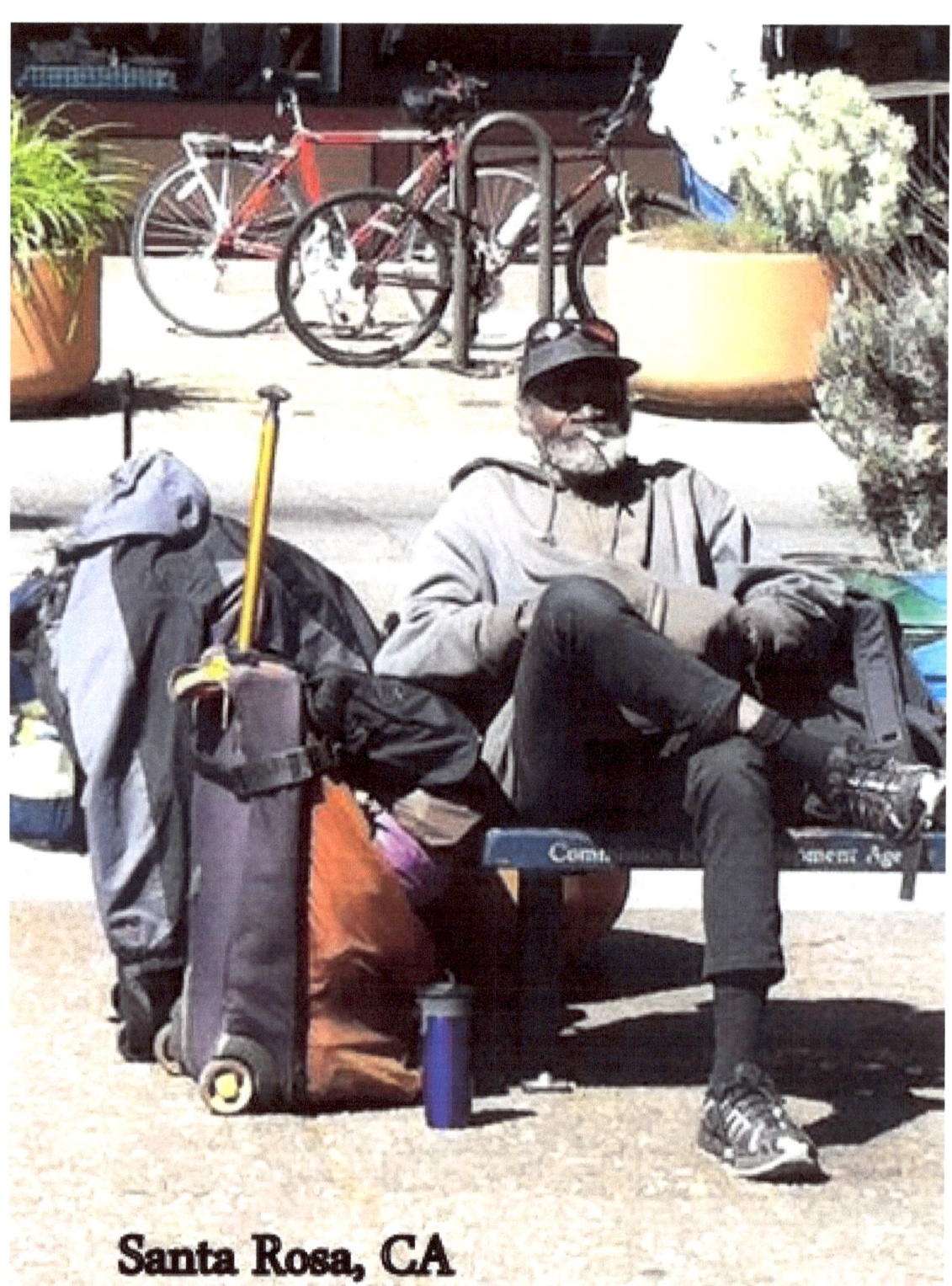

Santa Rosa, CA

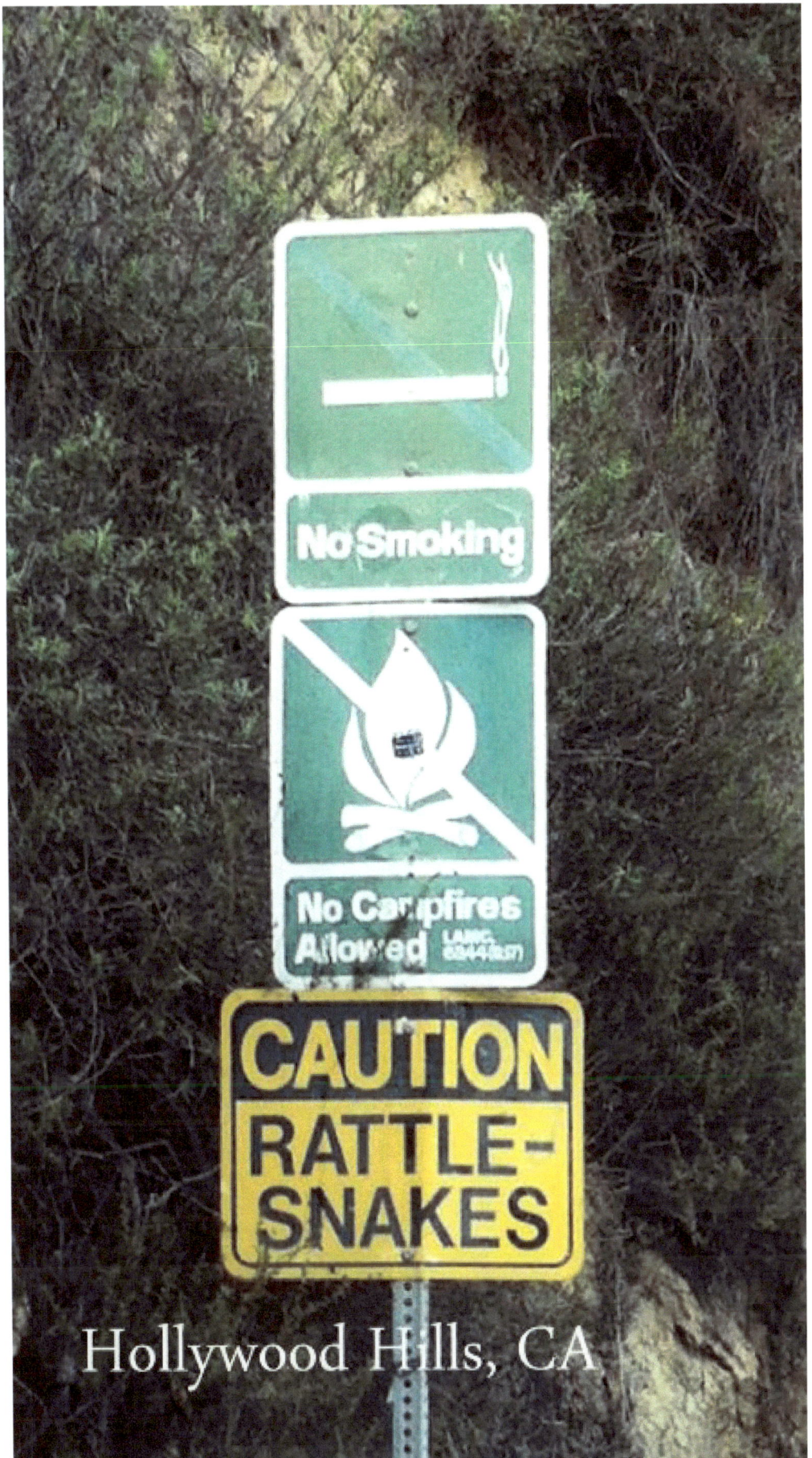

Hollywood Hills, CA

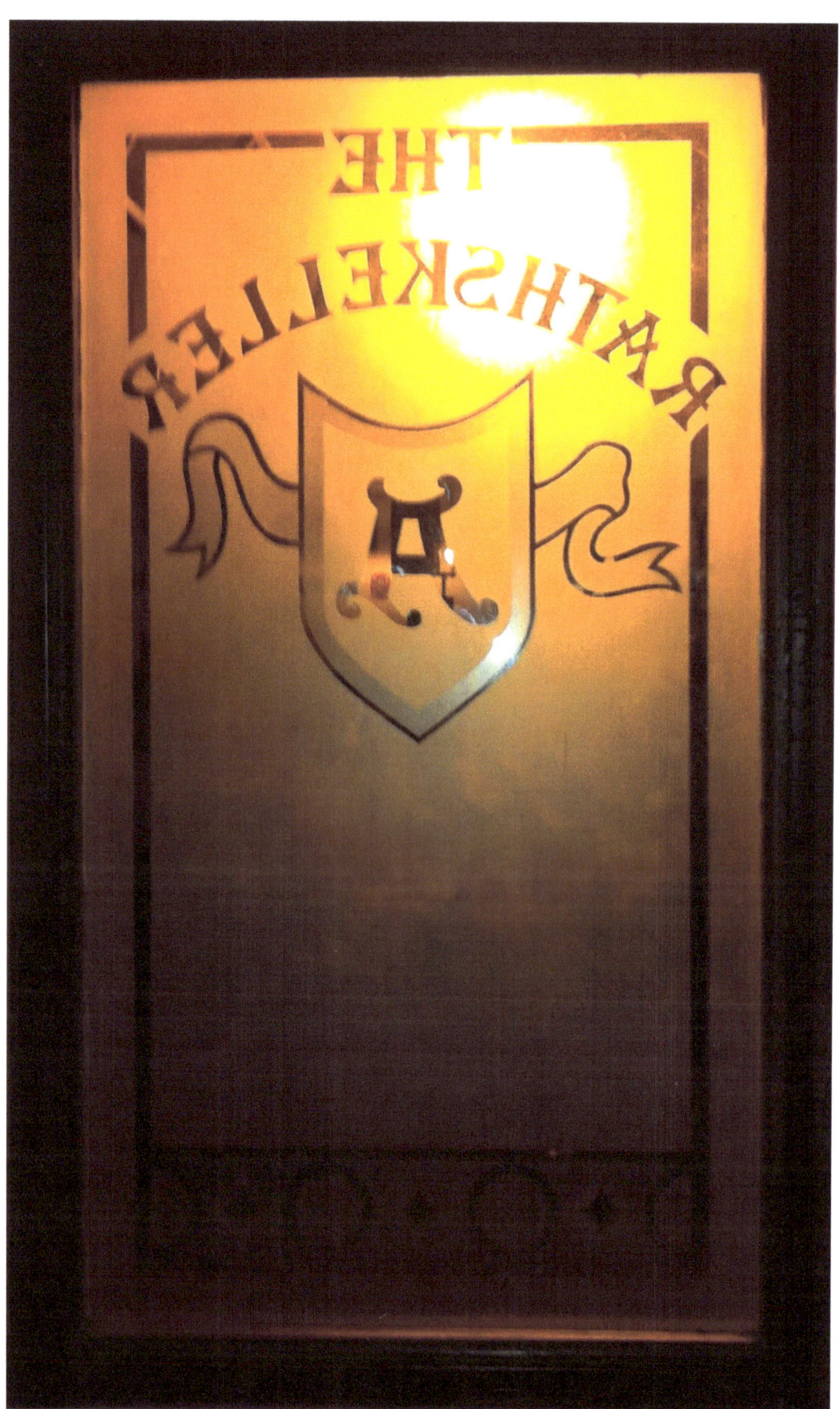

Indiana

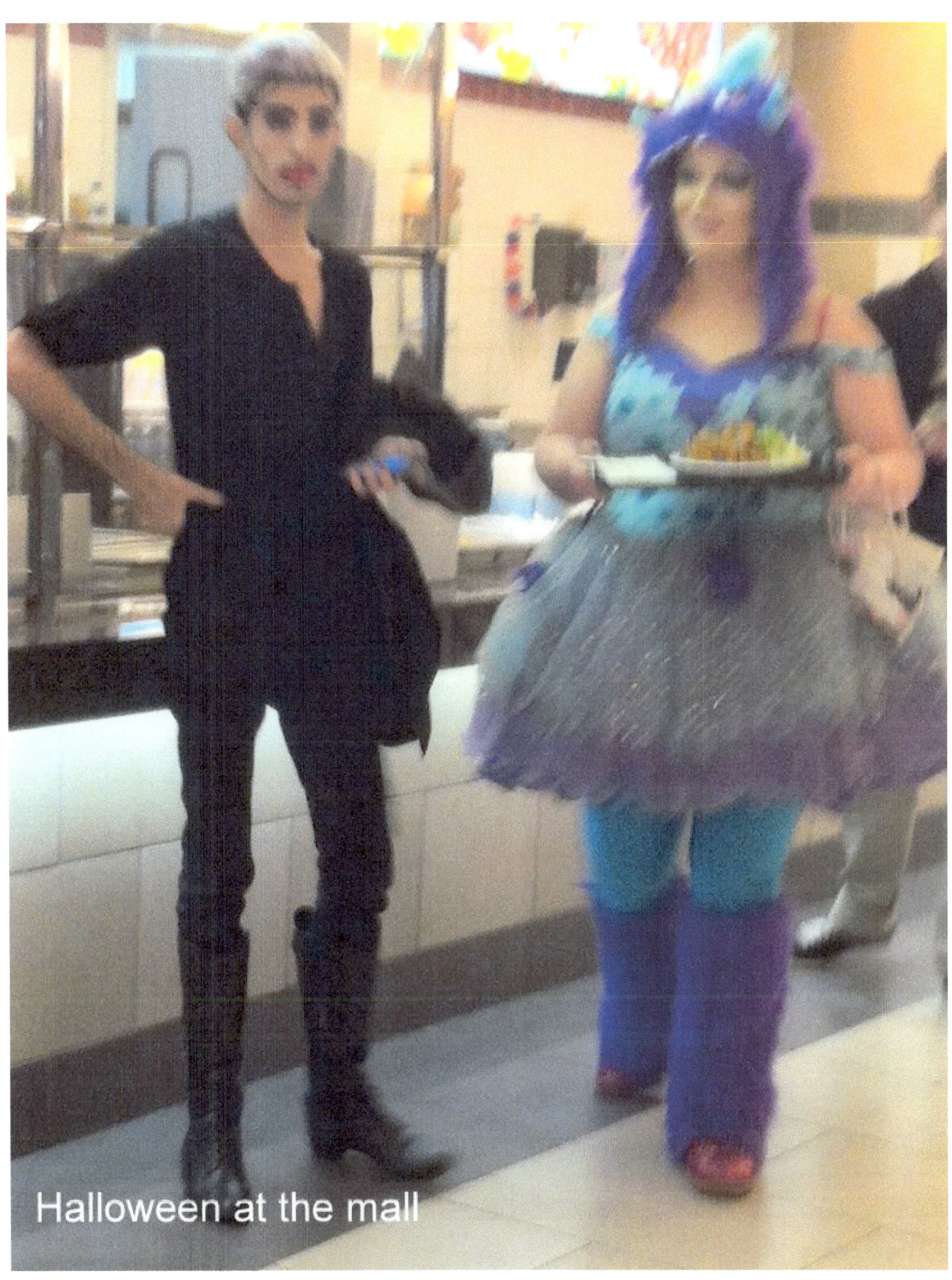

Halloween at the mall

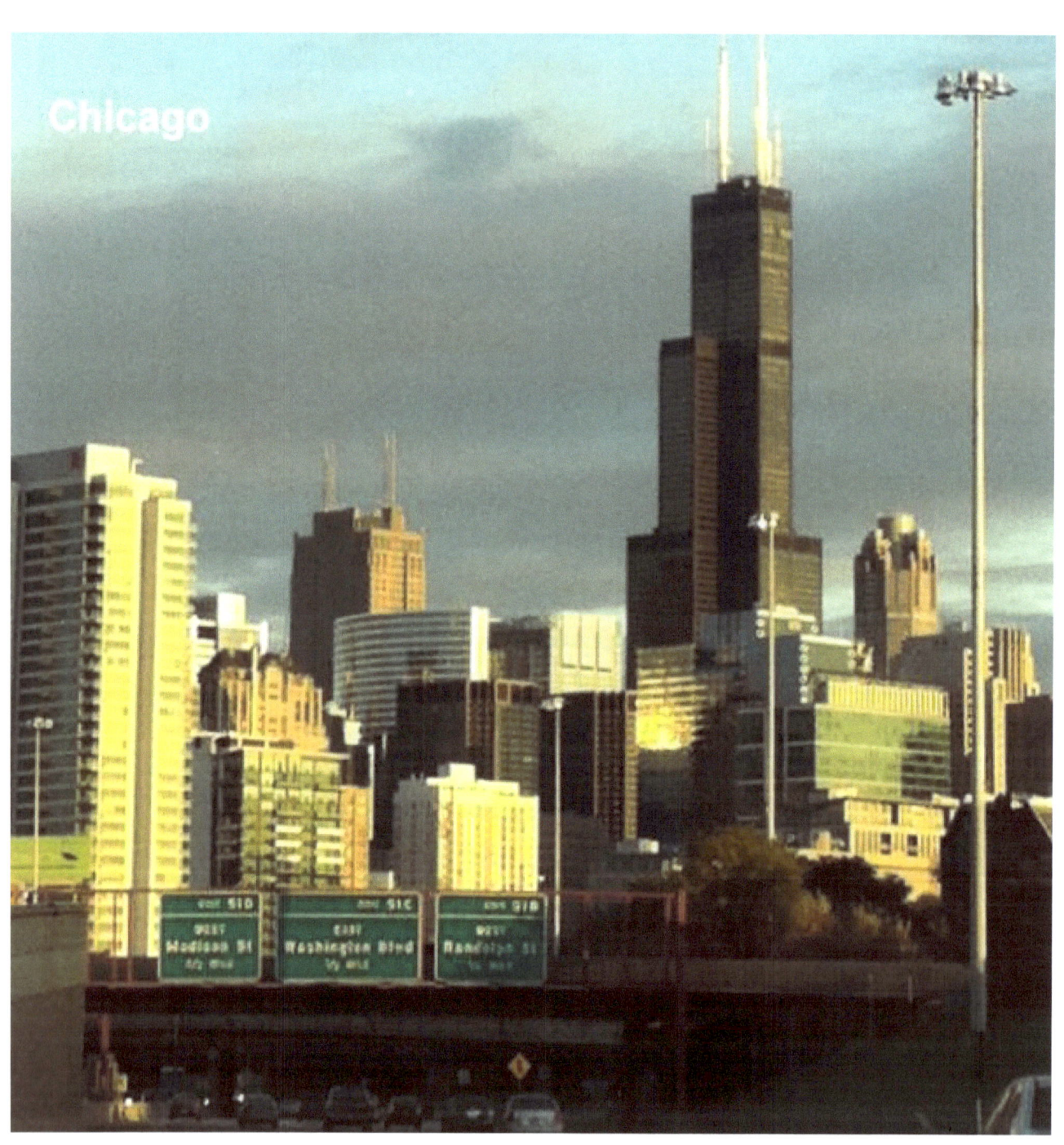

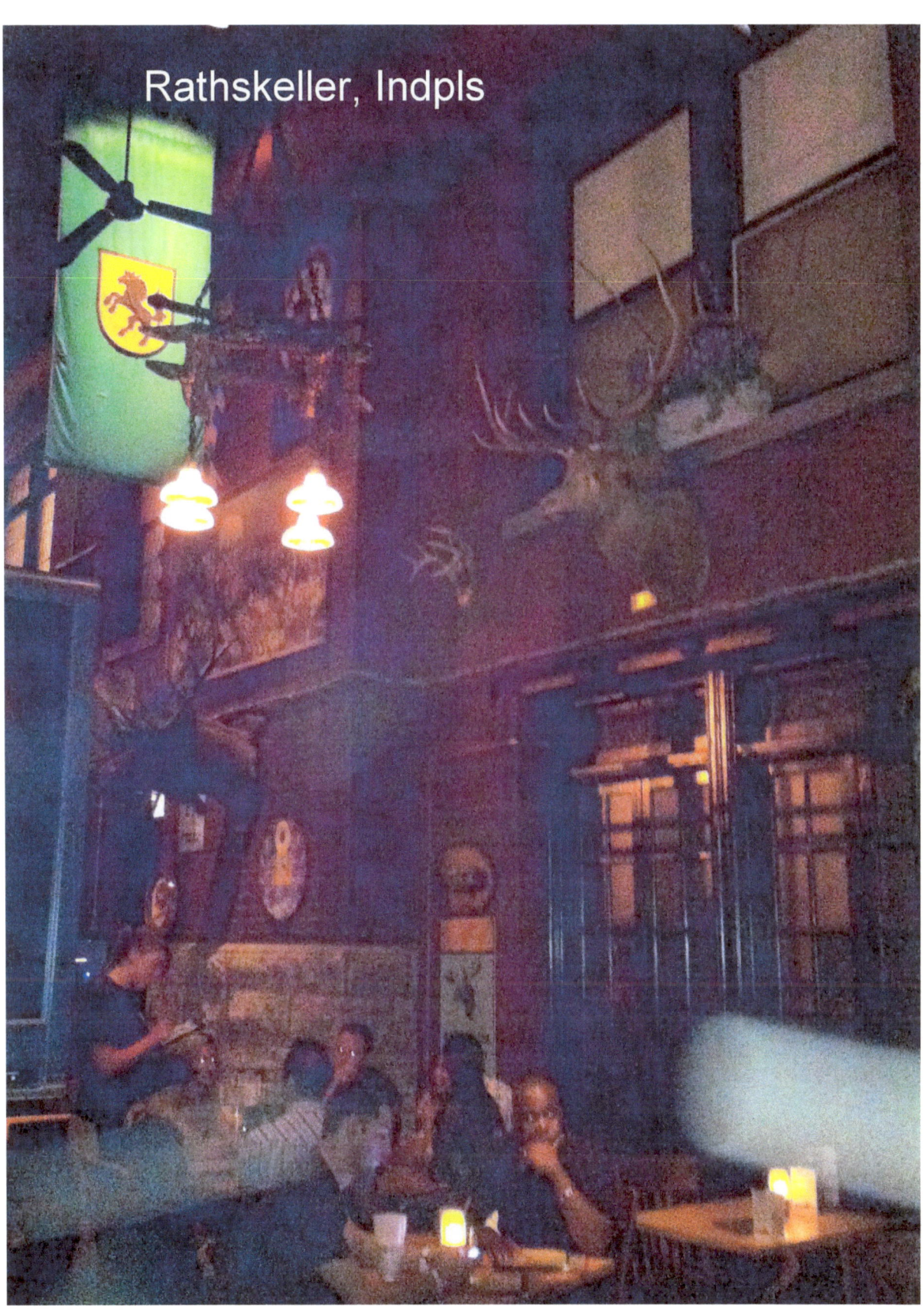

Rathskeller, Indpls

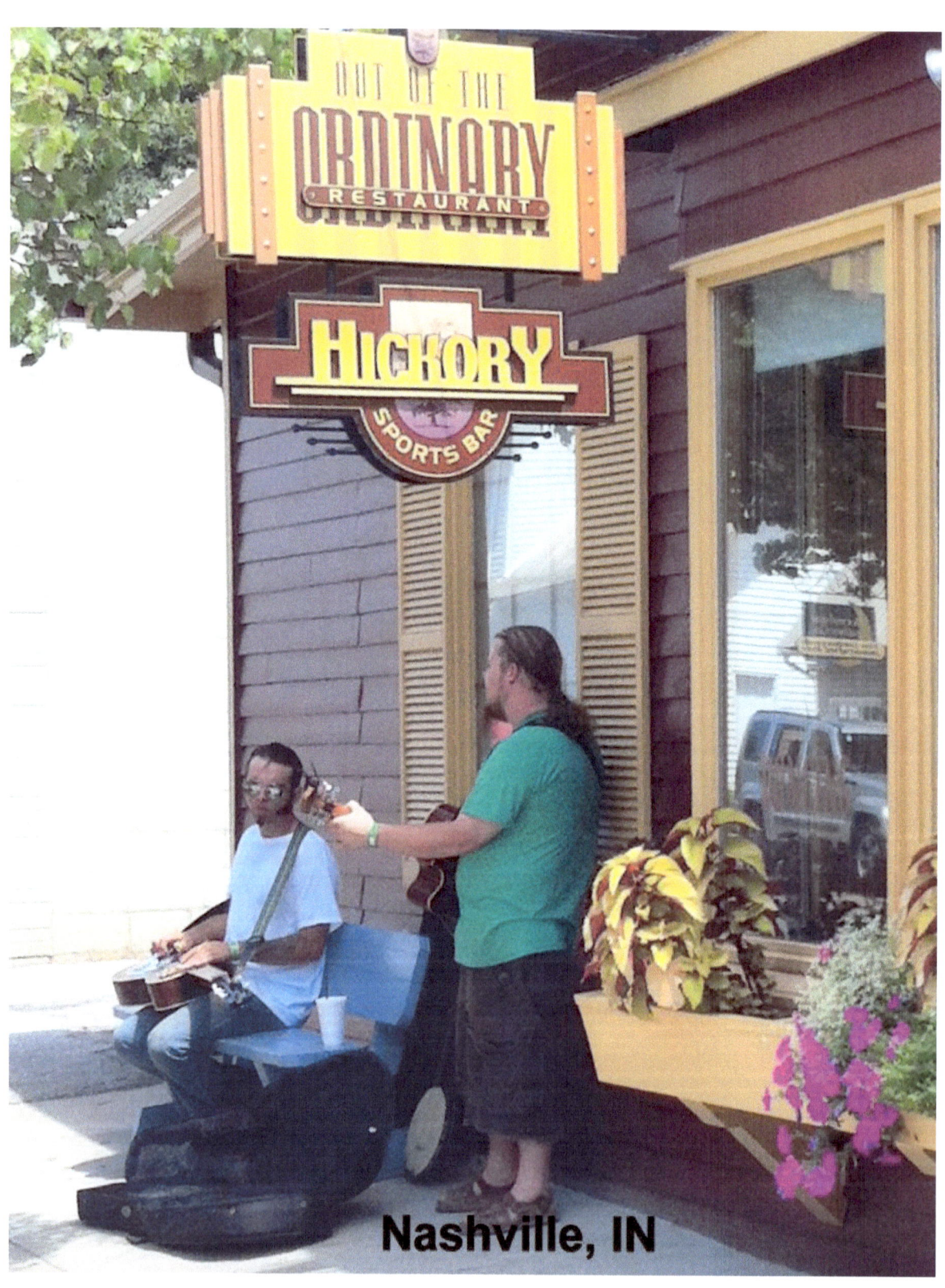

Nashville, IN

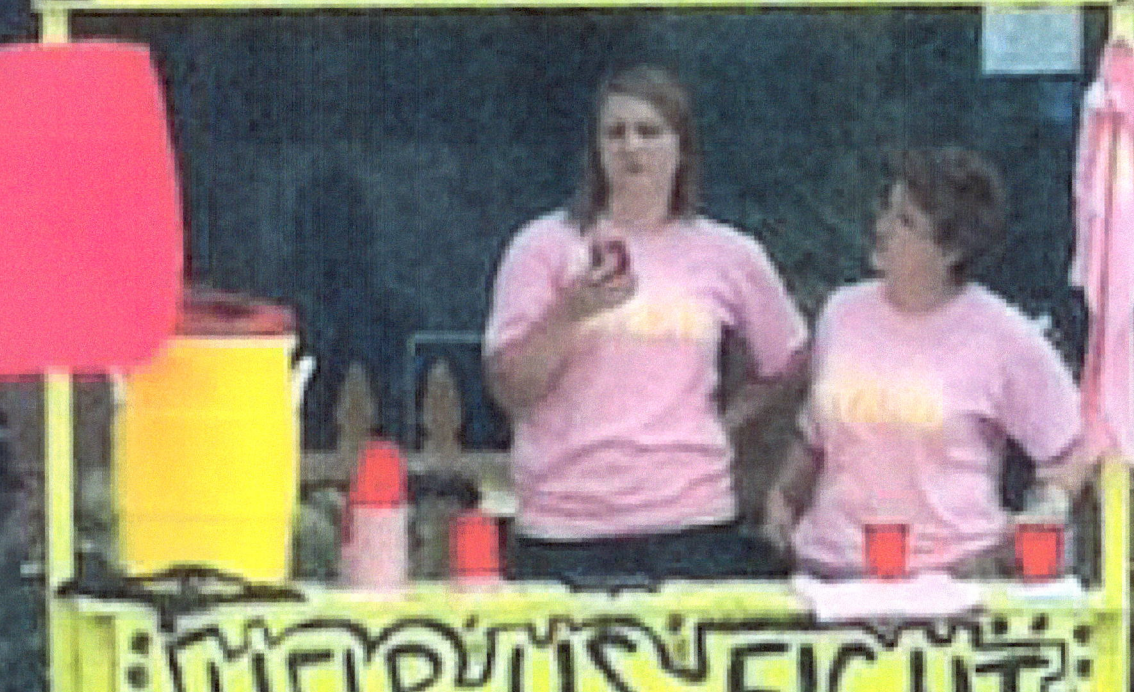

ALEX'S lemonade STAND

HELP US FIGHT CHILDHOOD CANCER

Indiana

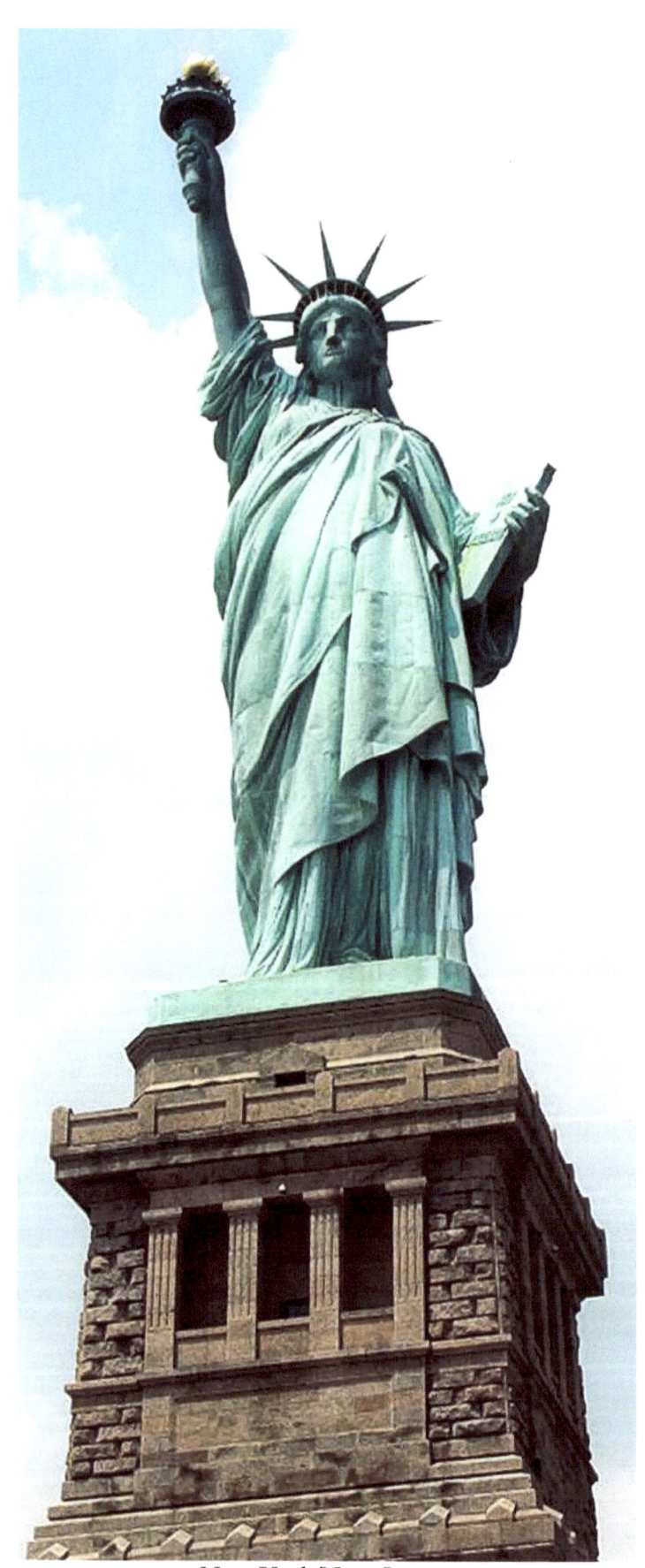

New York/New Jersey

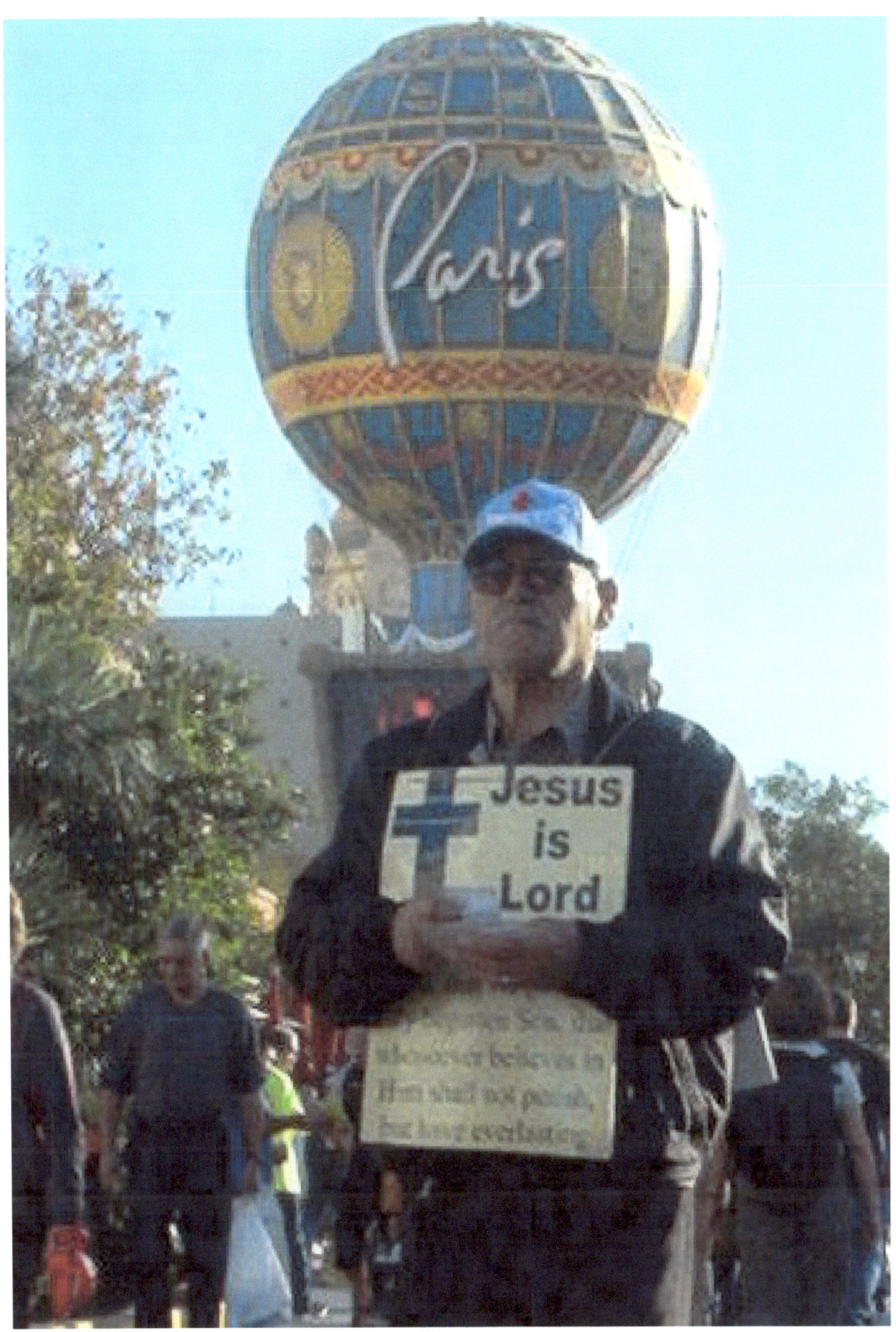

Vegas

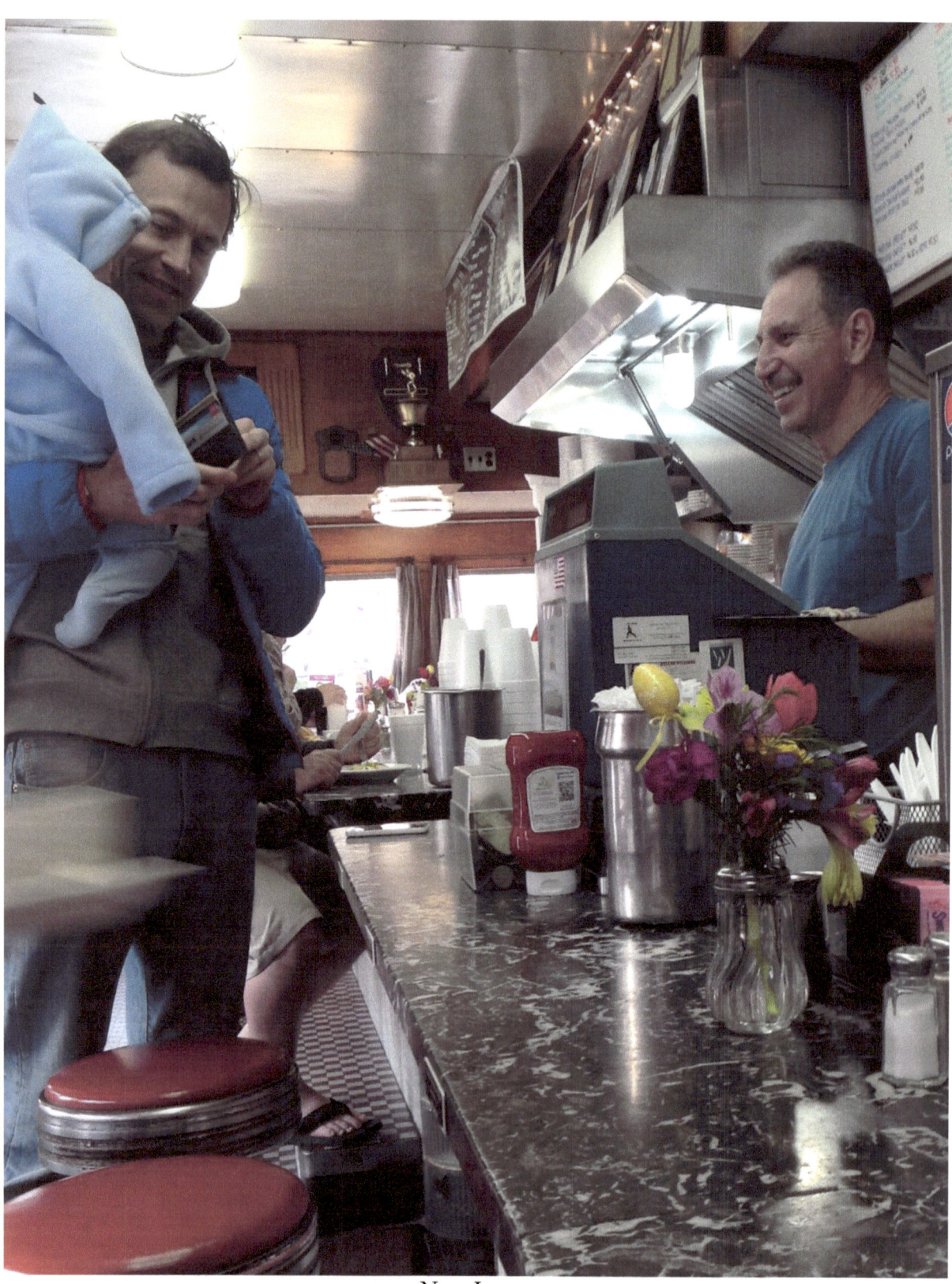

New Jersey

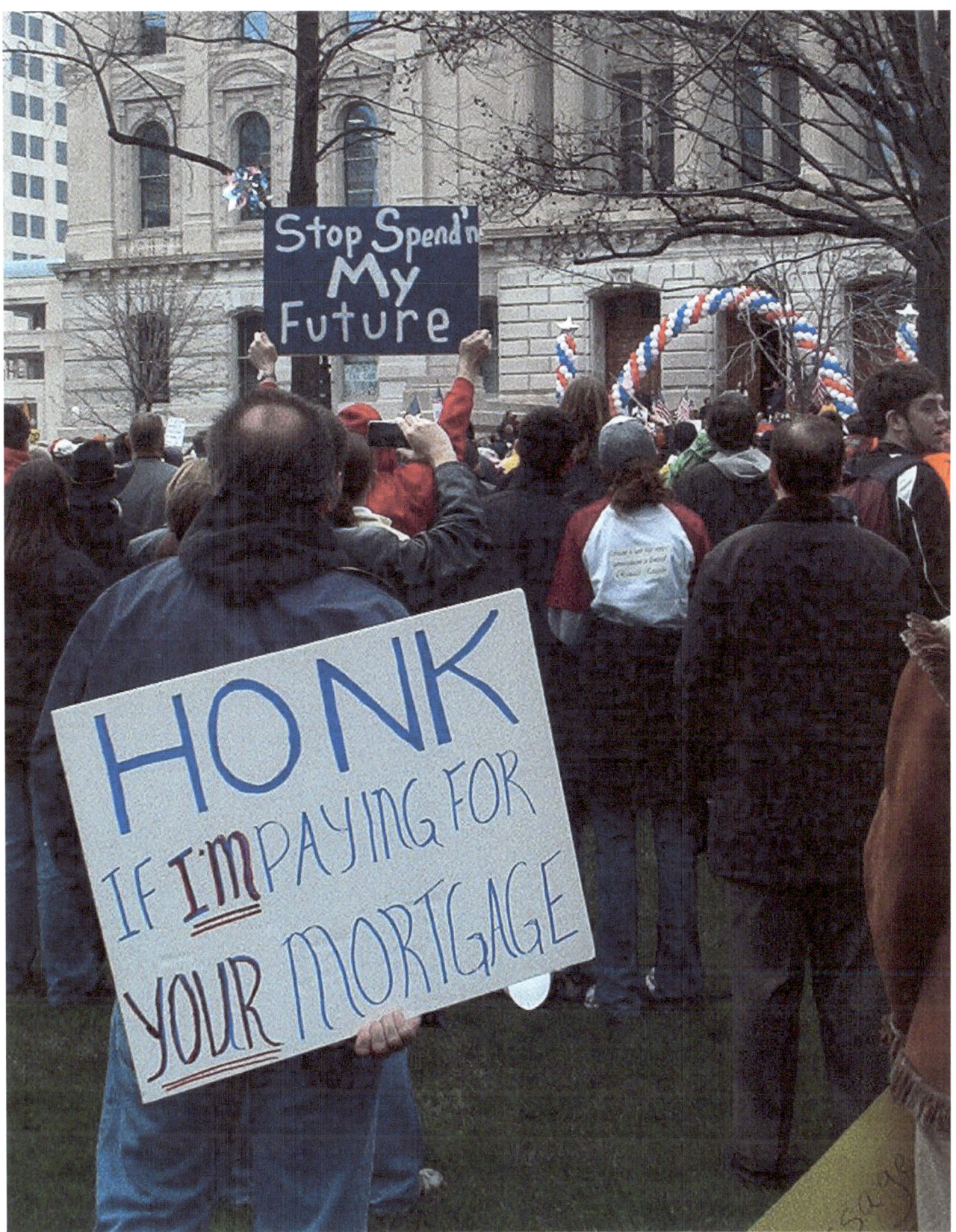

Tea Party Indianapolis

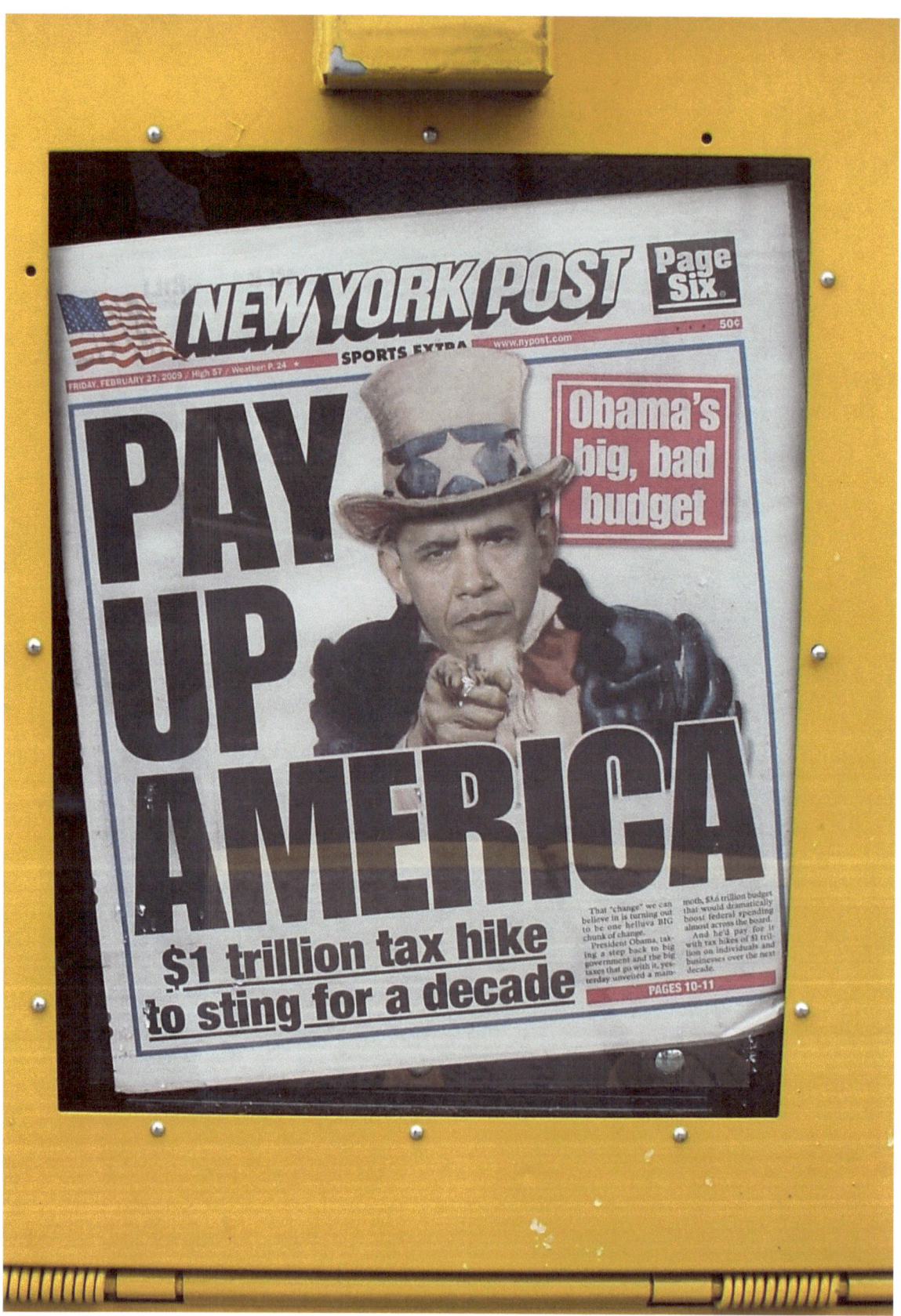

New Jersey

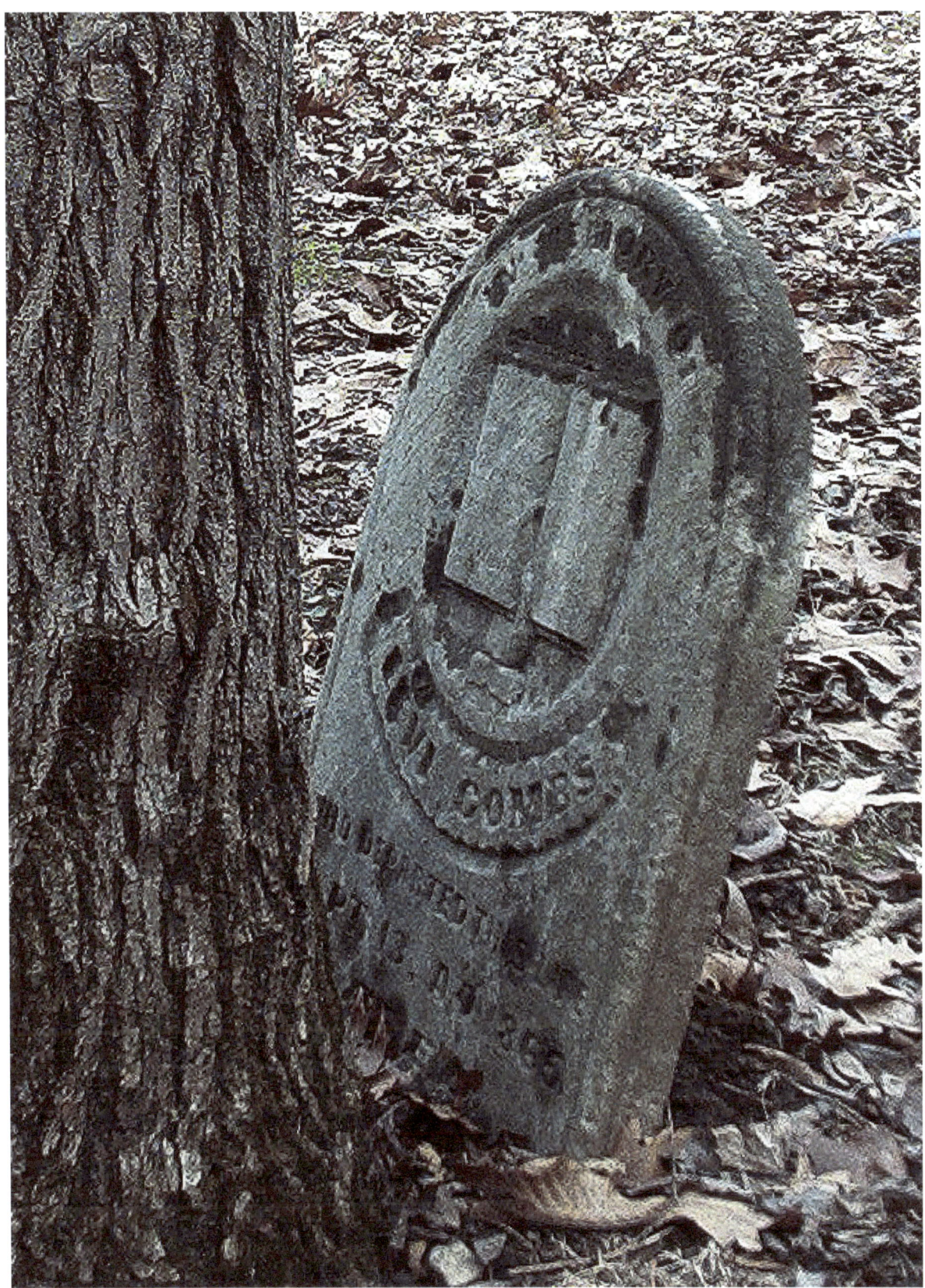
Indianapolis

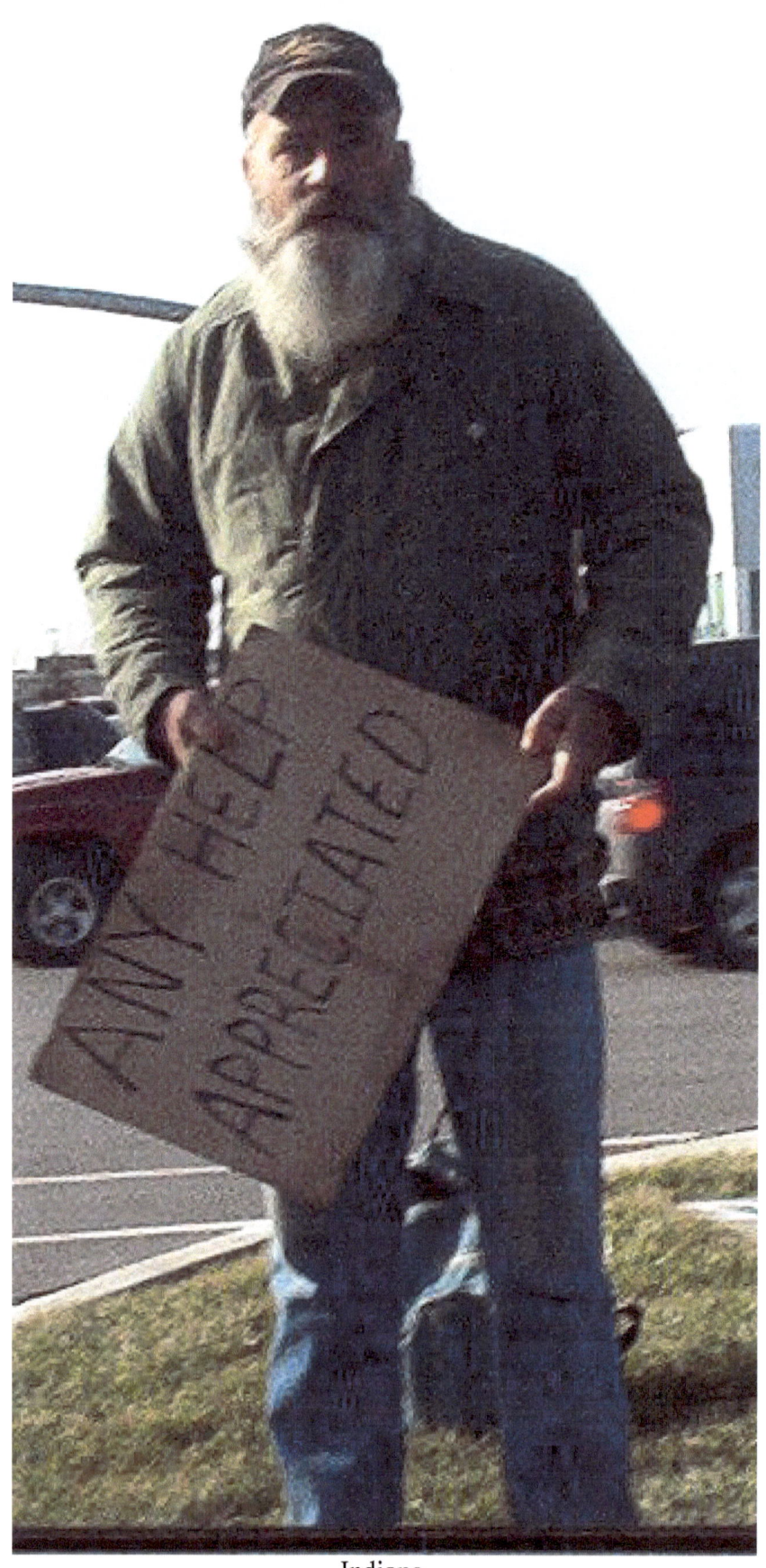

Indiana

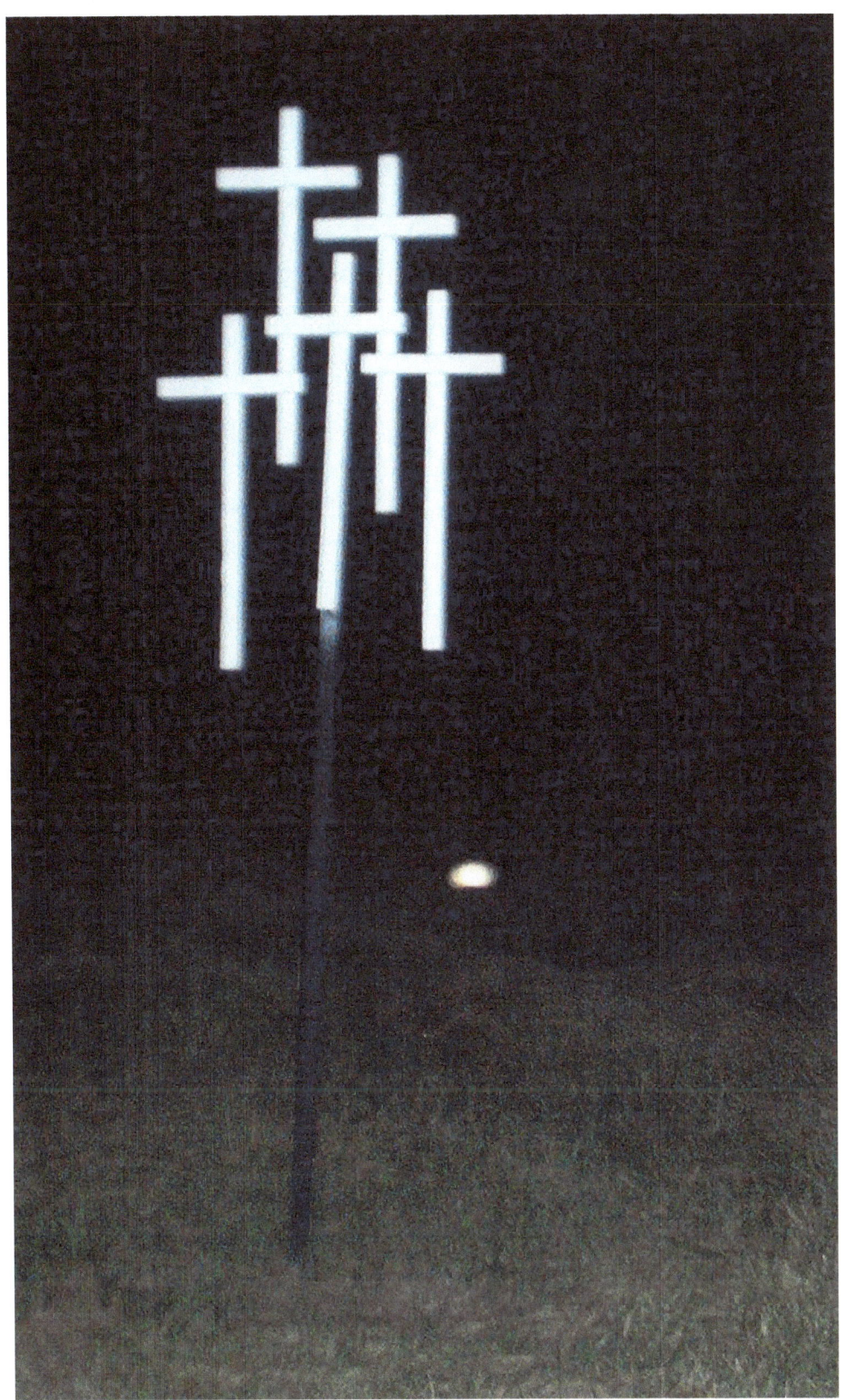

… Sad aftermath, Indiana

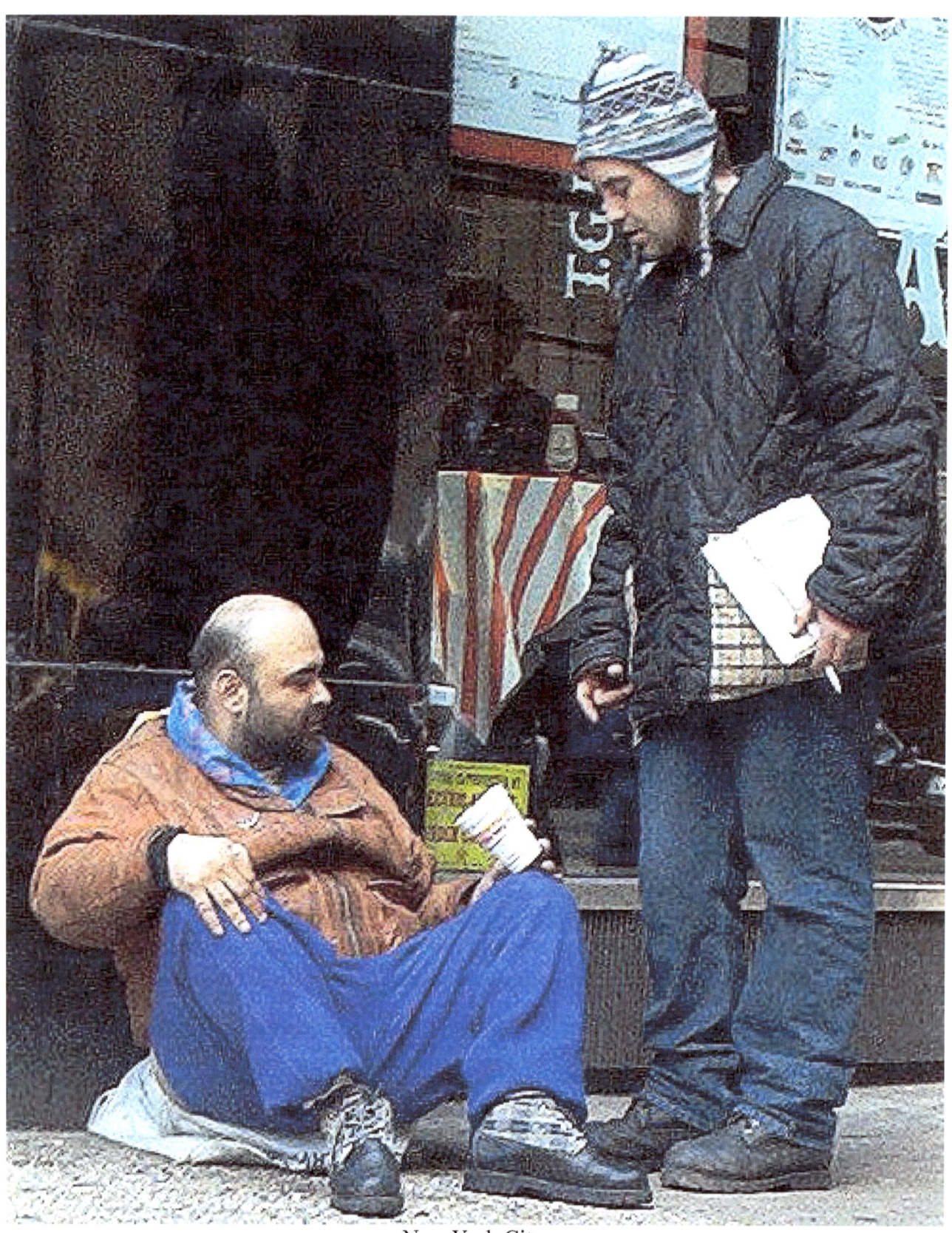

New York City

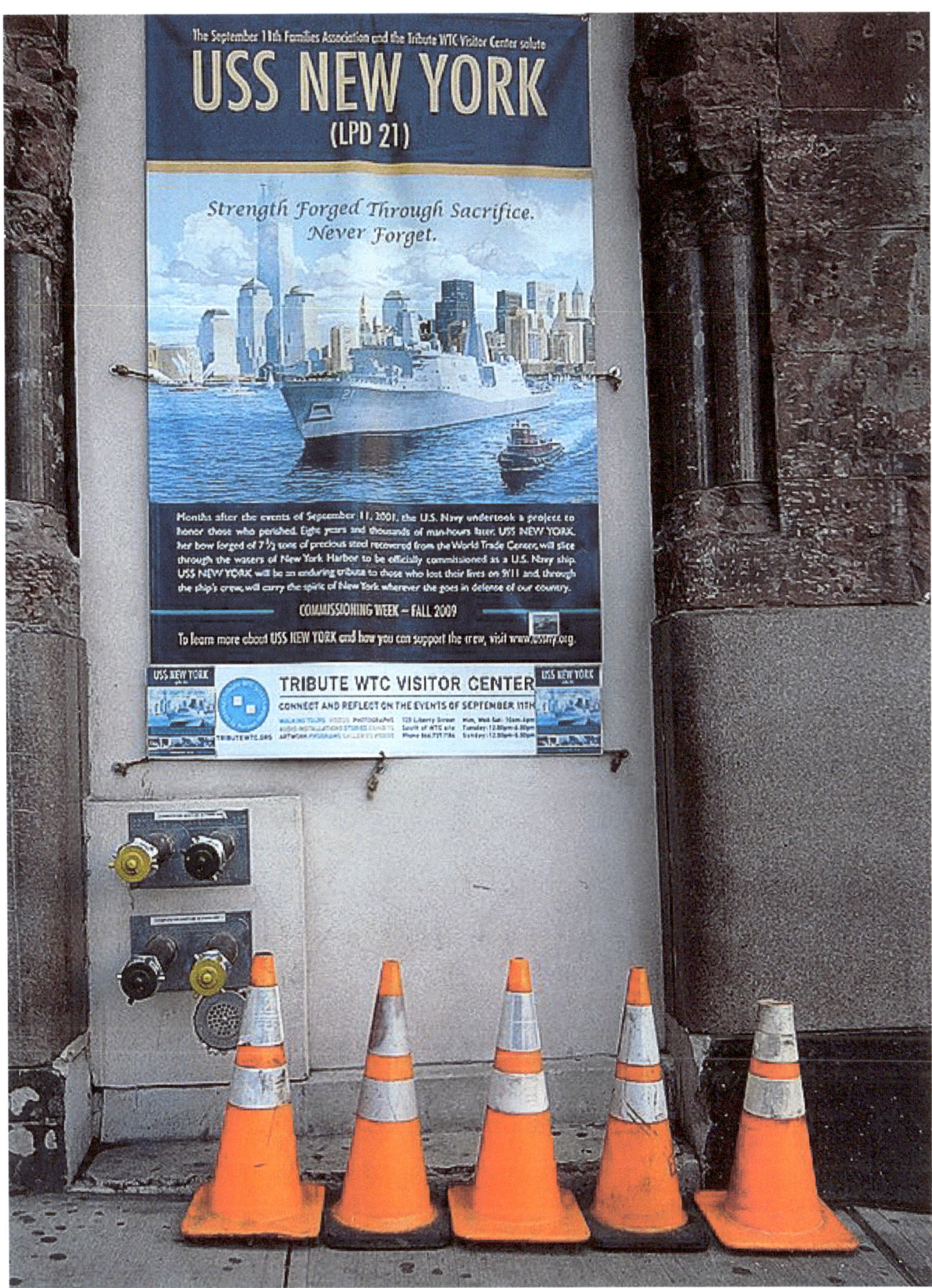

New York City by Ground Zero

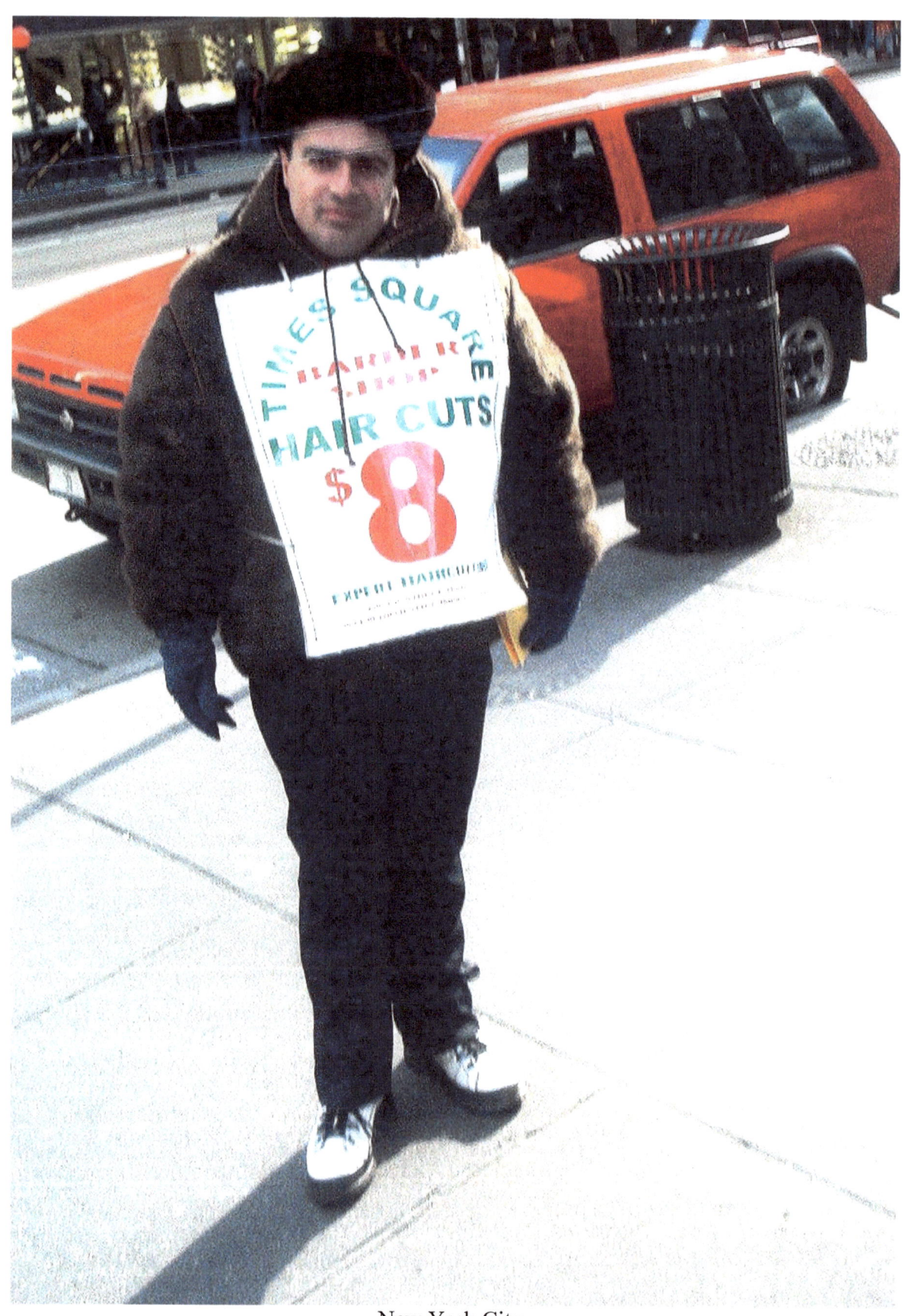

New York City

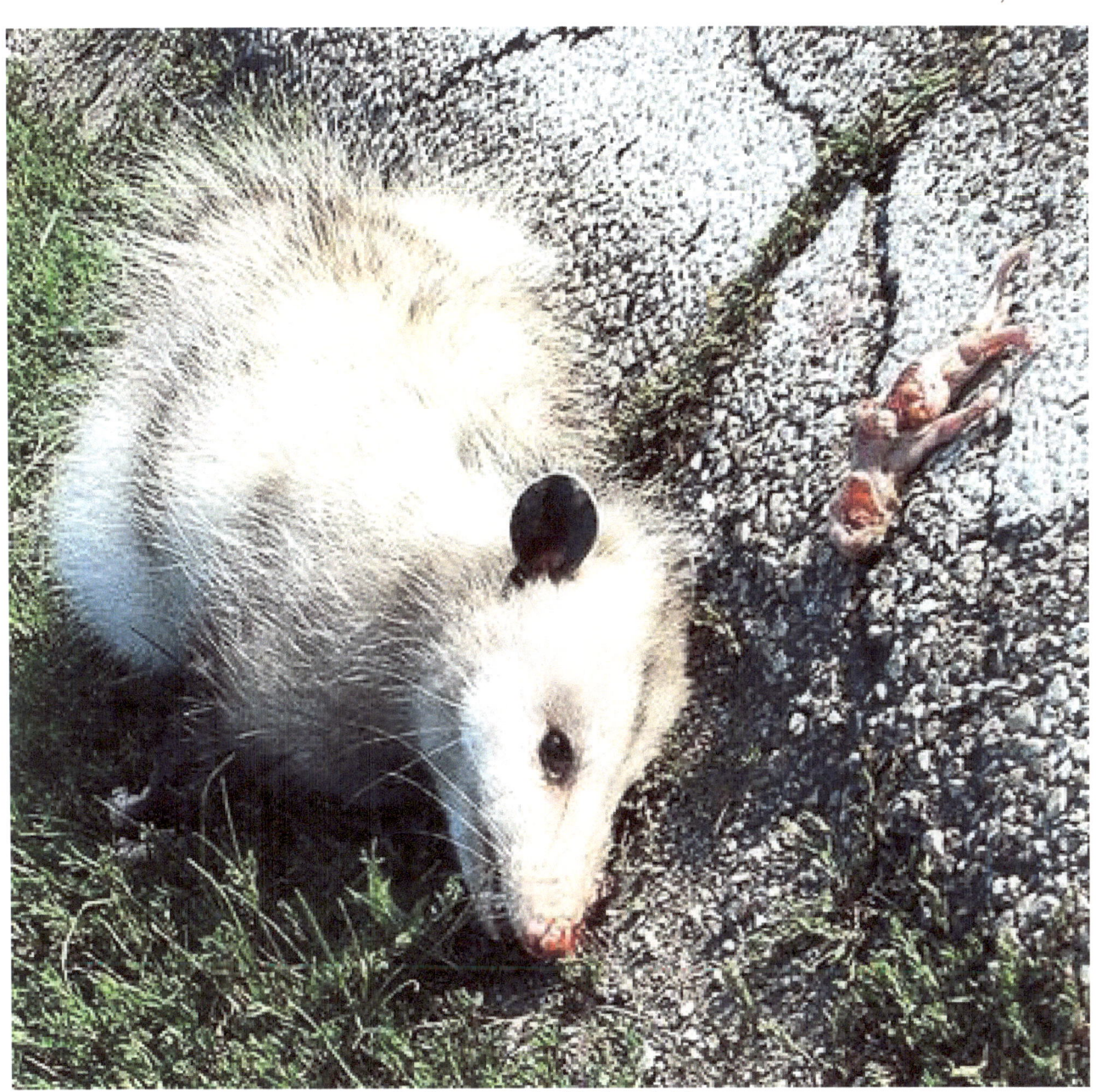

Indiana… a double homicide.

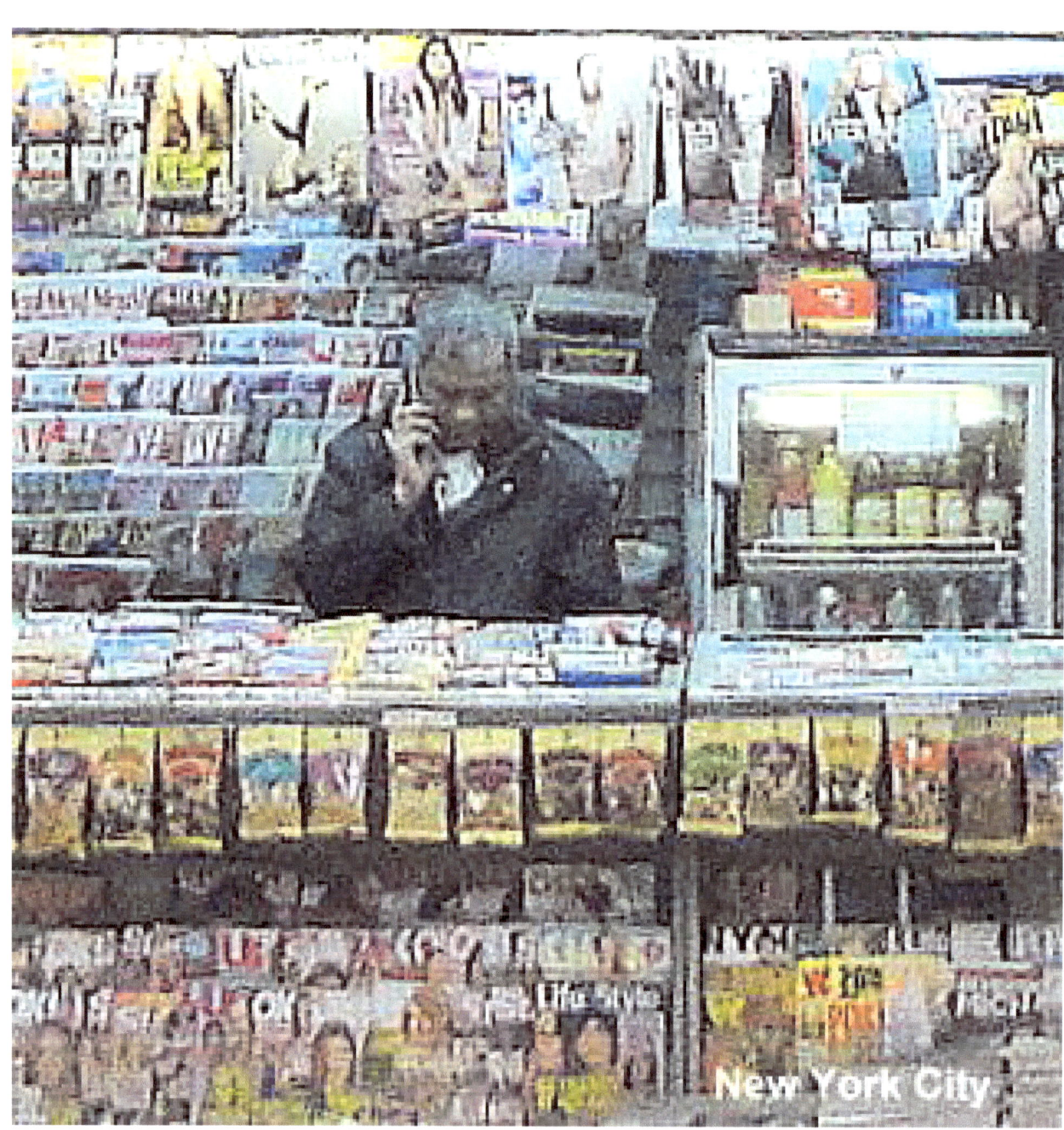

New York City

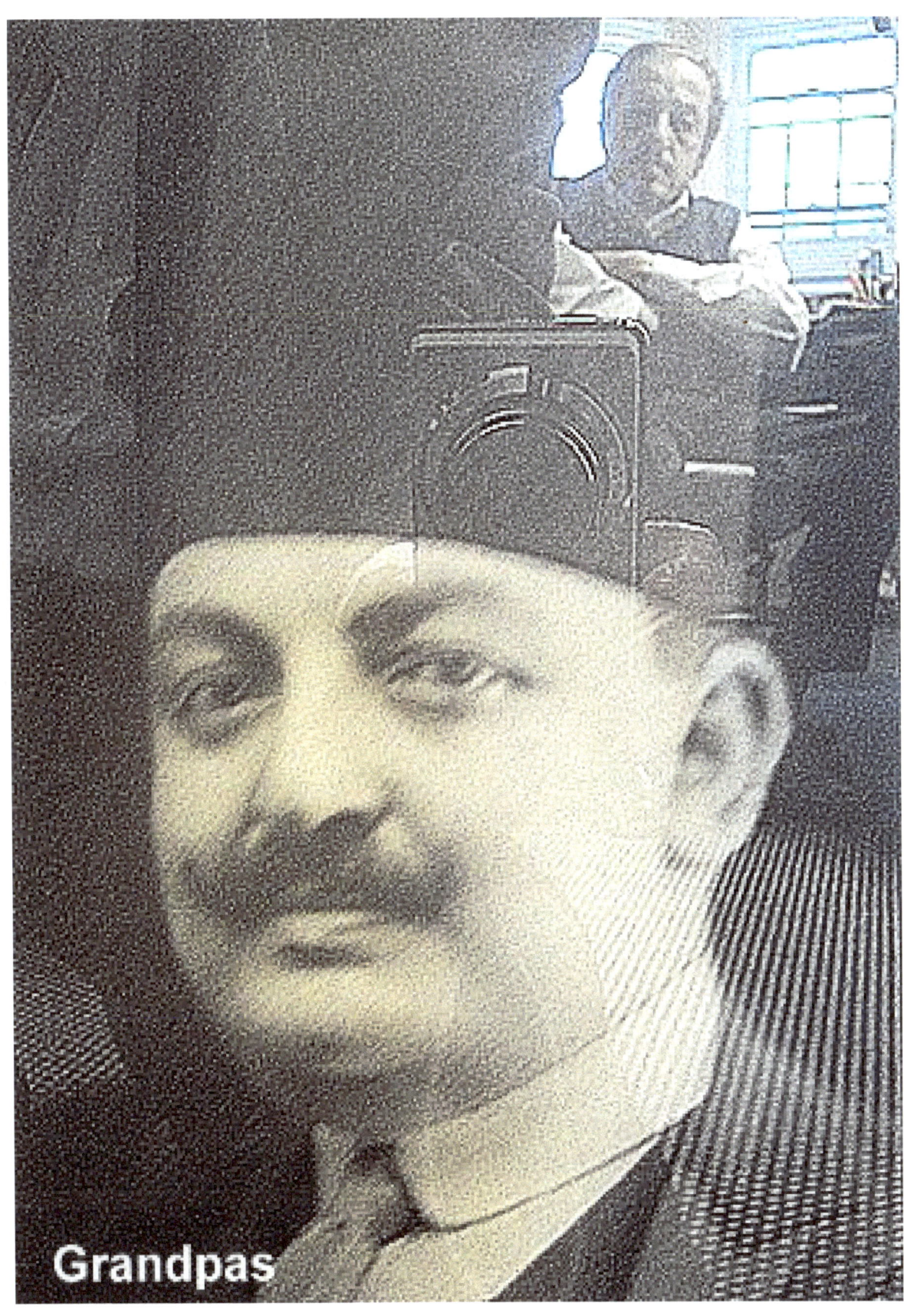

Grandpas

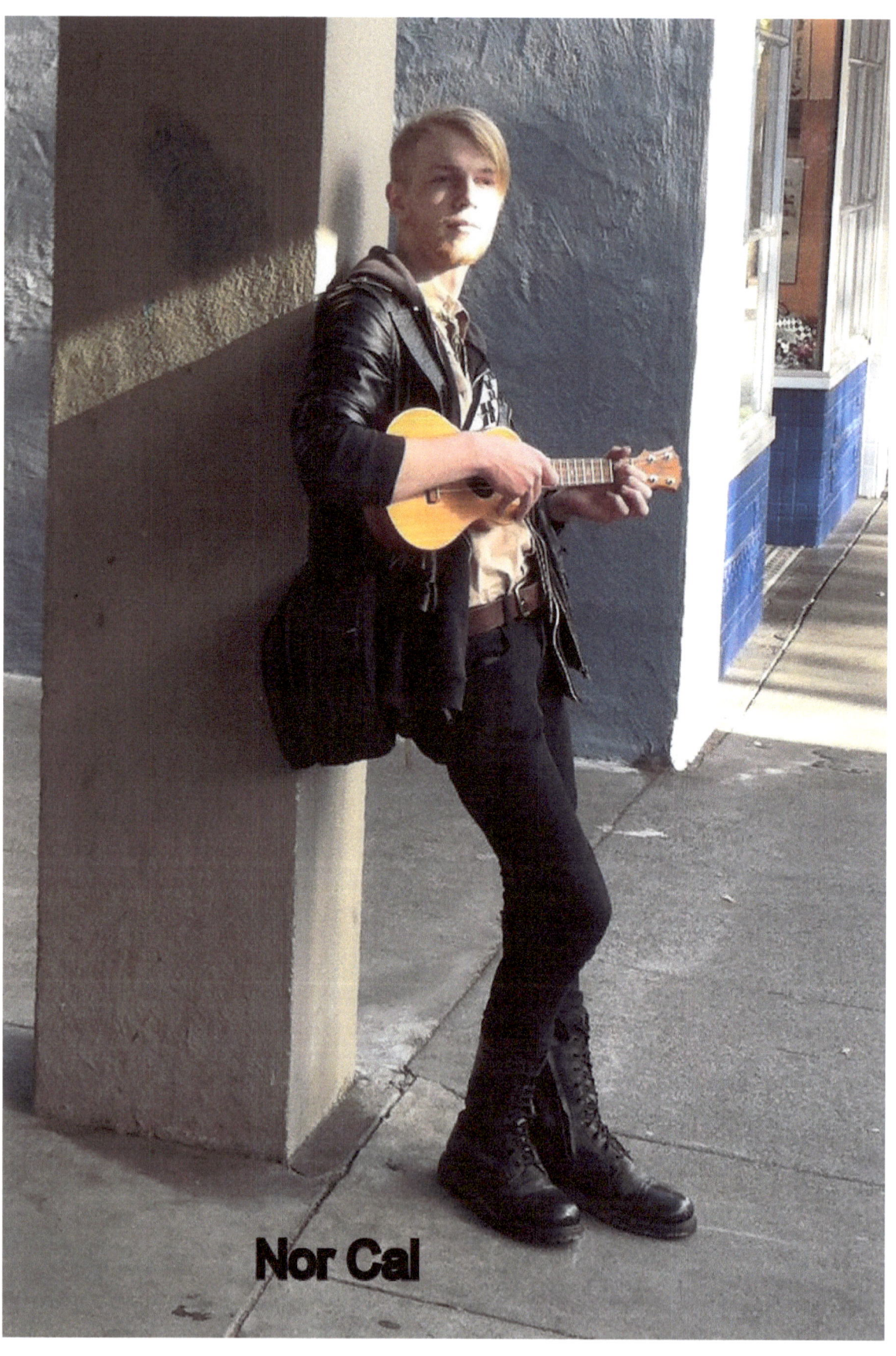

Nor Cal

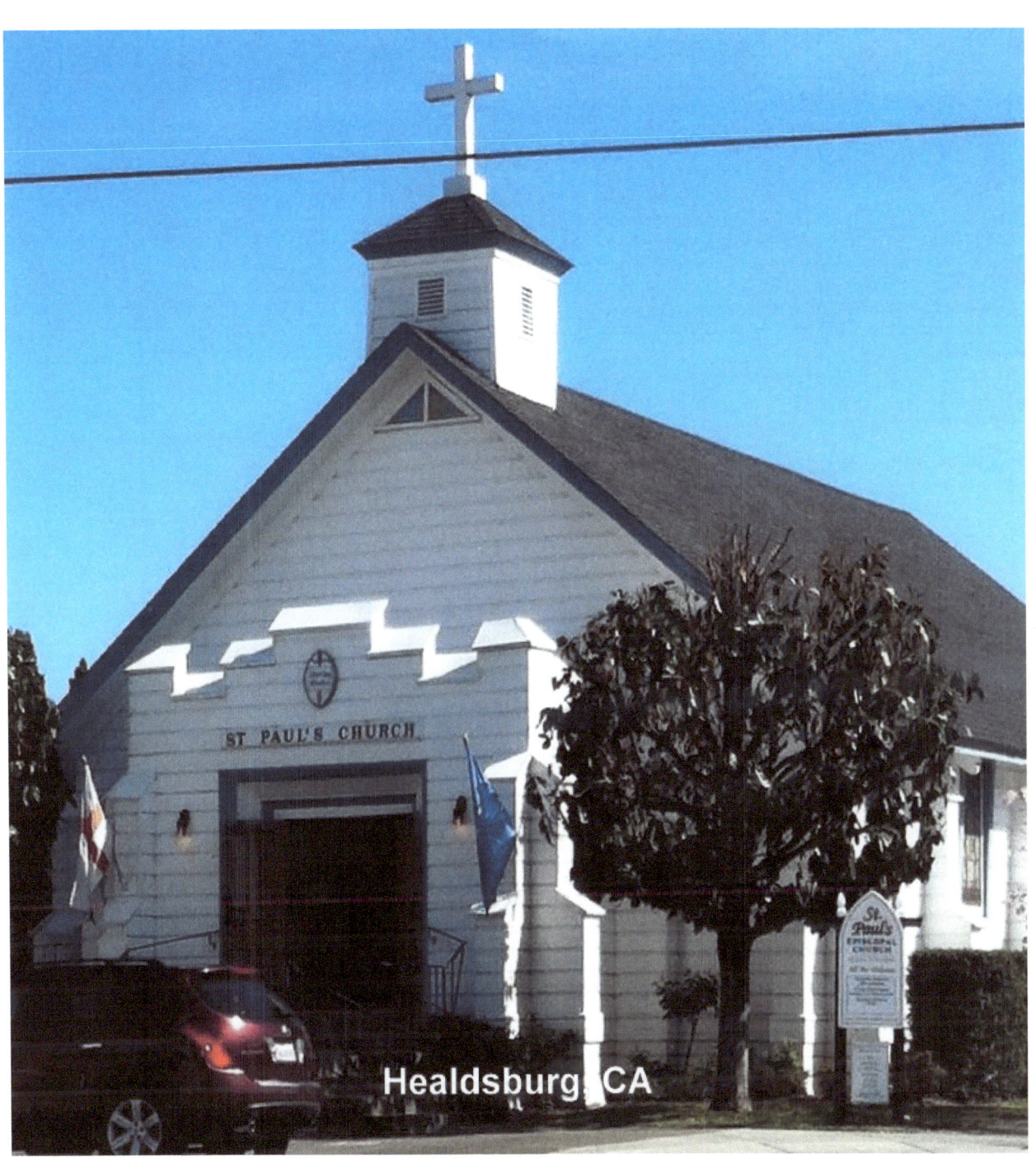

Healdsburg, CA

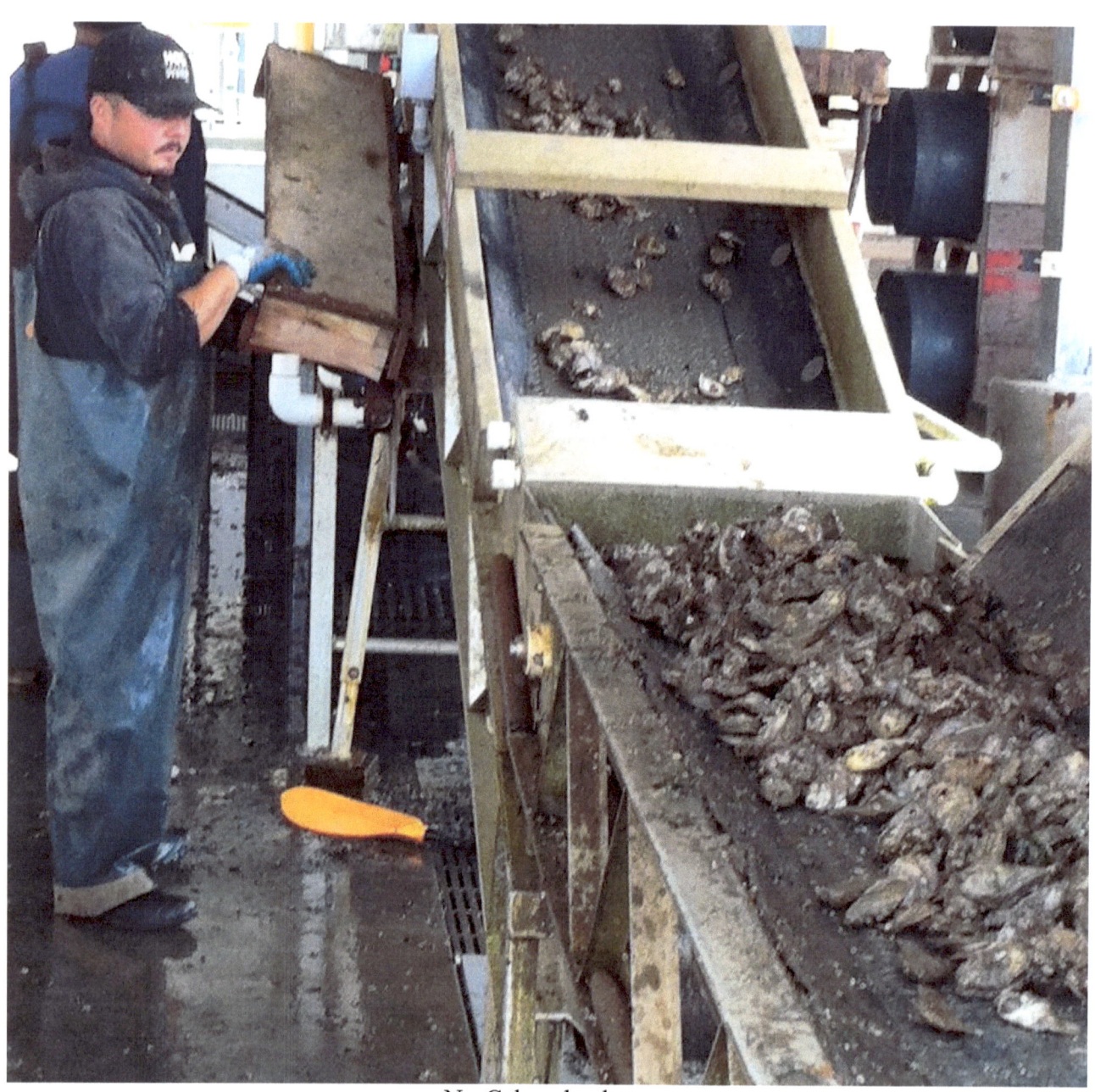

NorCal… shuckers

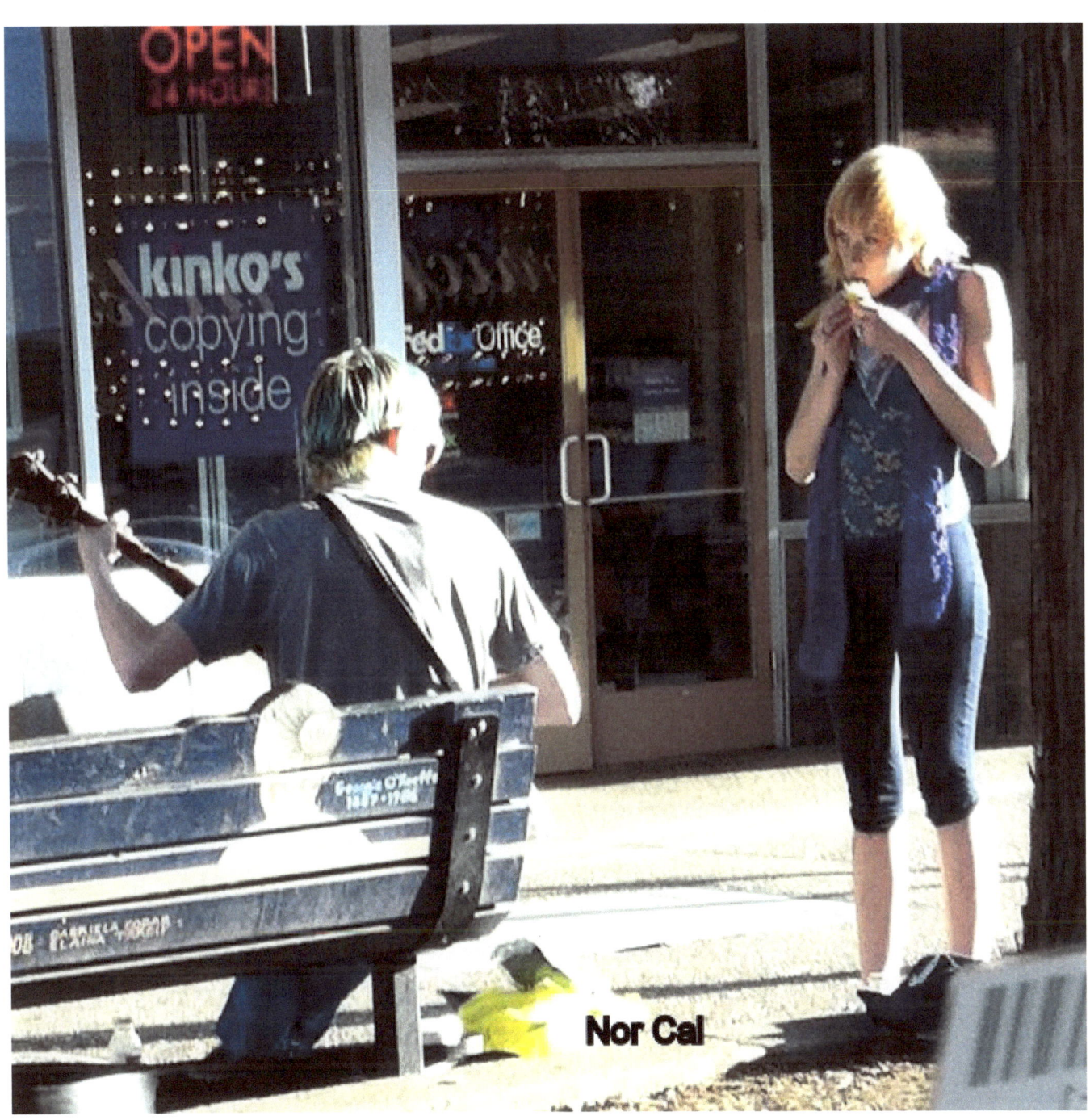

Nor Cal

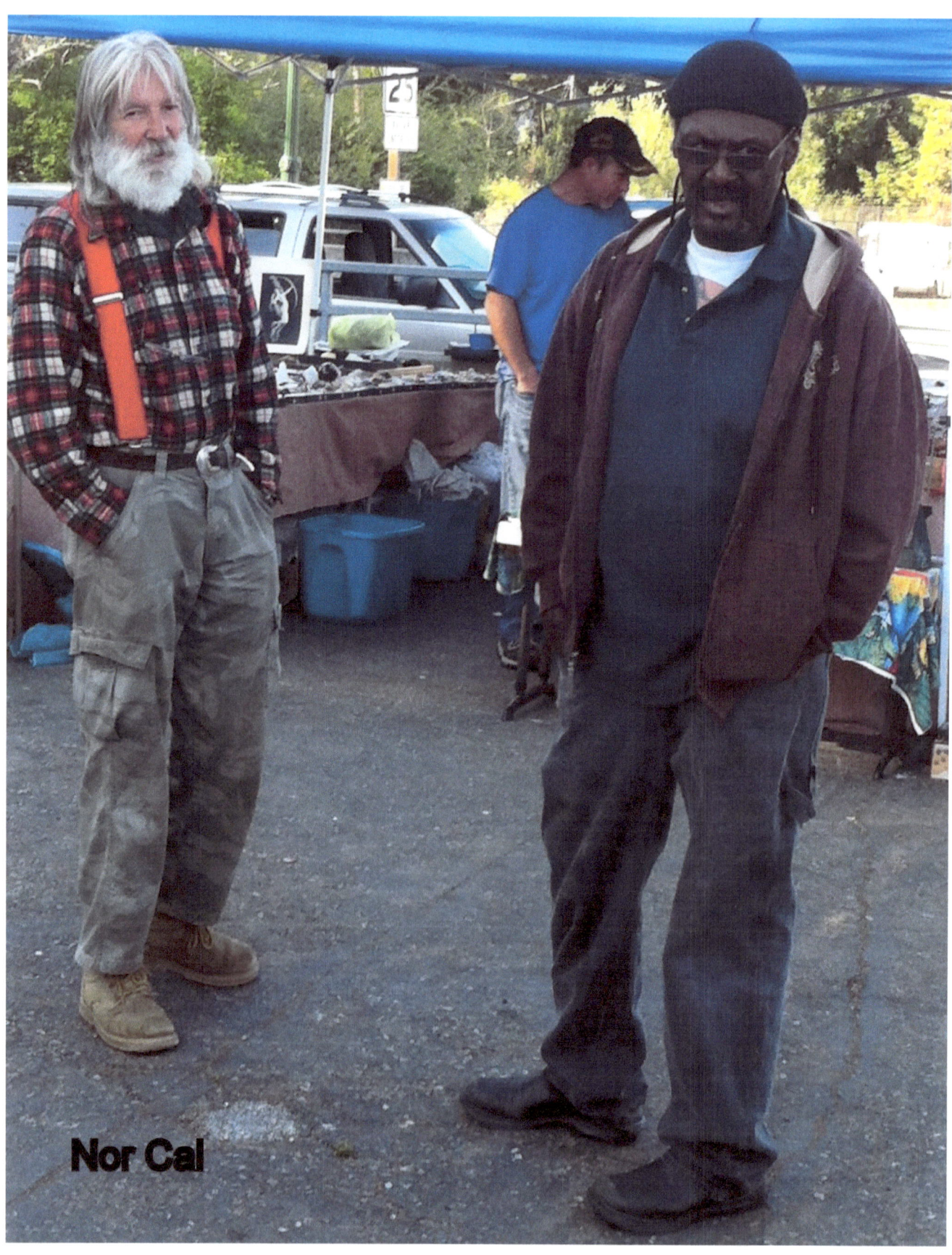

Nor Cal

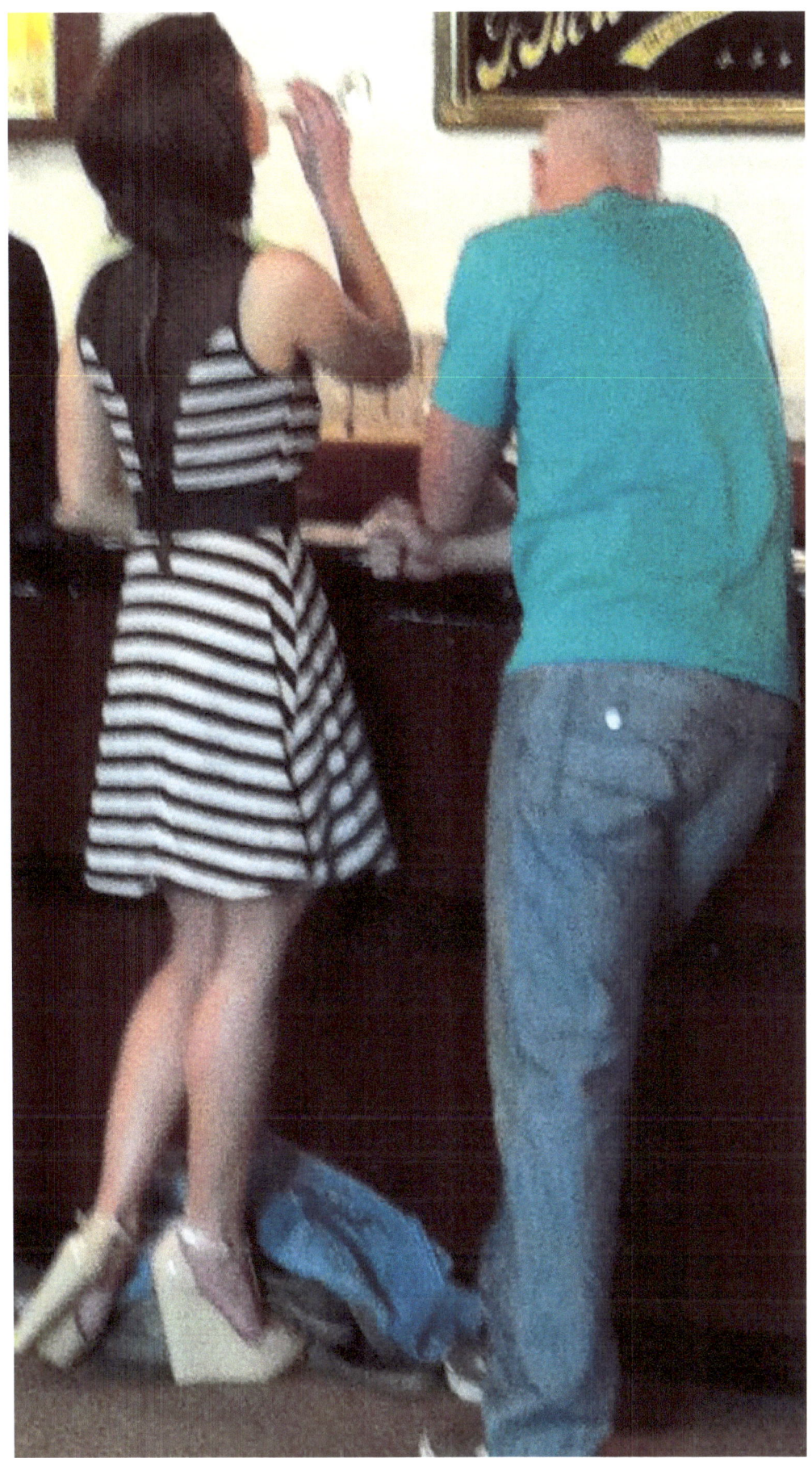

NorCal

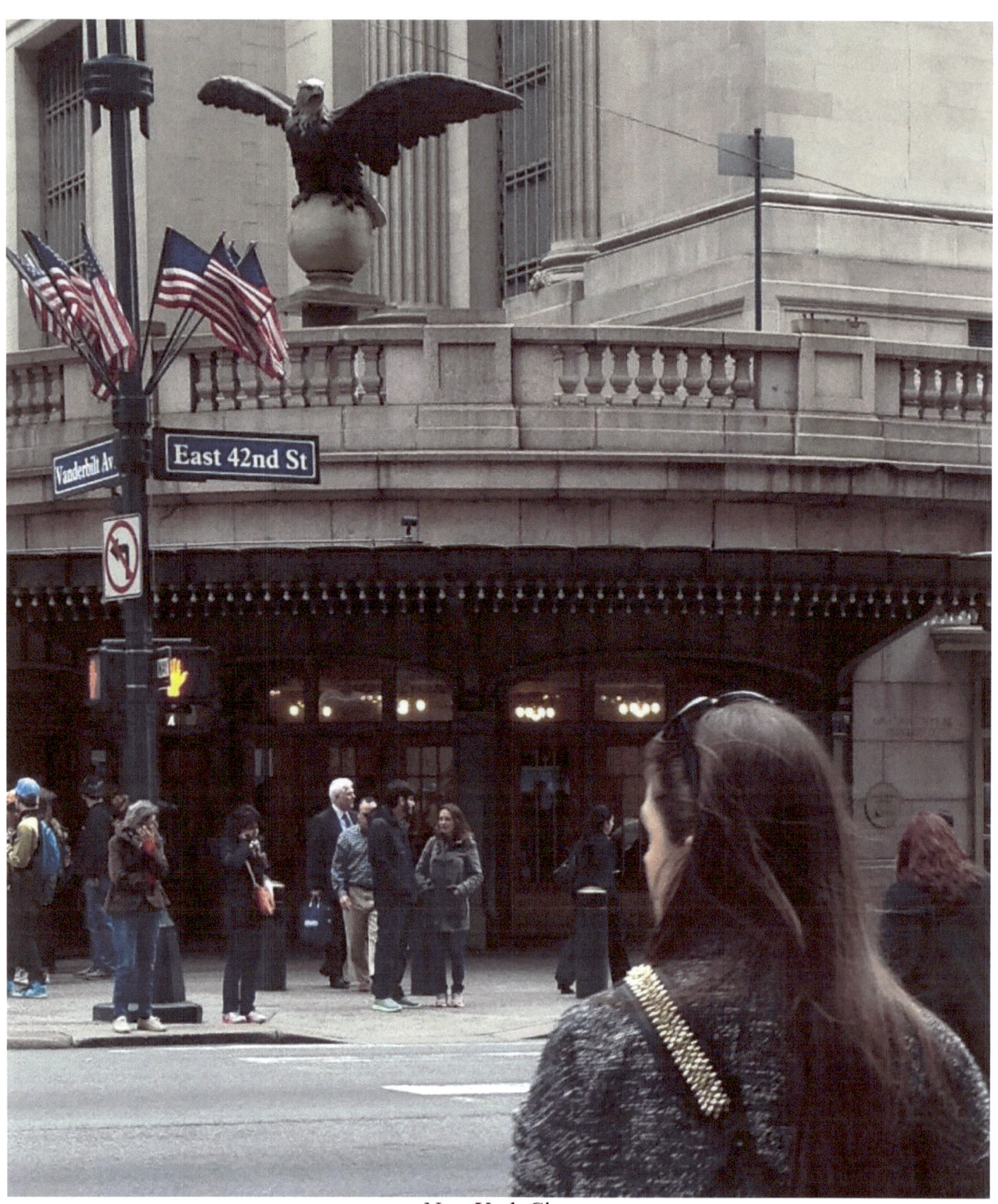

New York City

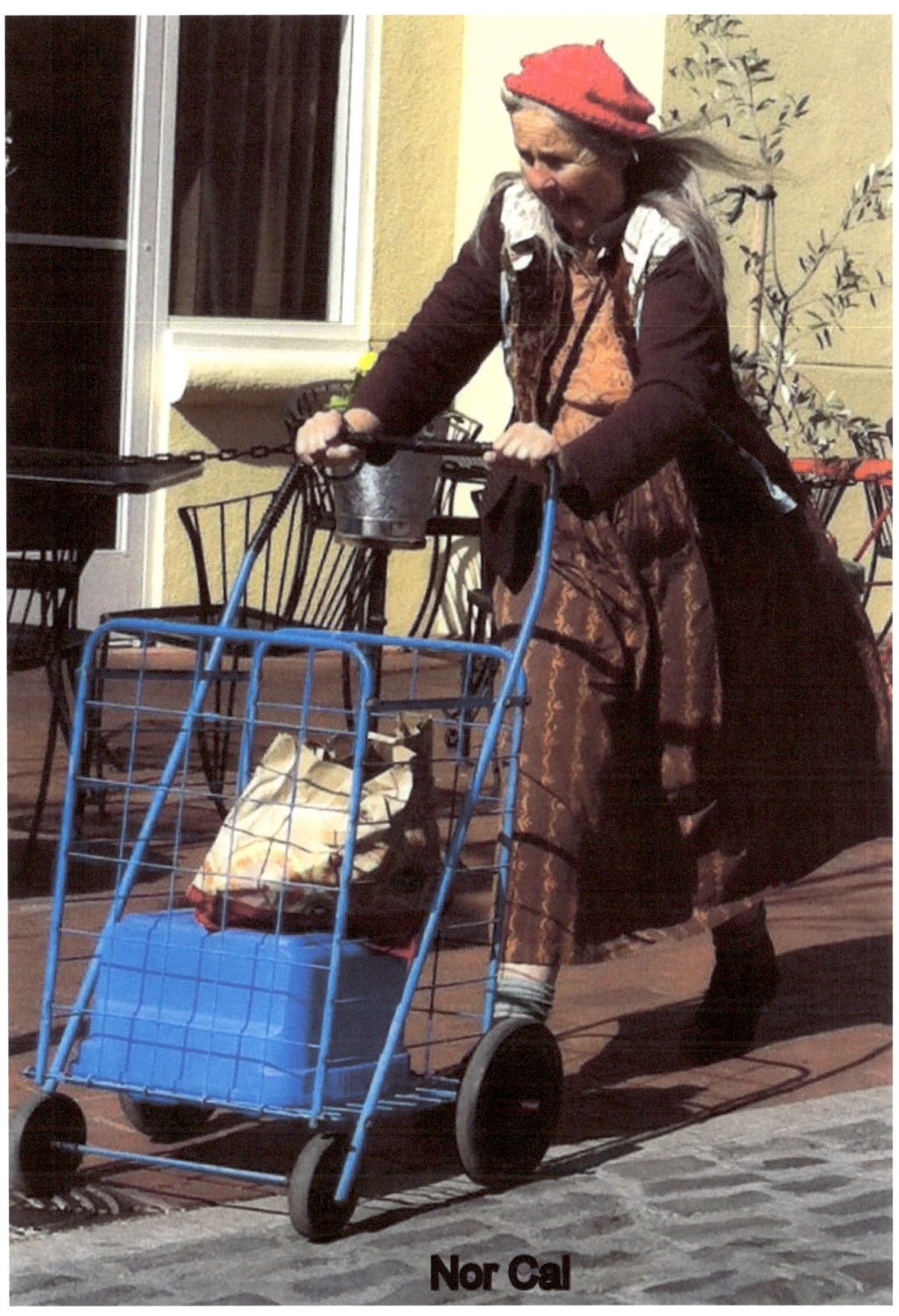

Nor Cal

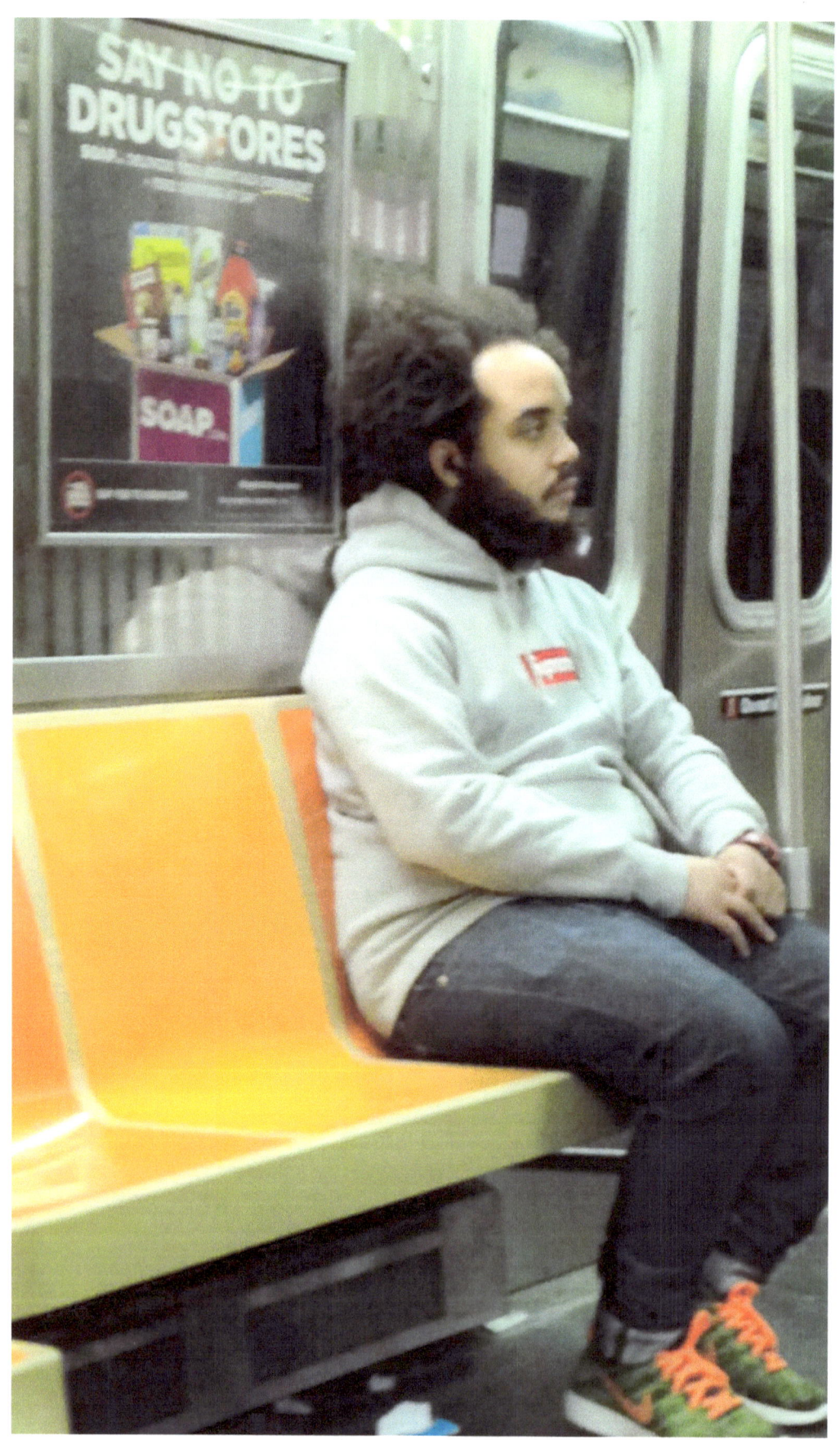

New York City

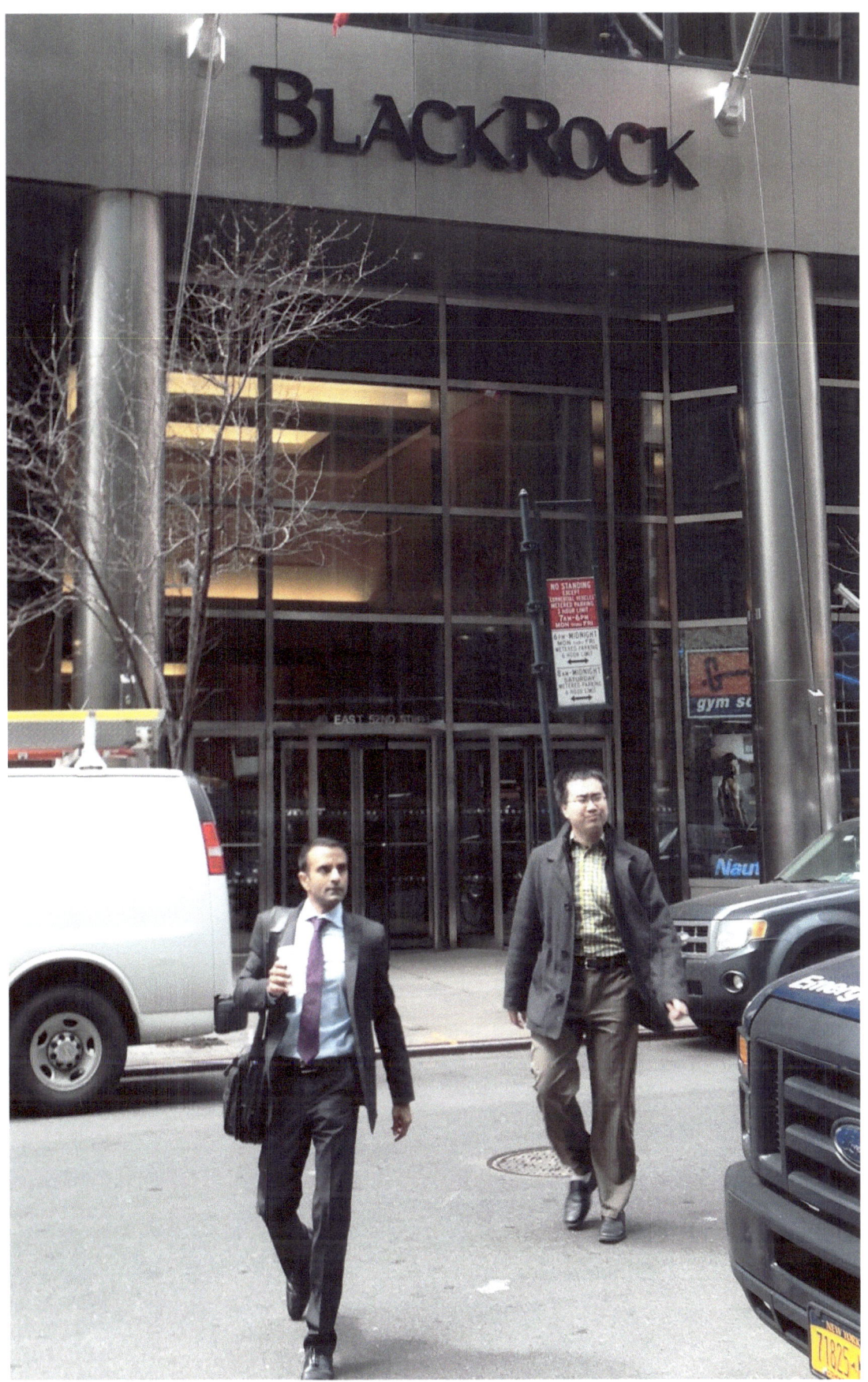

… the seat of power

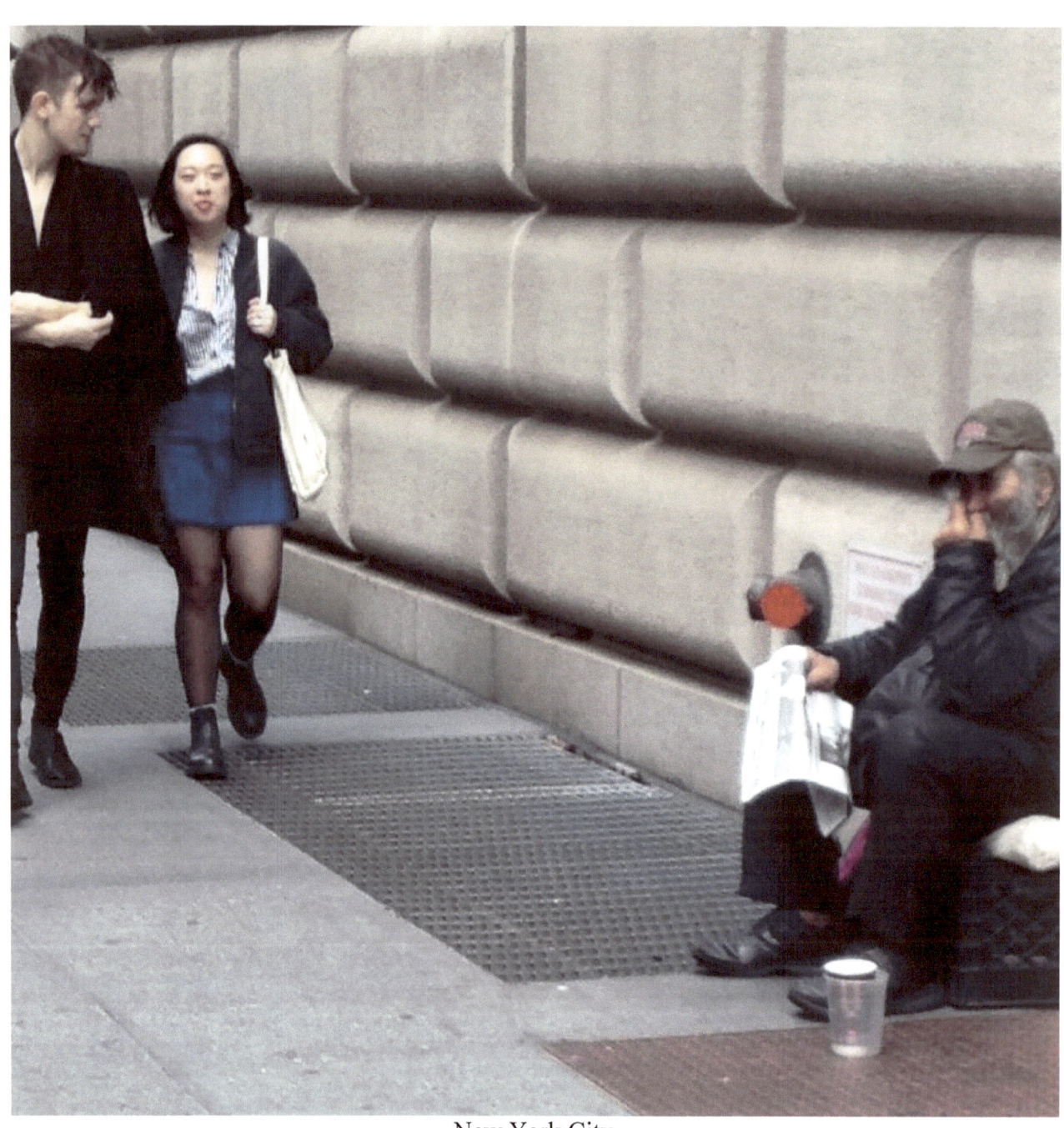

New York City

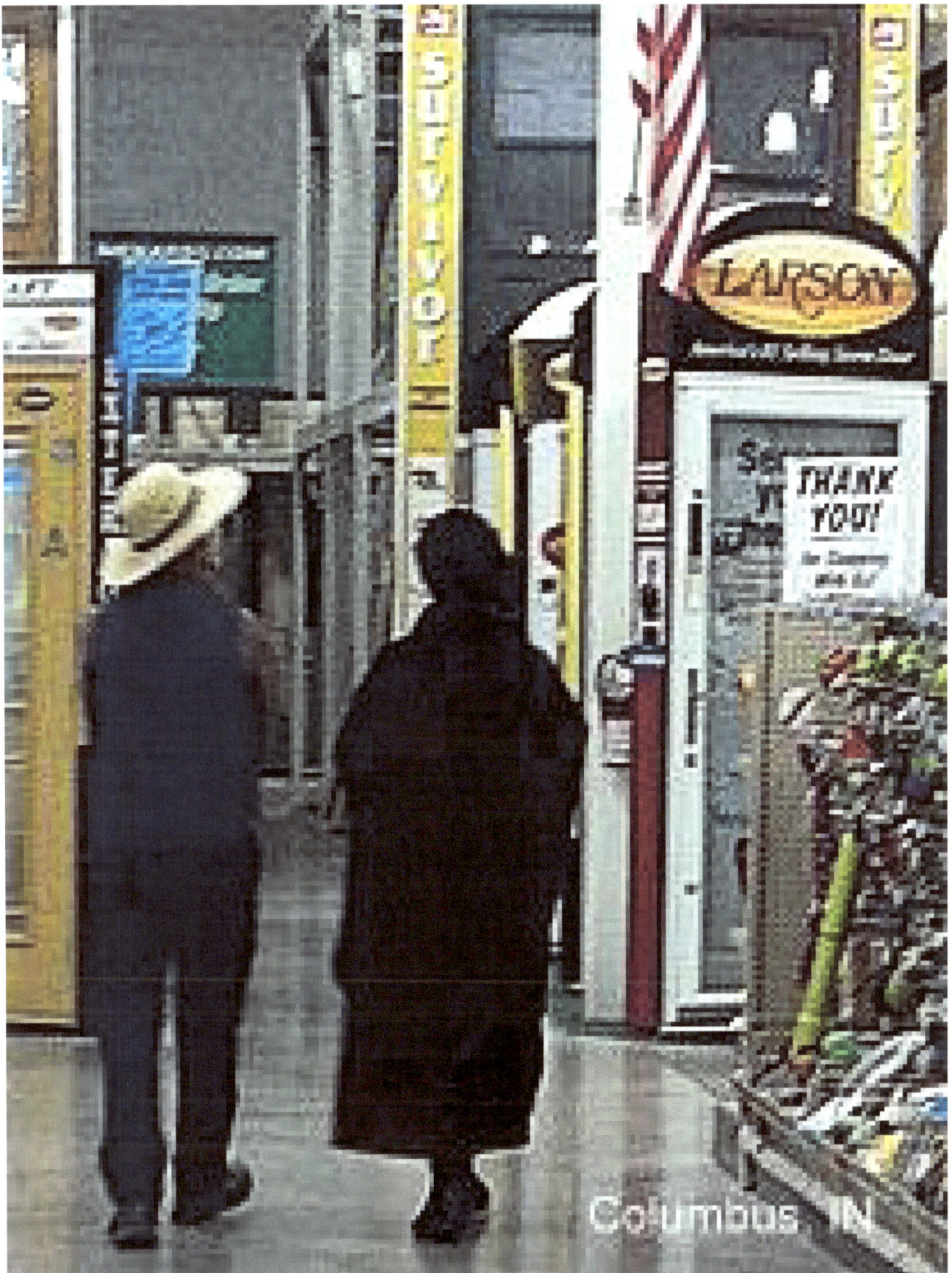
Columbus IN

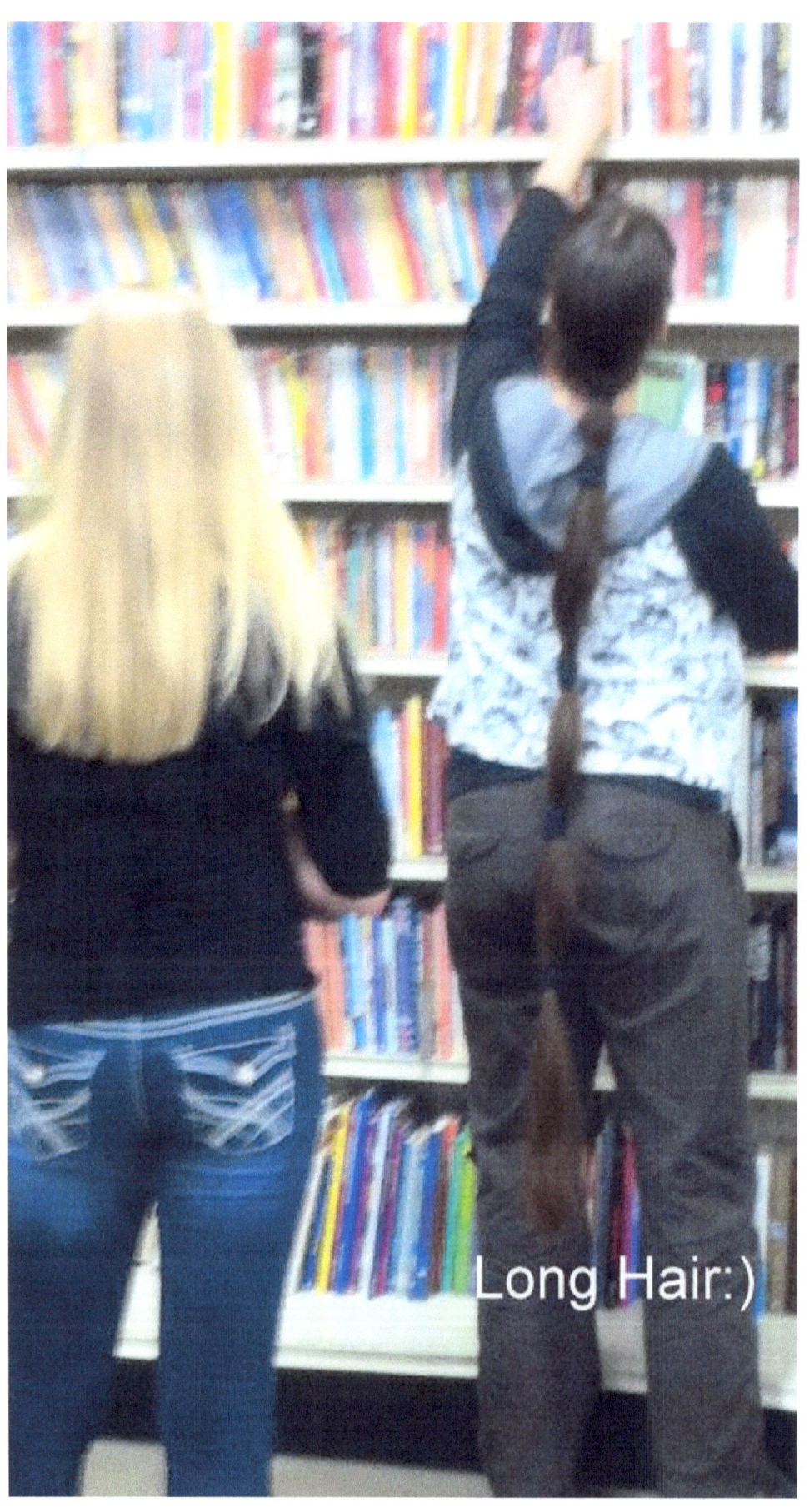

Long Hair:)

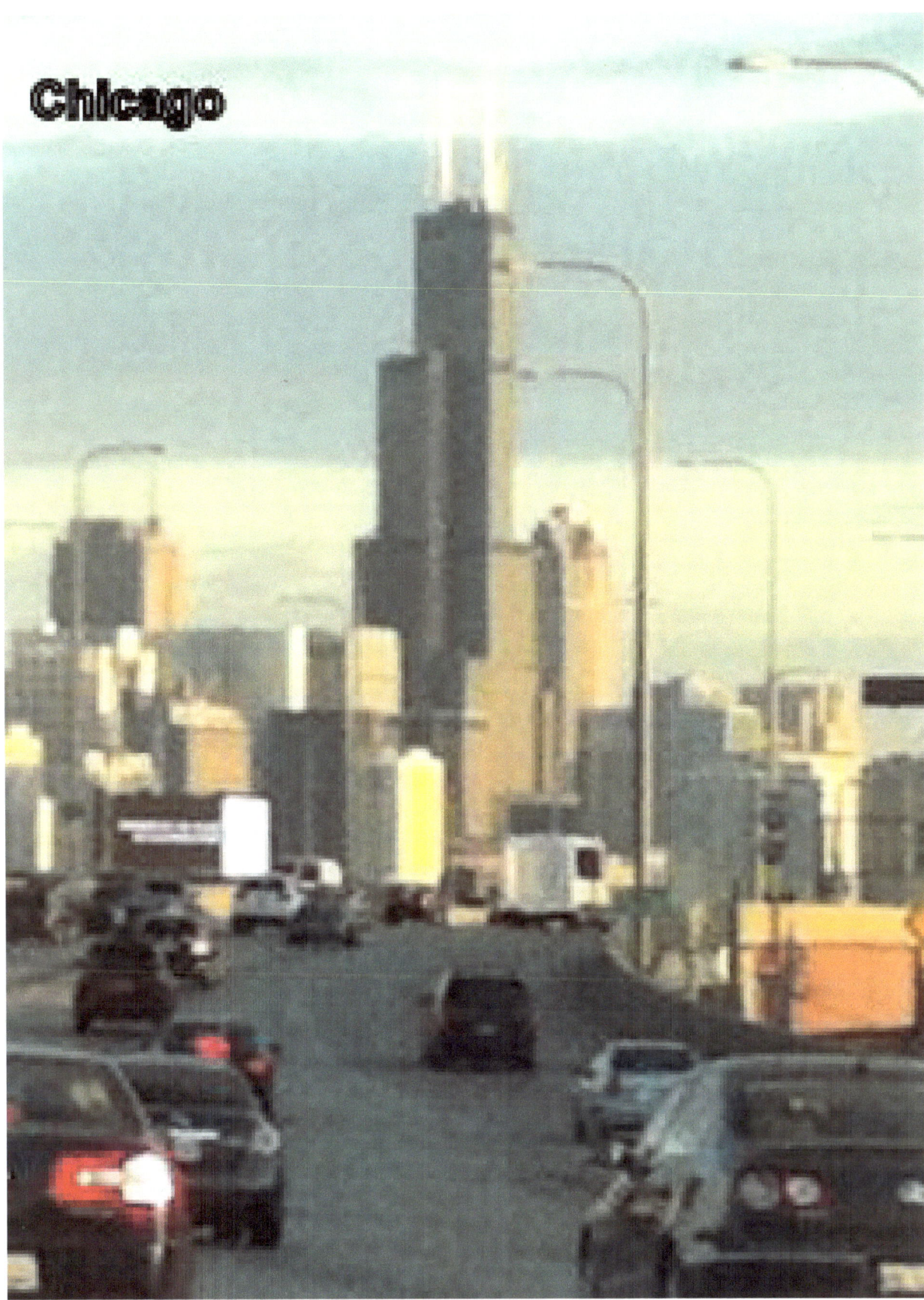

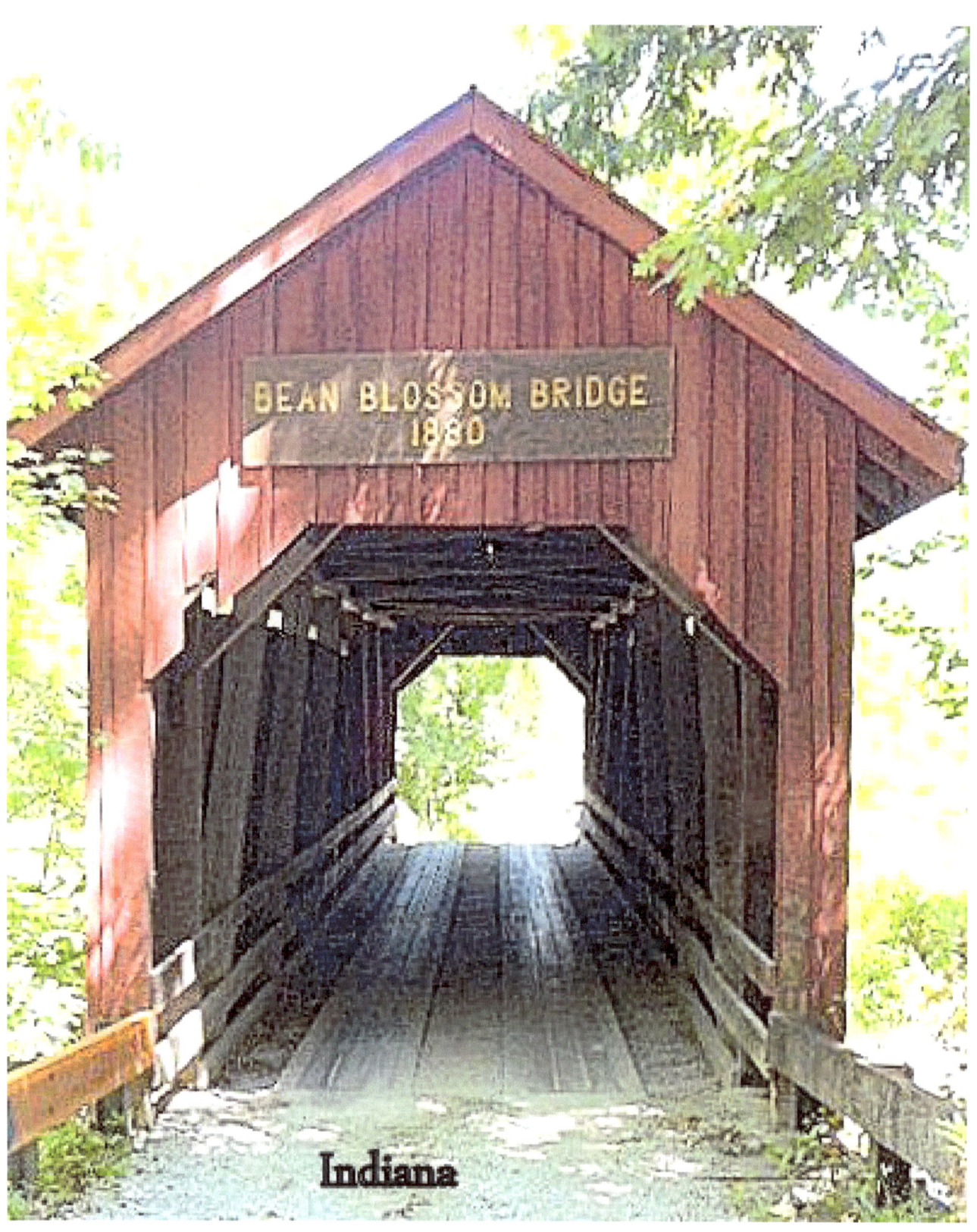

Indiana

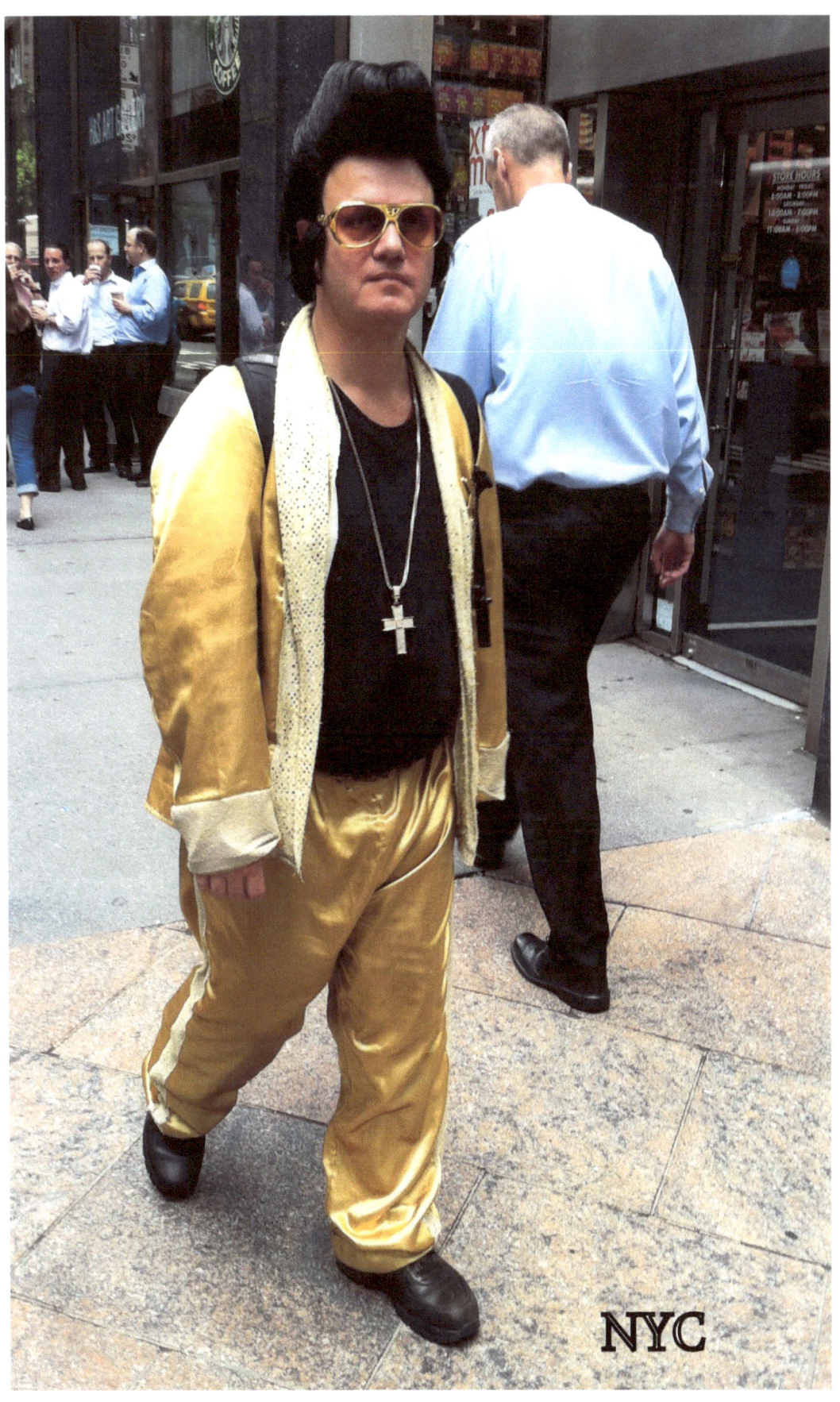

NYC

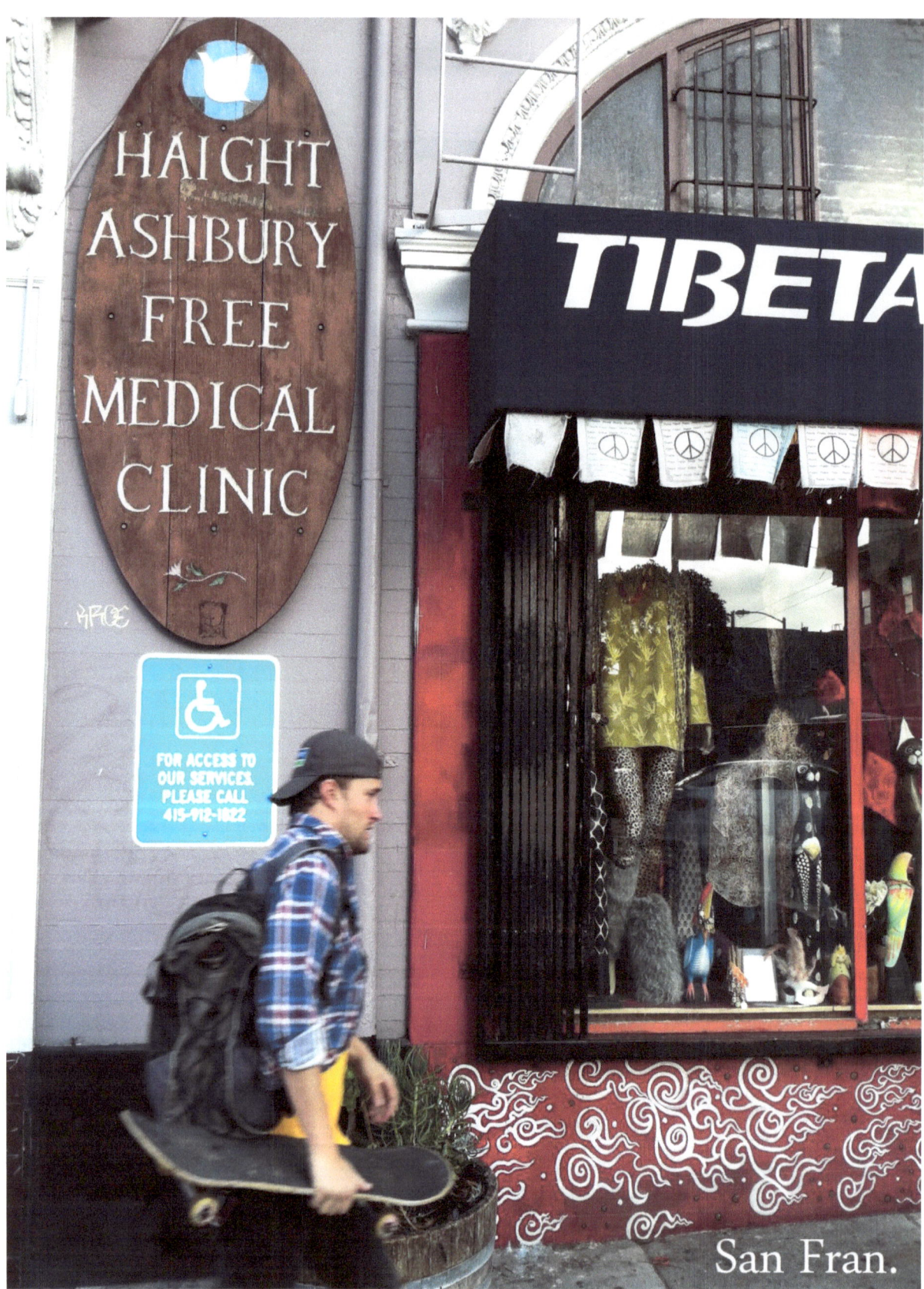

HAIGHT
ASHBURY
FREE
MEDICAL
CLINIC

FOR ACCESS TO
OUR SERVICES
PLEASE CALL
415-912-1822

TIBETA

San Fran.

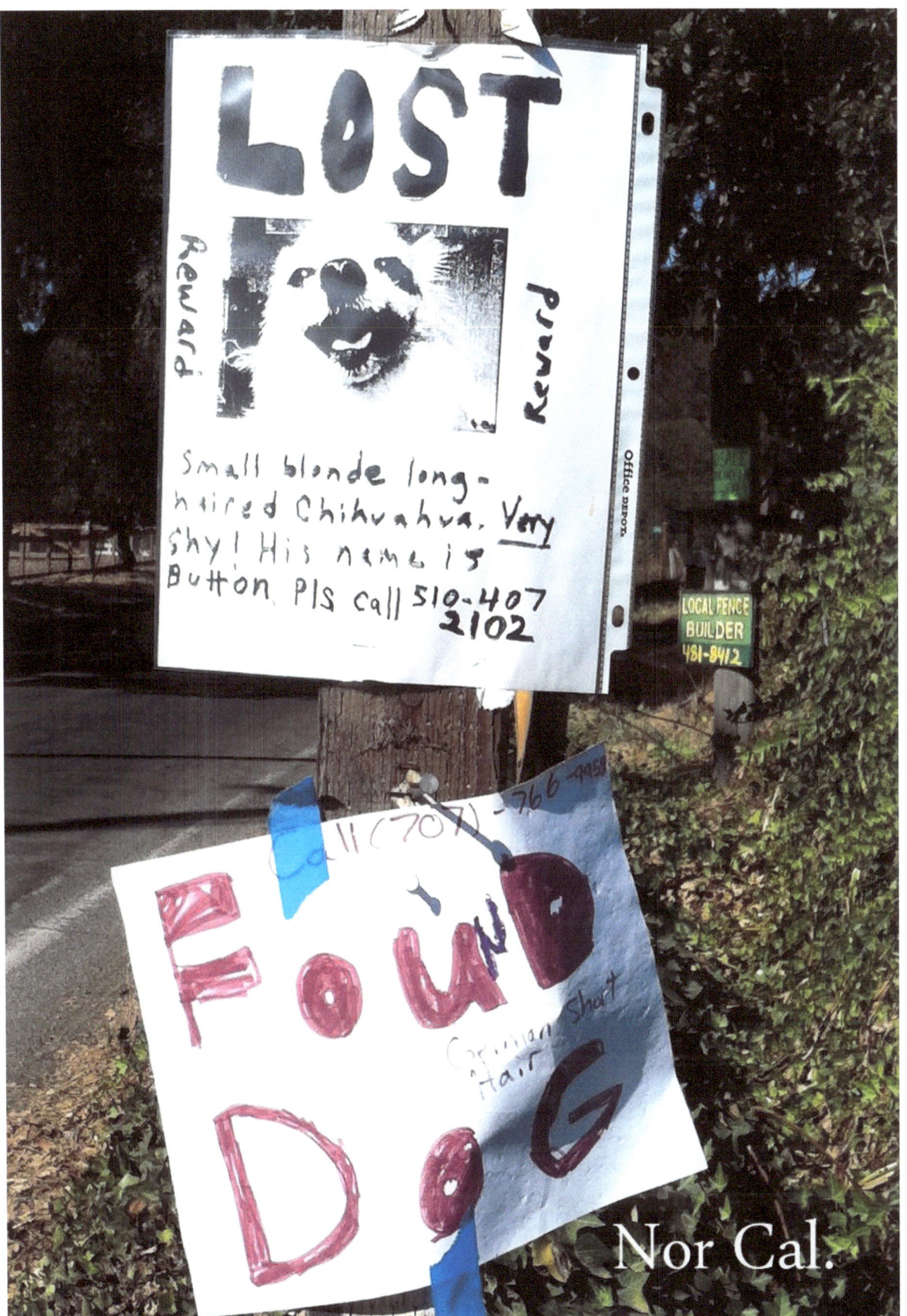

Nor Cal.

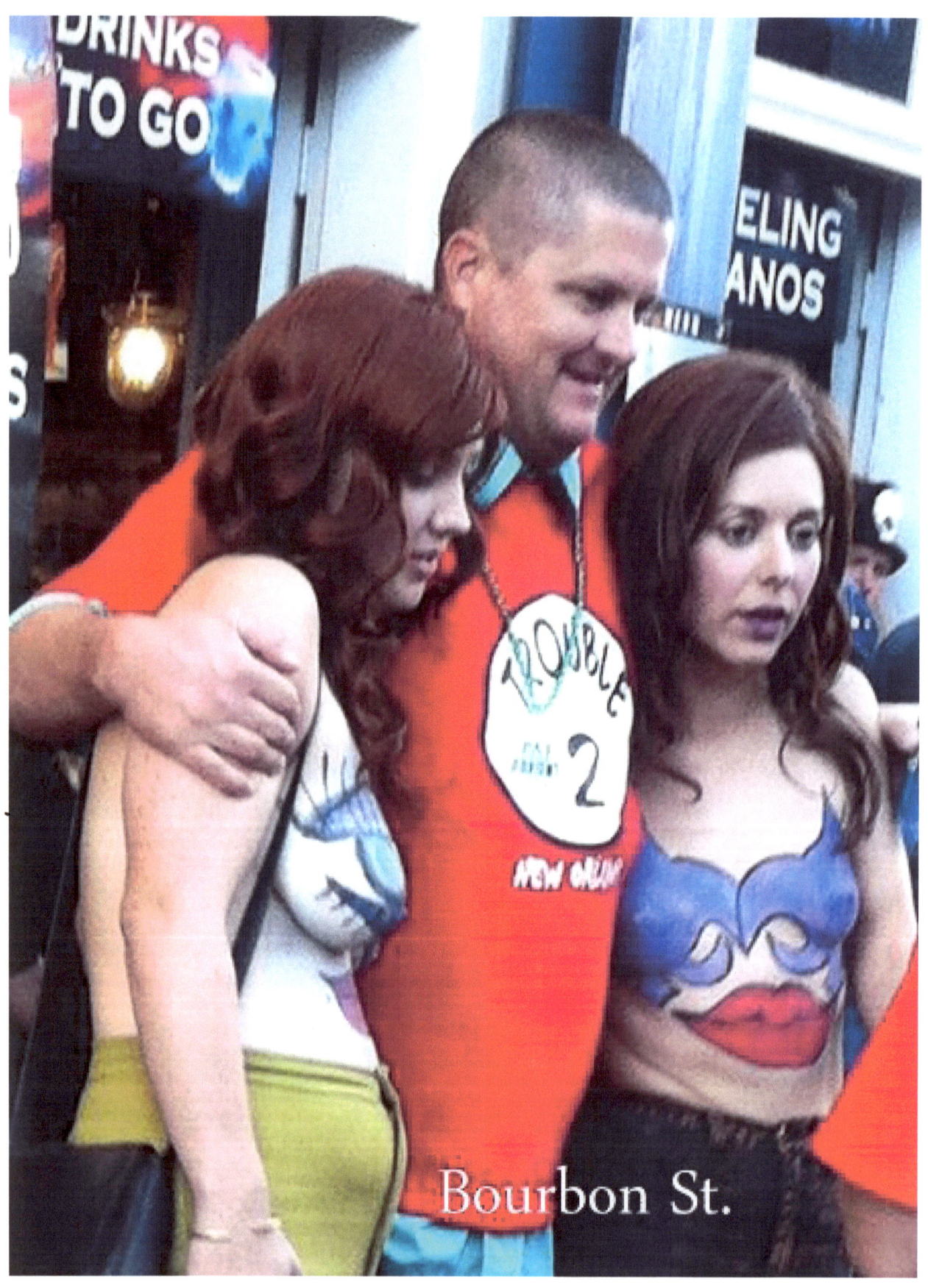

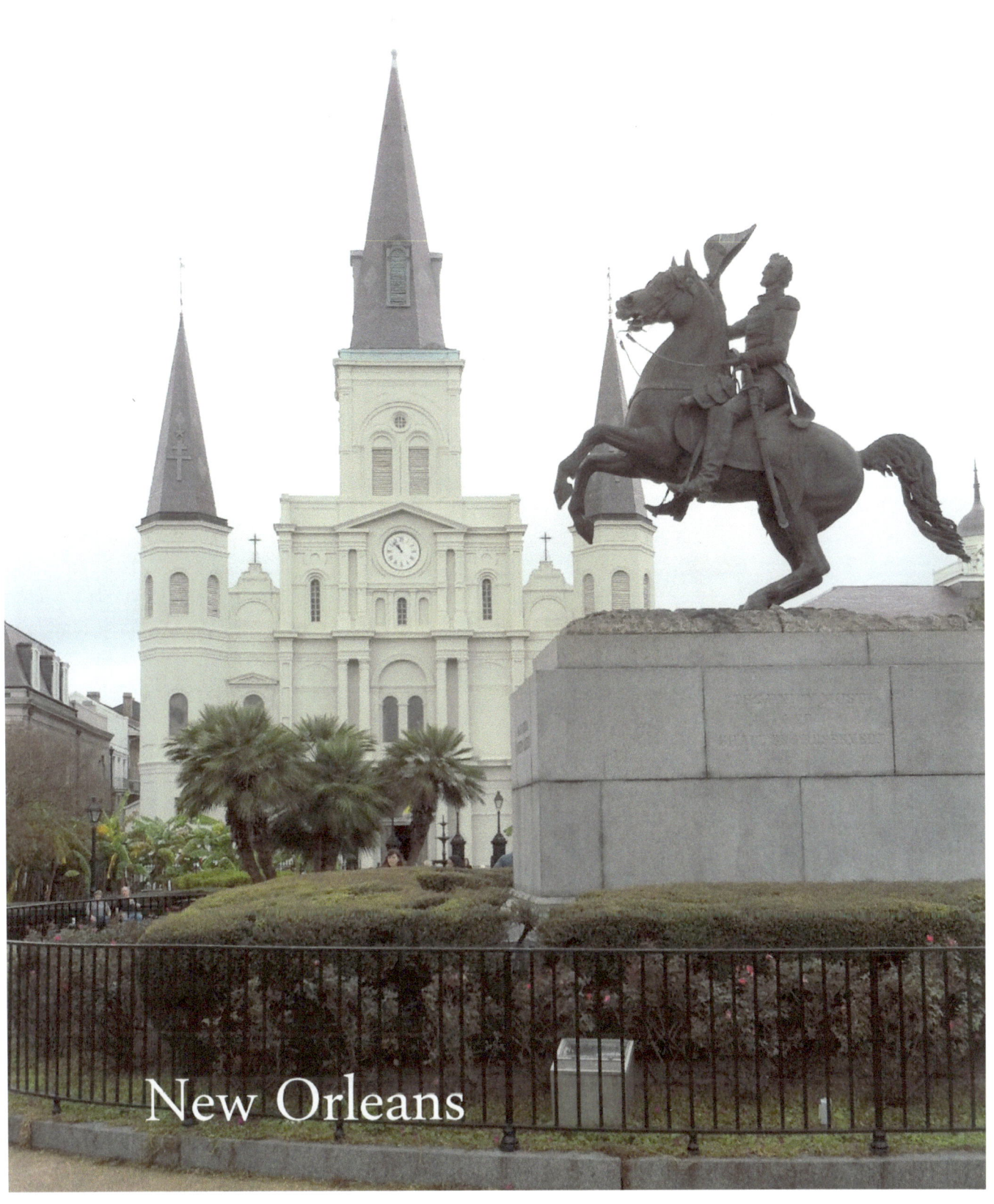

New Orleans

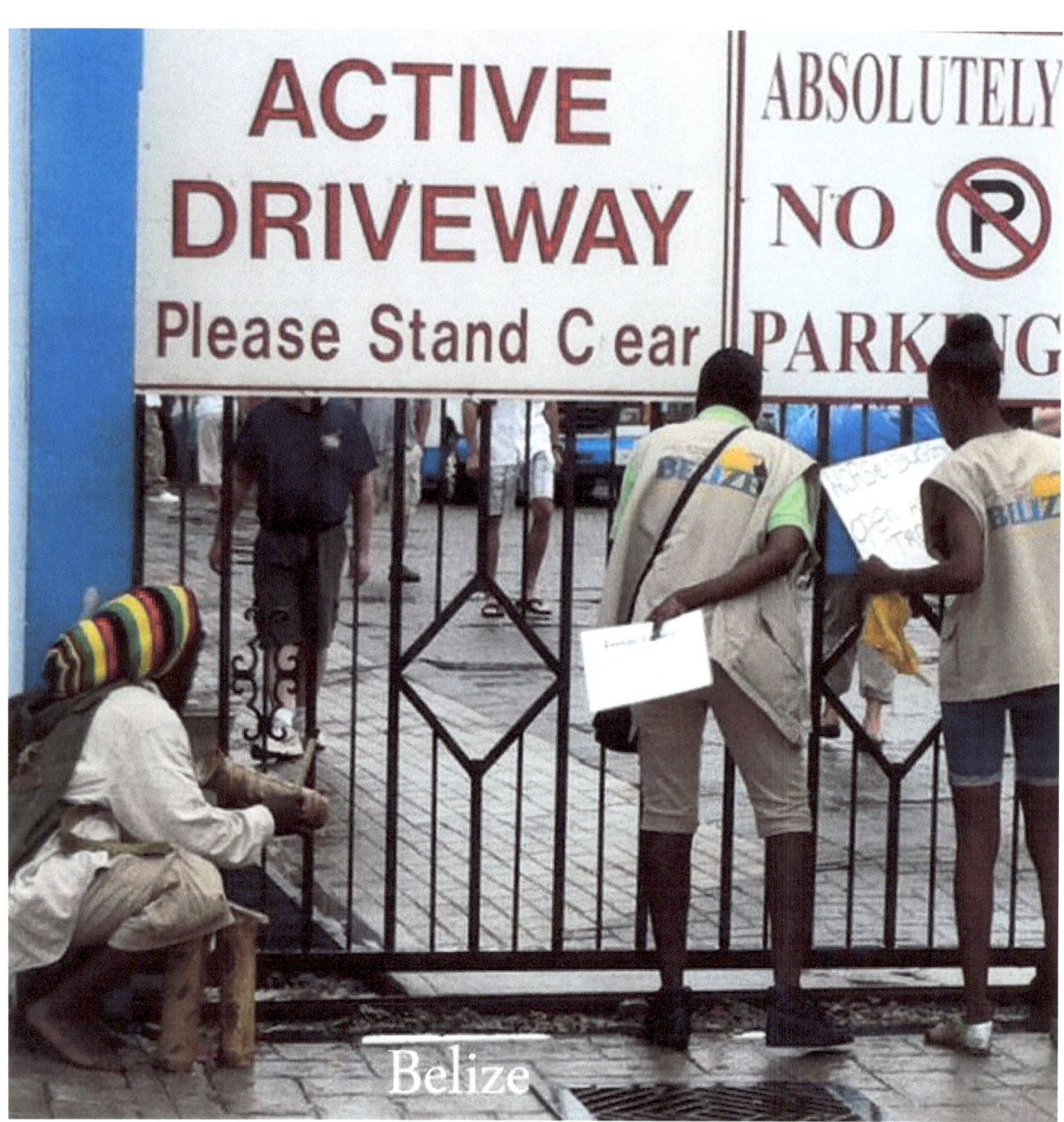

Belize

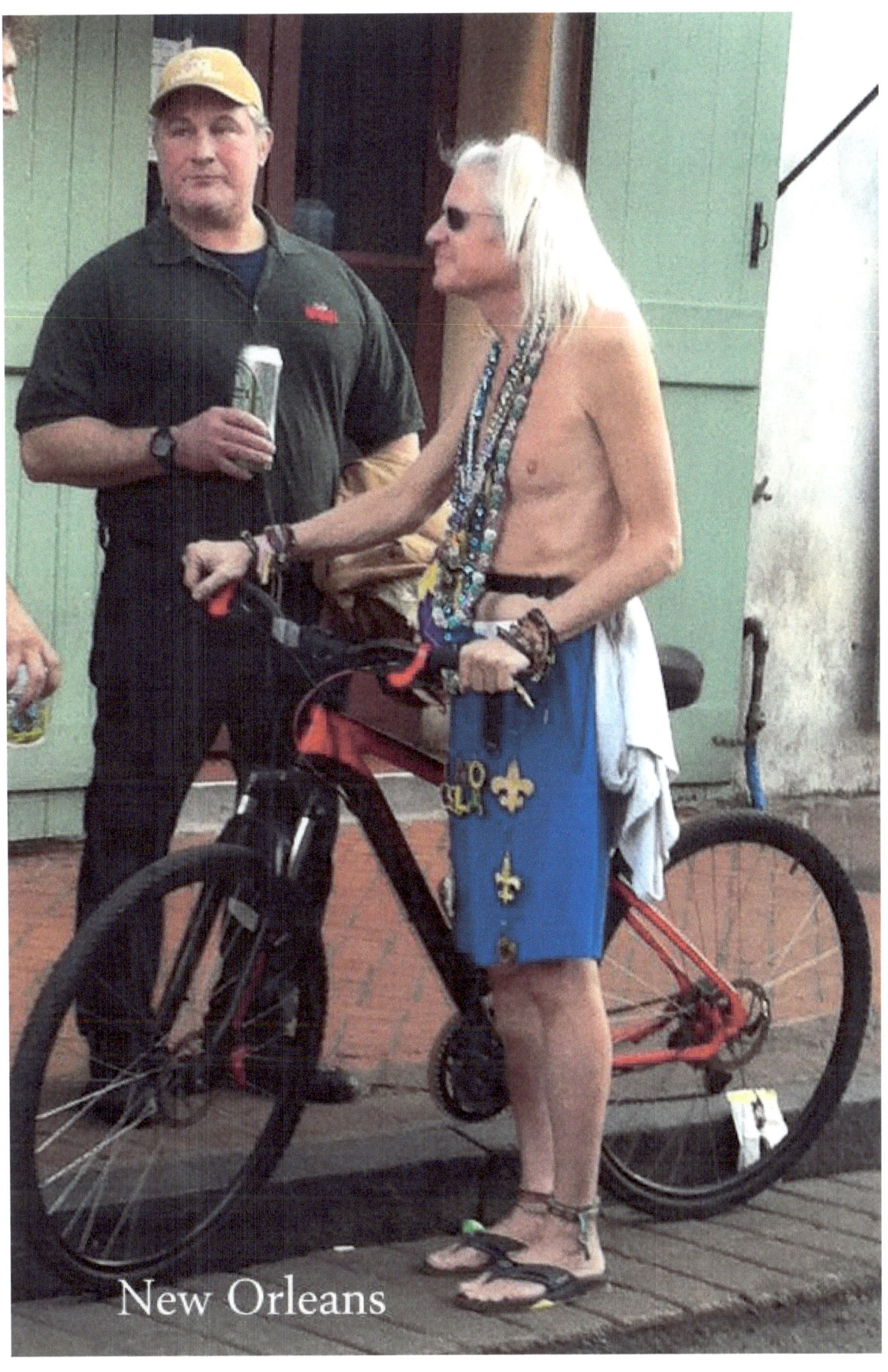

New Orleans

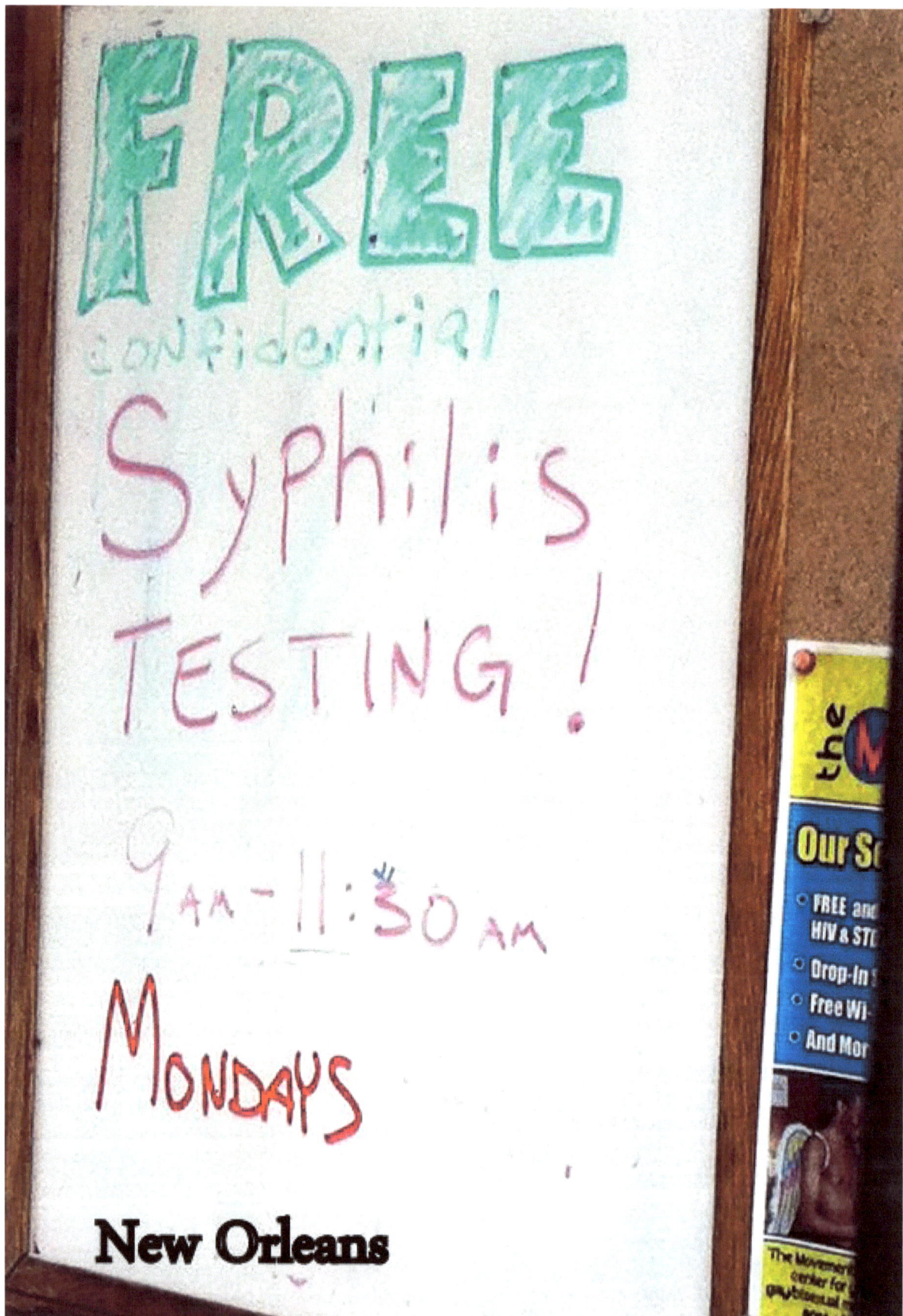

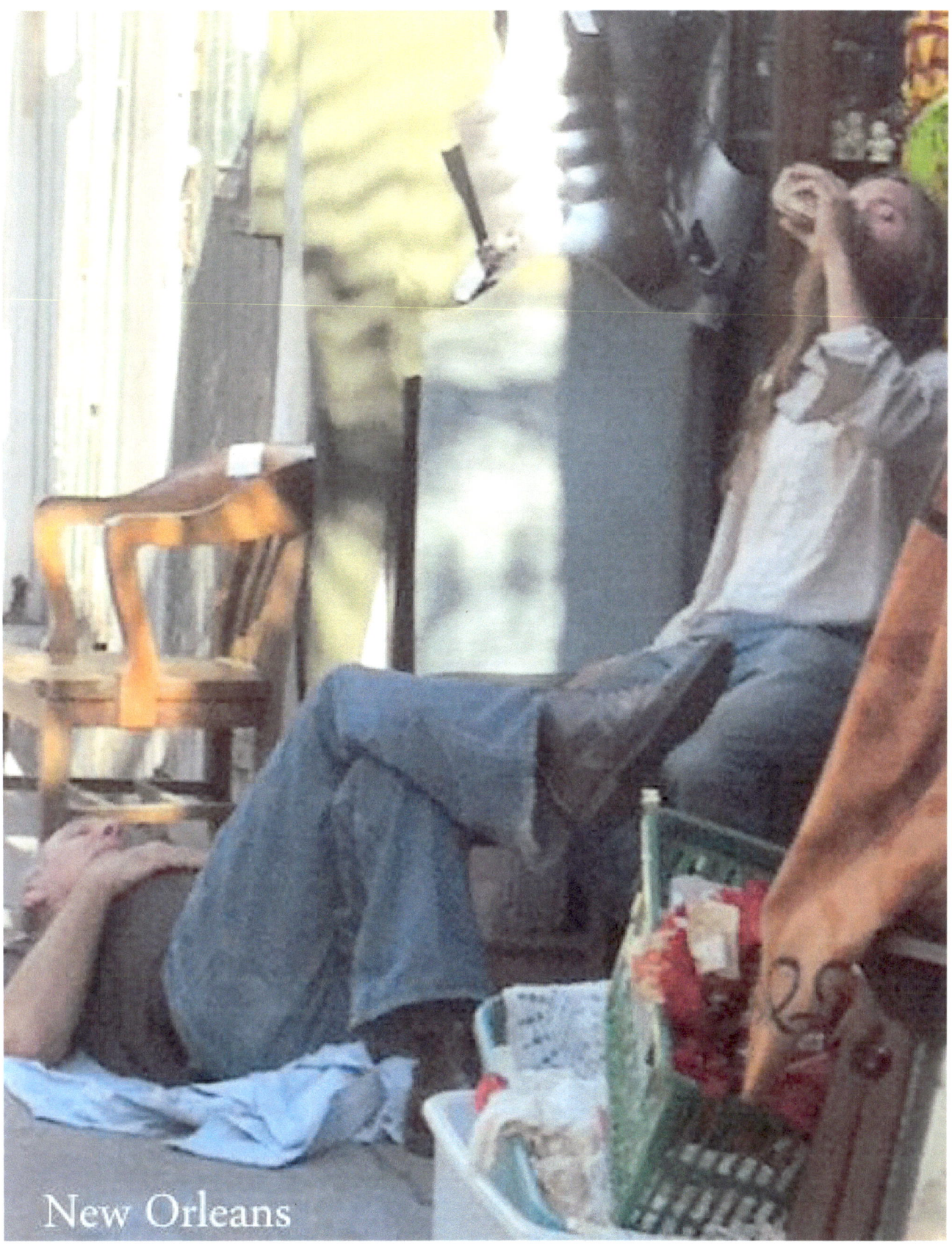

New Orleans

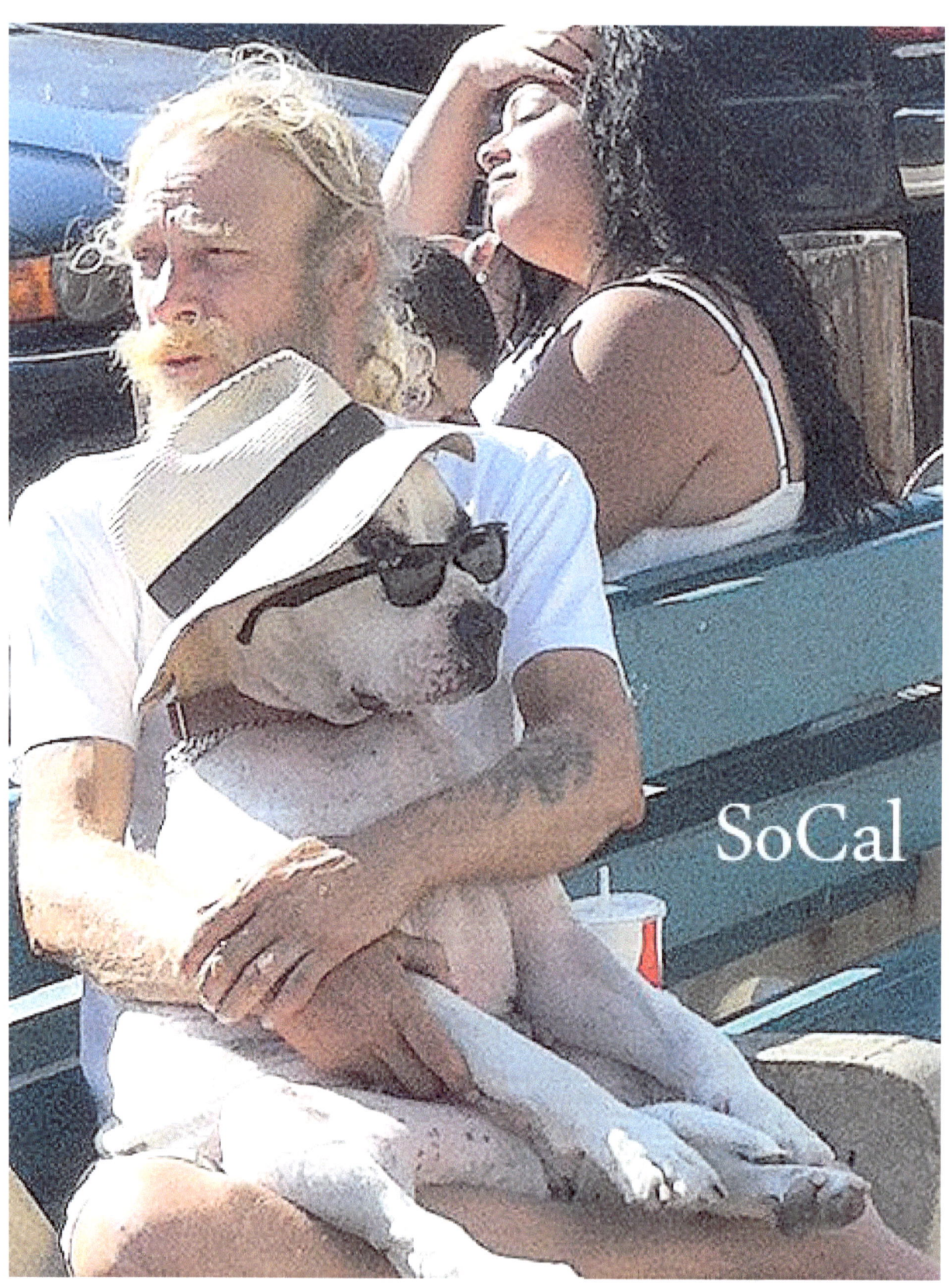

SoCal

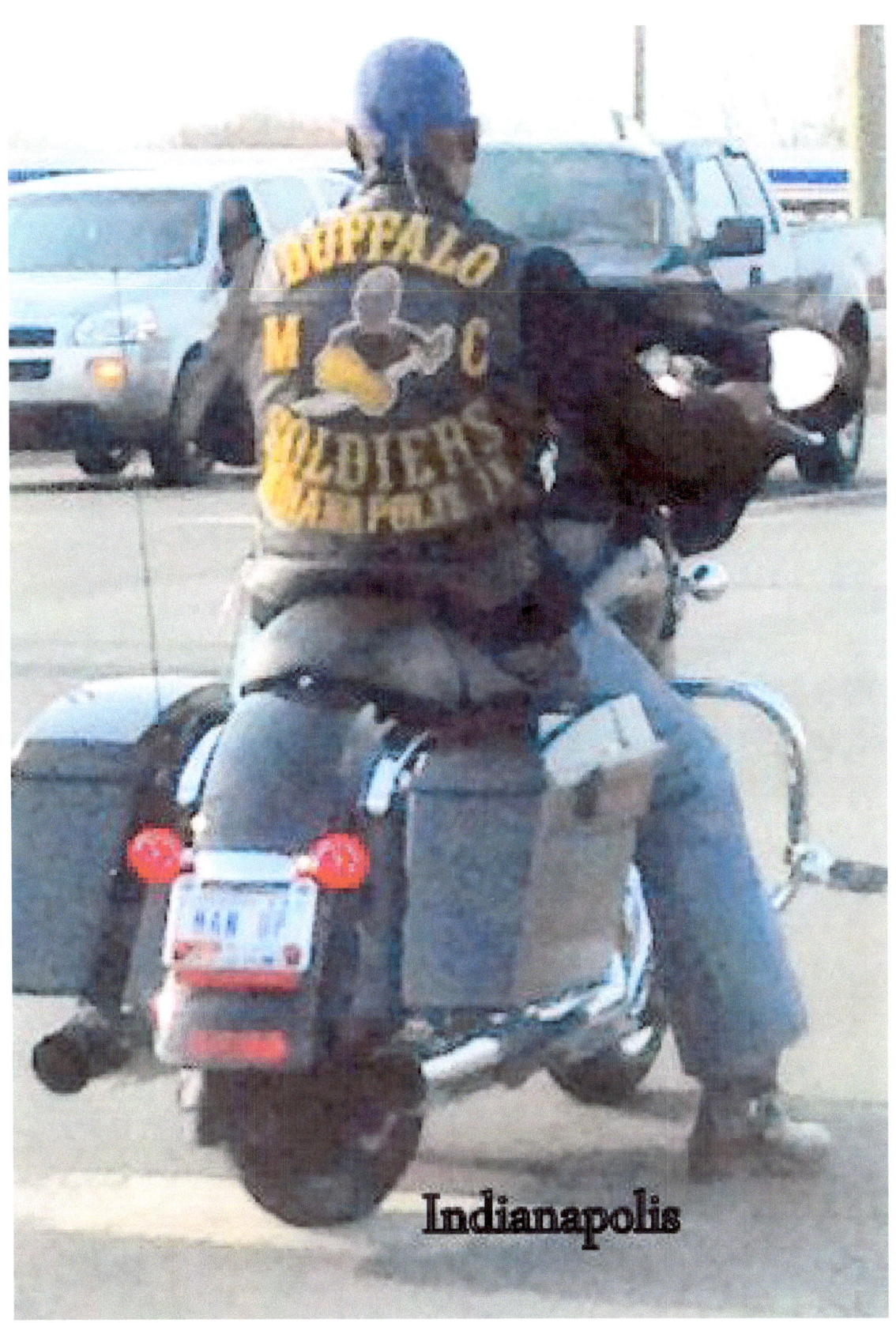

Indianapolis

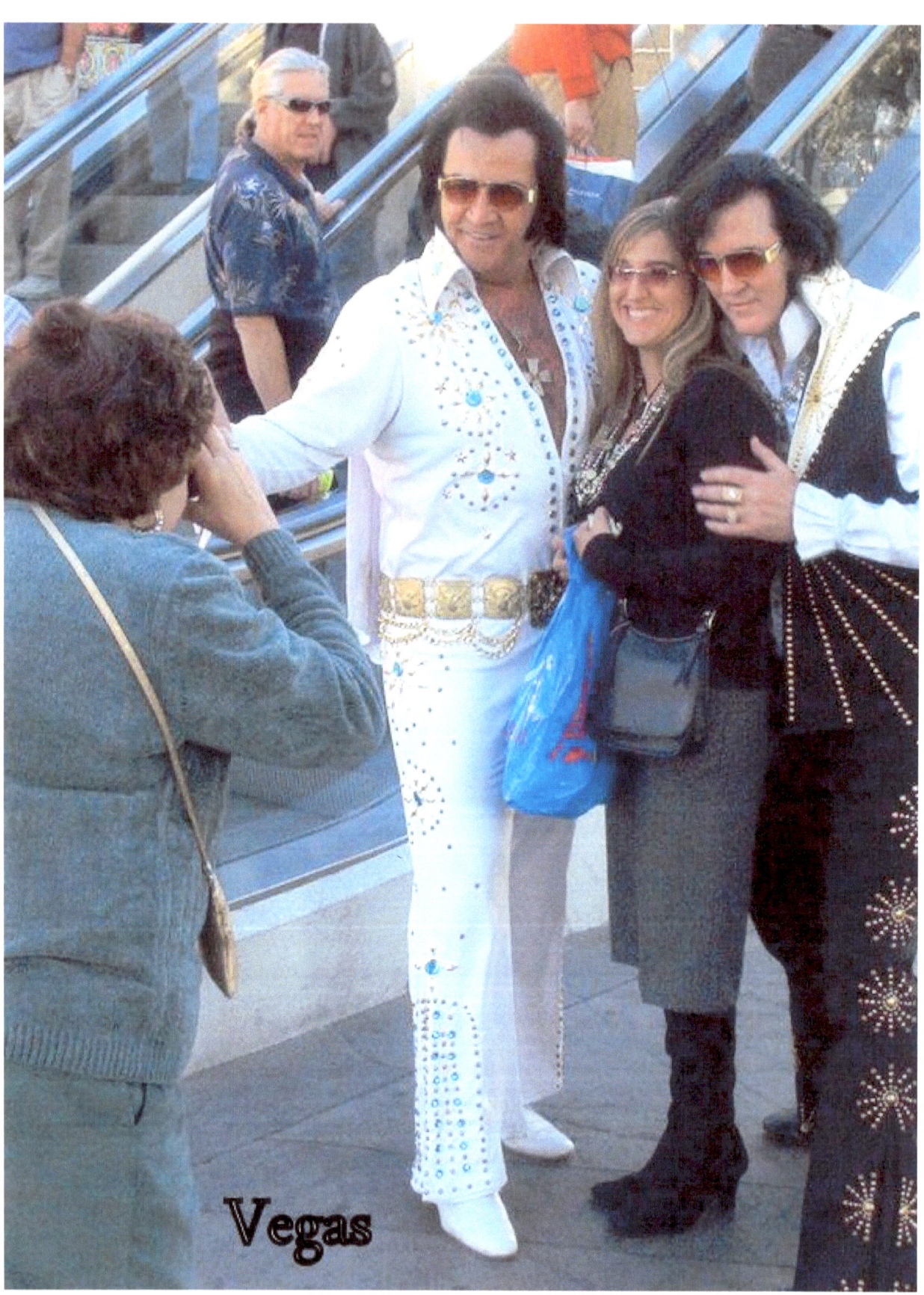

Vegas

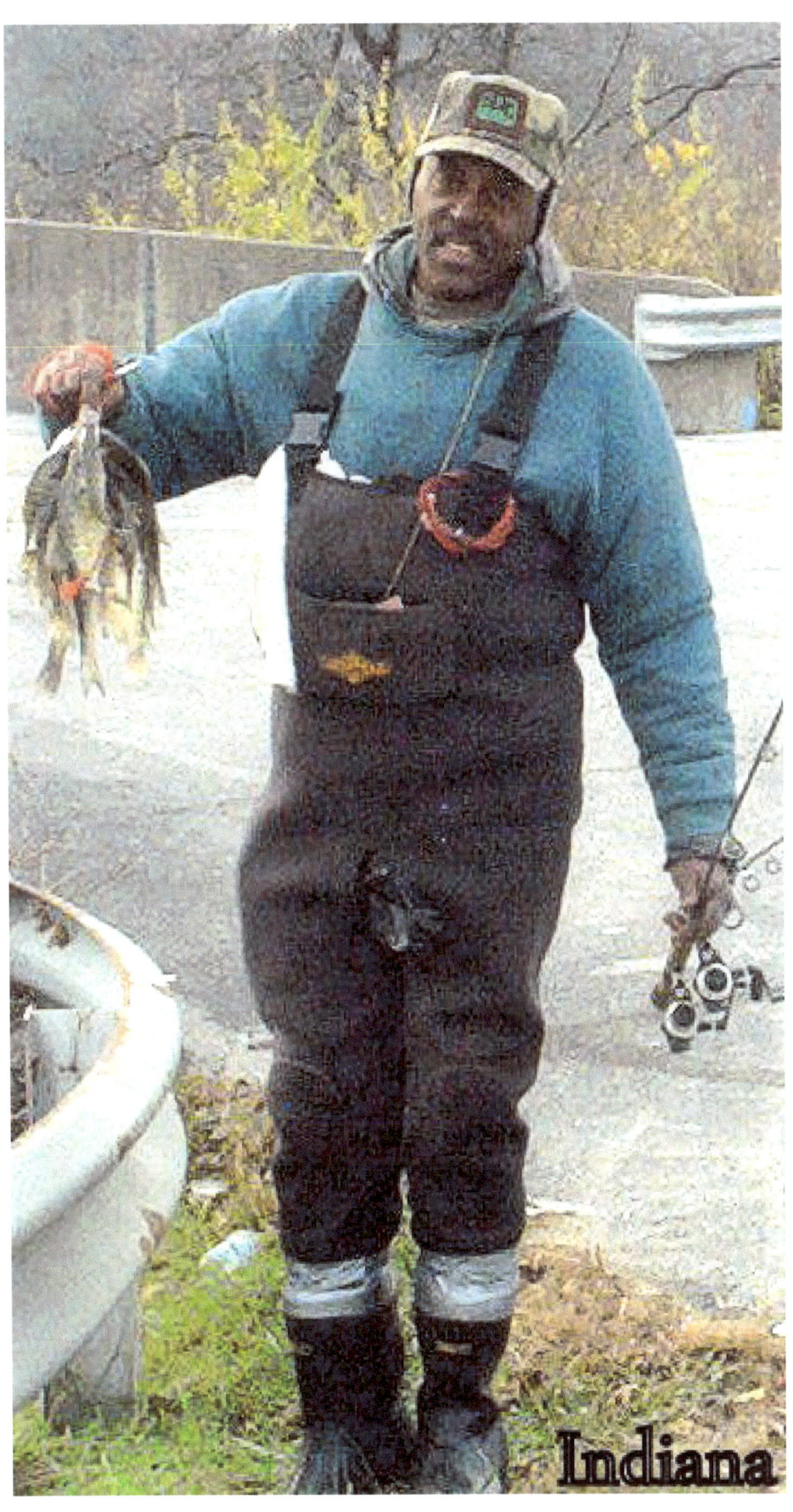

Indiana

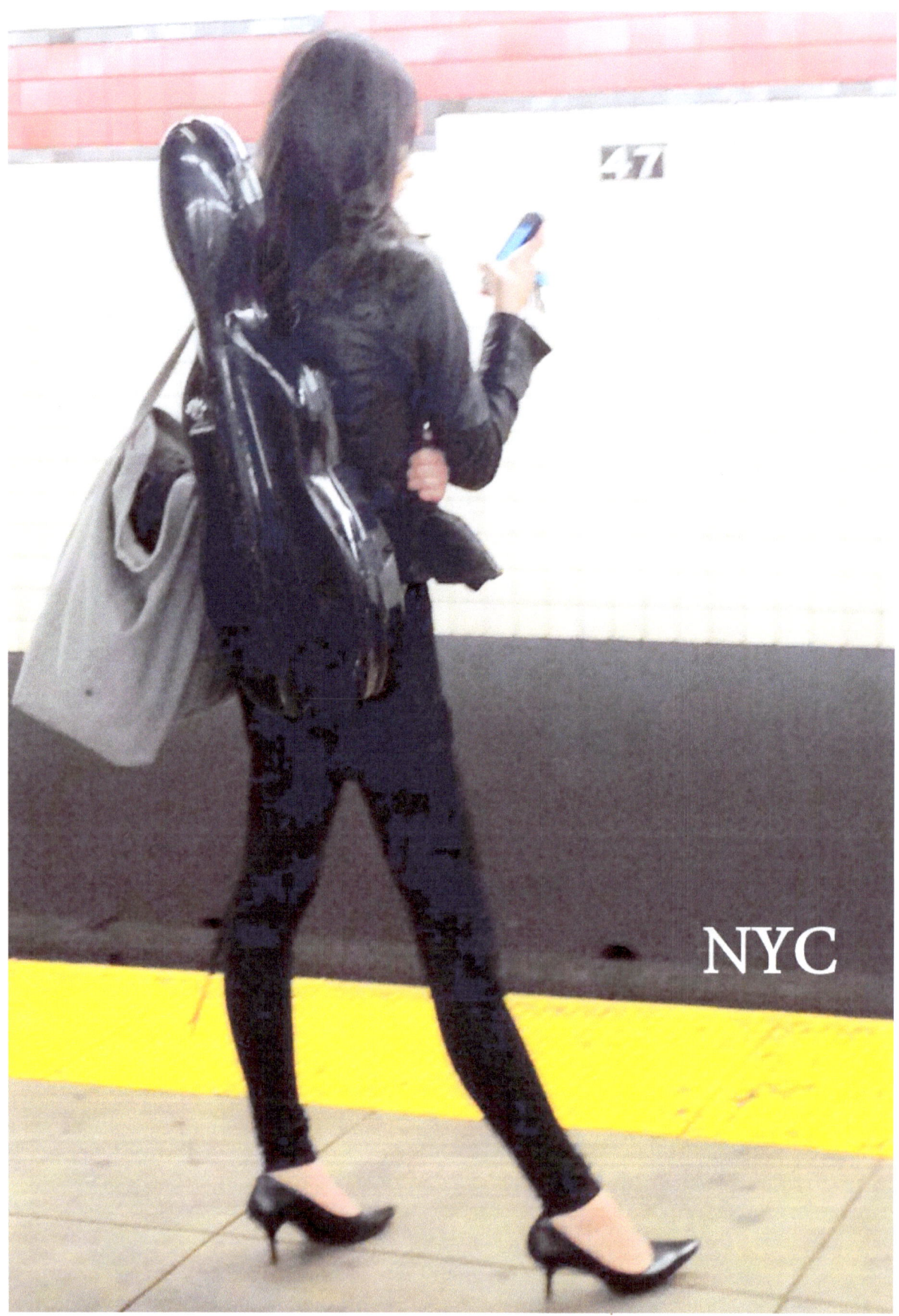

NYC

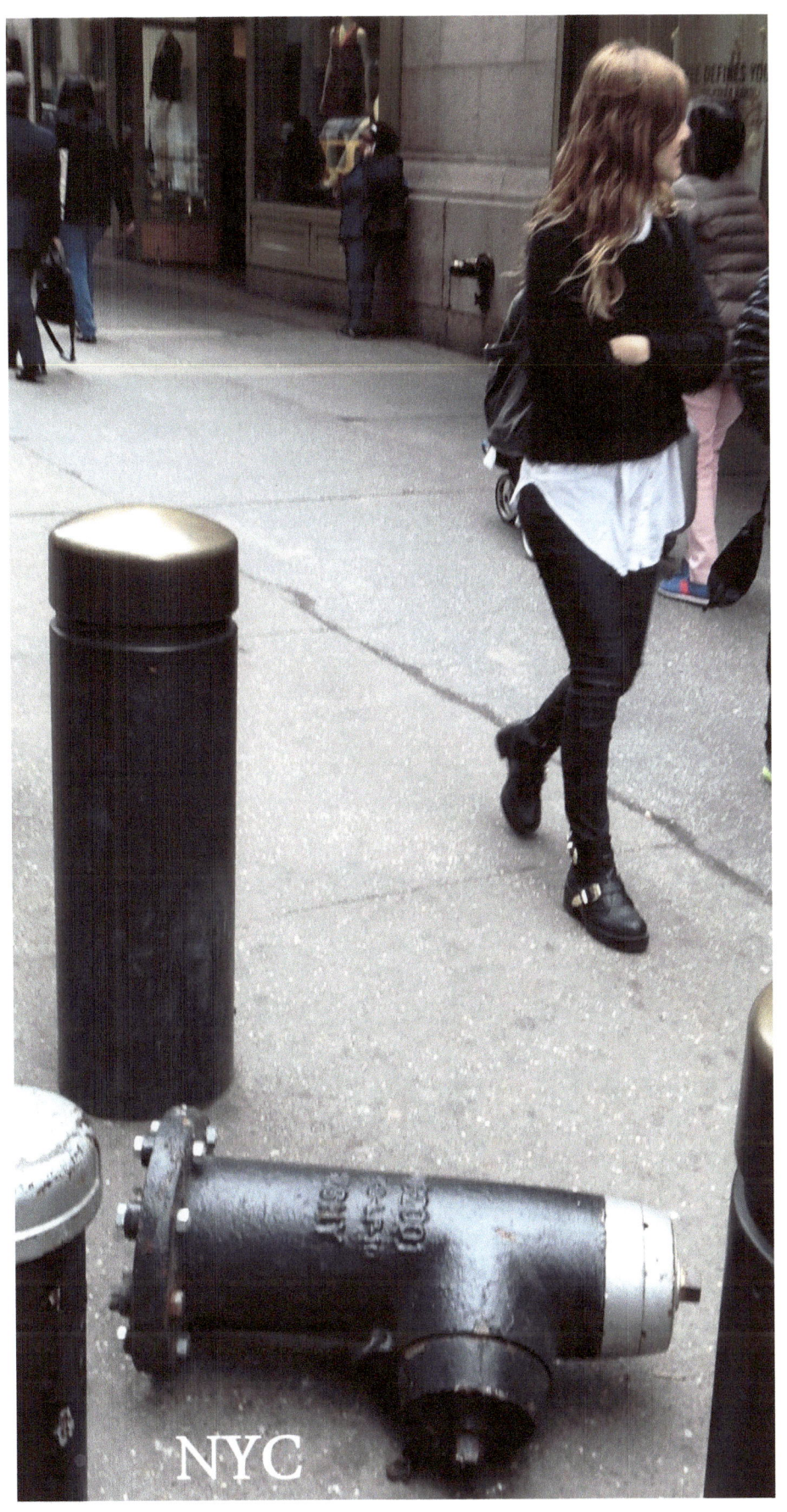

NYC

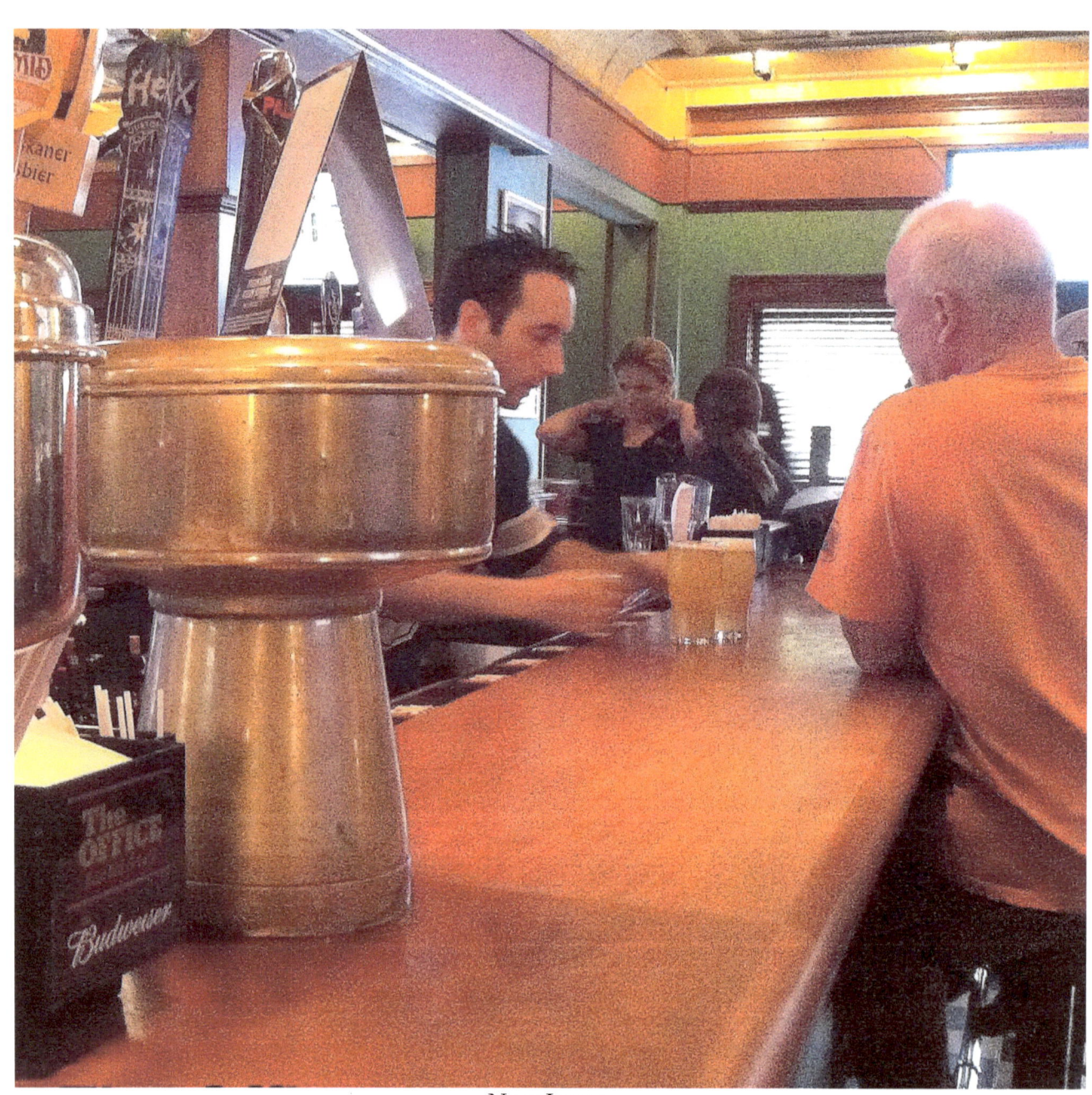

New Jersey

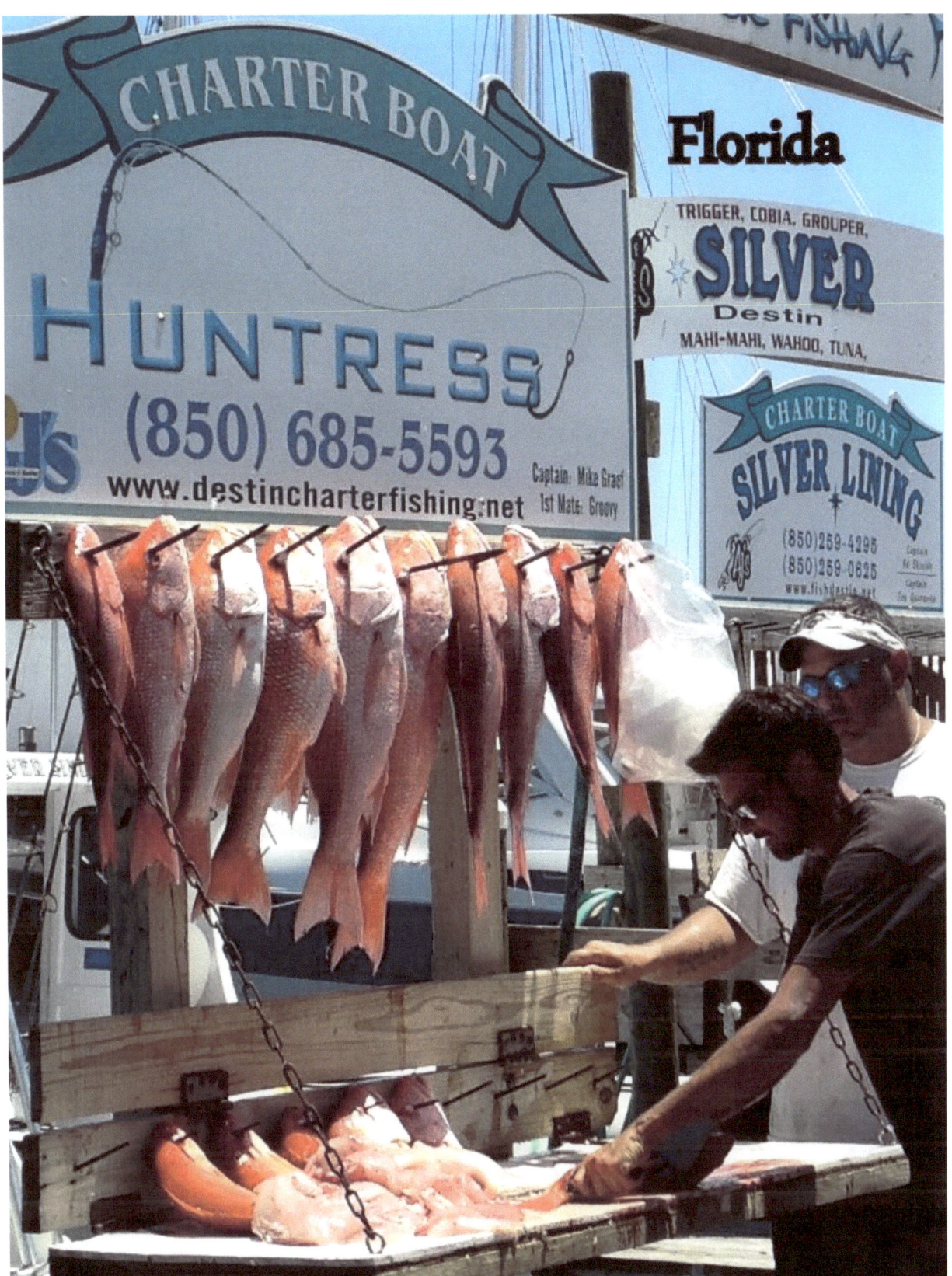

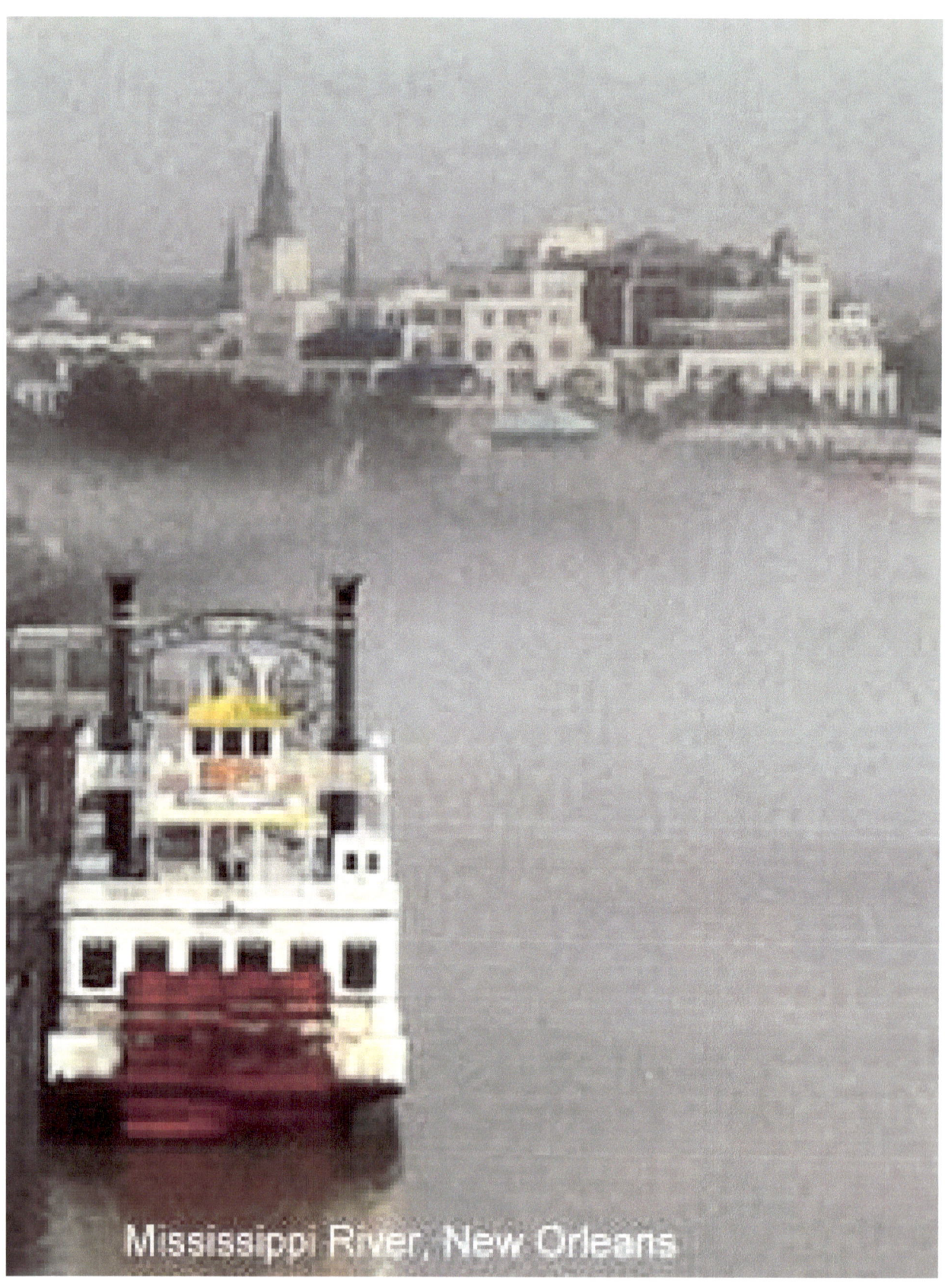

Mississippi River, New Orleans

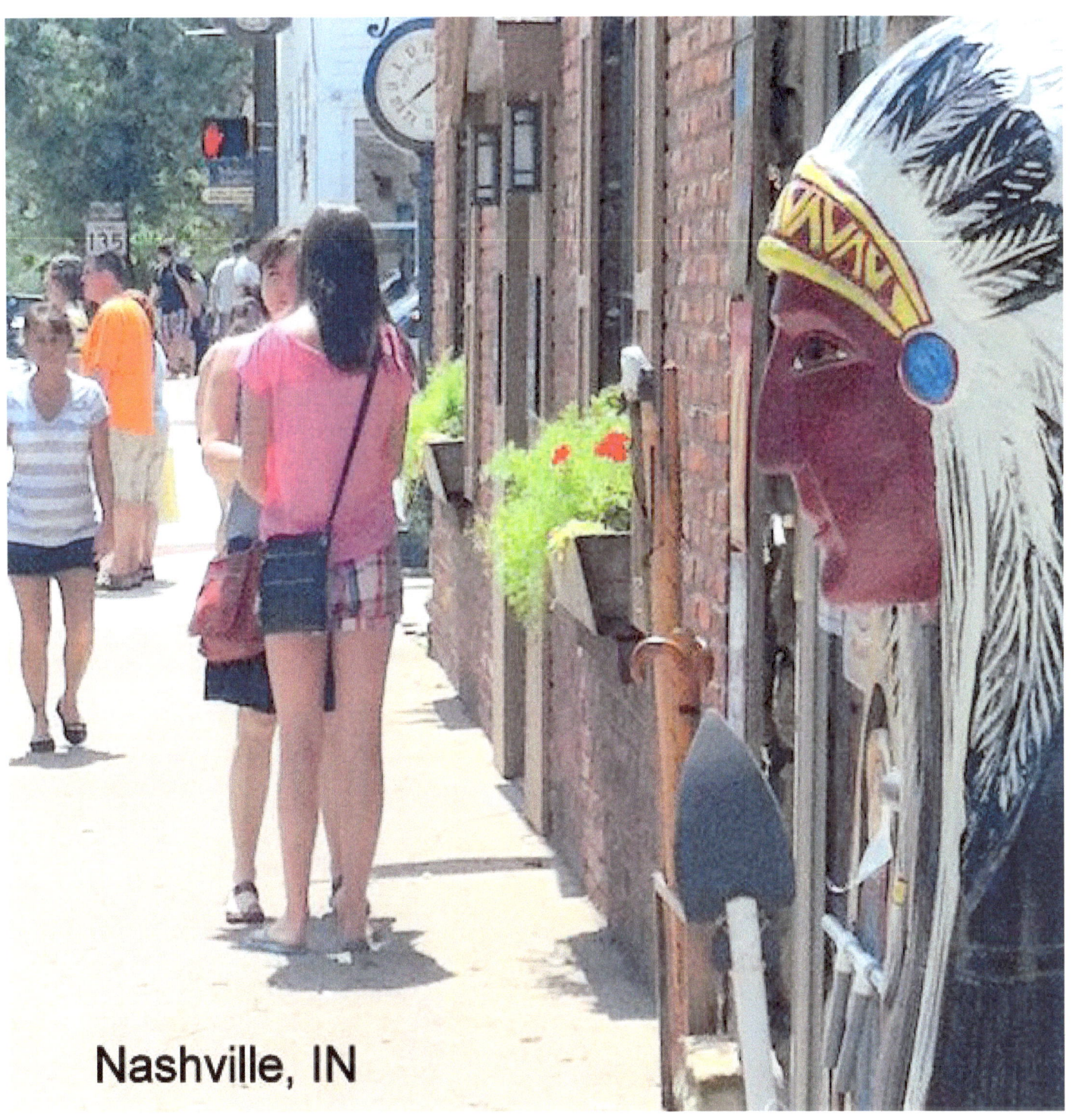
Nashville, IN

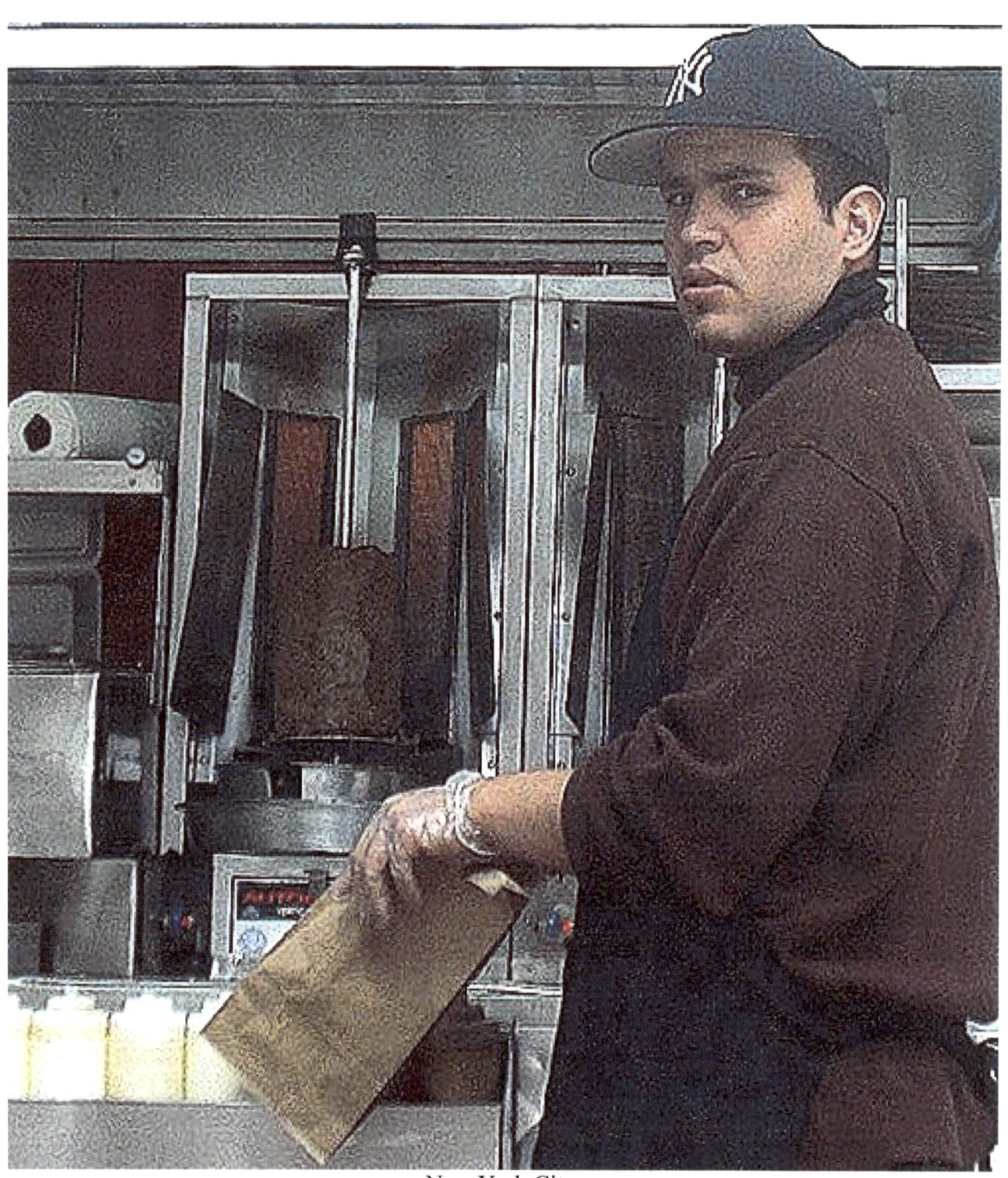

New York City

SEPTEMBER 11, 2001

*We Shall Never Forget Our Friends And Neighbors
Who Went To Work That Morning,
But Did Not Return To Us That Night.*

*May This Tree Serve As A Living Memorial
To The Following Community Members Who Died
In The Tragic Attack On The World Trade Center.*

DAVID B. BRADY
MARK R. BRUCE
THOMAS R. CLARK
JAMES L. CONNOR
KEVIN R. CROTTY
THOMAS GLASSER
ROBERT A. LAWRENCE, JR.
A. TODD RANCKE
CLIVE "IAN" THOMPSON

*Planted By The City Of Summit
July 11, 2002*

New Jersey

ARE YOU WRINKLED
WITH BURDEN

COME ON INTO CHURCH
FOR A FAITH LIFT

Indiana

BAPTIST CHURCH

GOD NEVER MET A
SINNER HE DOES NOT
LOVE

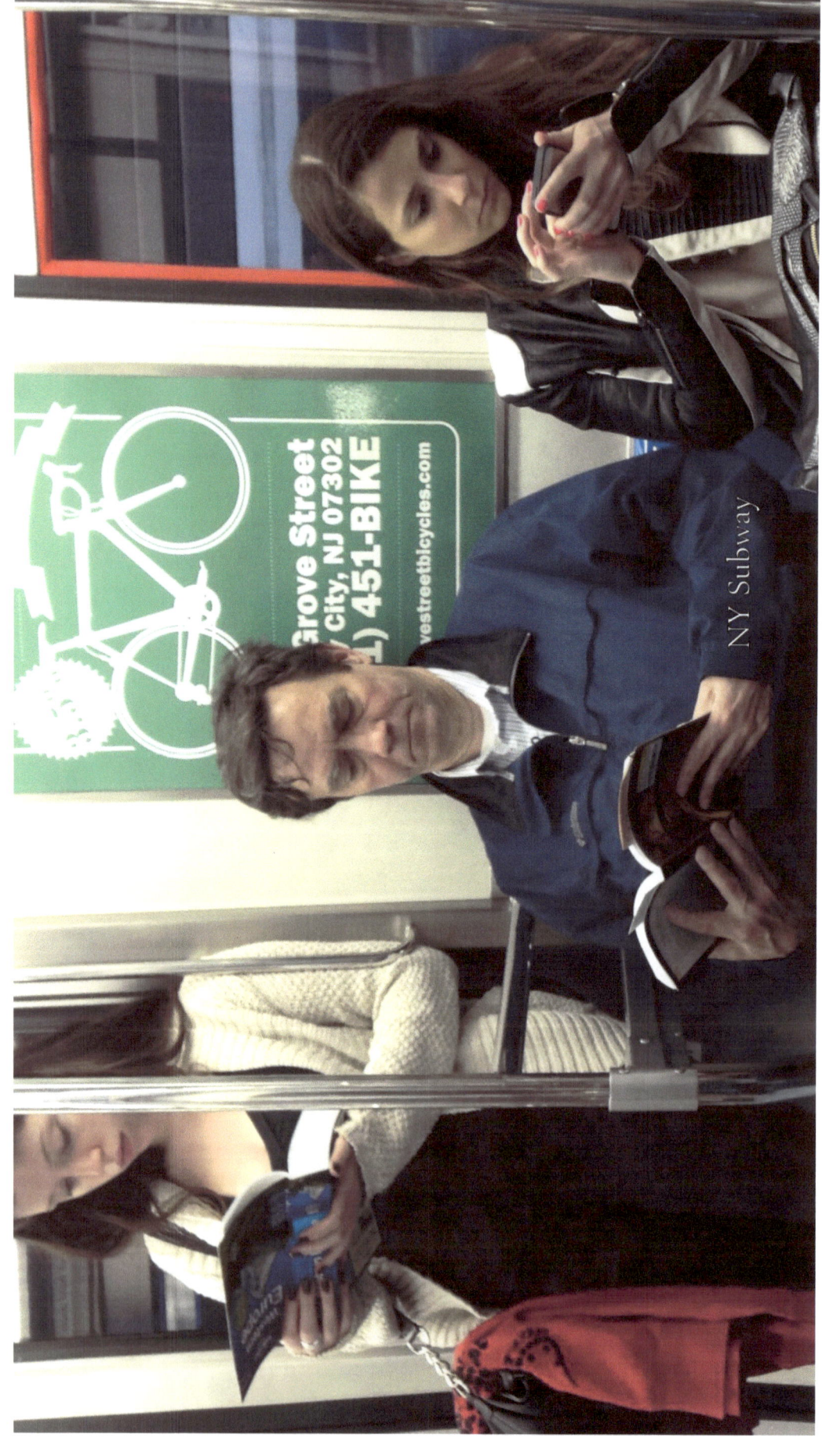

NY Subway

THE GREATEST CHRISTMAS GIFT EVER GIVEN WAS THE LORD JESUS

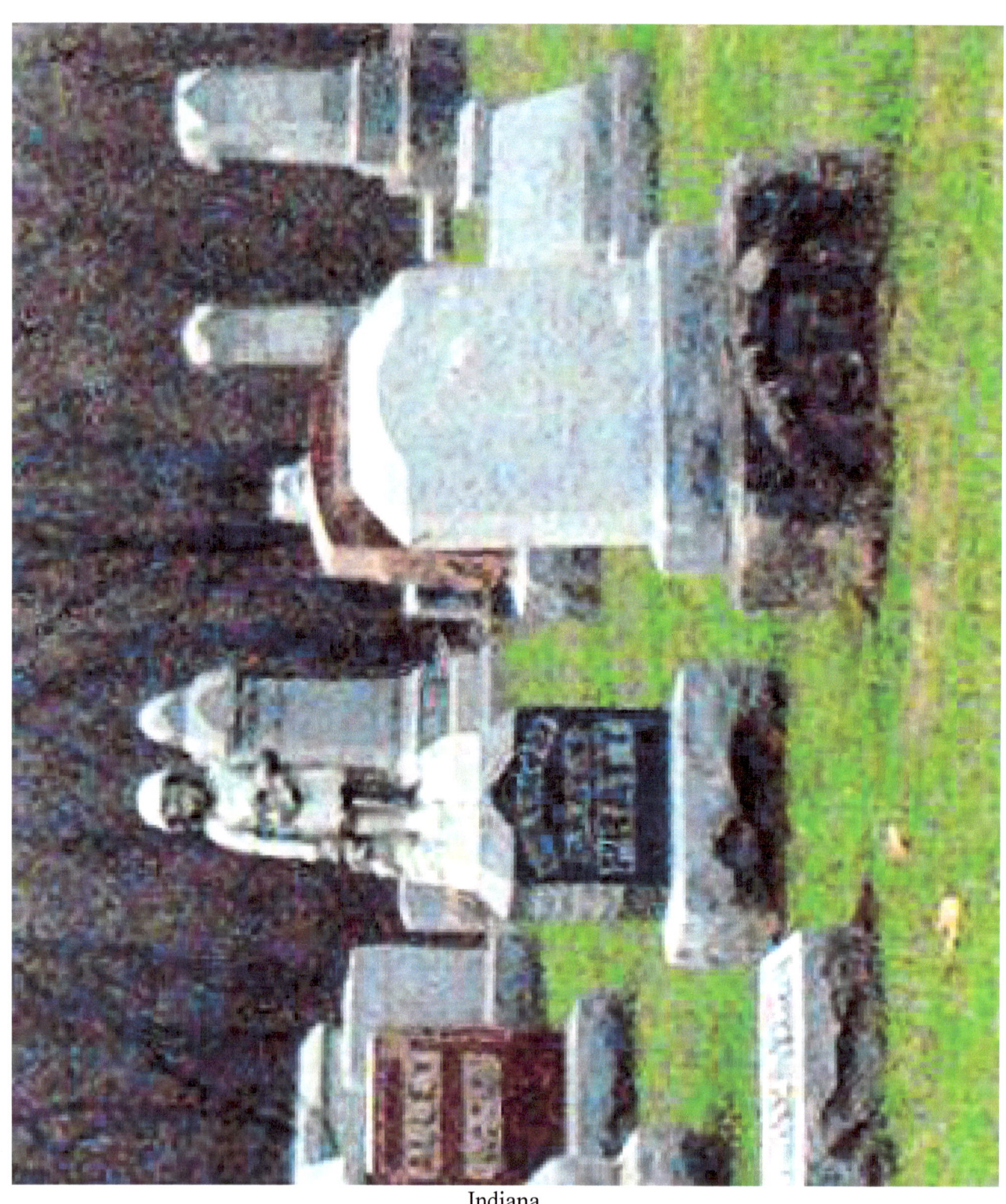

Indiana

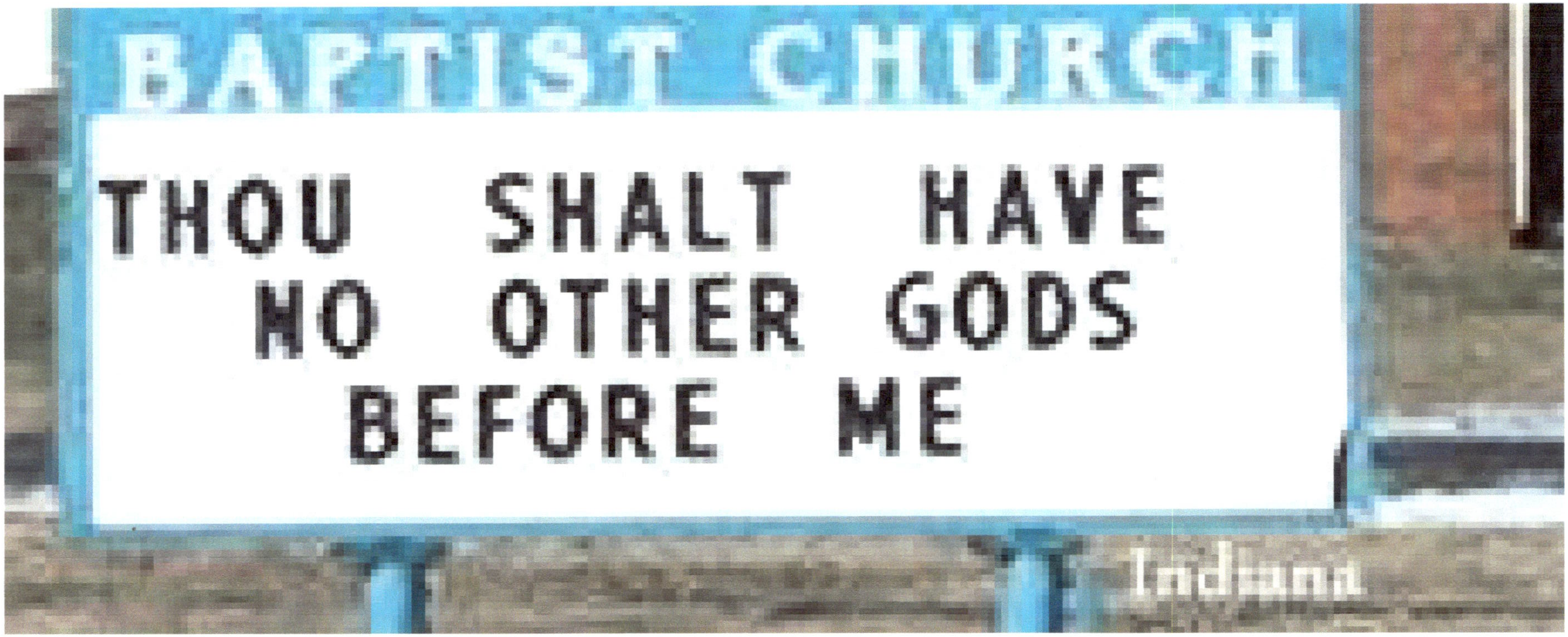

BAPTIST CHURCH

THOU SHALT HAVE
NO OTHER GODS
BEFORE ME

Indiana

WHEN WE SEE

HIM

WE WILL

KNOW

HIM

Indiana

ADVENT PENANCE SERVICE TUES. 6:30

Indiana

LOVE... THE LORD IS ON THE WAY

Indiana

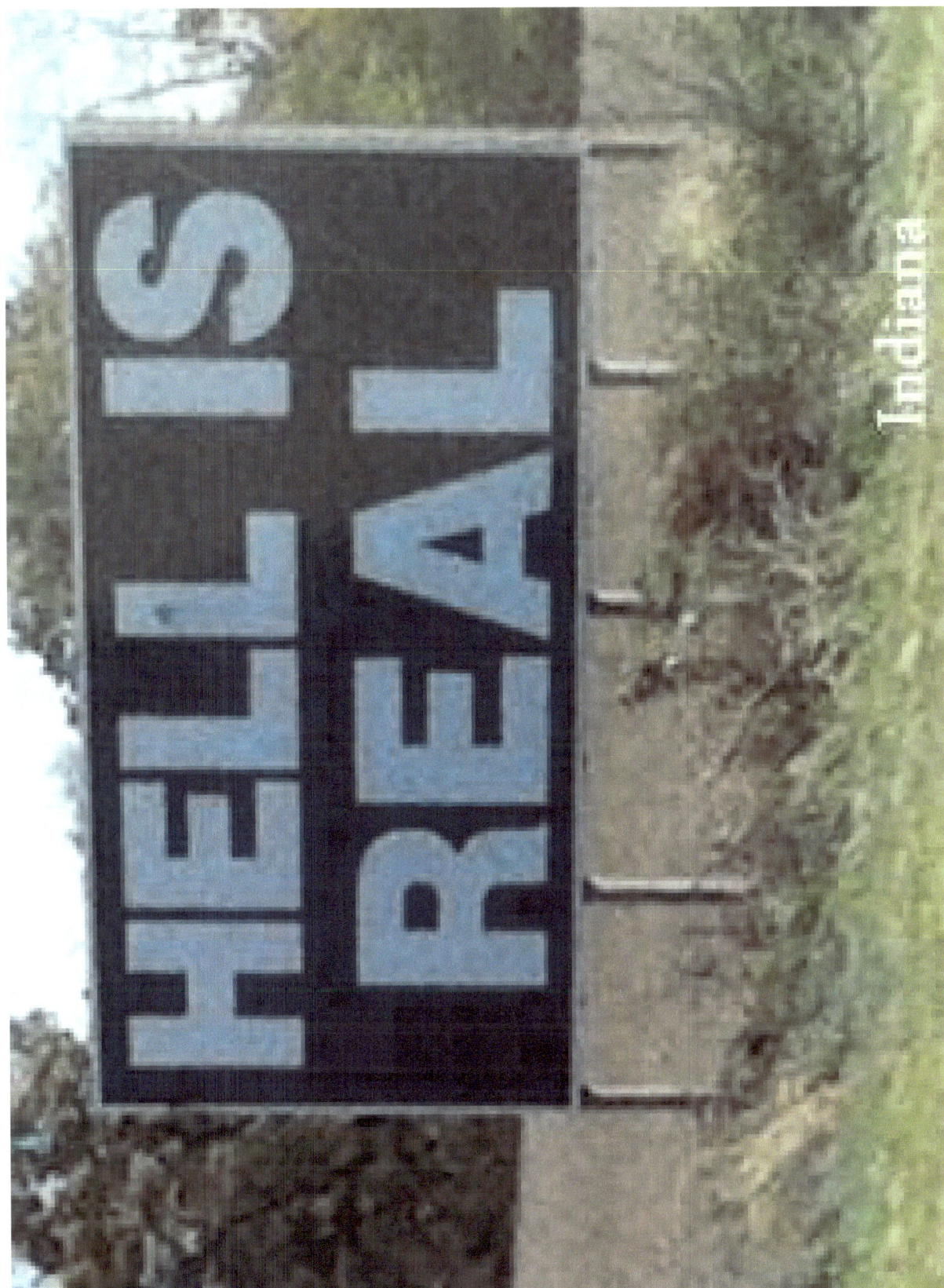

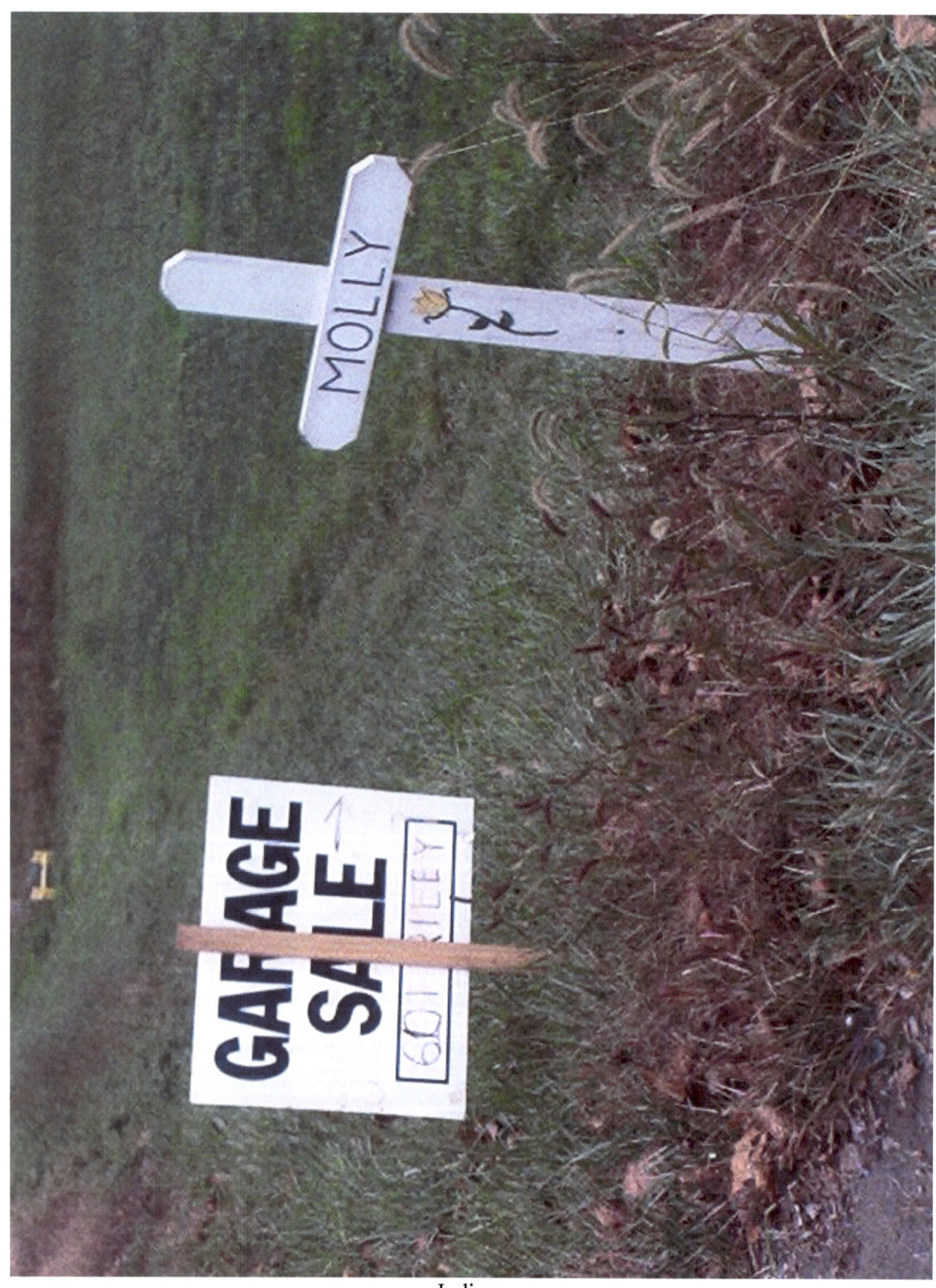

Indiana

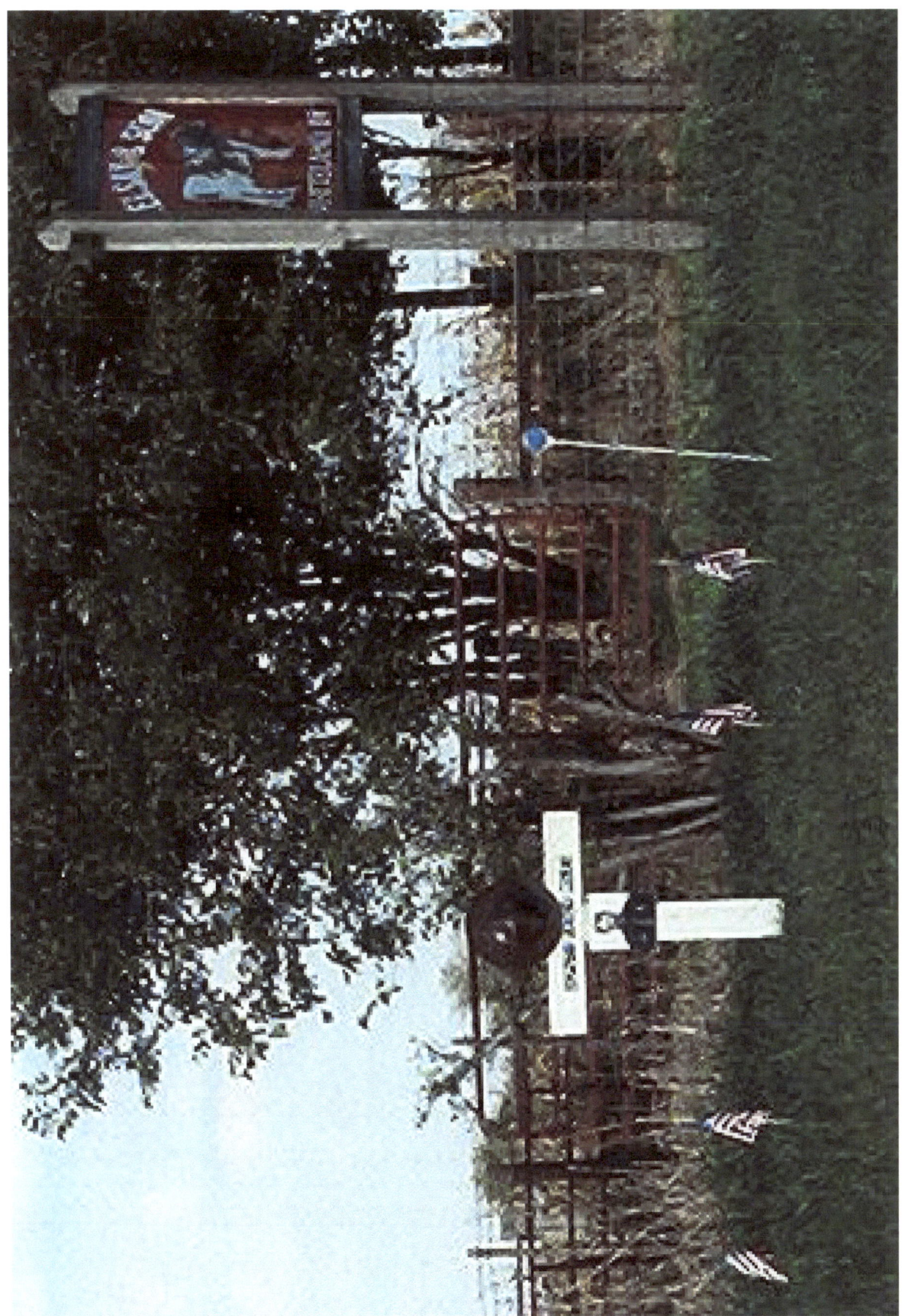

Indiana

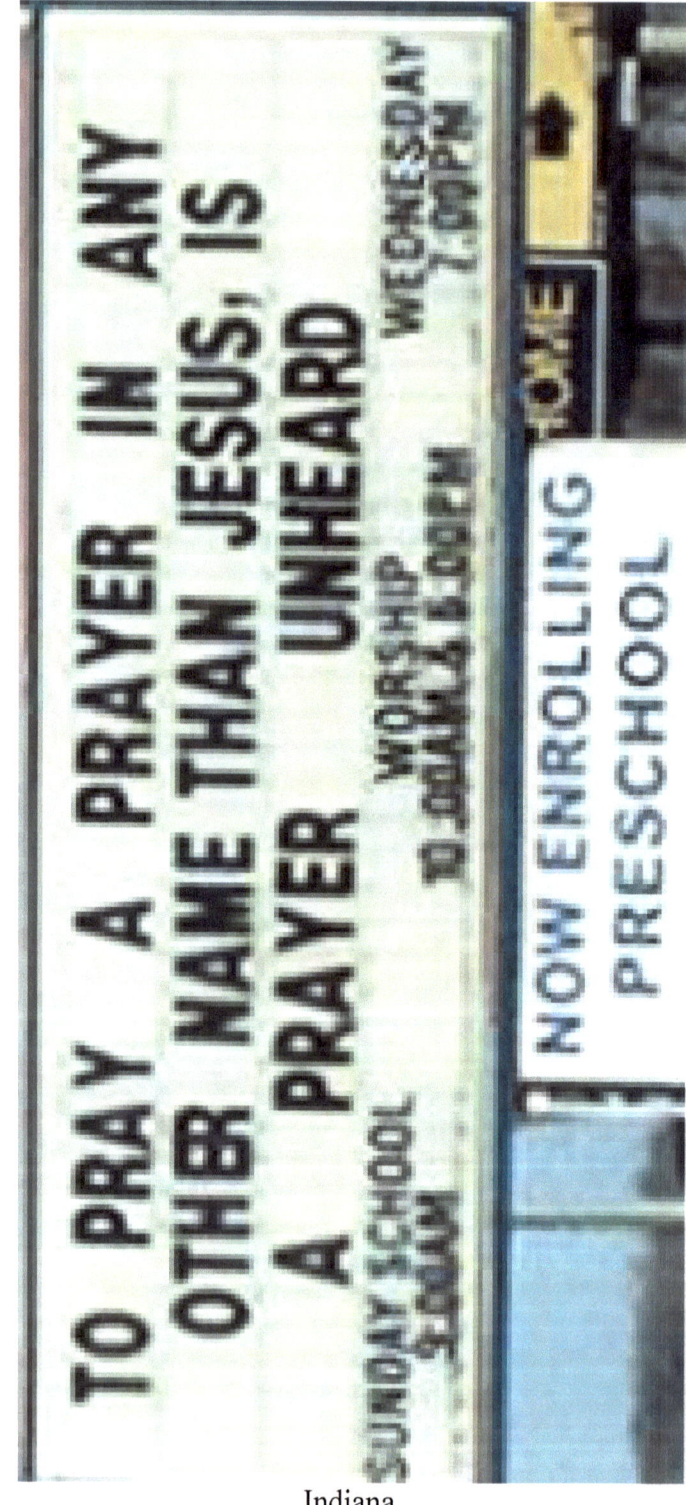

TO PRAY A PRAYER IN ANY
OTHER NAME THAN JESUS, IS
A PRAYER UNHEARD

SUNDAY SCHOOL
9:00 AM

WORSHIP
10:00 AM & 6:00 PM

WEDNESDAY
7:00 PM

NOW ENROLLING
PRESCHOOL

Indiana

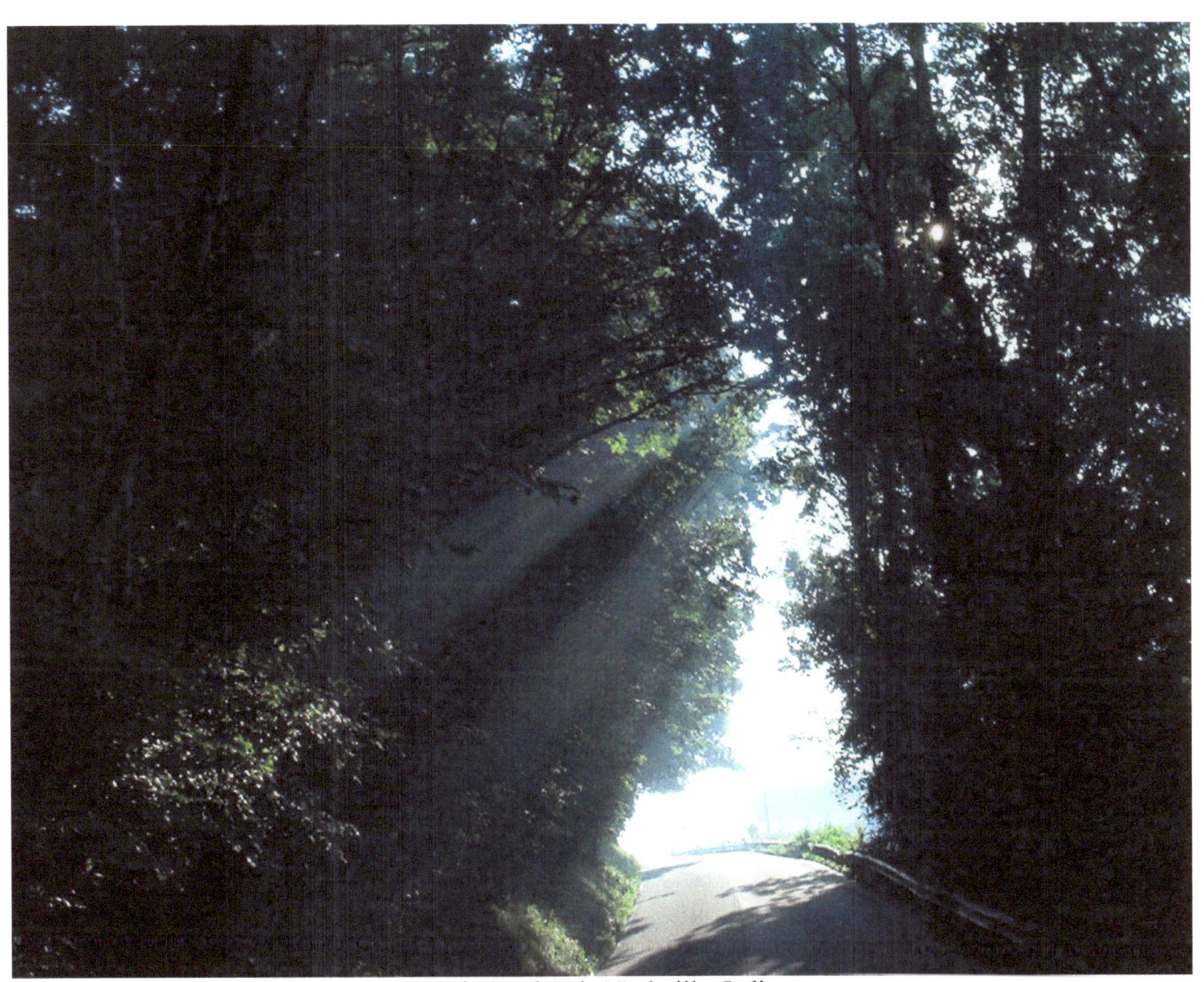

Salt Creek Rd., Nashville, Indiana

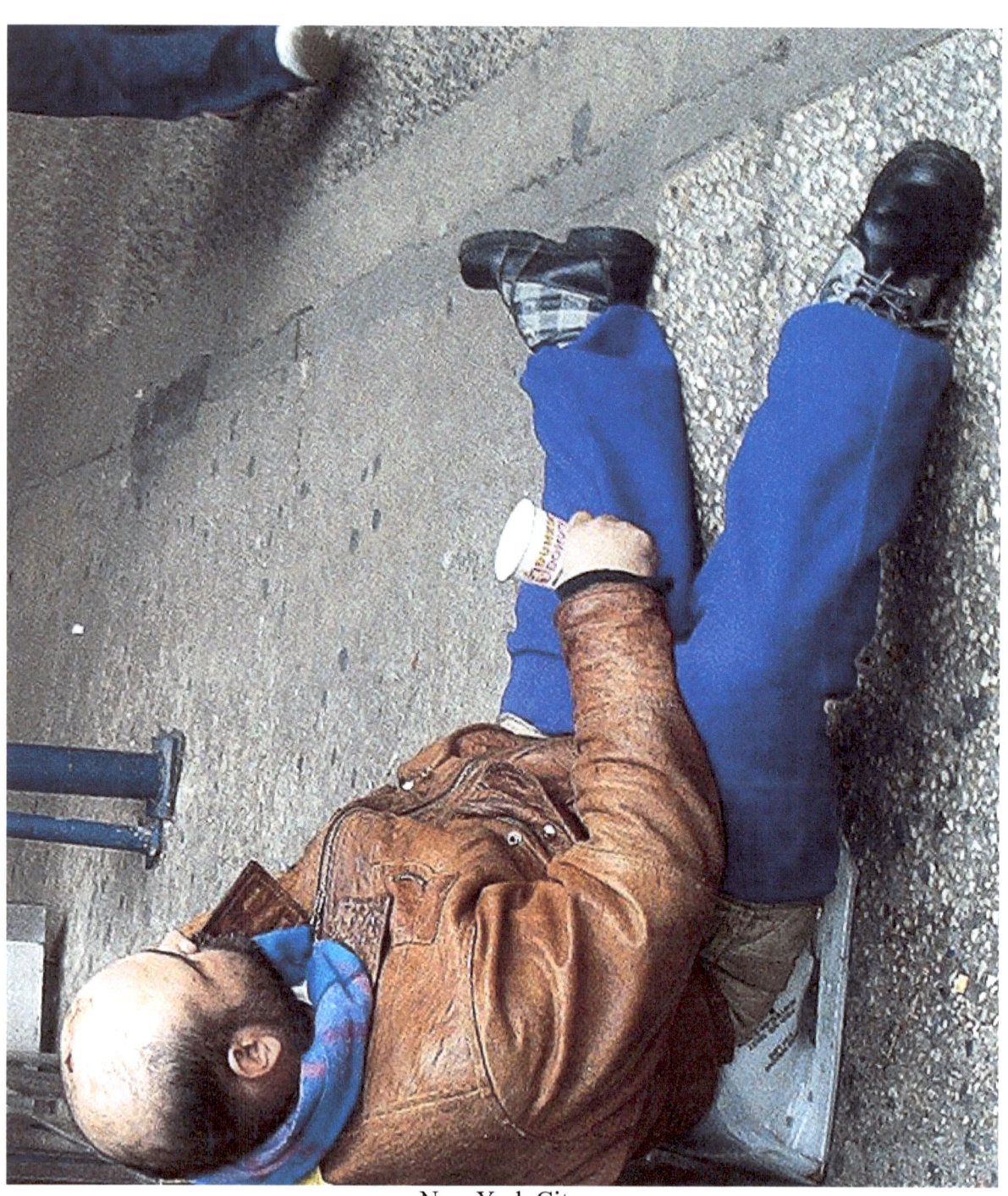

New York City

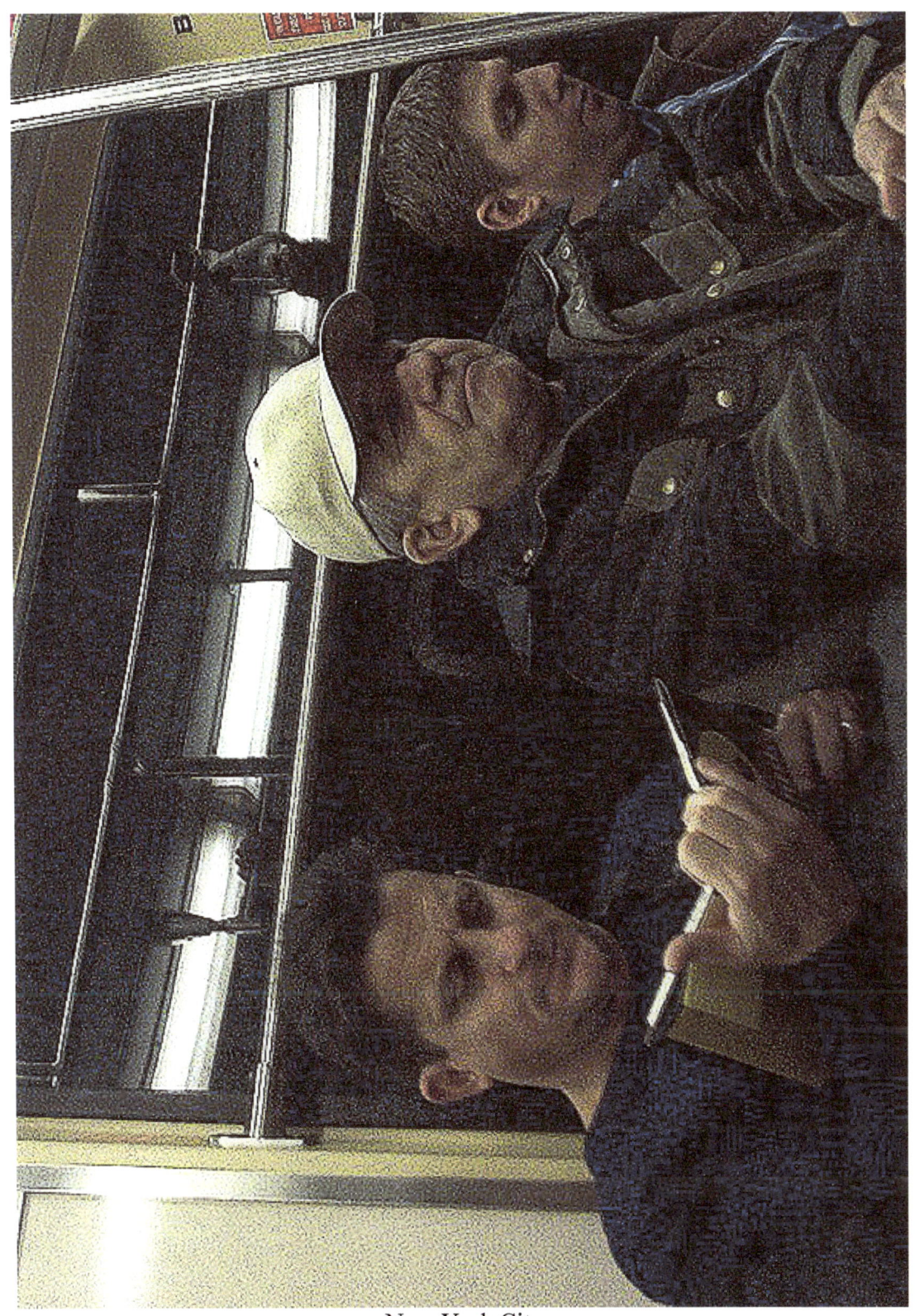

New York City

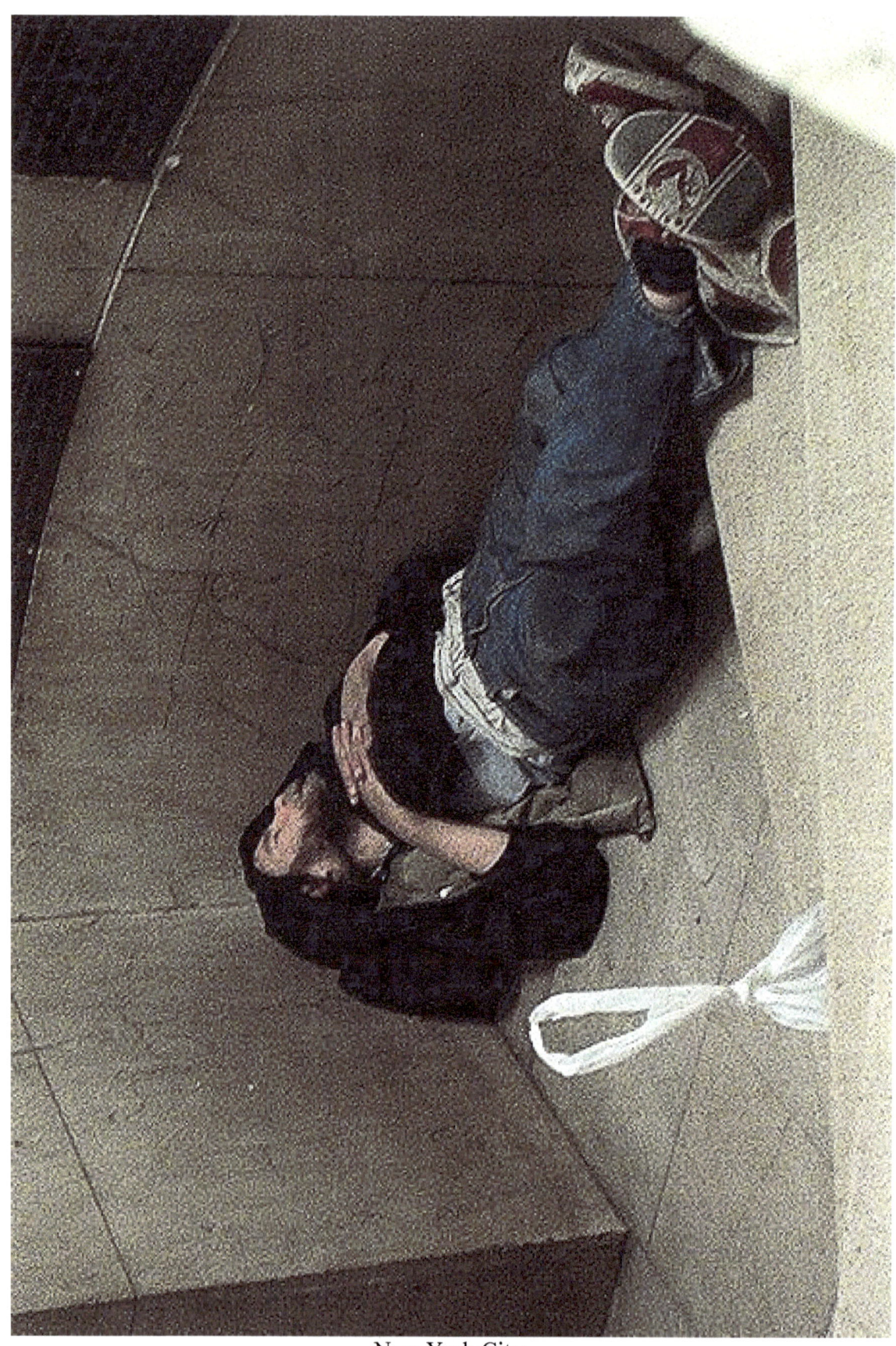

New York City

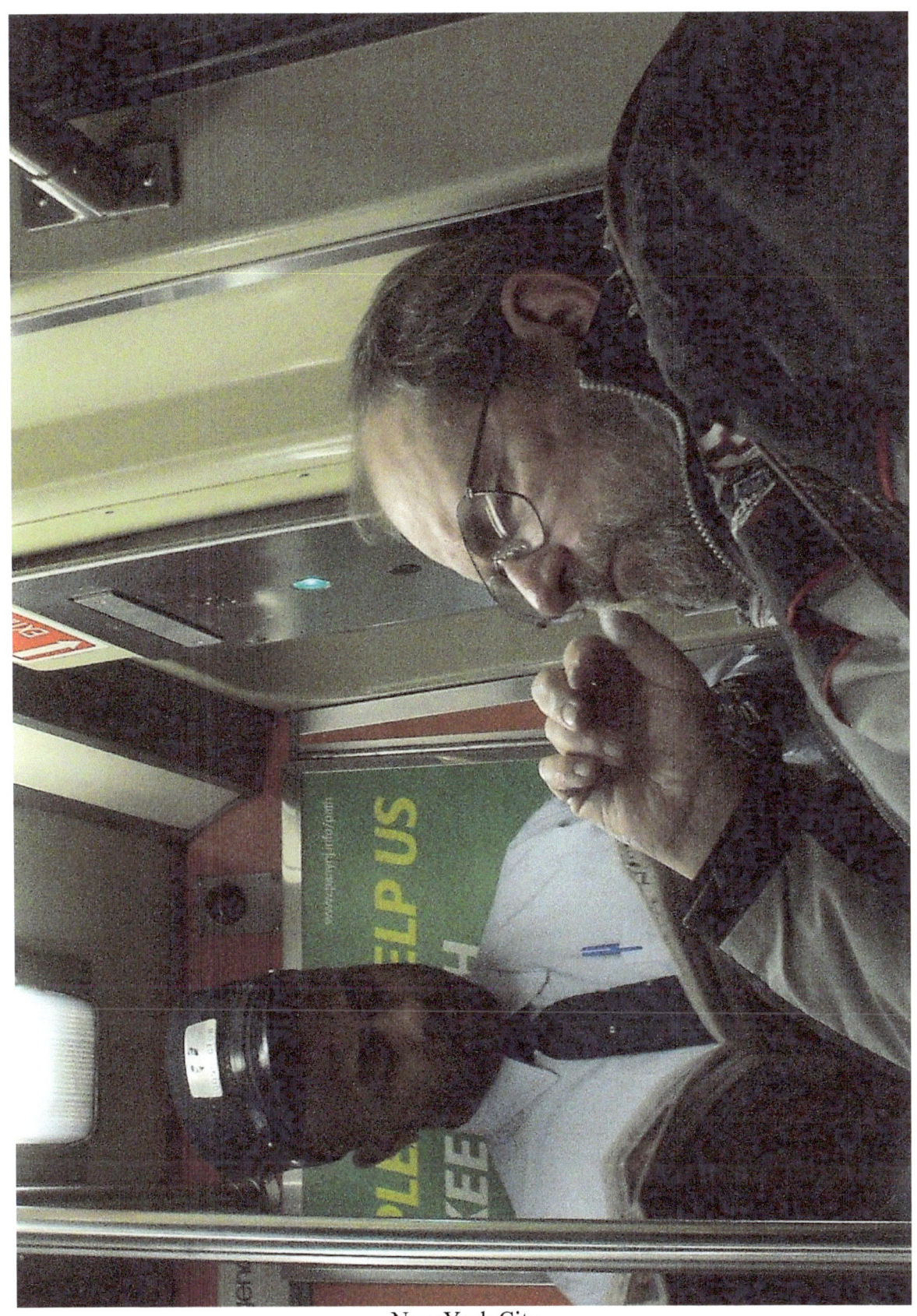

New York City

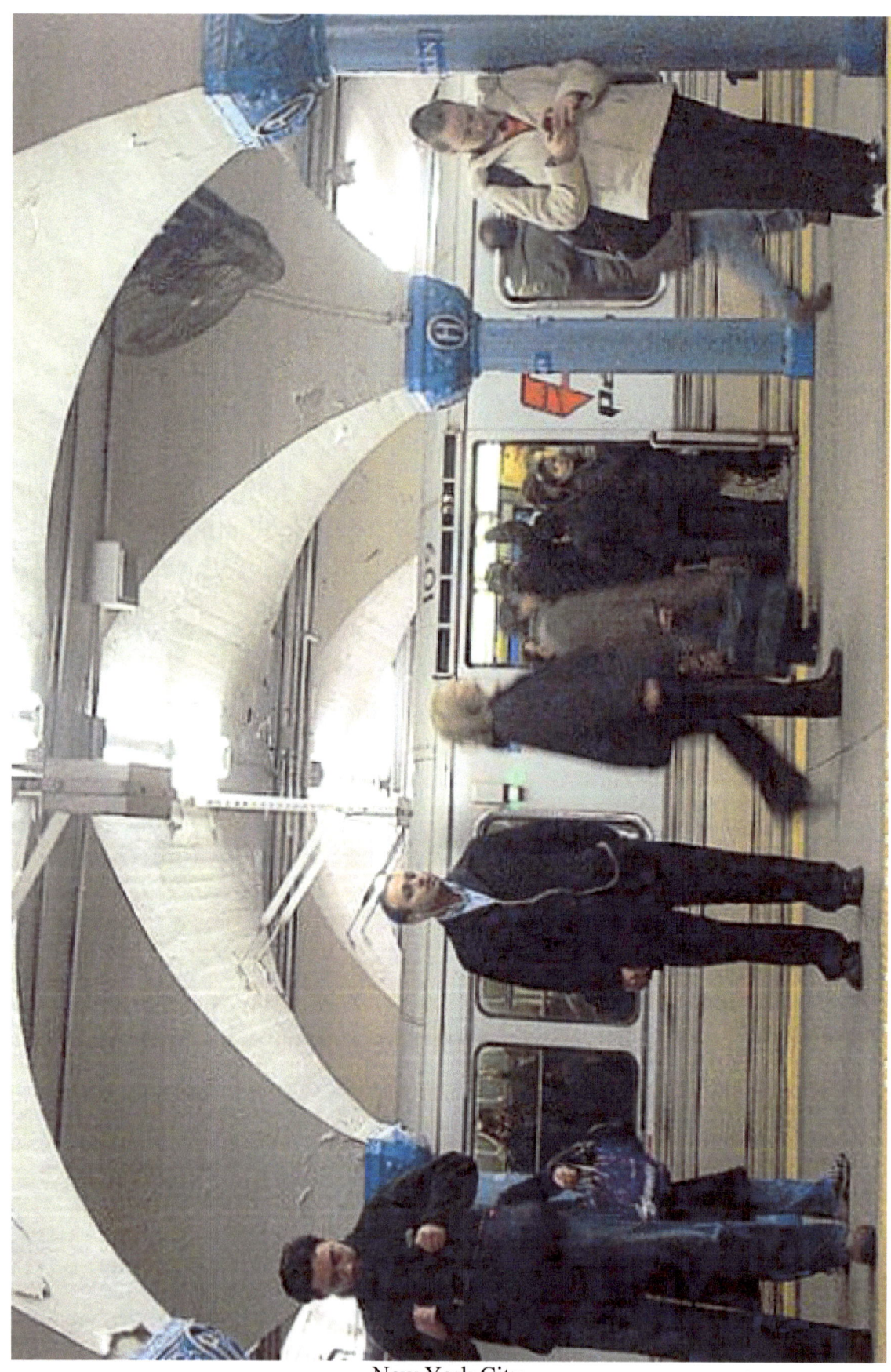

New York City

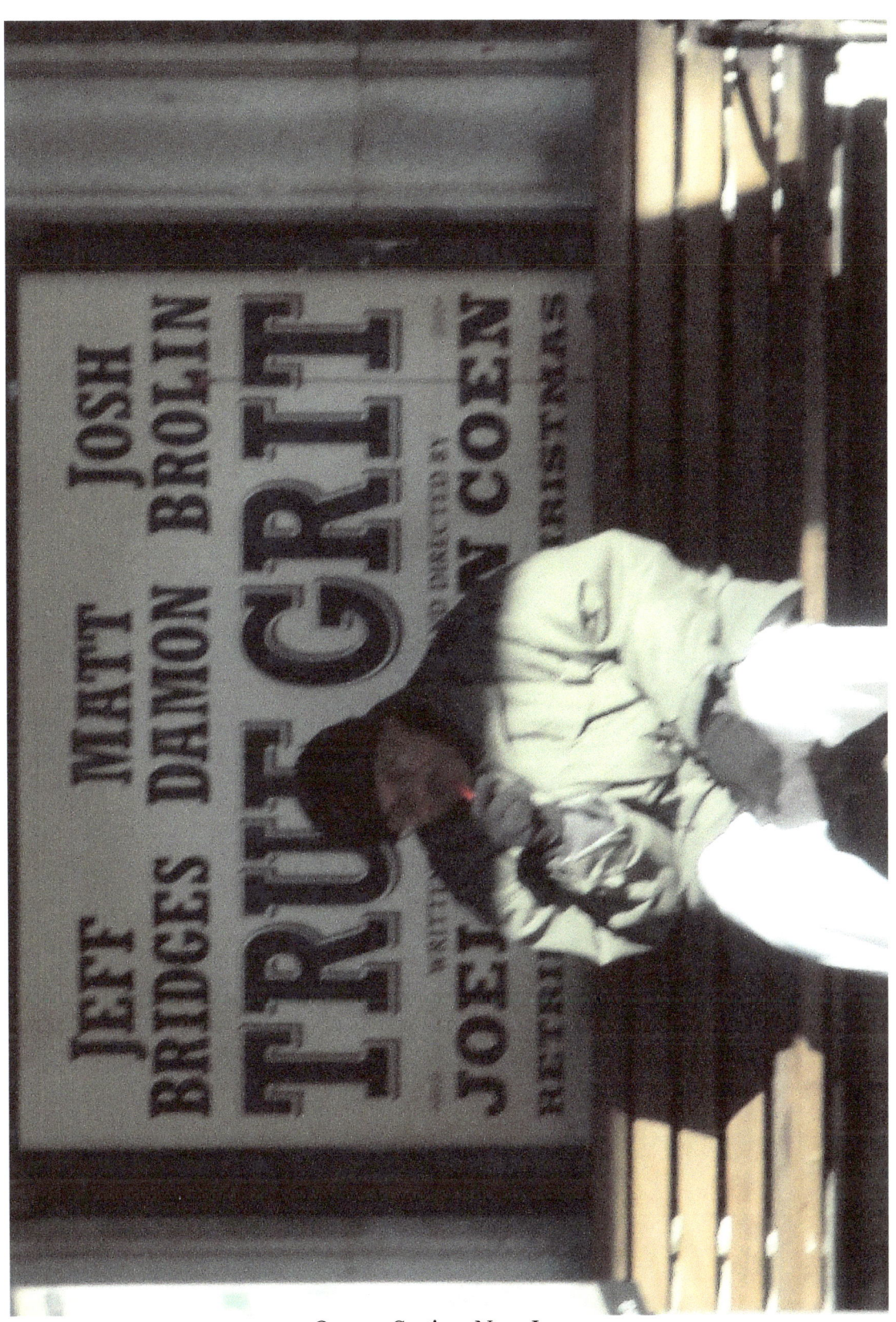

Orange Station, New Jersey

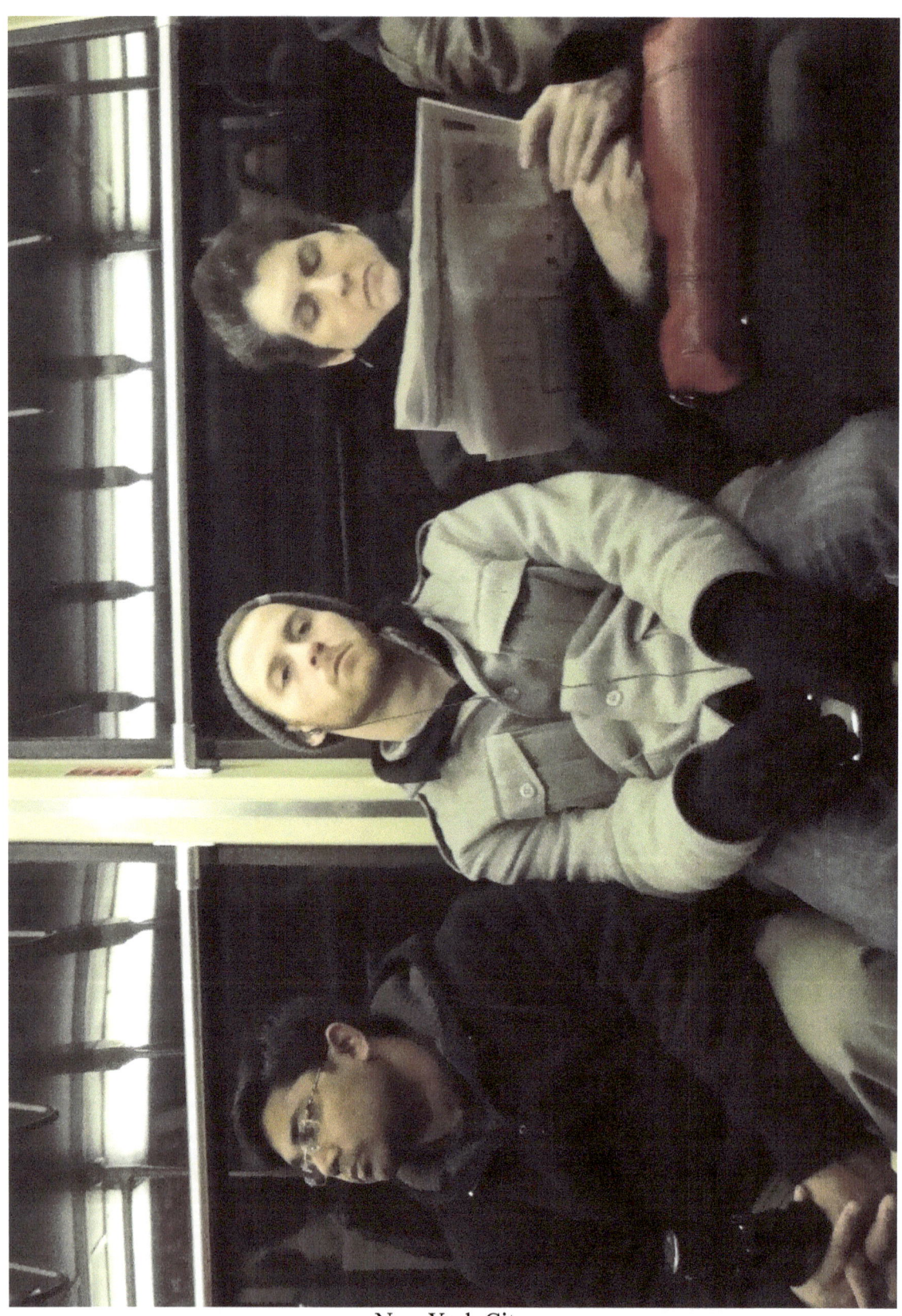

New York City

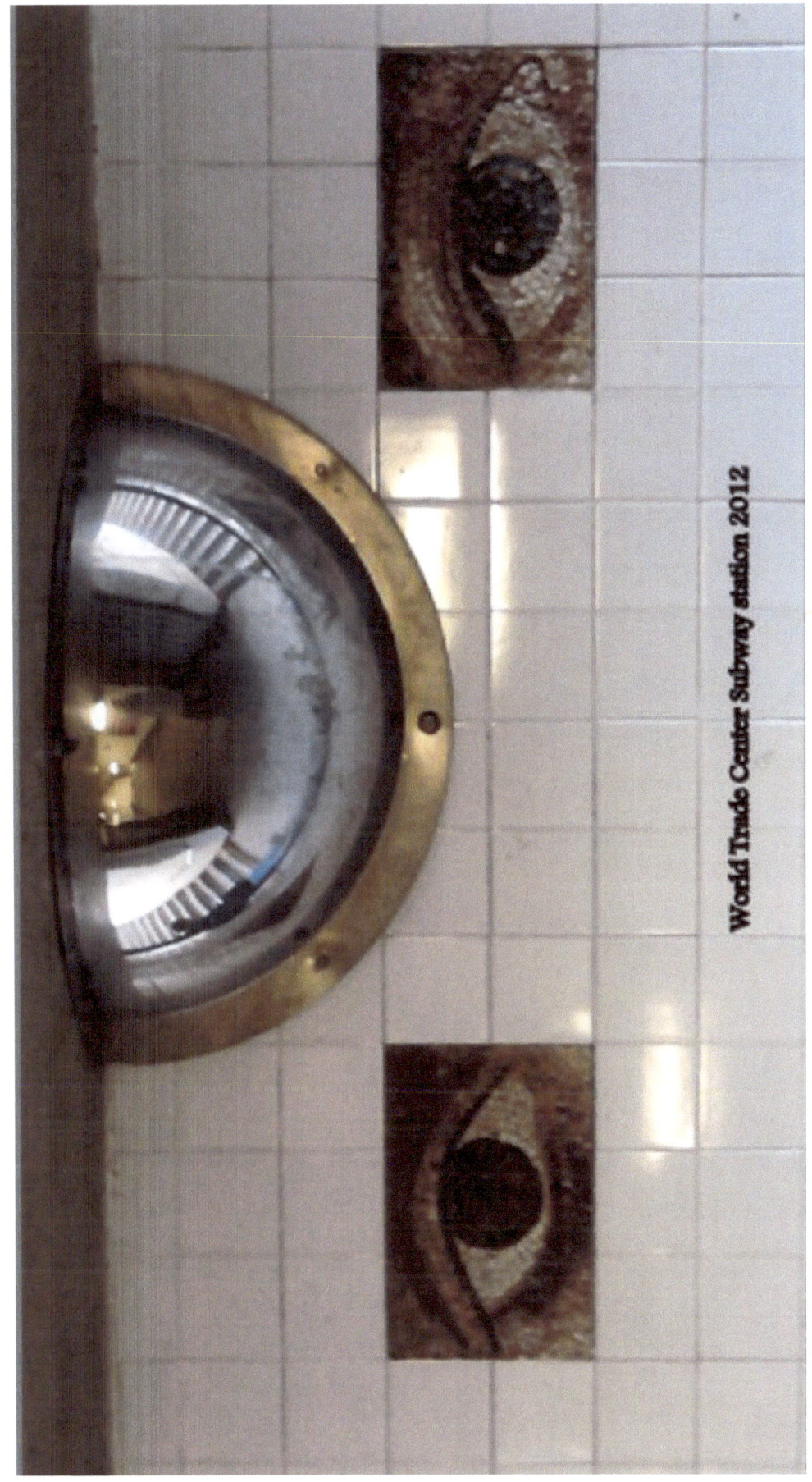

World Trade Center Subway station 2012

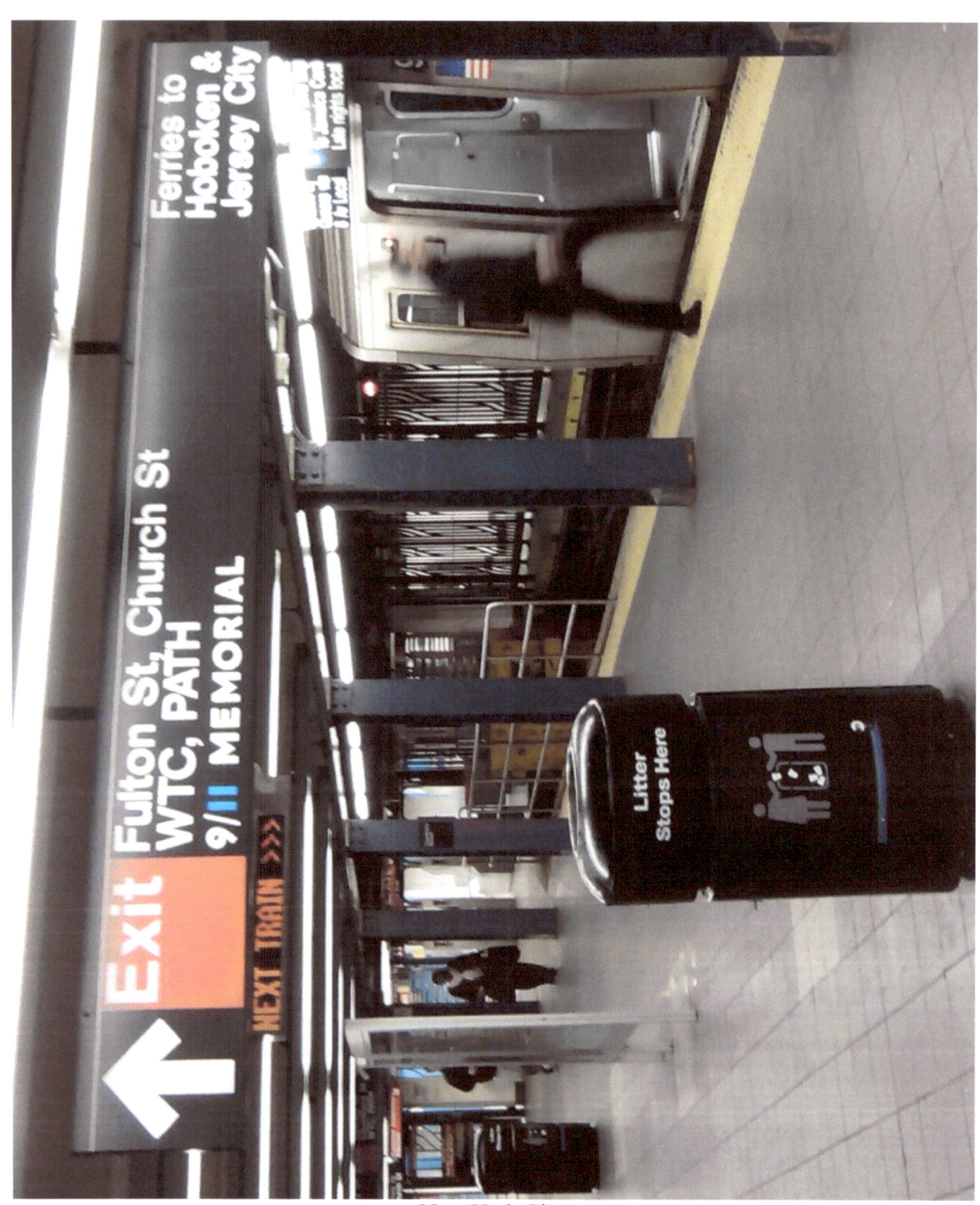

New York City

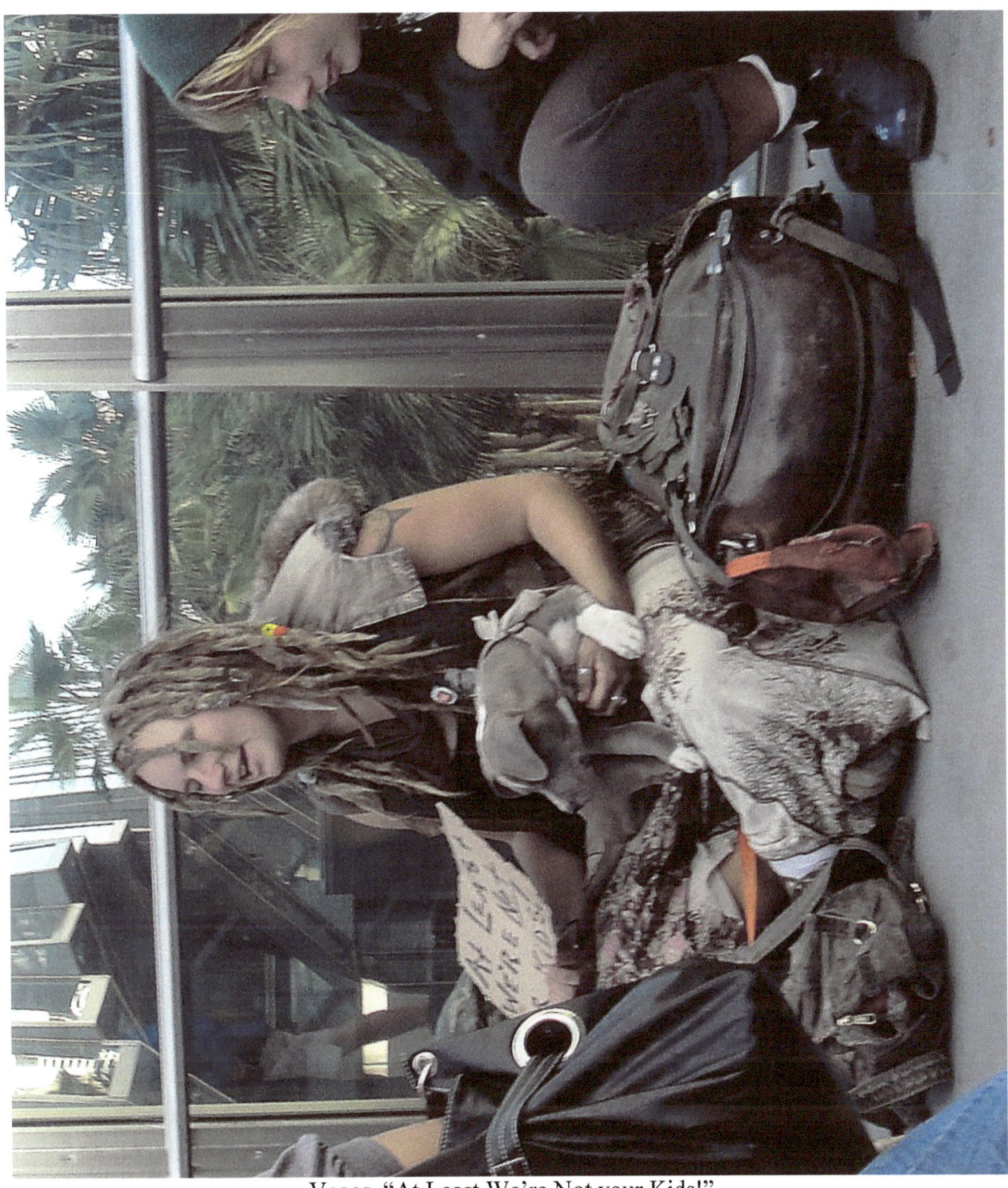

Vegas "At Least We're Not your Kids!"

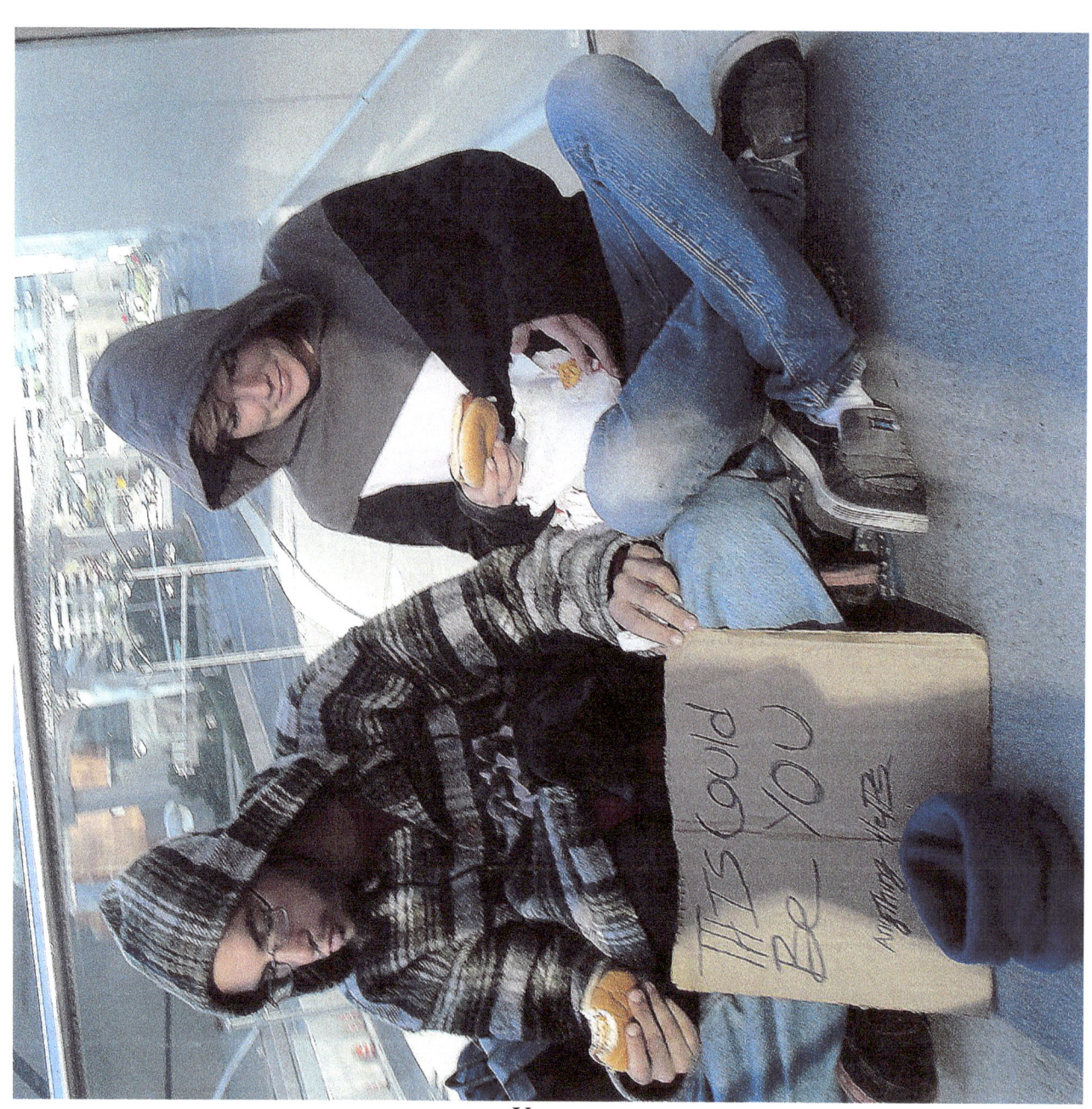

Vegas

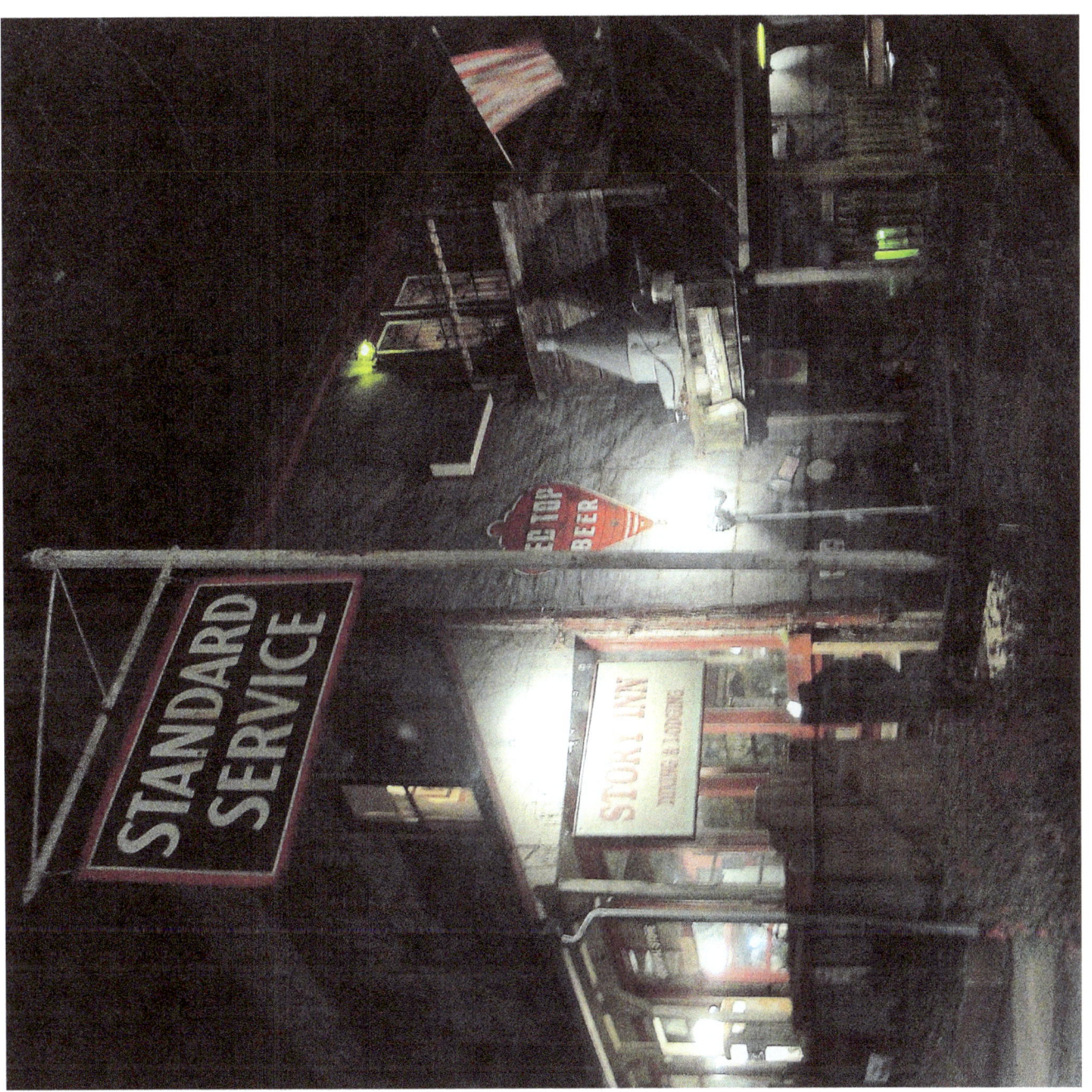

Indiana

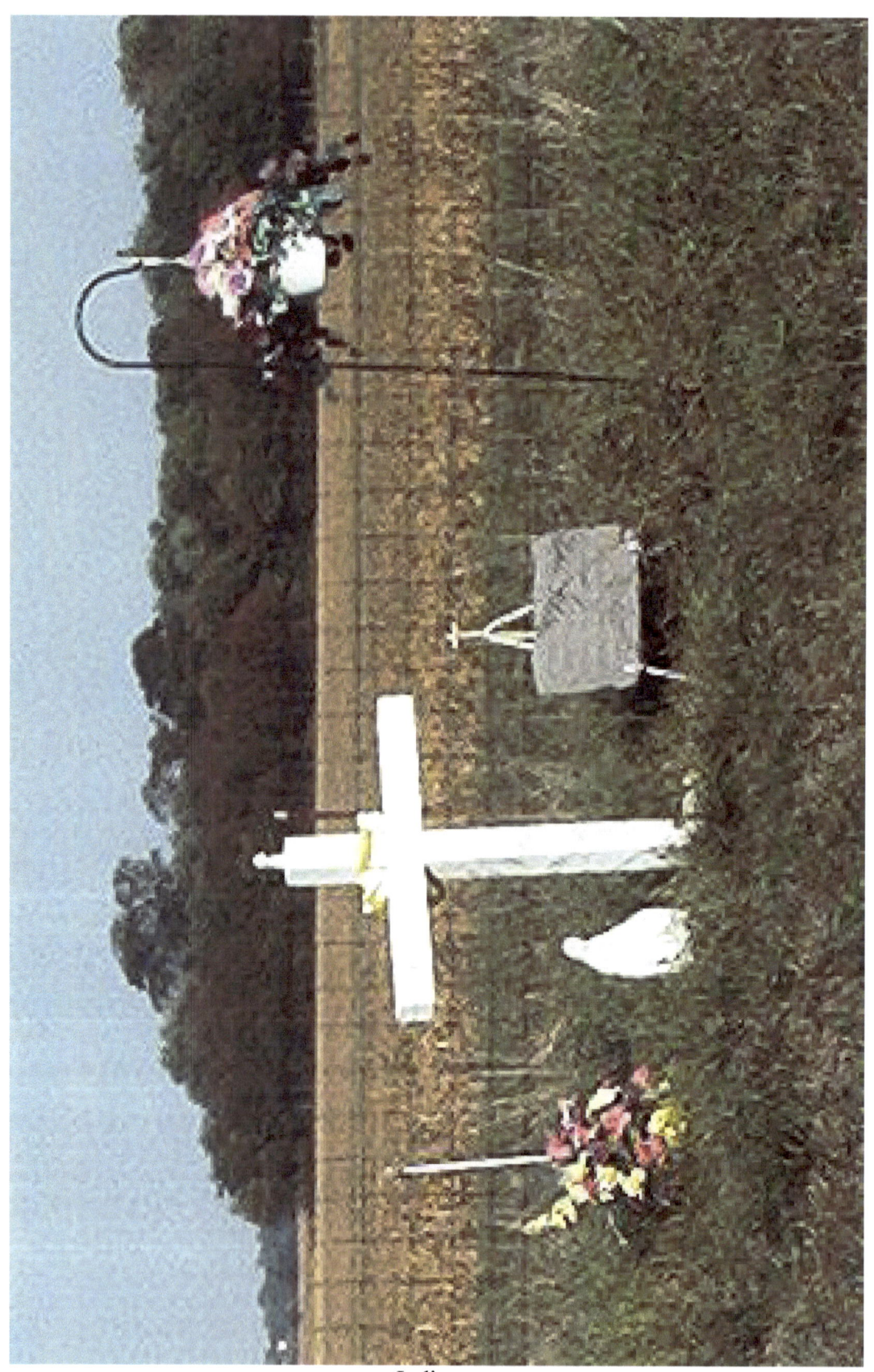

Indiana

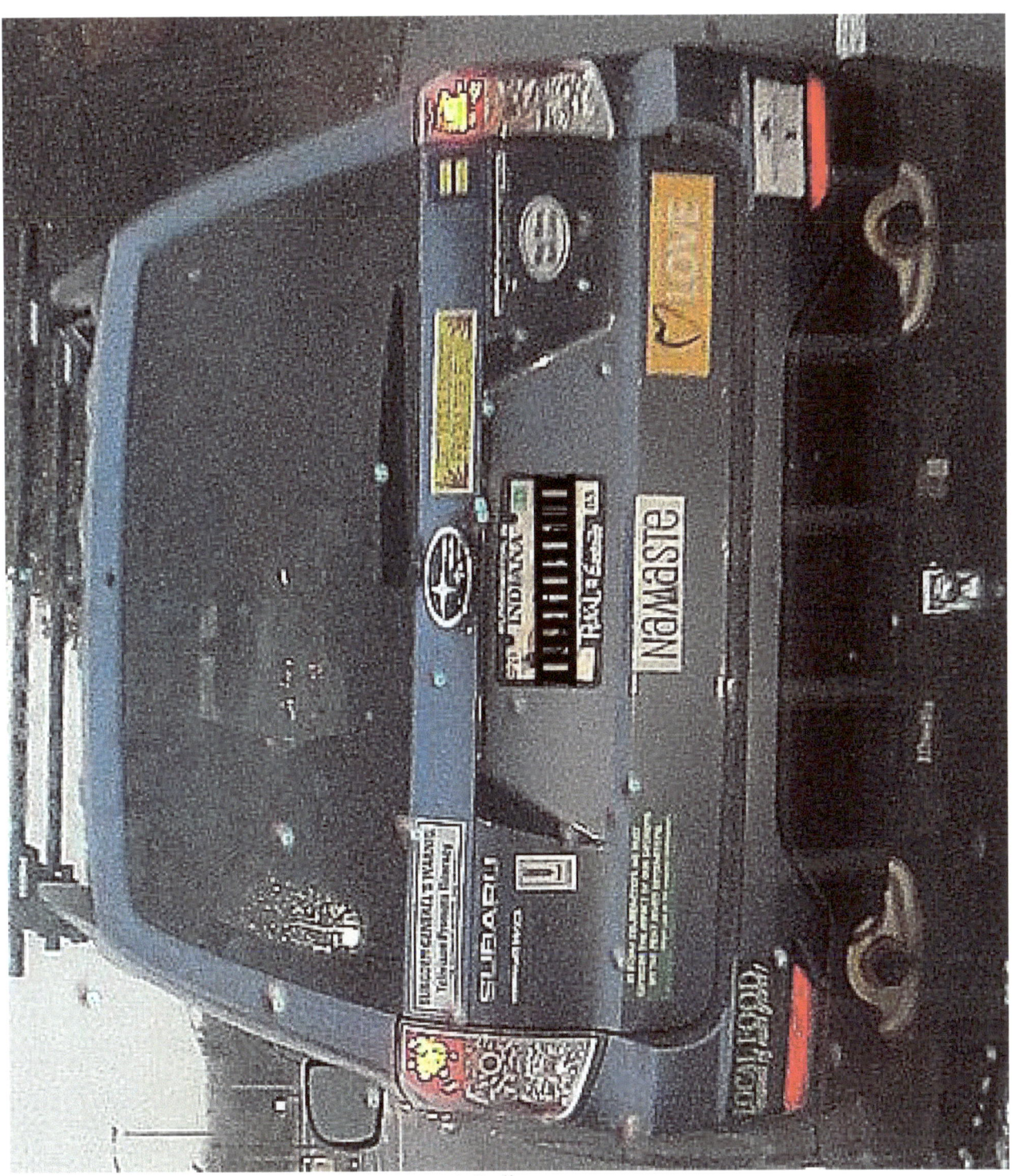

Indiana

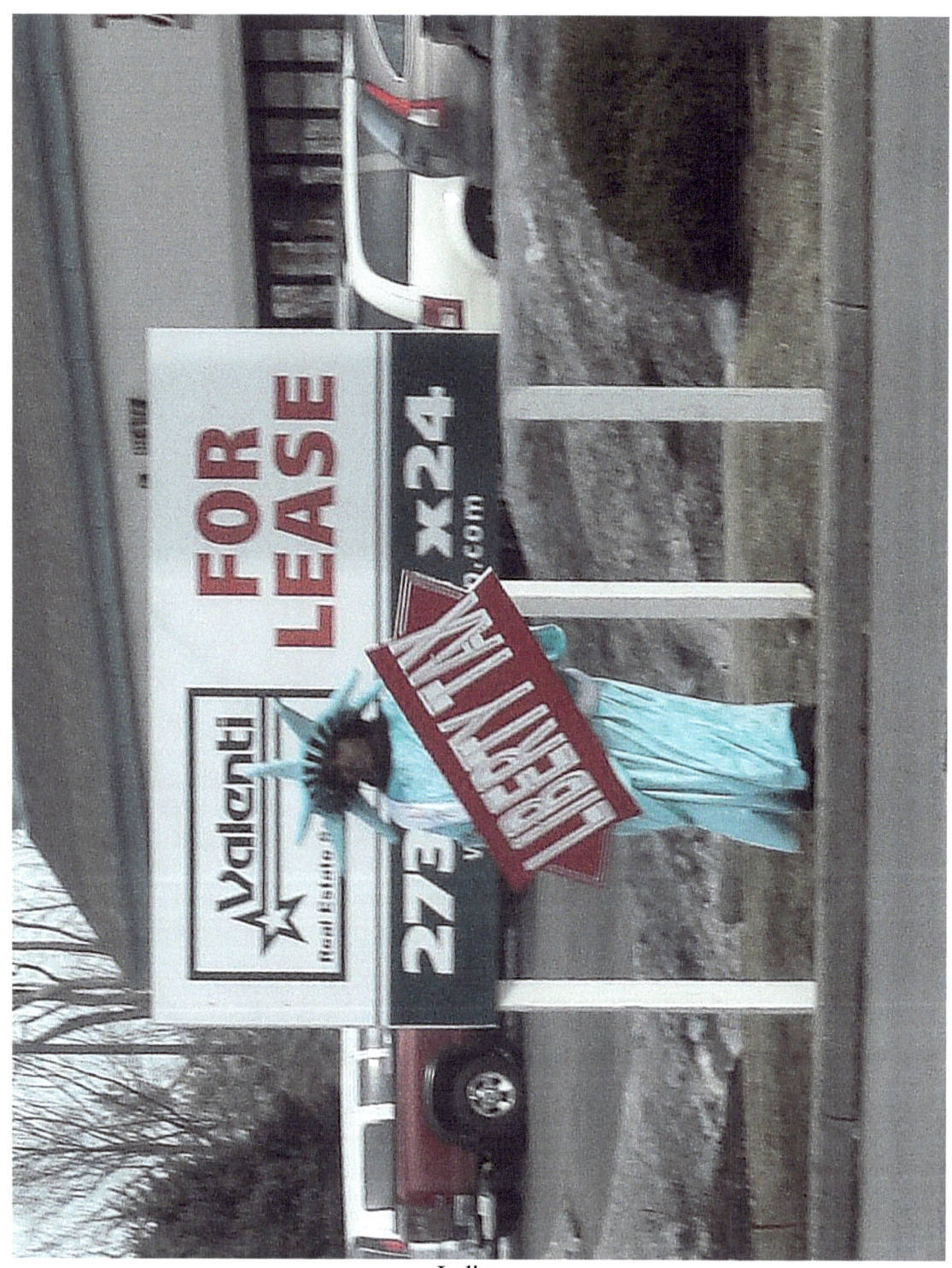

Indiana
(We've all seen him ☺)

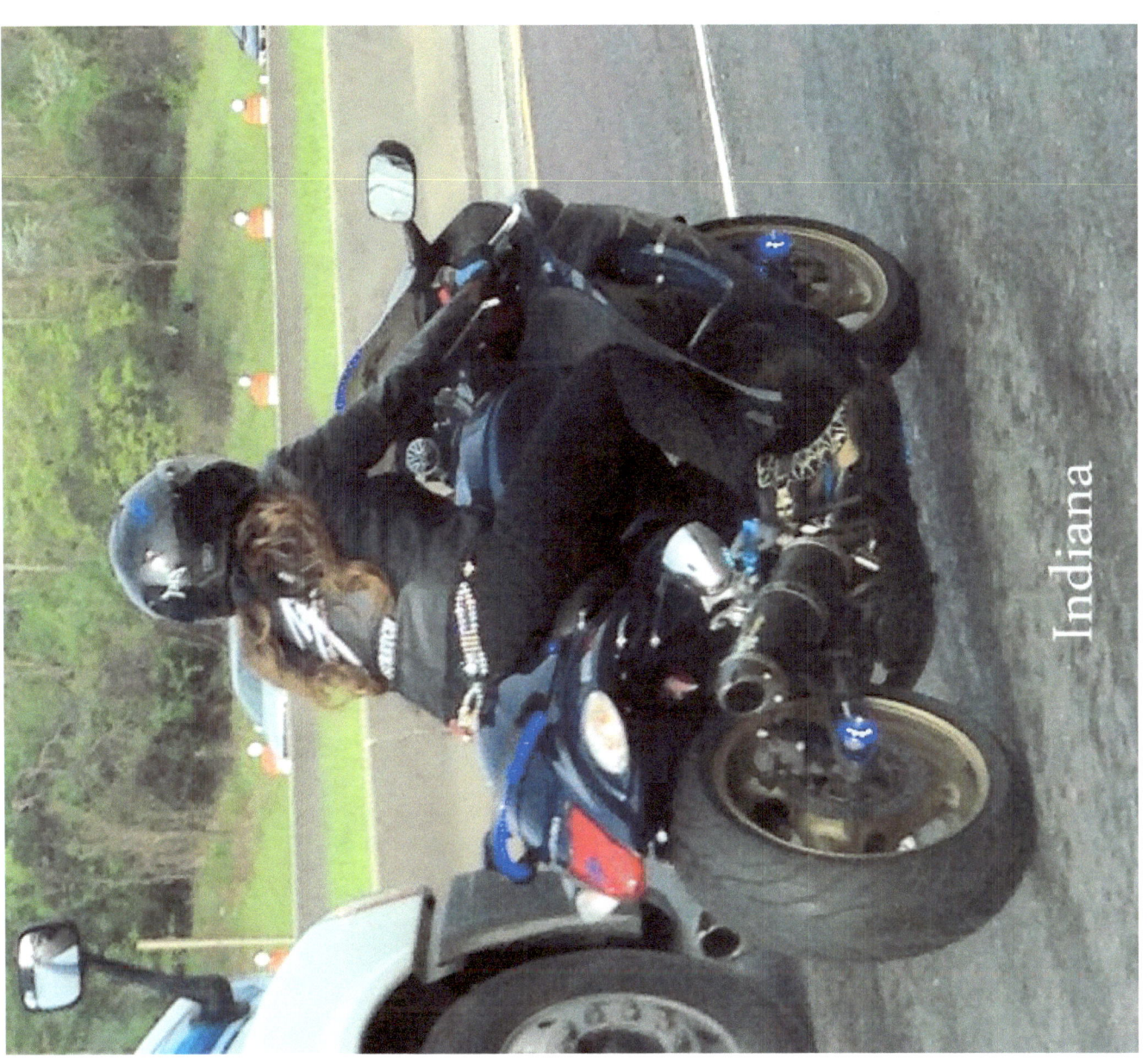

Indiana

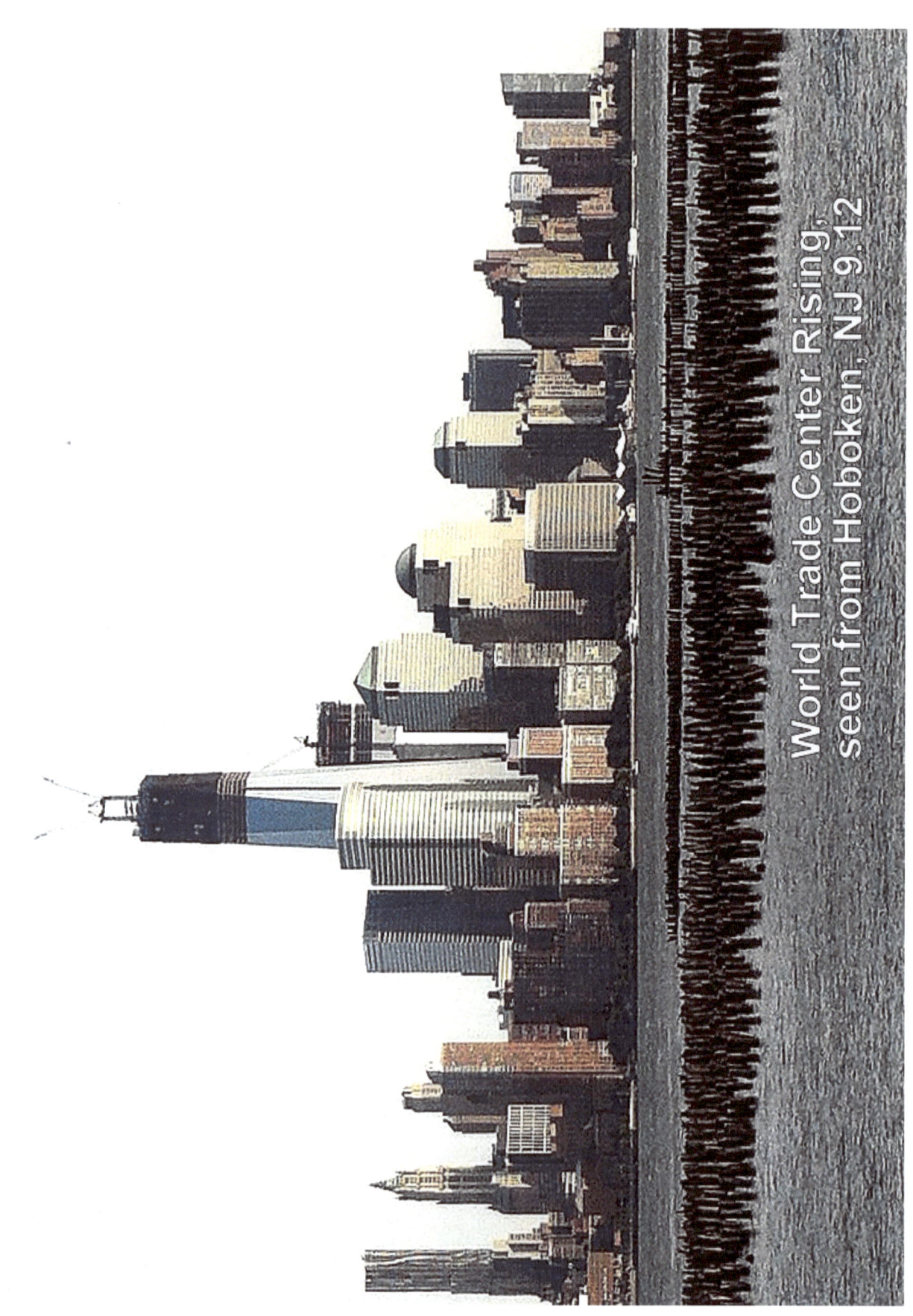

World Trade Center Rising,
seen from Hoboken, NJ 9.12

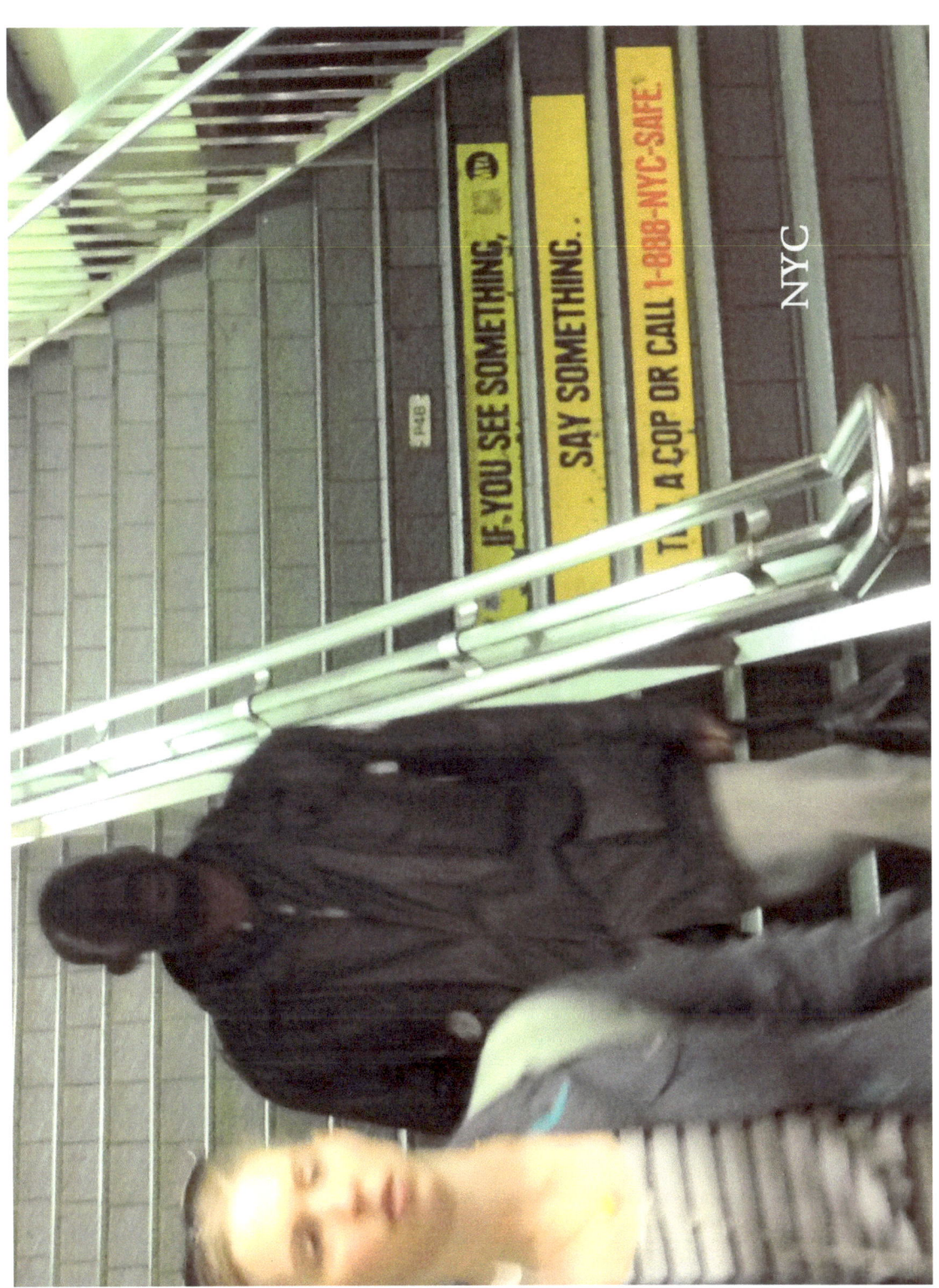

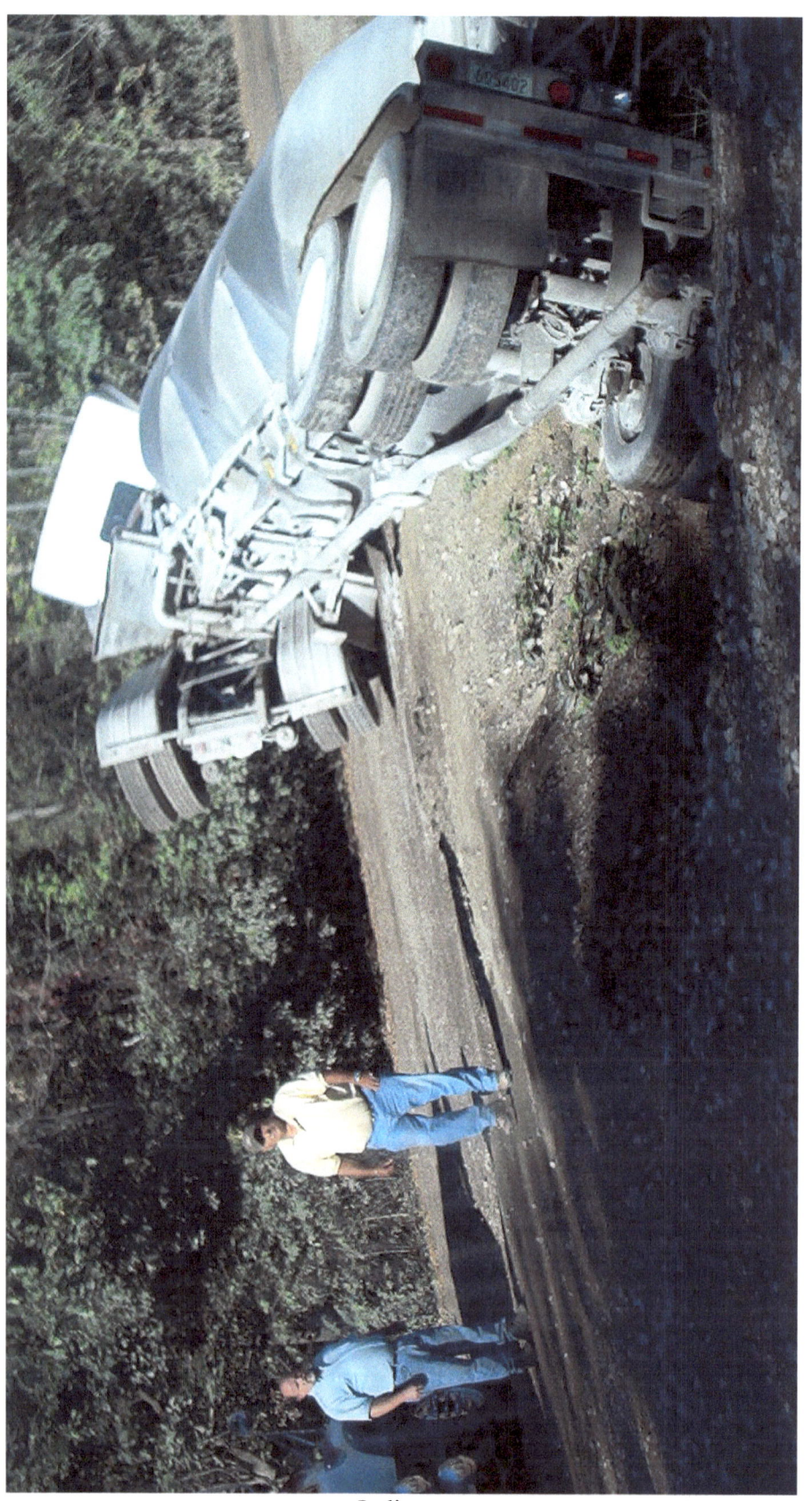

Indiana

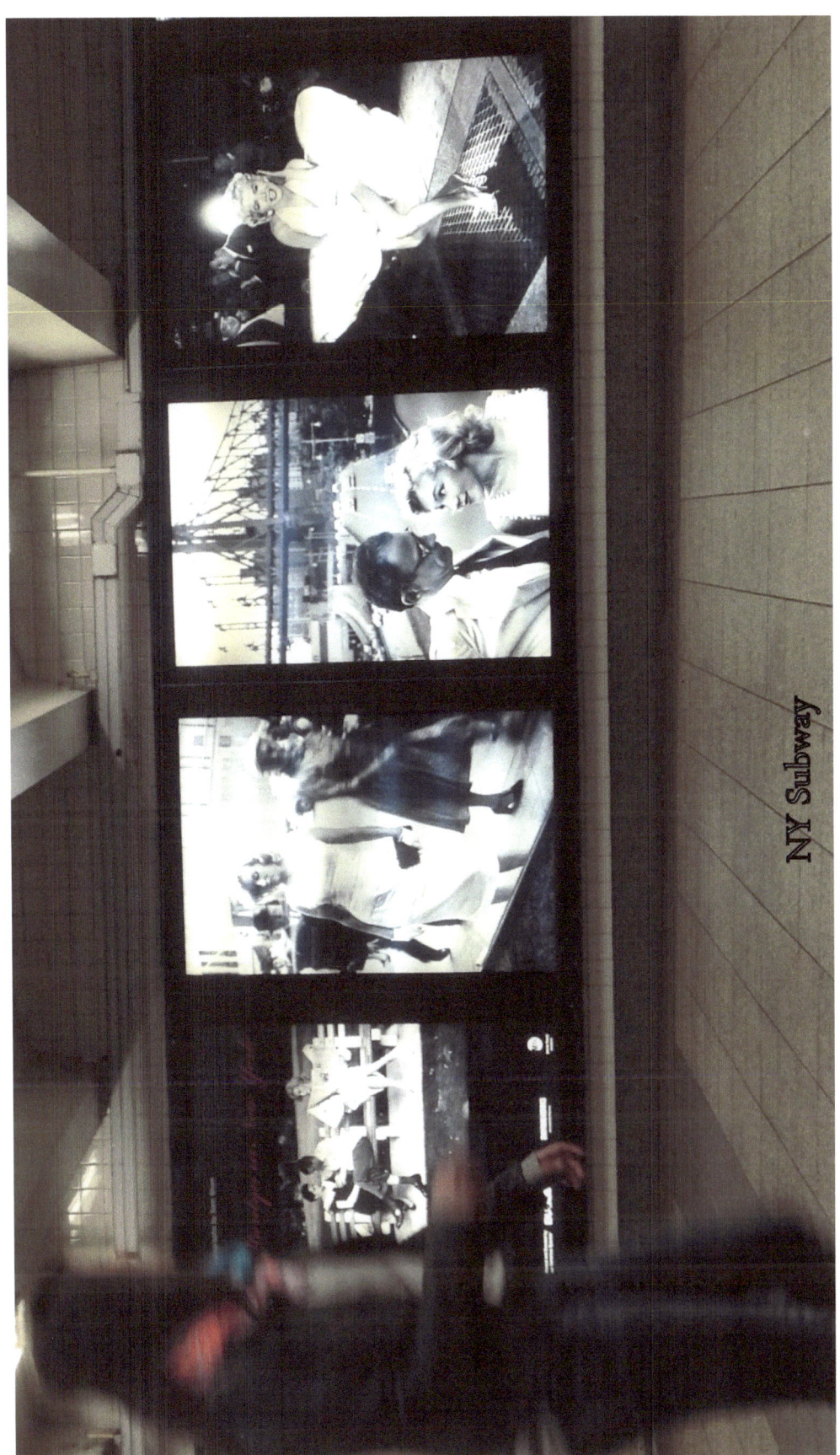

NY Subway

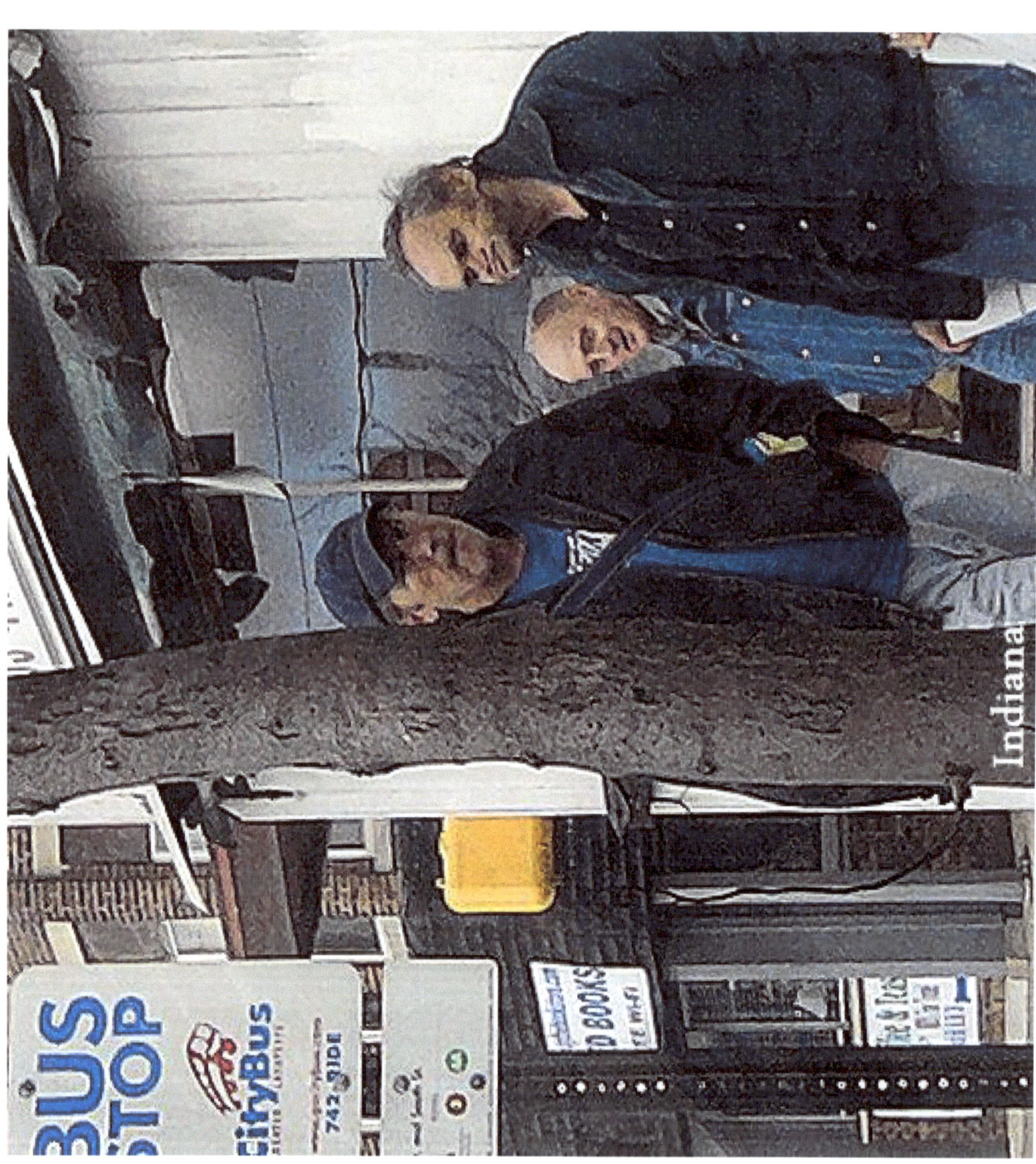

After you die,
You will meet God.

855-FOR-TRUTH

Indiana

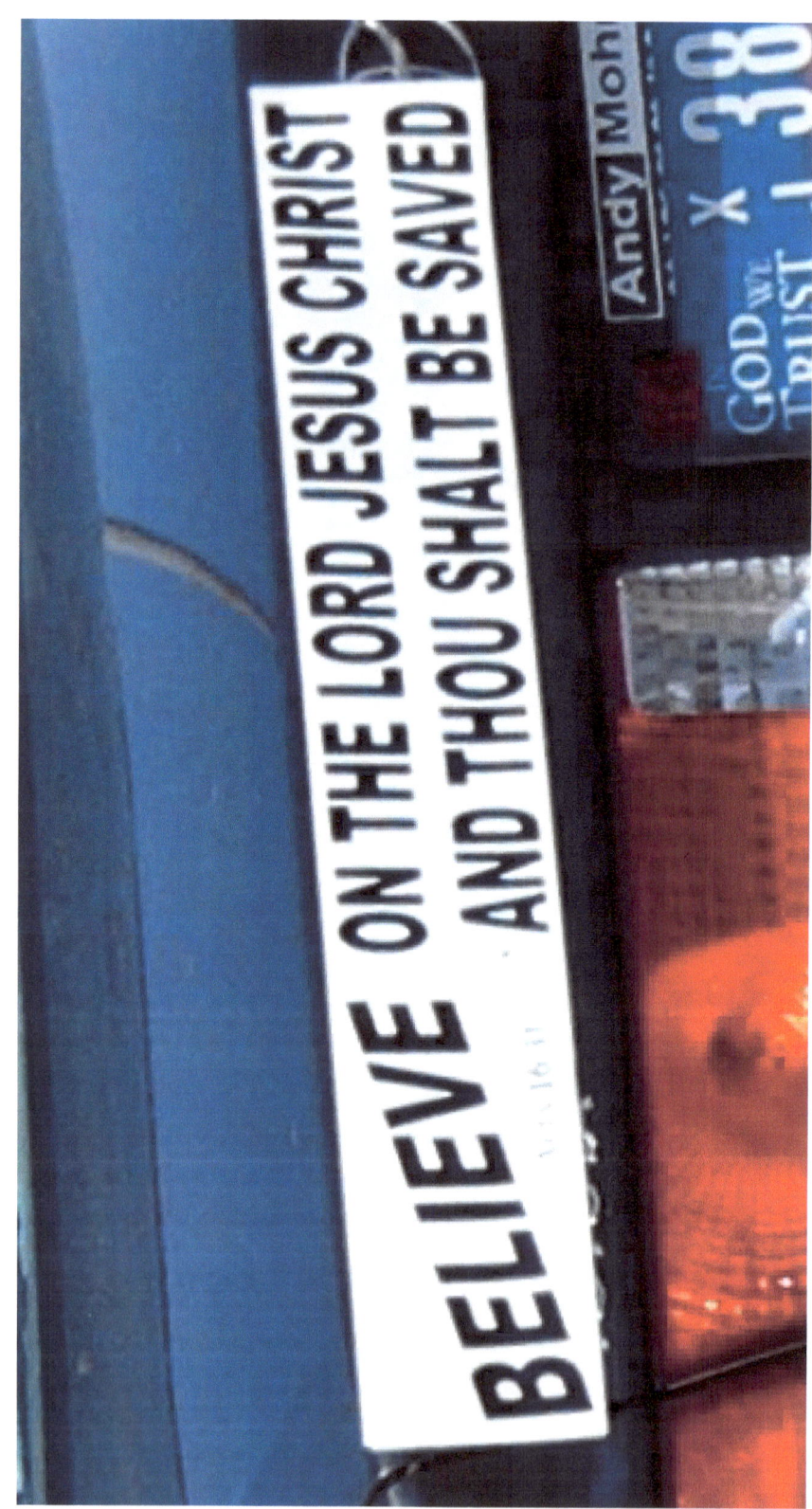

Indiana

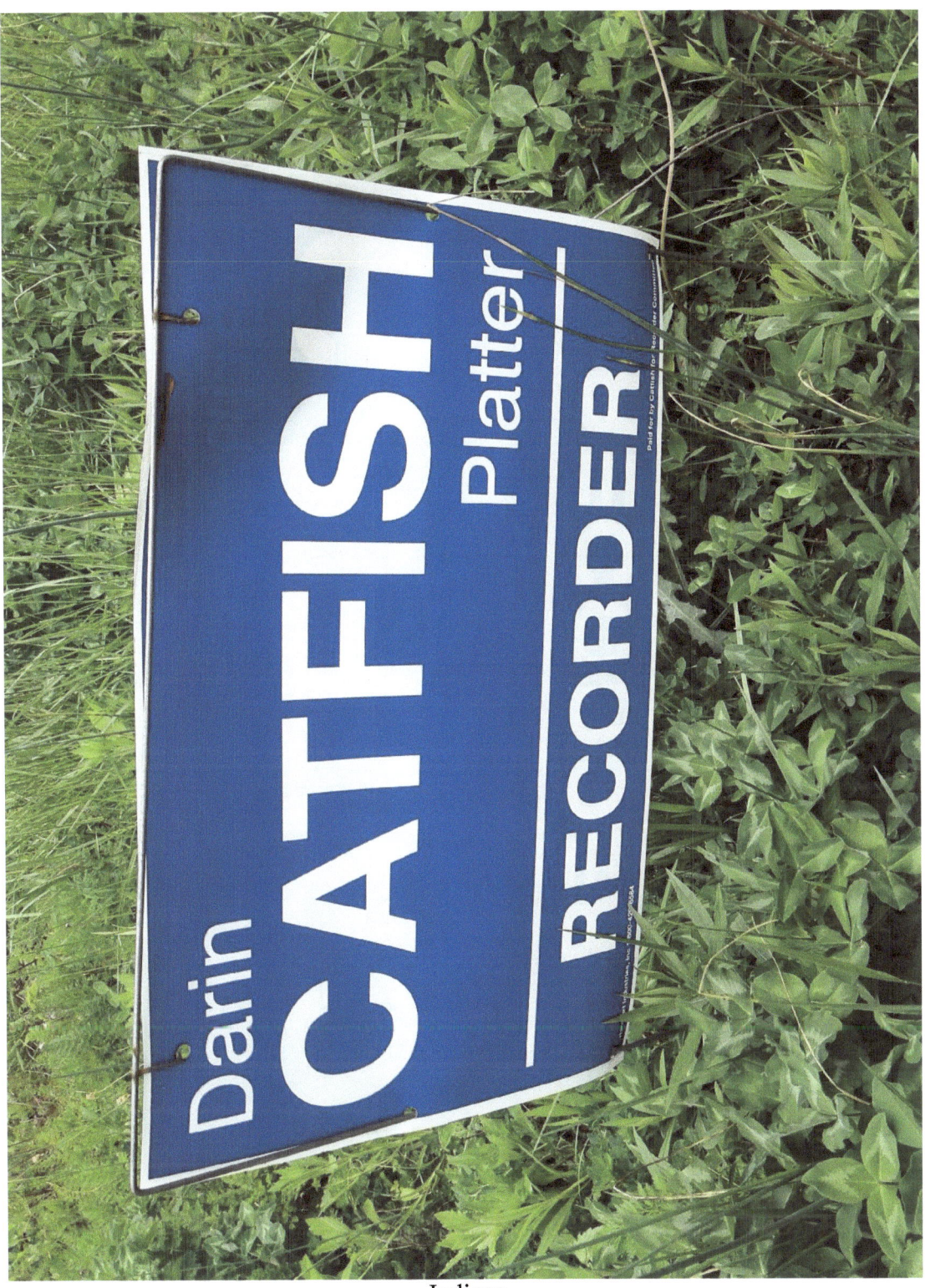

Indiana

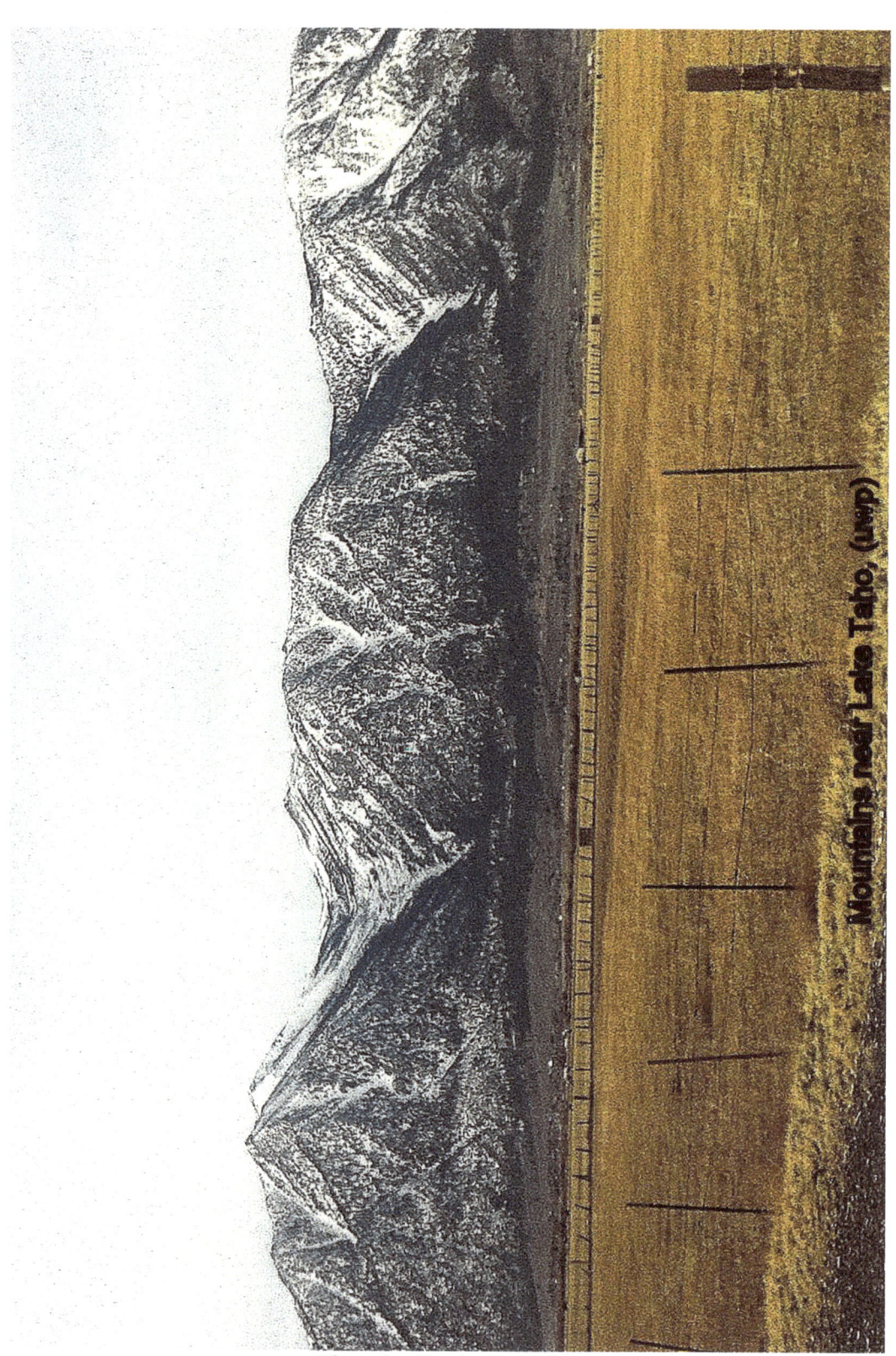

Mountains near Lake Taho₂ (uwp)

Photo by Kayla D. Eldib

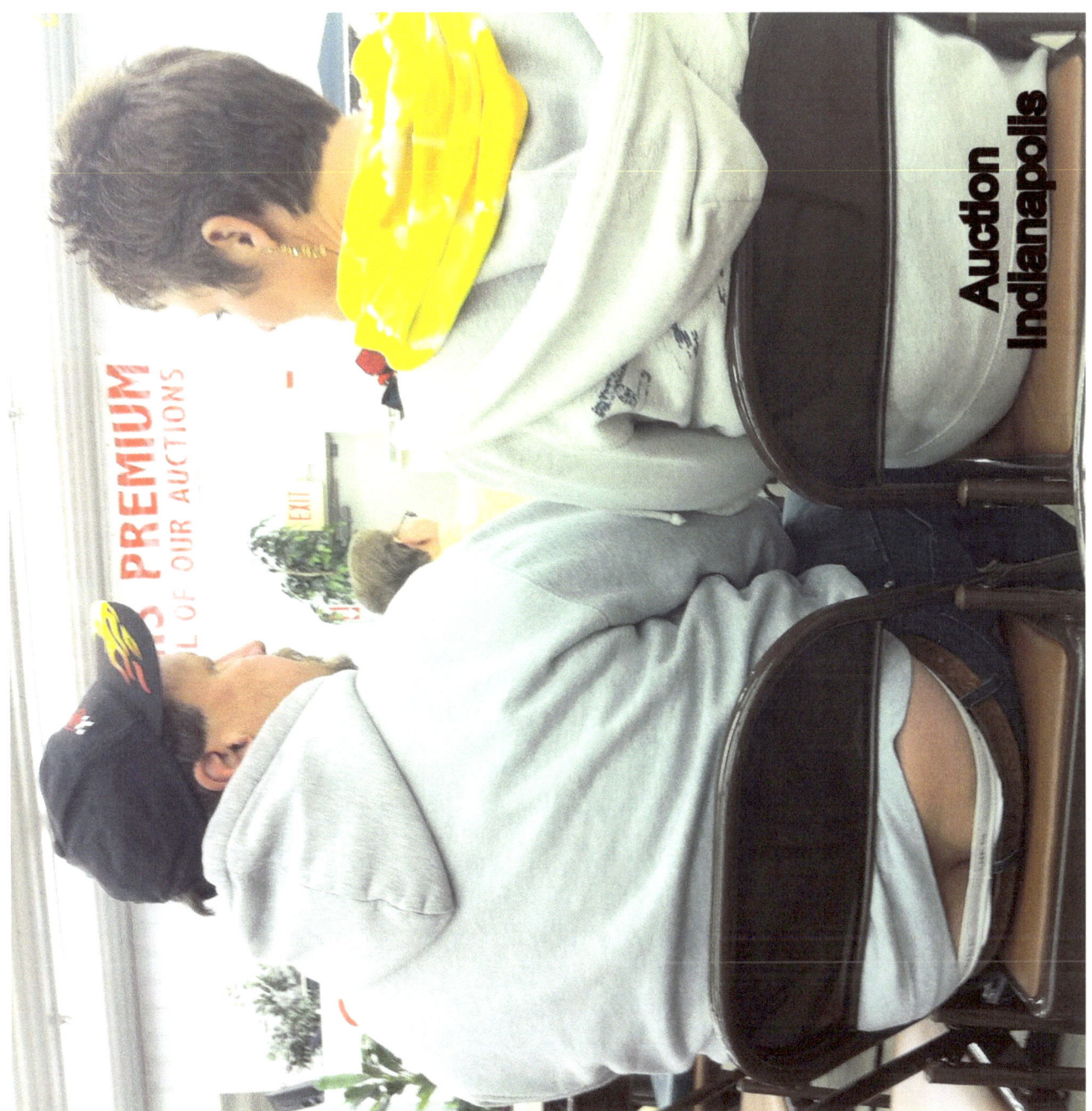

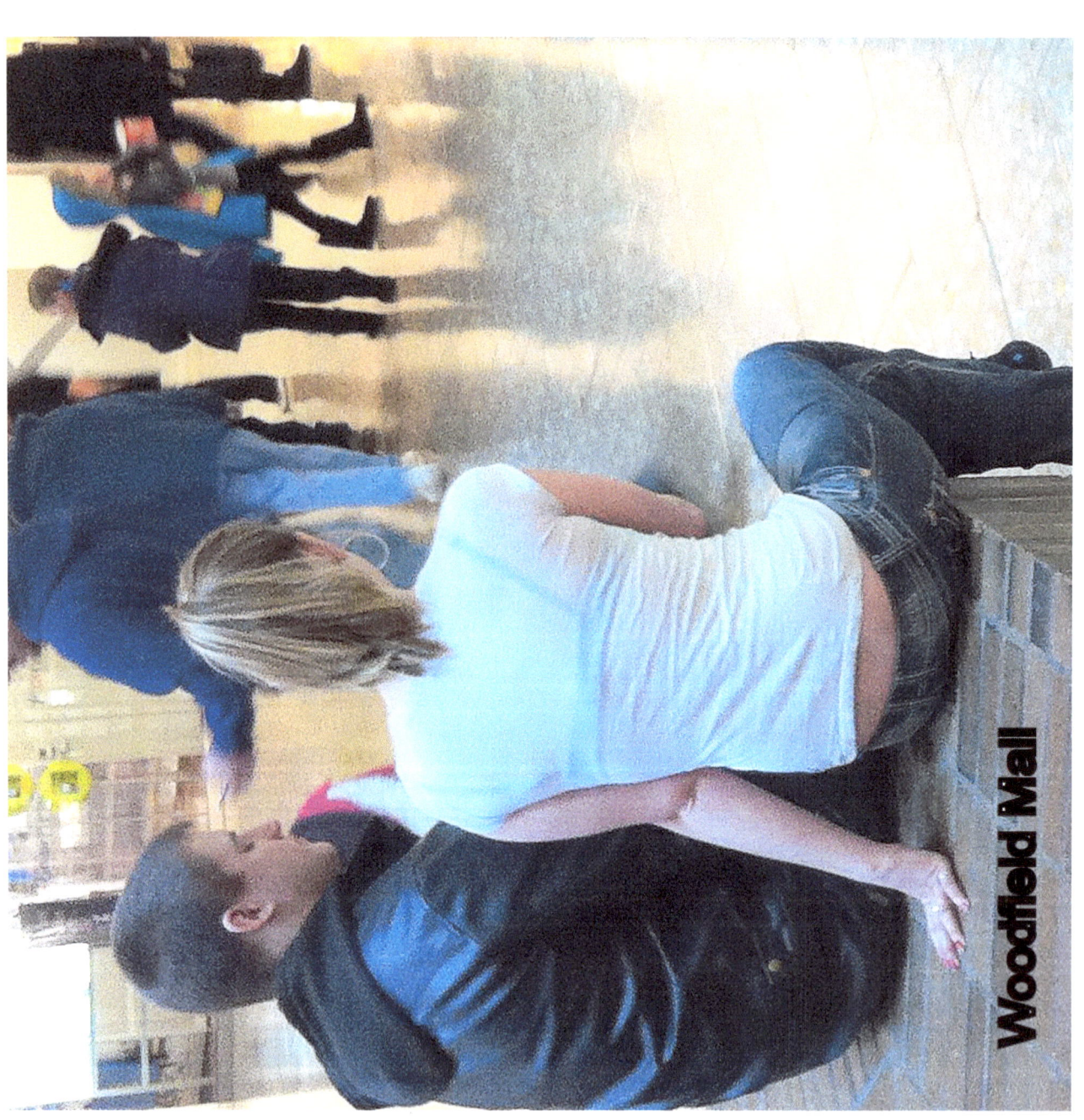

Woodfield Mall

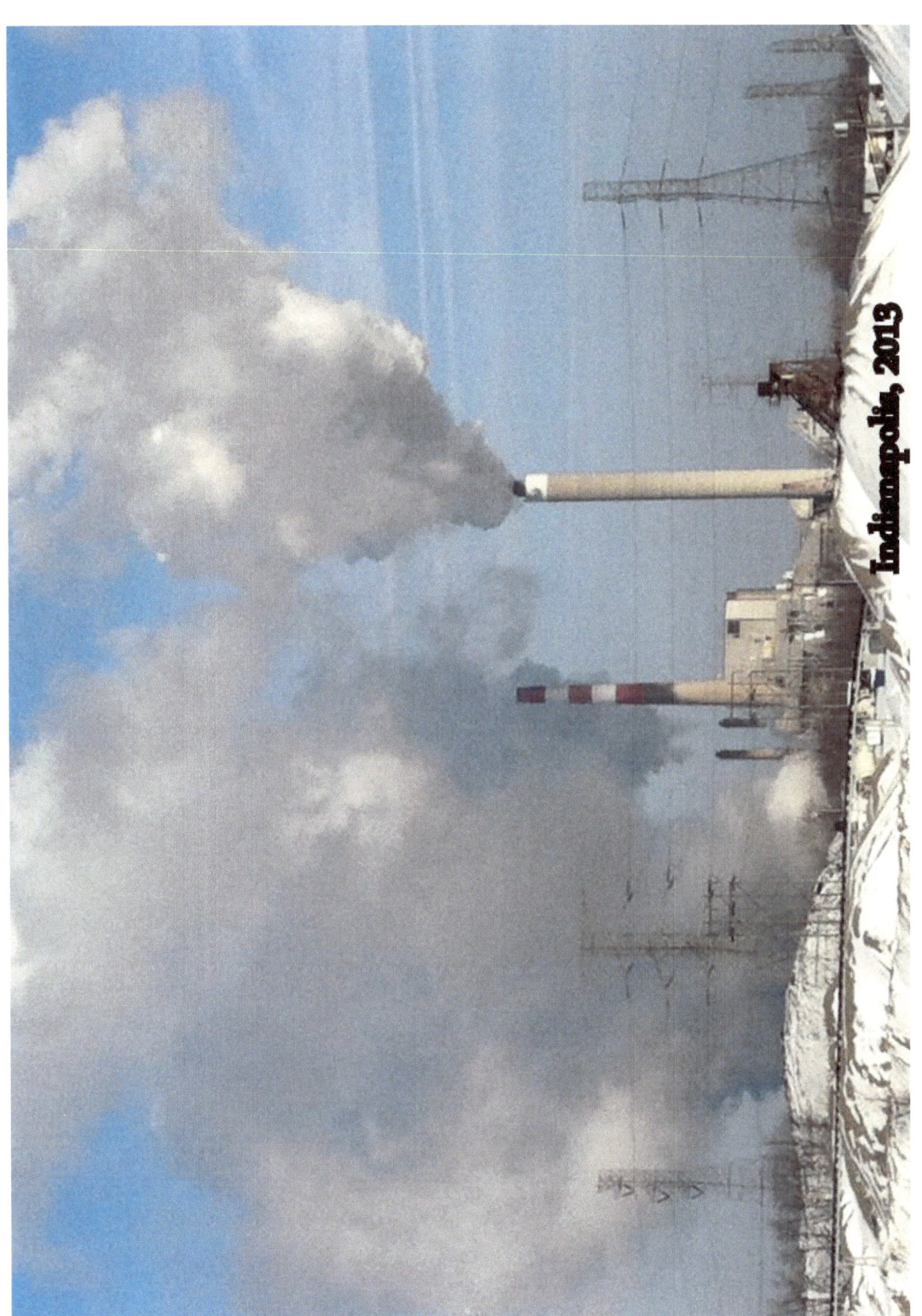

Indianapolis, 2013

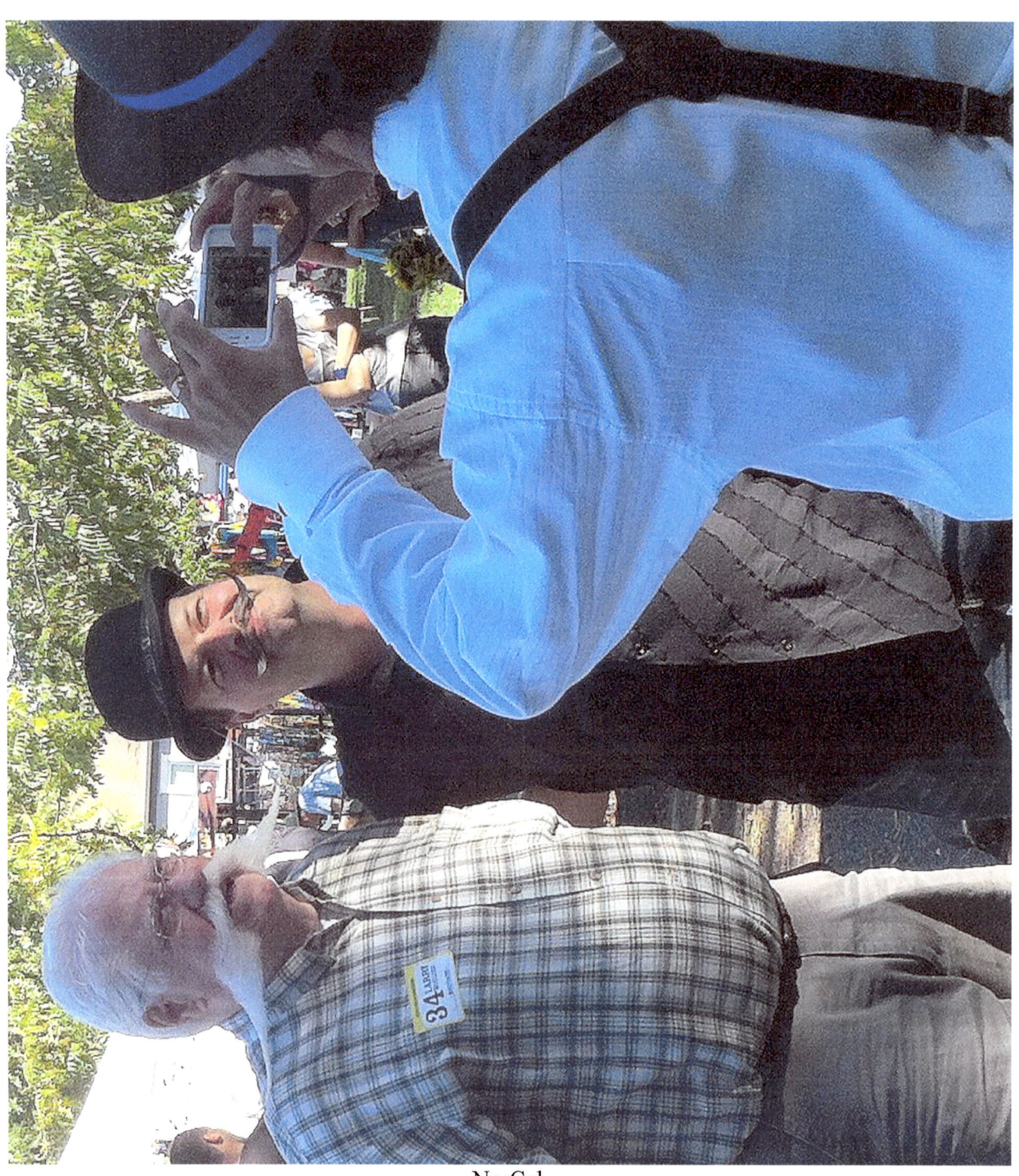

NorCal

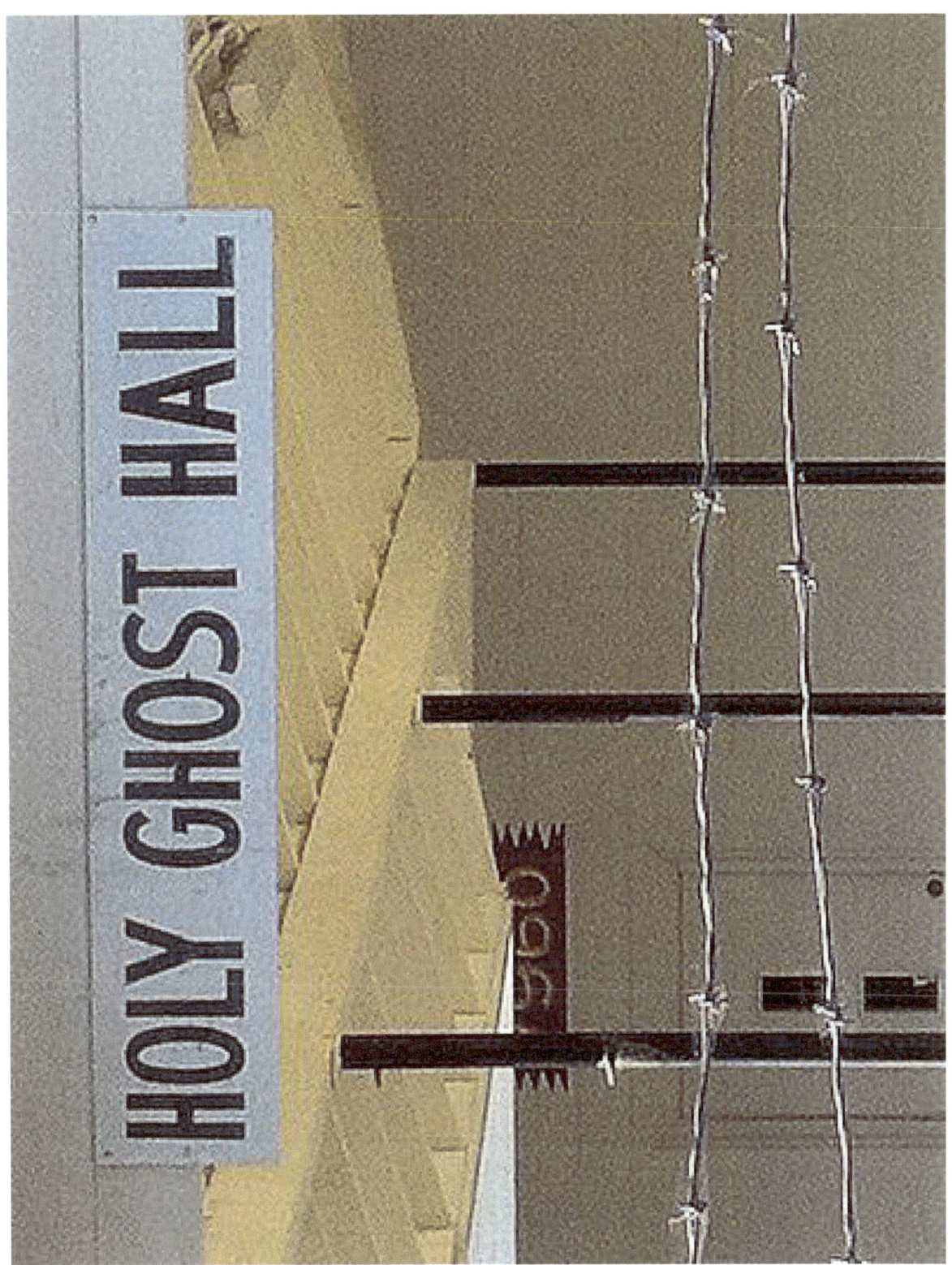

NorCal

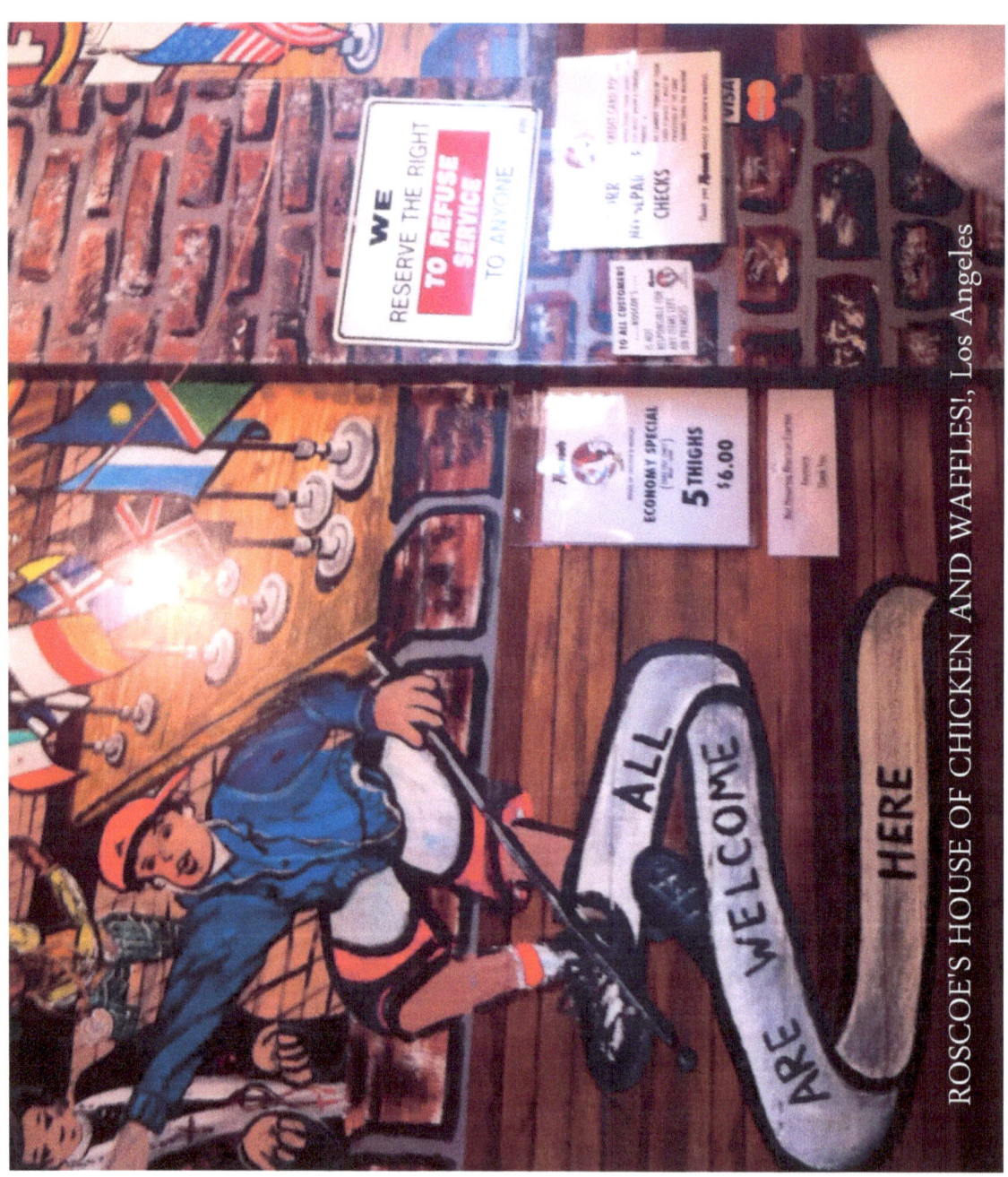

ROSCOE'S HOUSE OF CHICKEN AND WAFFLES!, Los Angeles

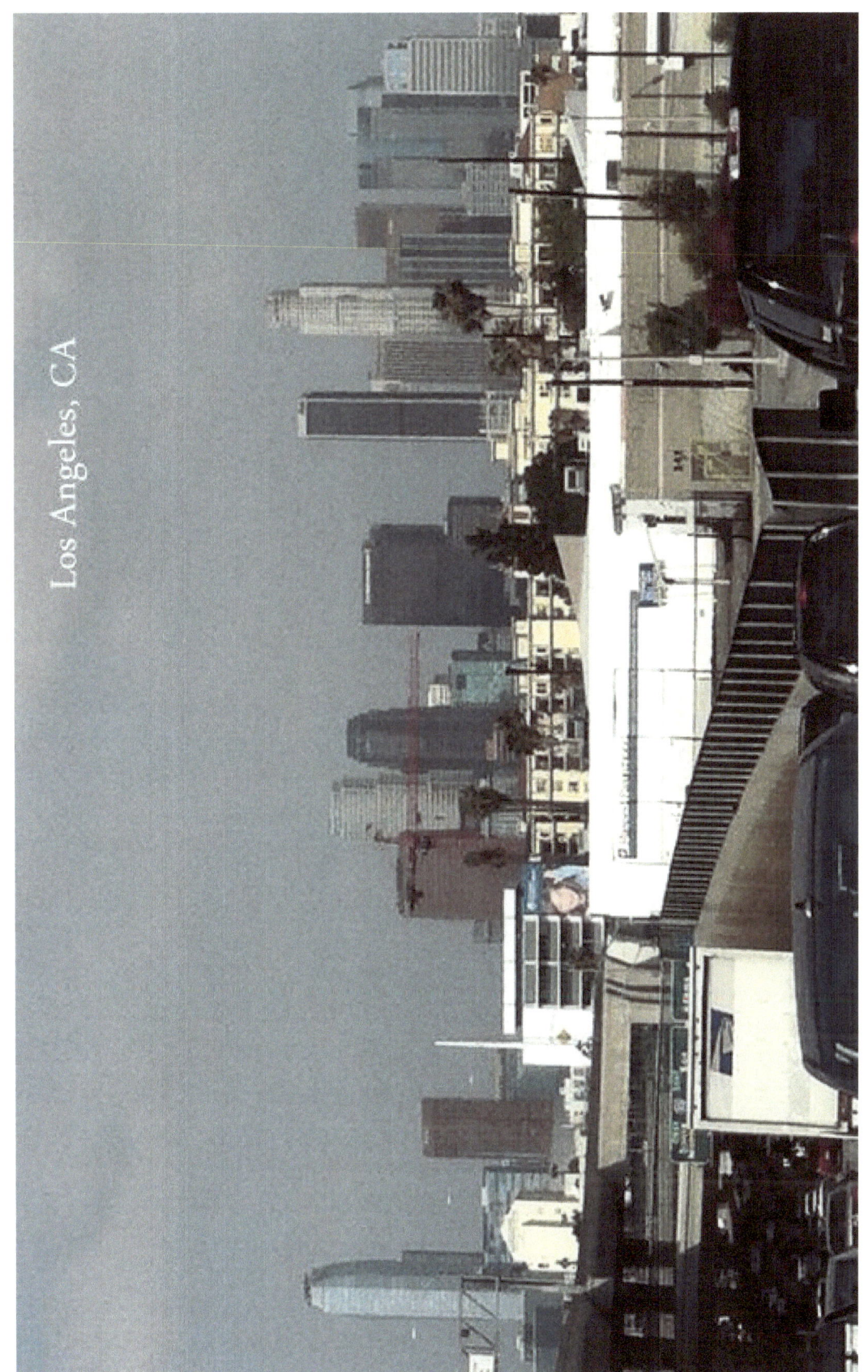

Los Angeles, CA

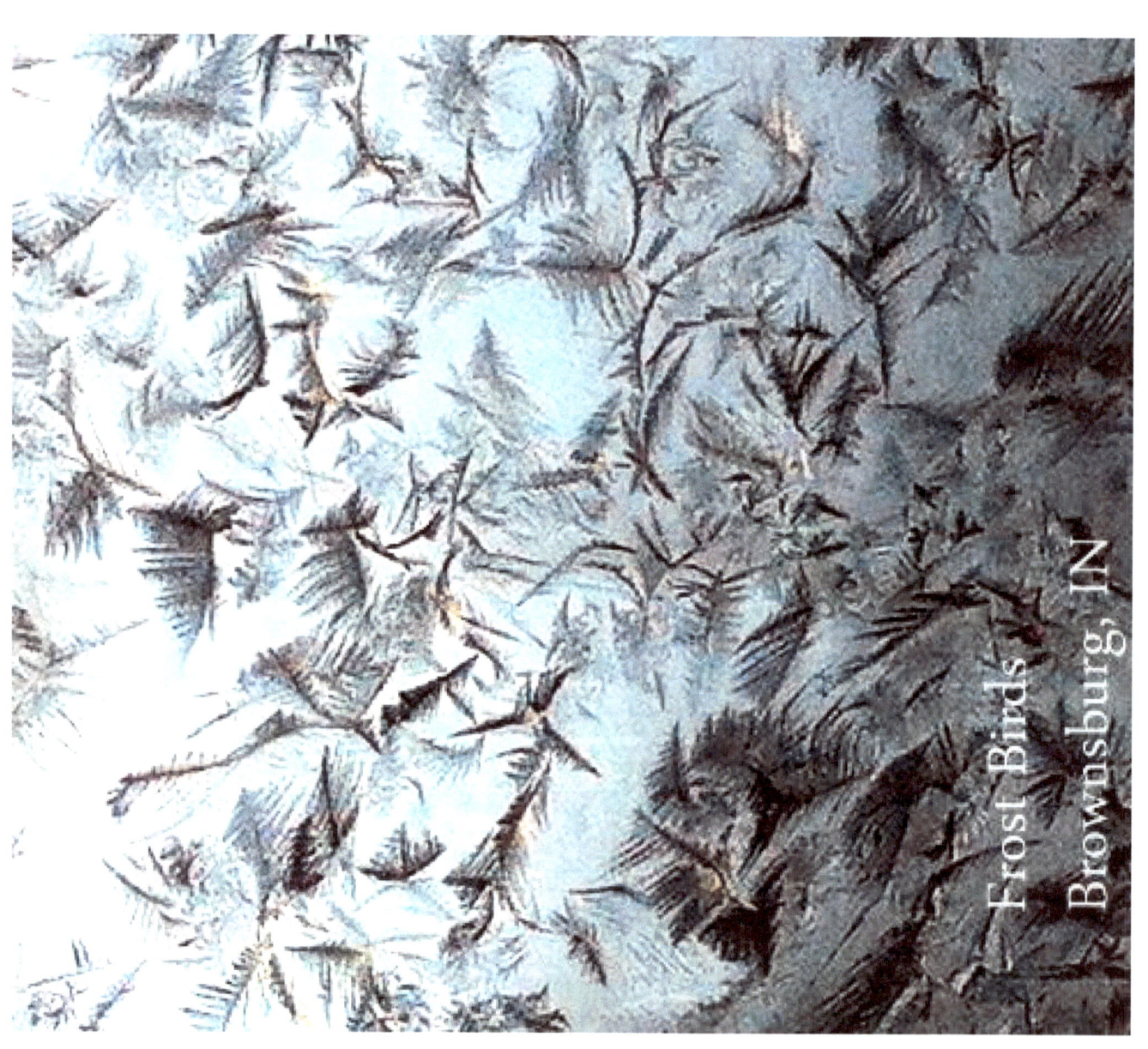

Frost Birds
Brownsburg, IN

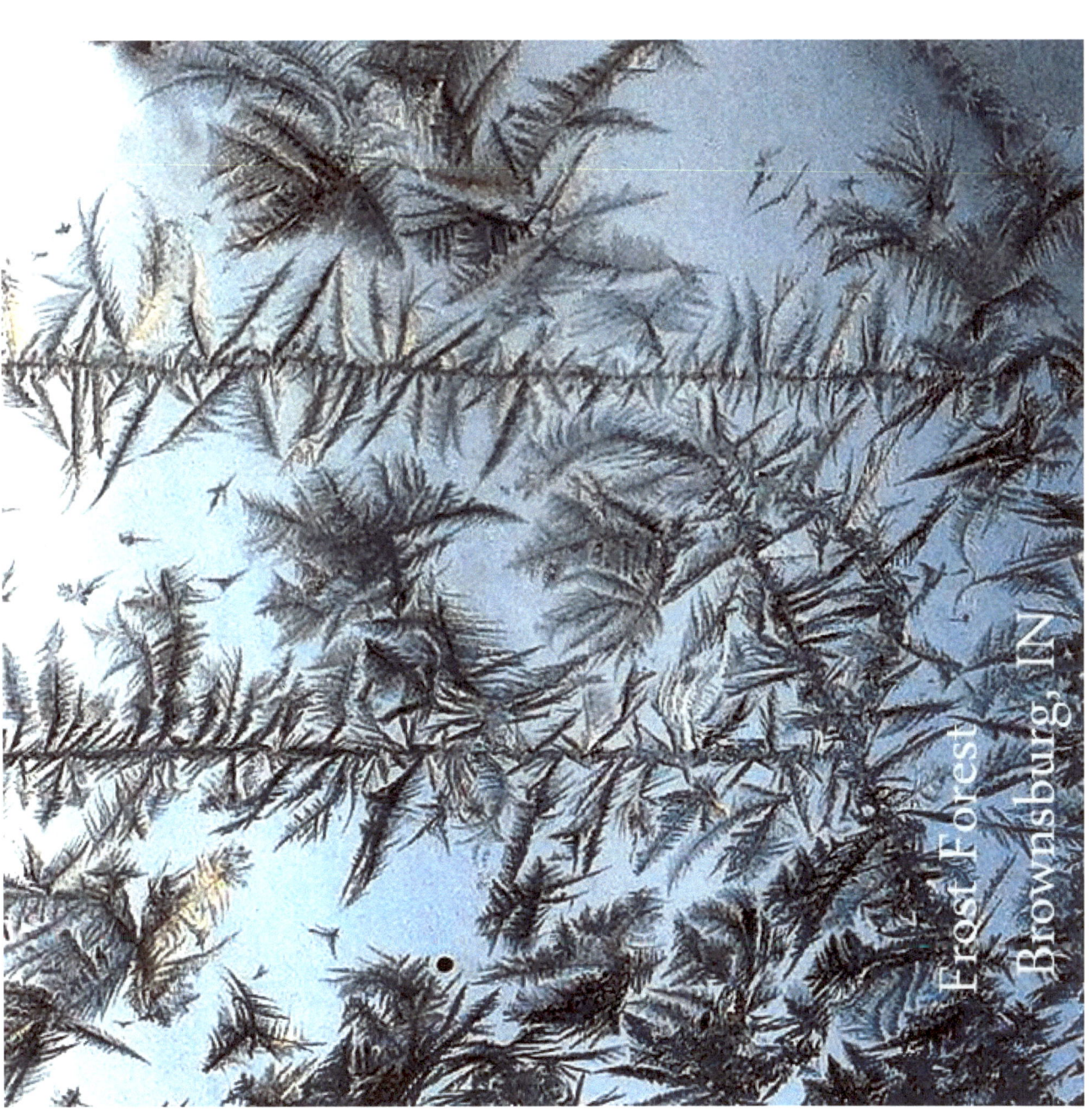

Frost Forest
Brownsburg, IN

Indiana

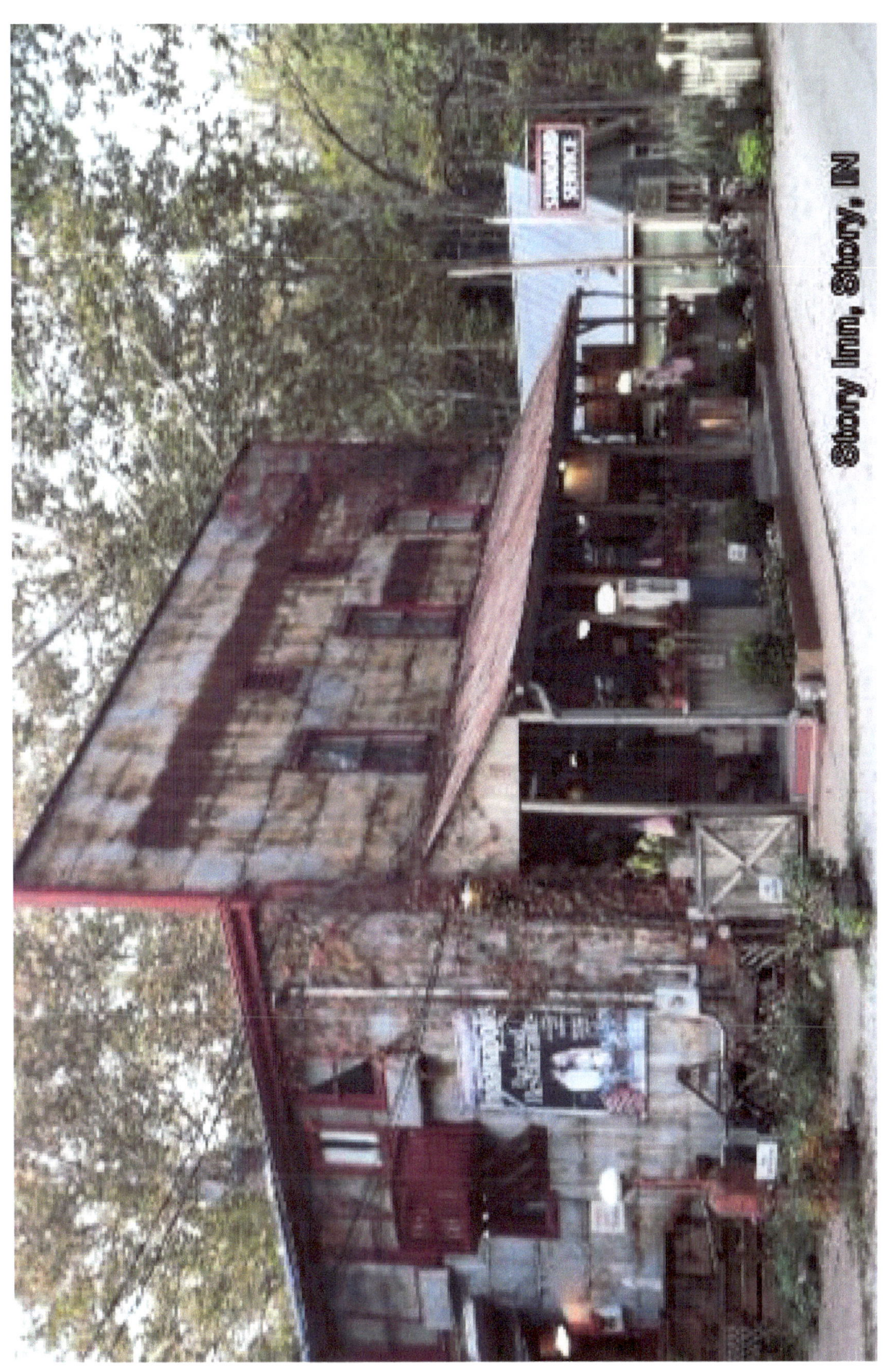

Story Inn, Story, IN

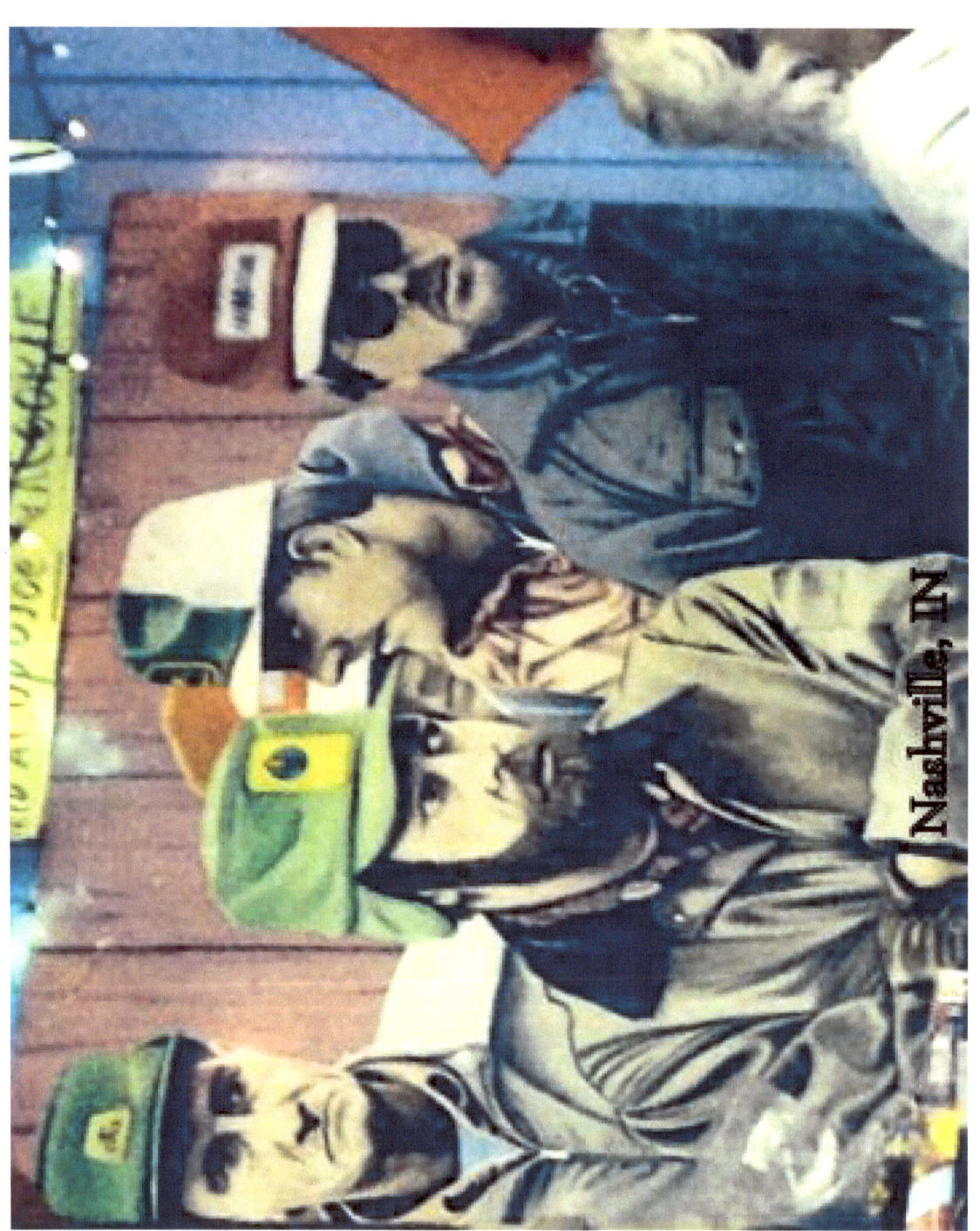

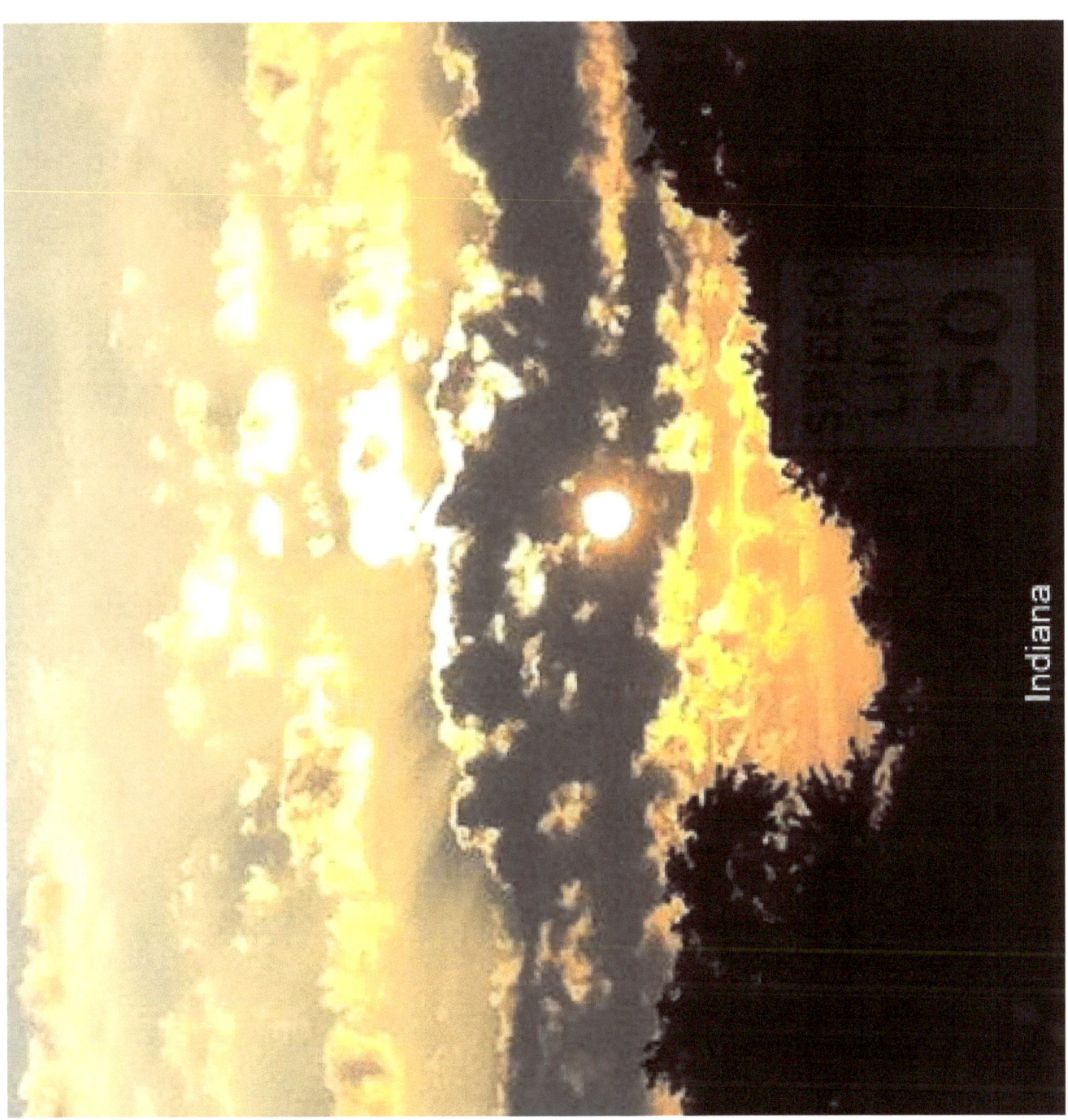

Indiana

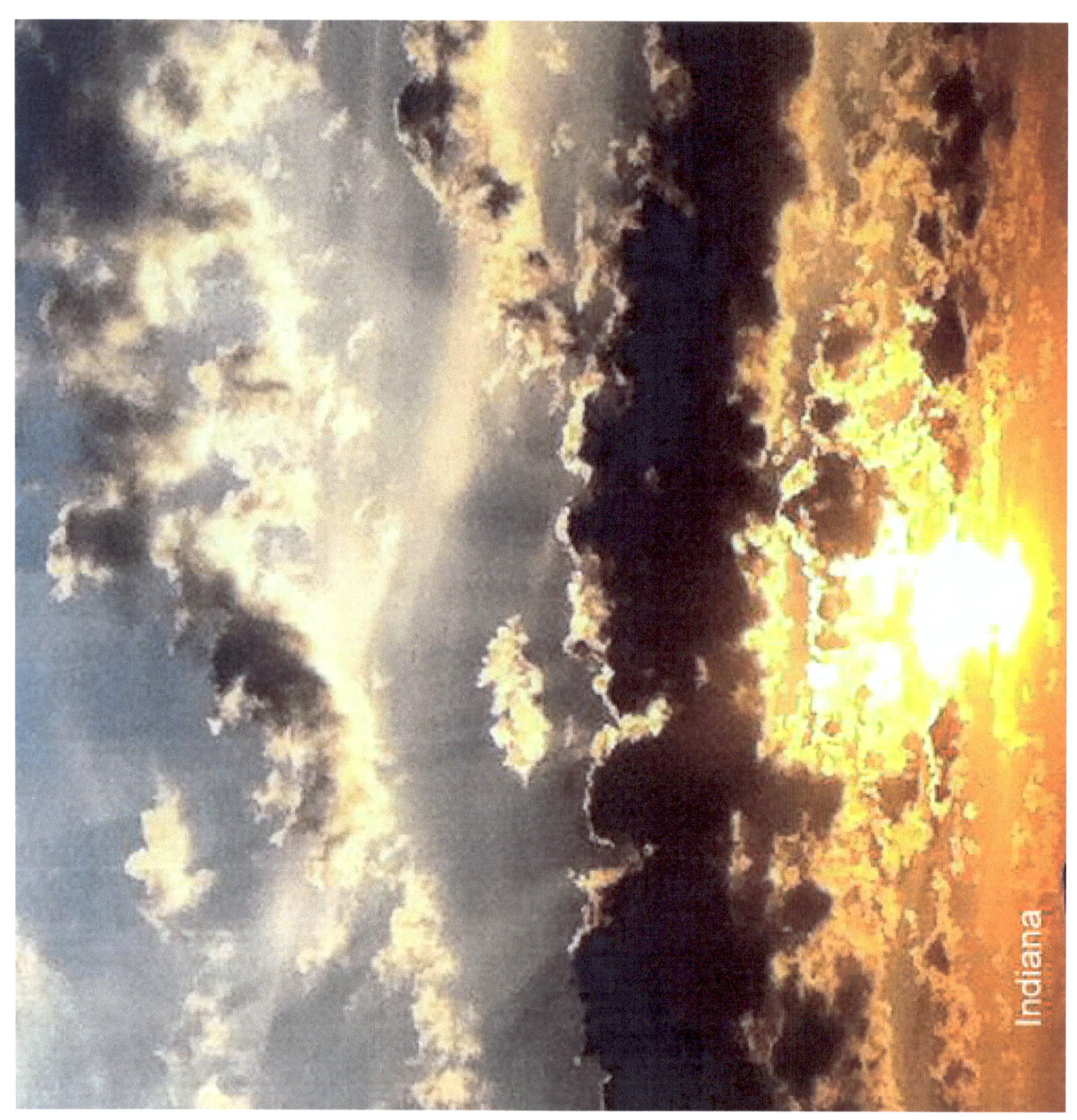

Indiana

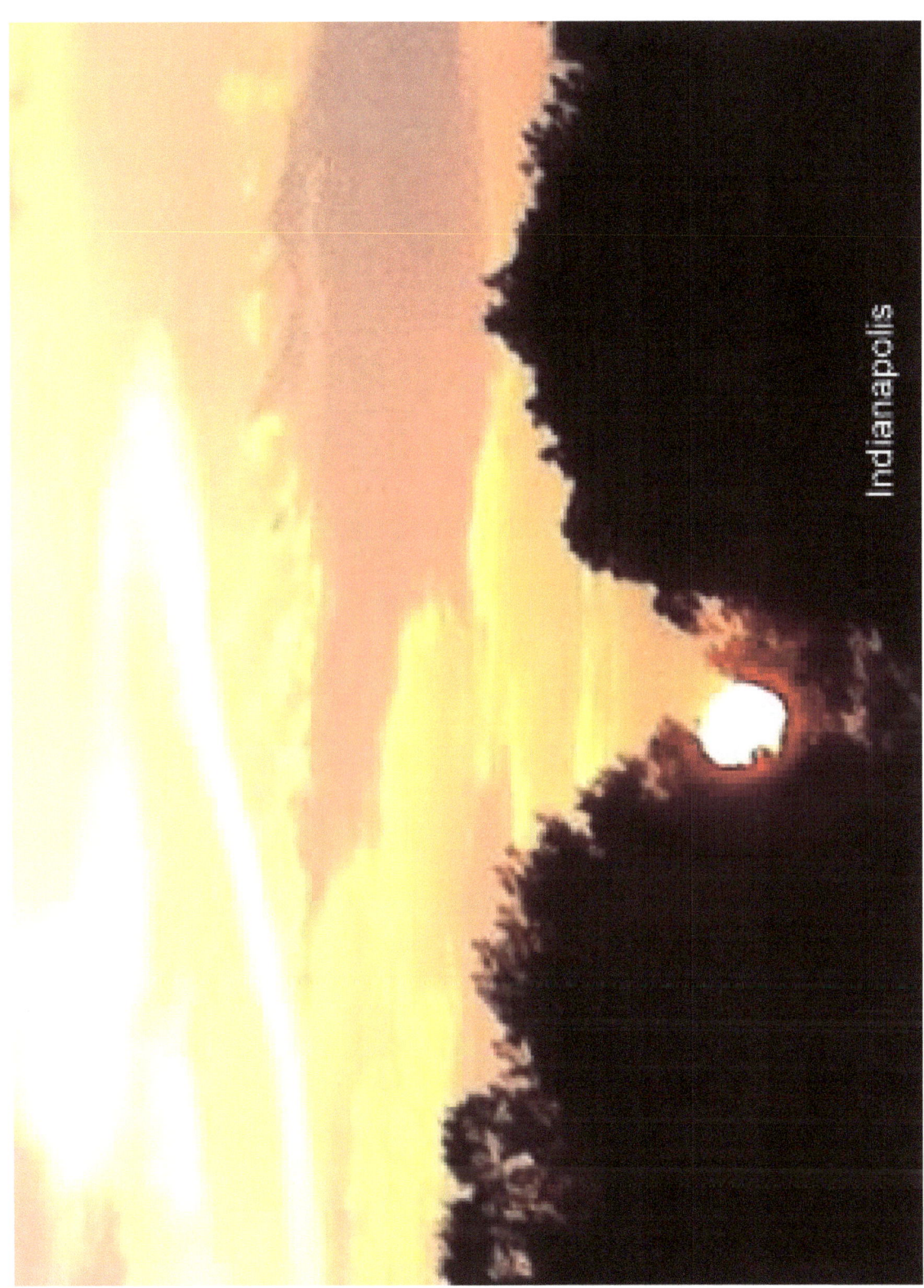

Indianapolis

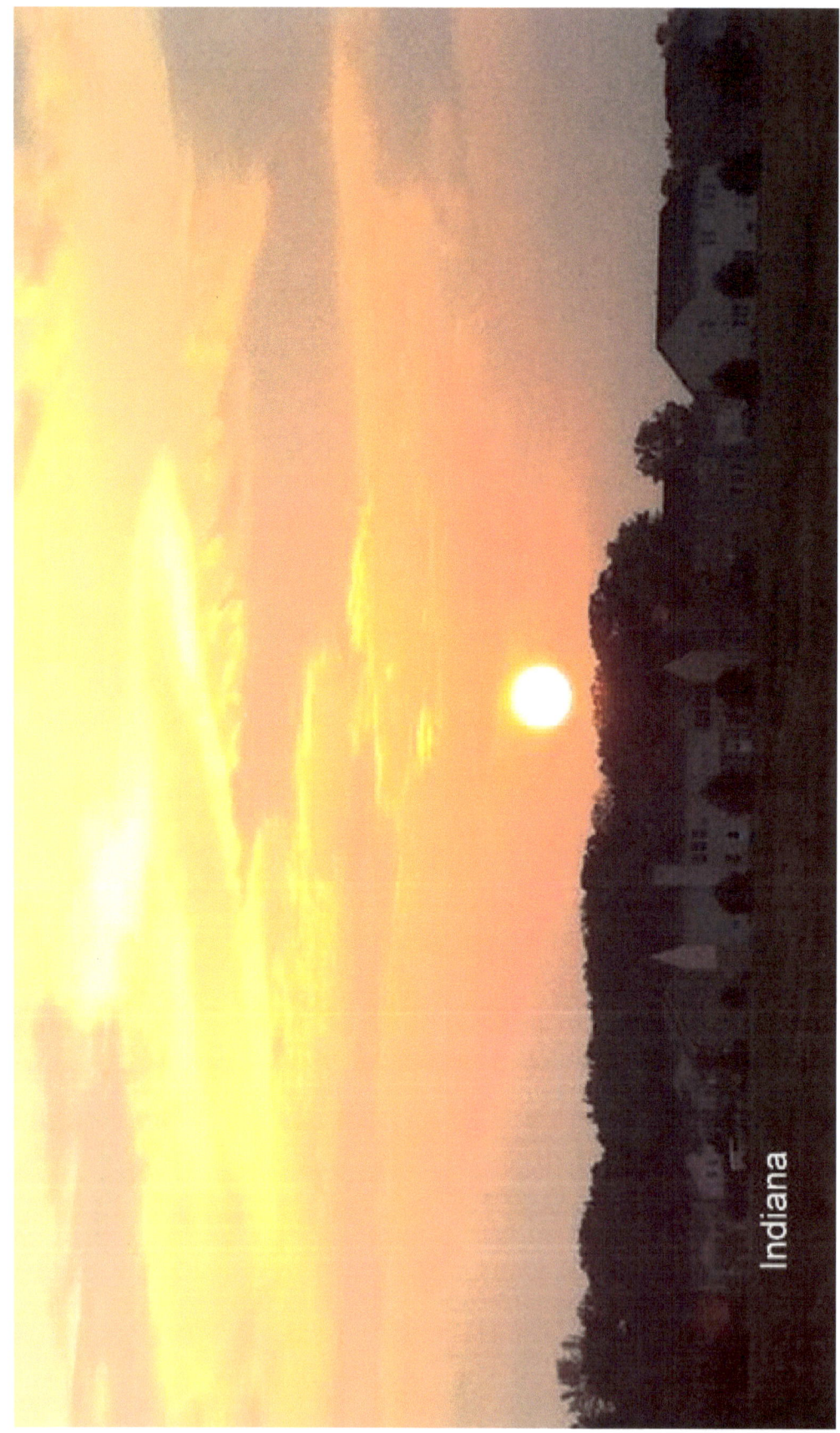

Indiana

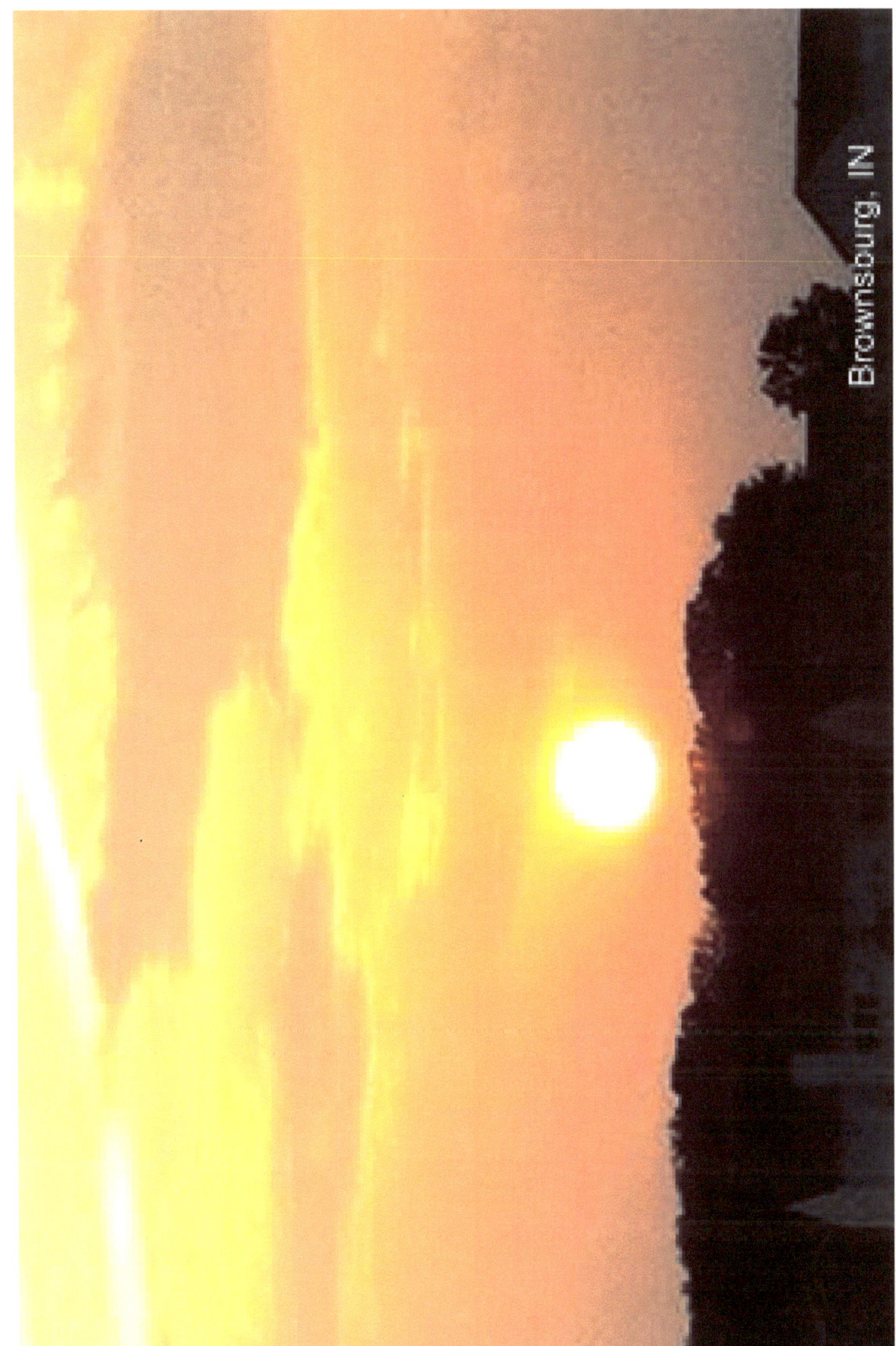

Brownsburg, IN

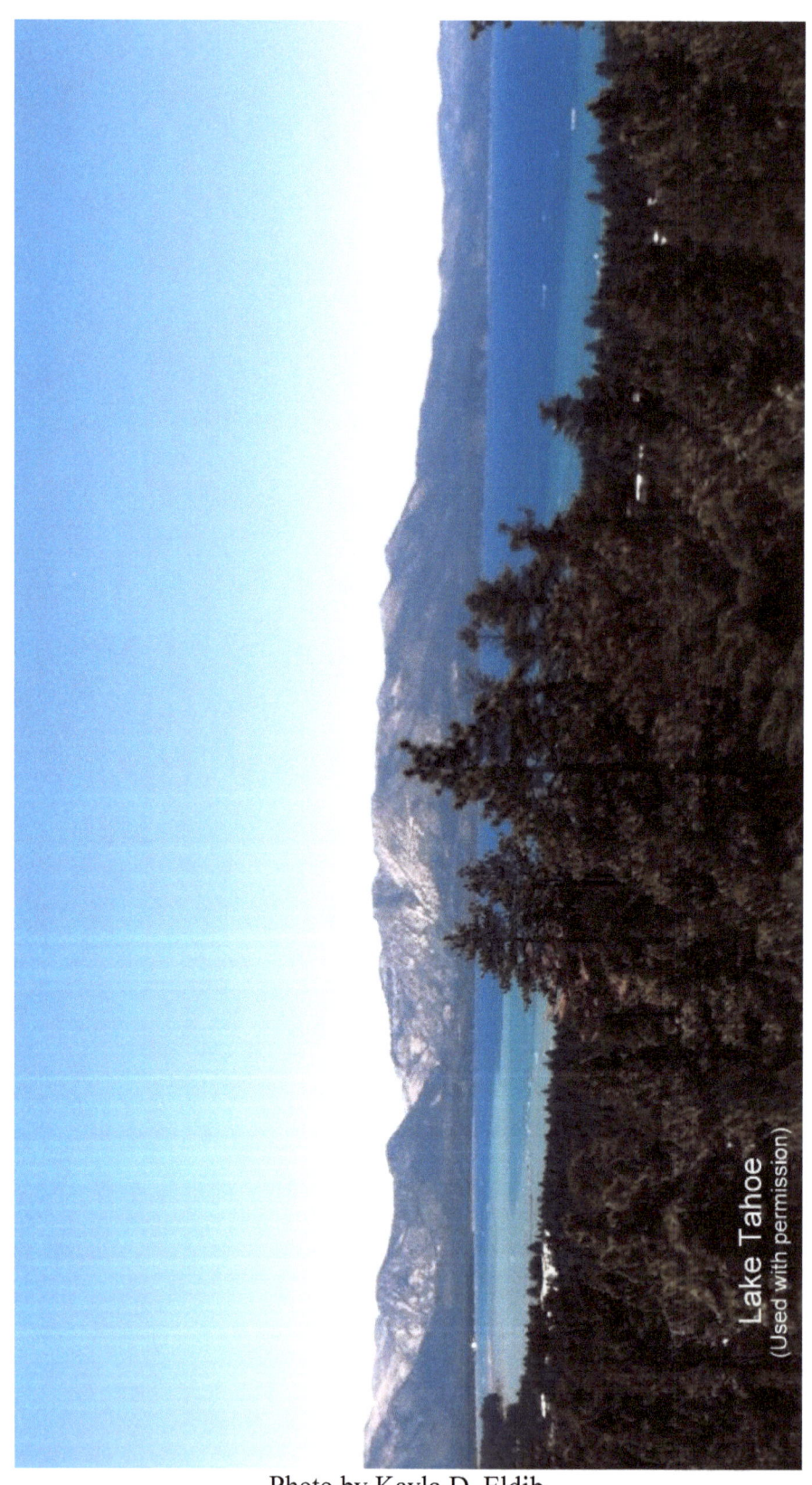

Lake Tahoe
(Used with permission)

Photo by Kayla D. Eldib

Indiana

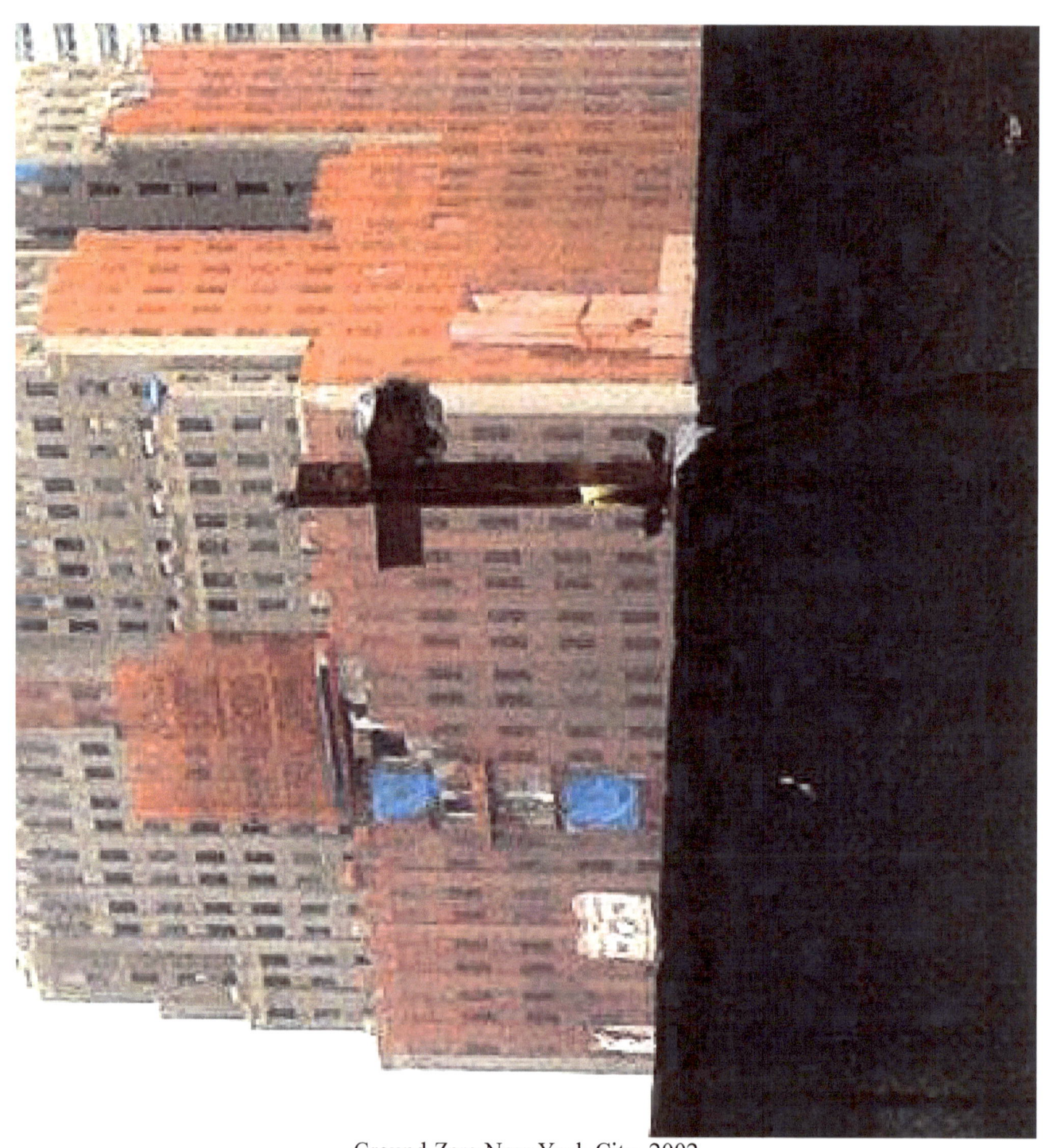

Ground Zero New York City, 2002

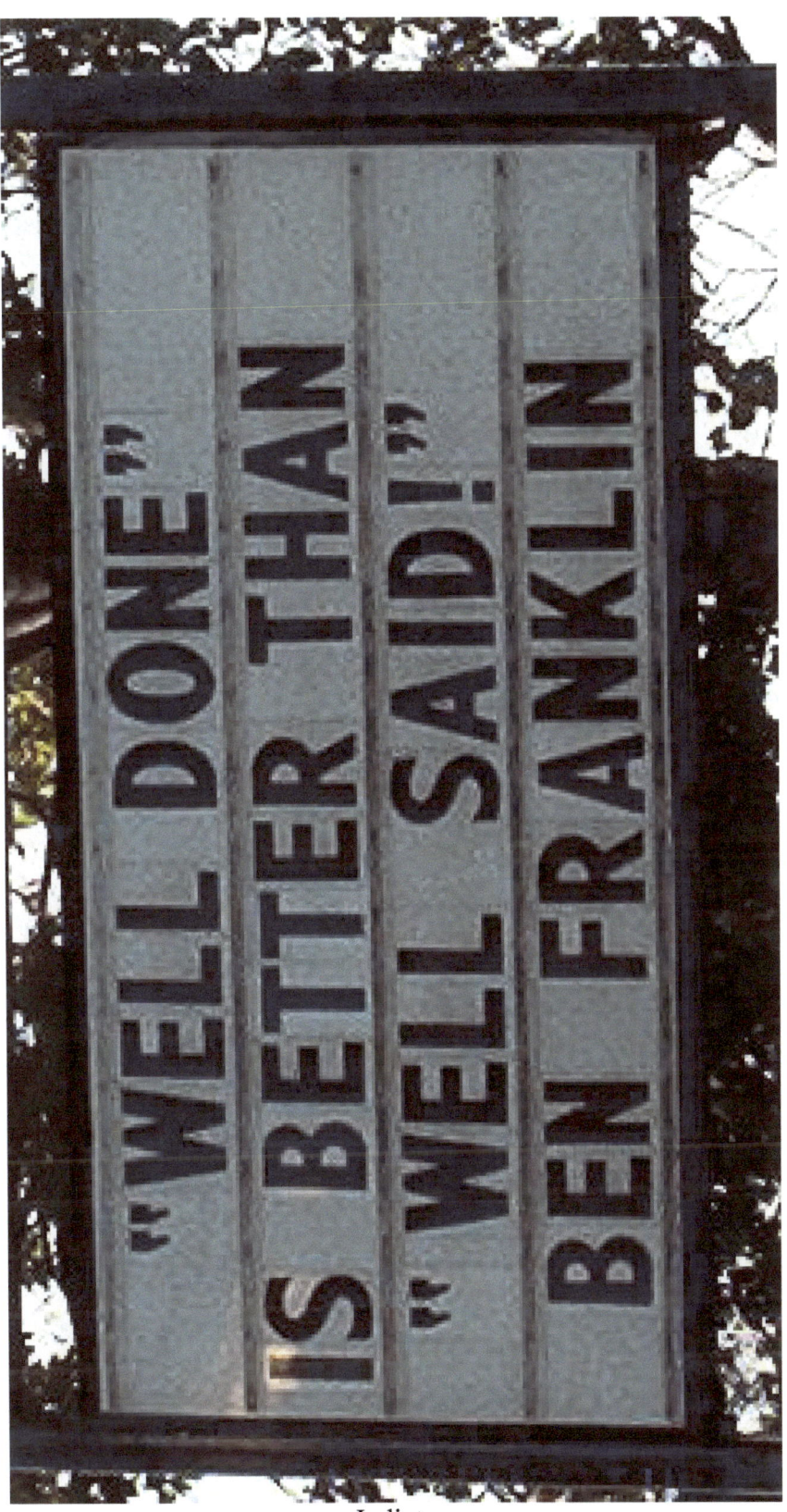

Indiana

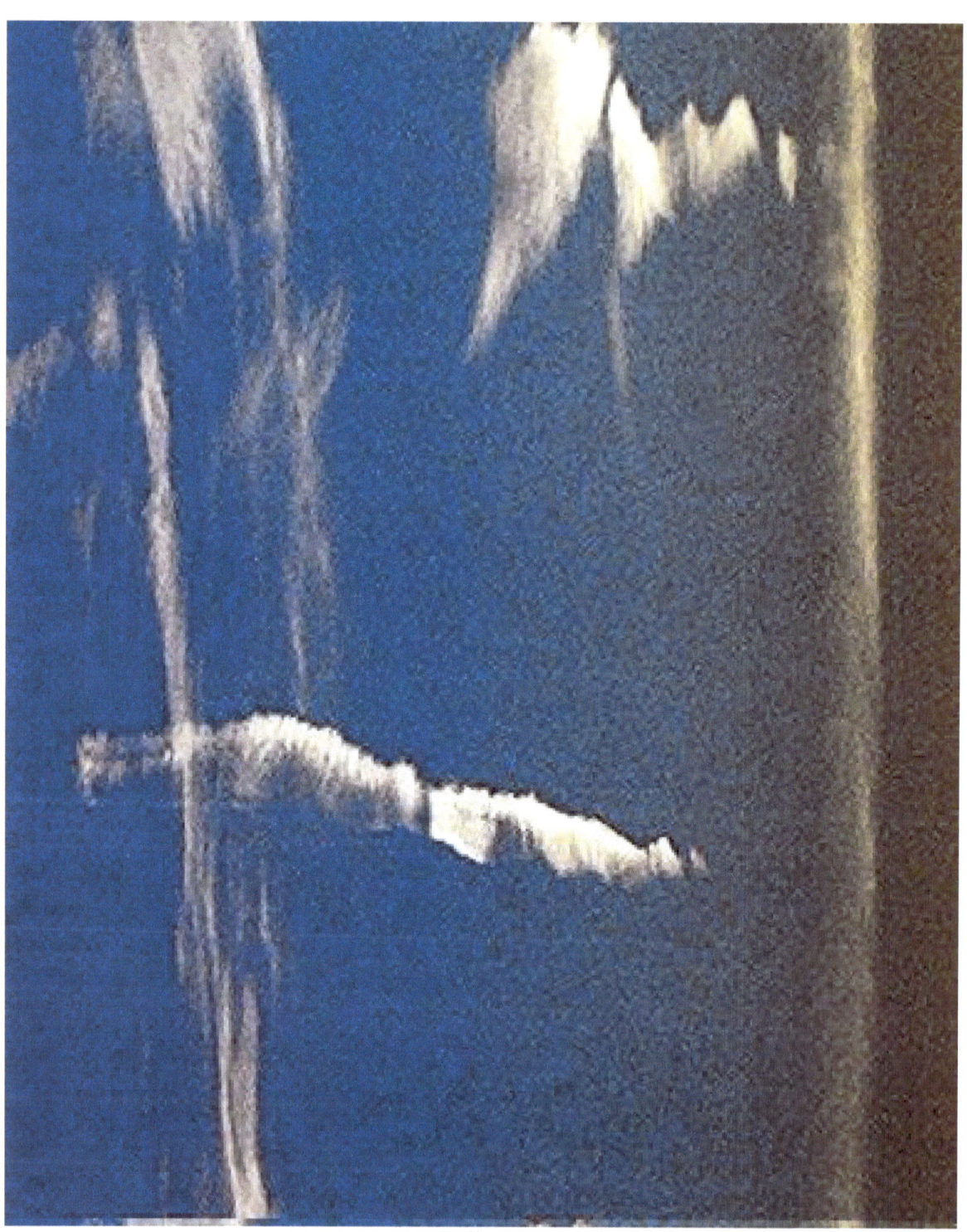

Indiana

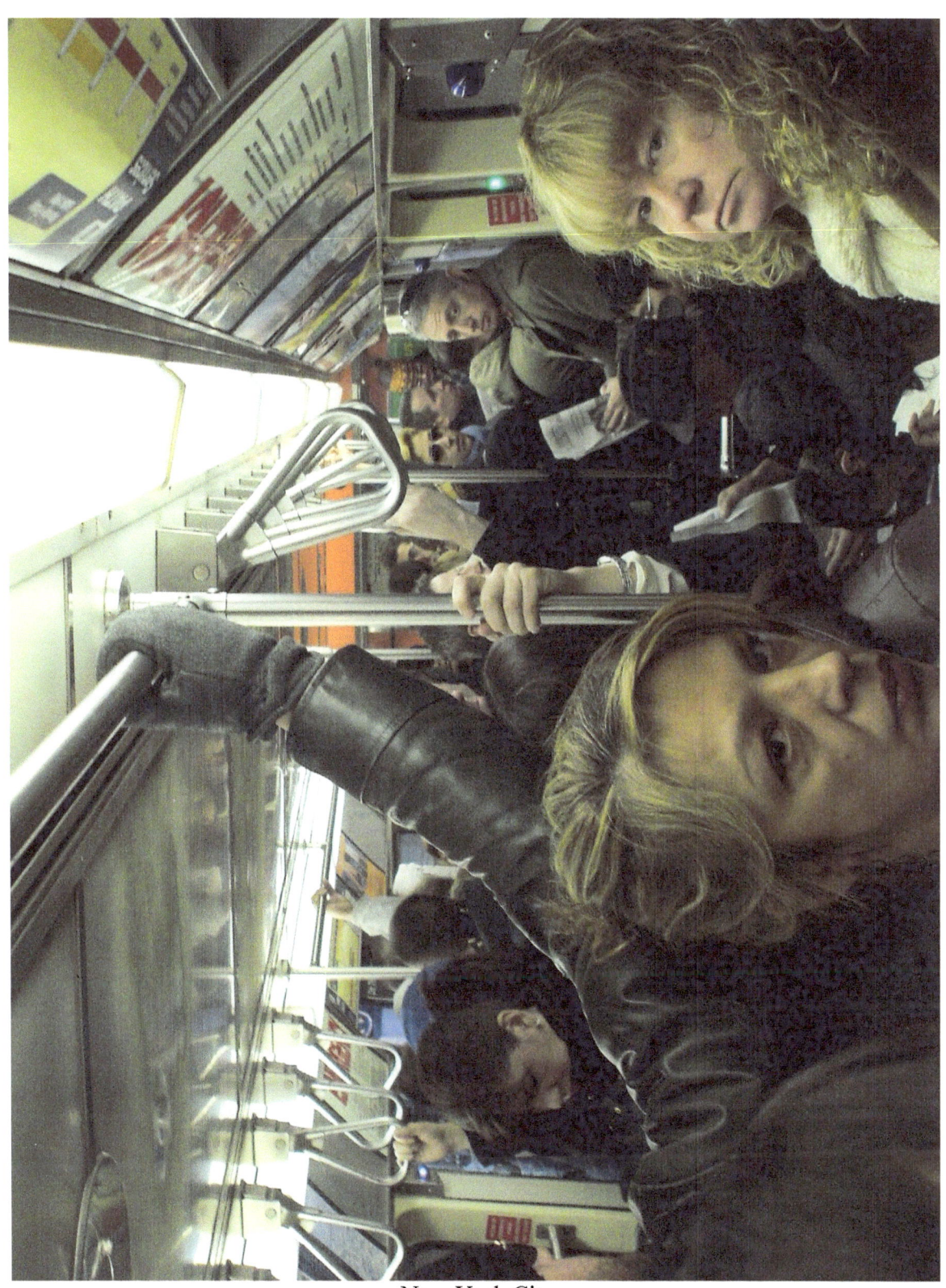

New York City

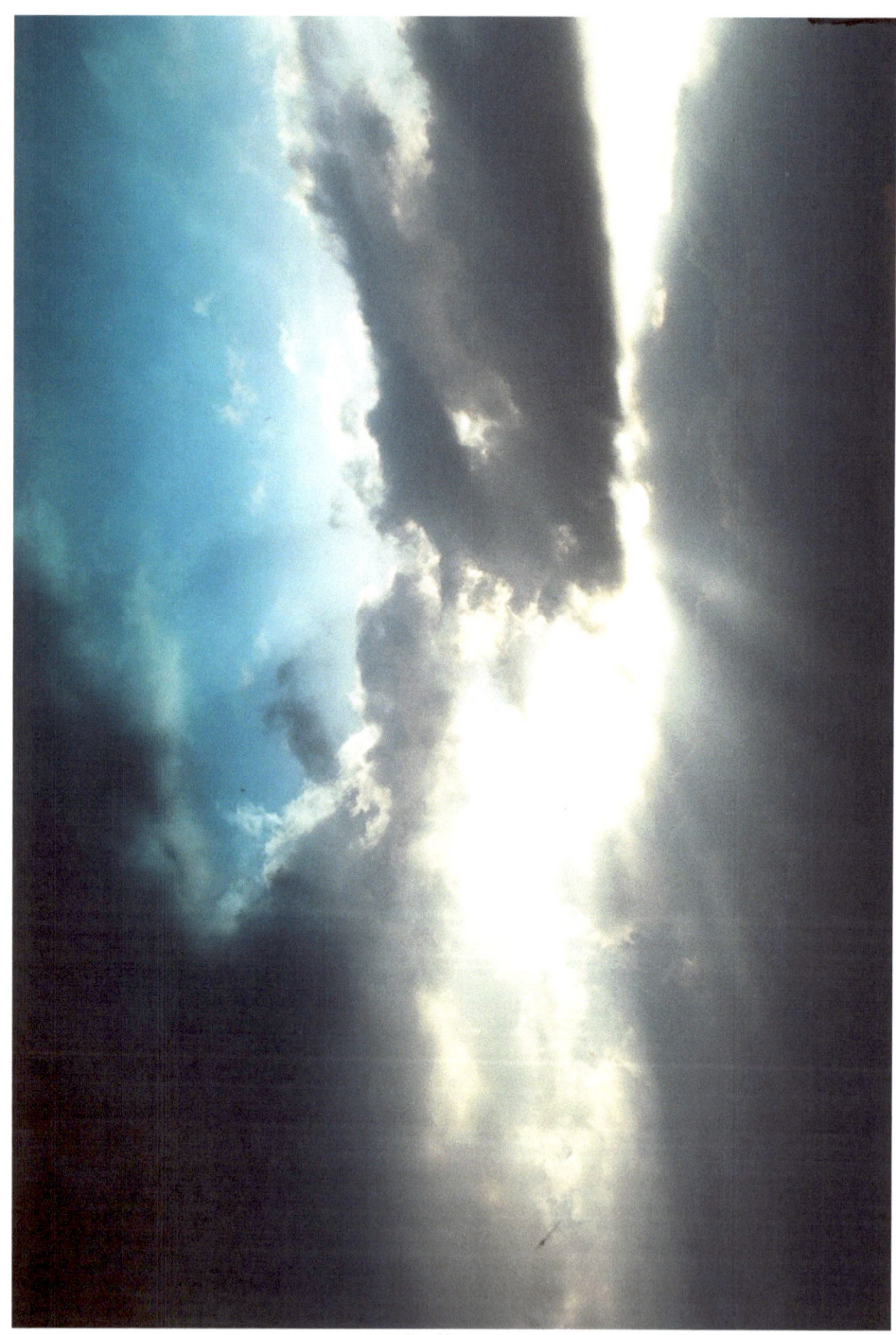

Indiana

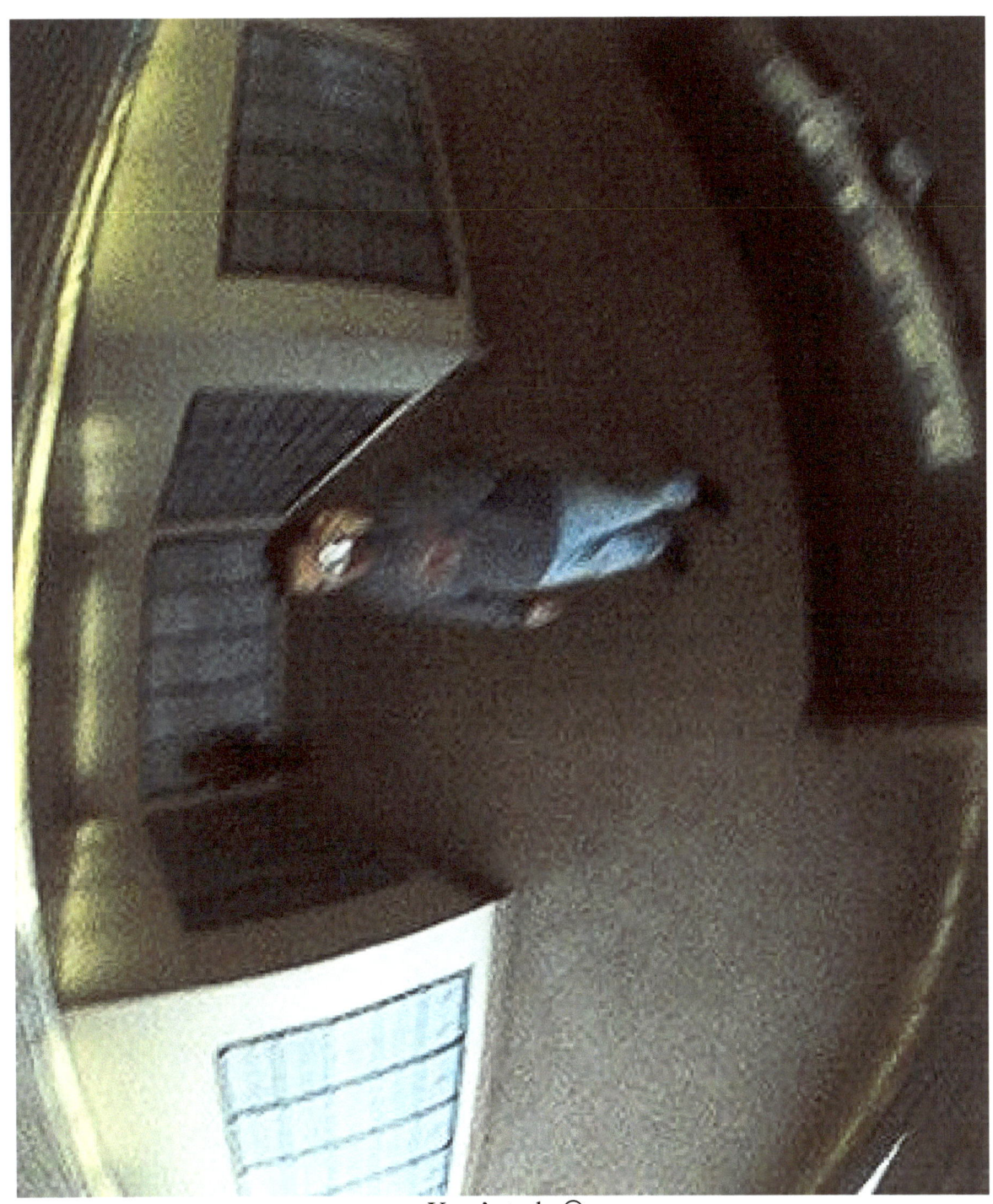

Your's truly ☺

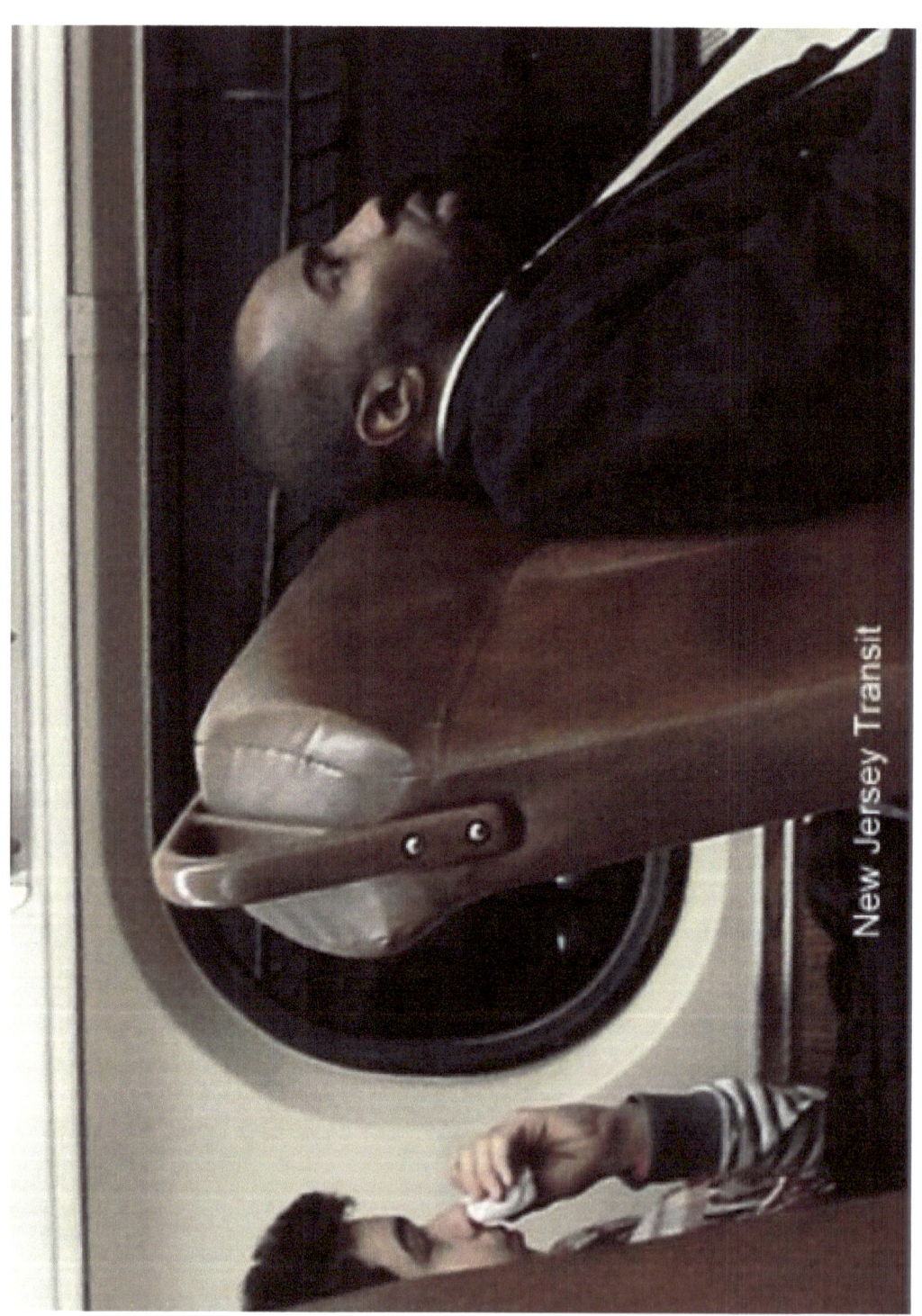

New Jersey Transit

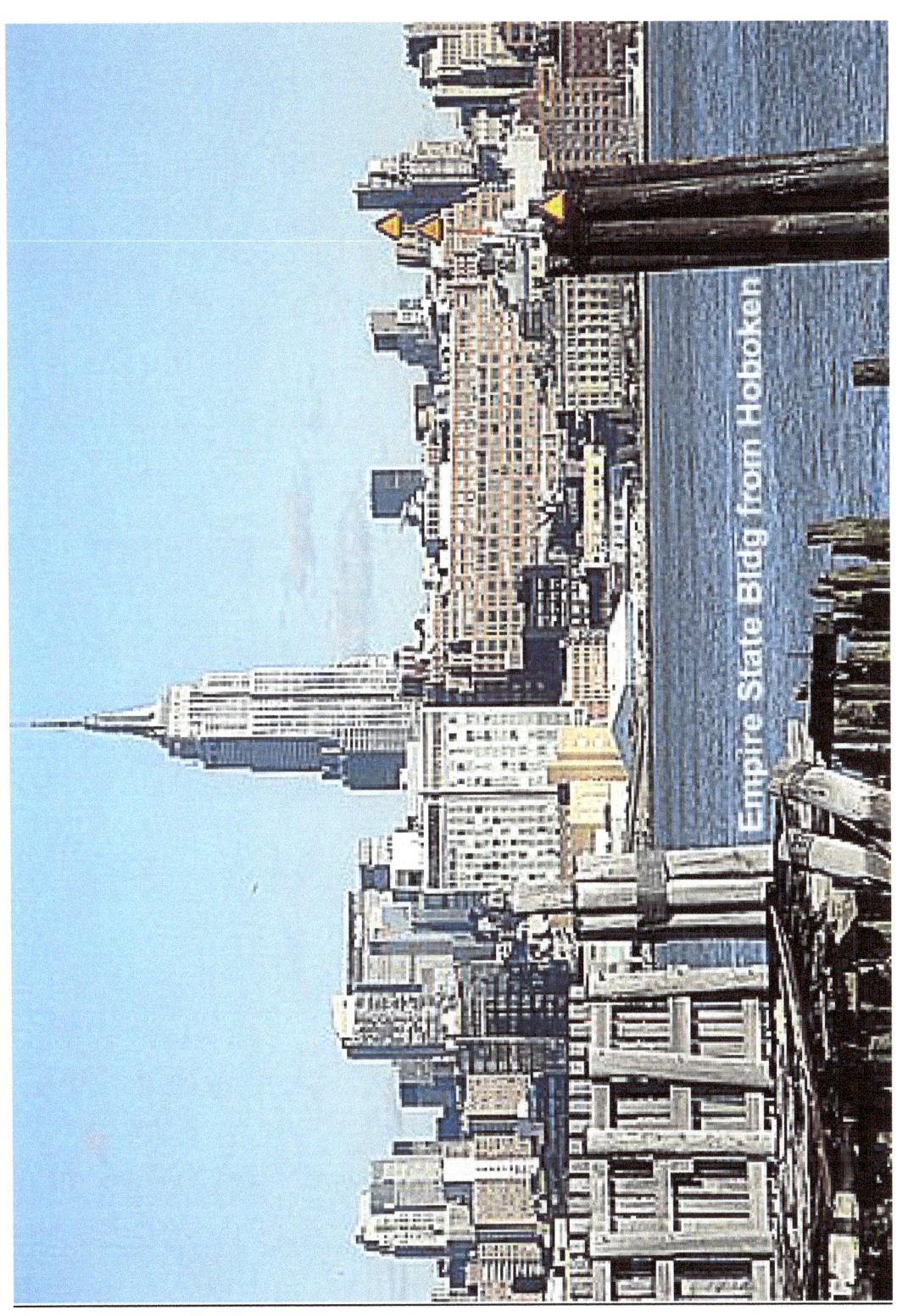

Empire State Bldg from Hoboken

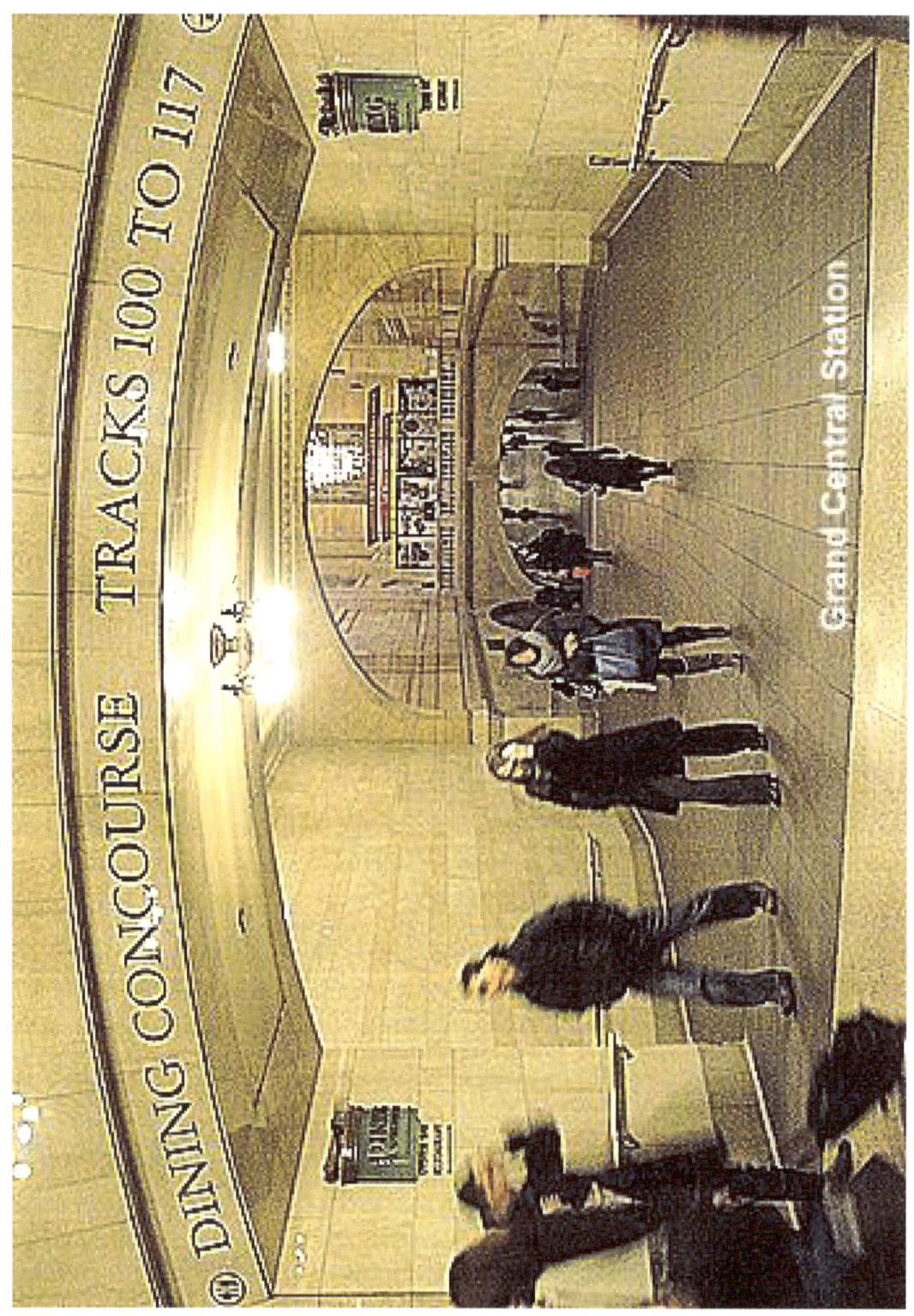

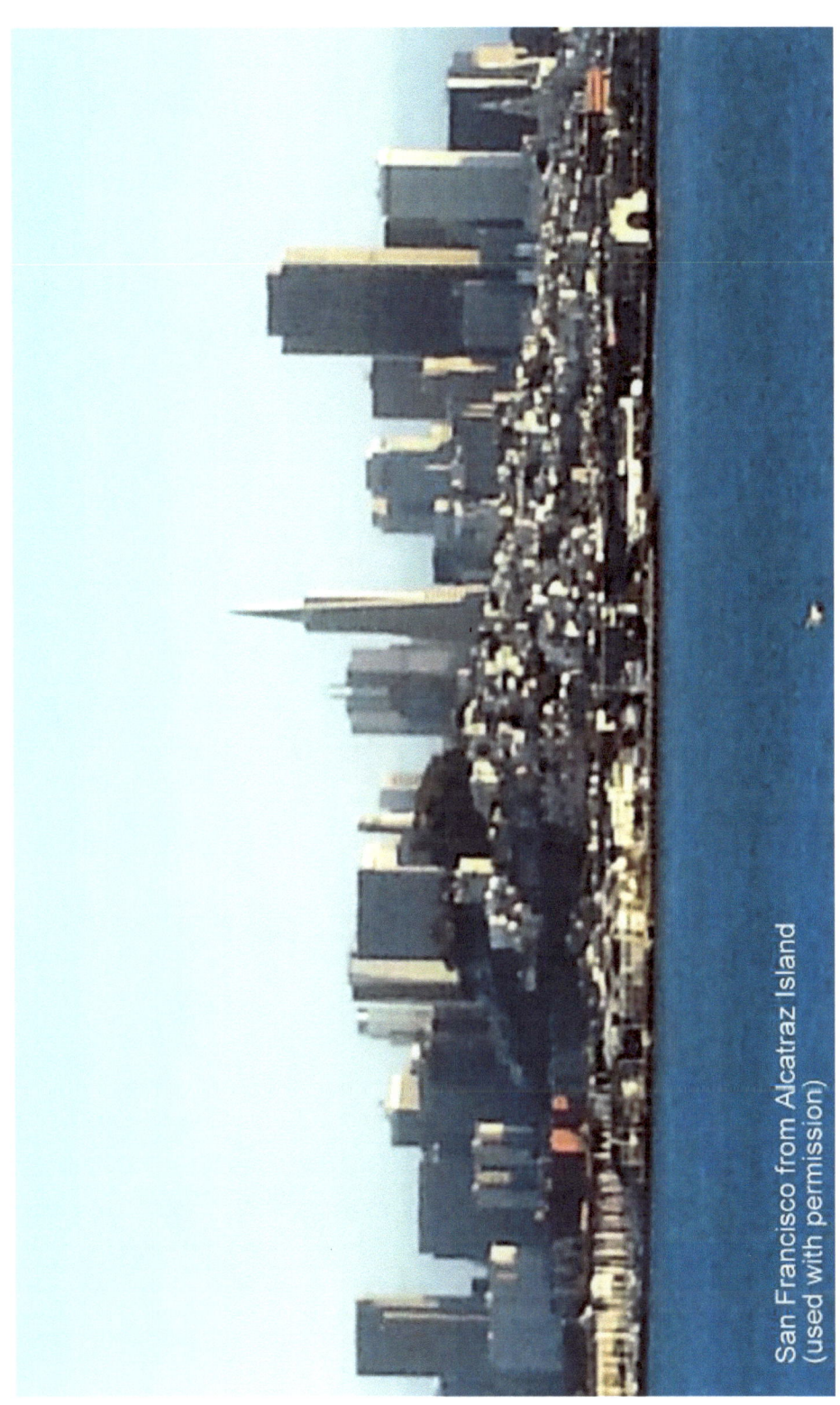

San Francisco from Alcatraz Island
(used with permission)

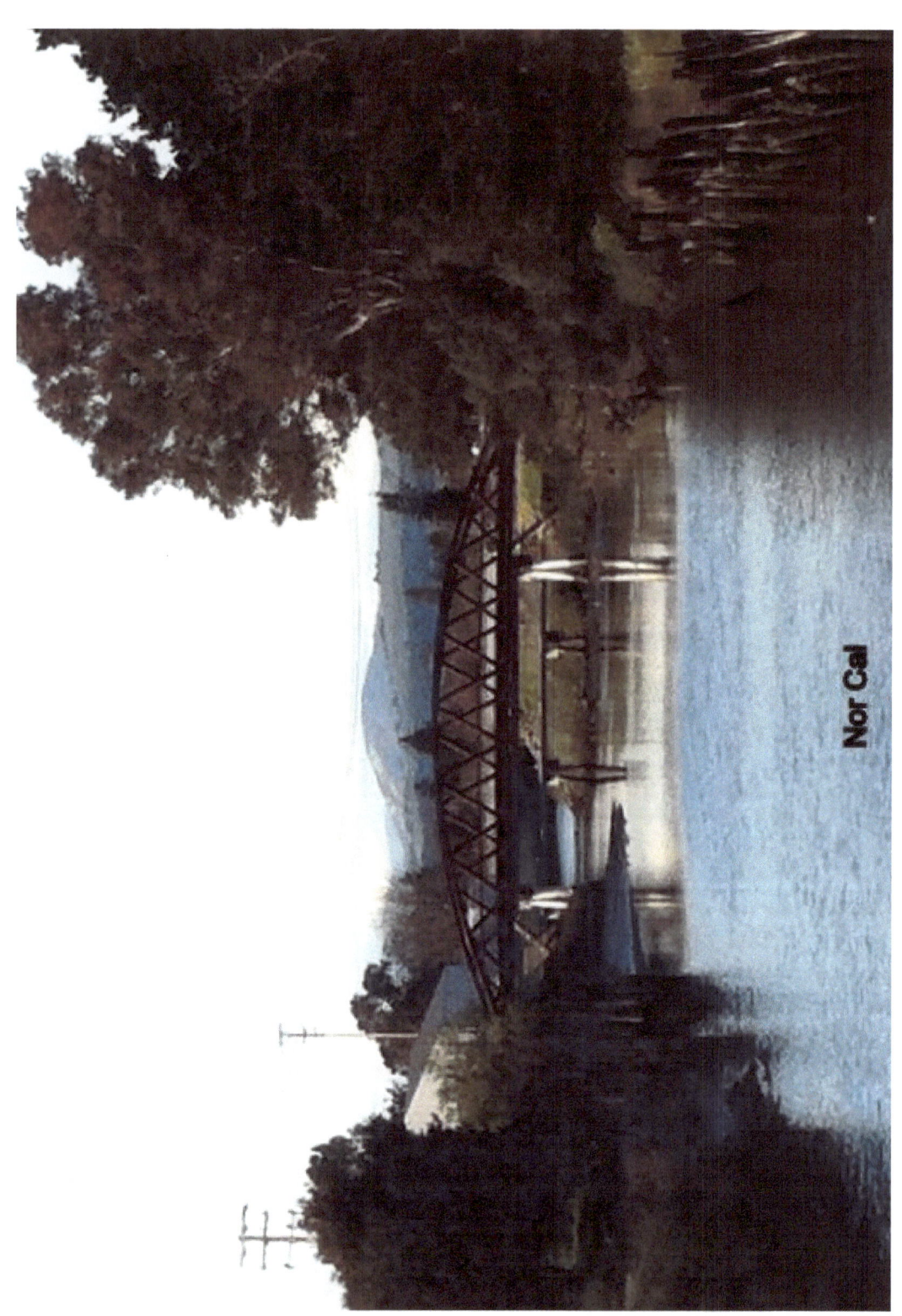

Nor Cal

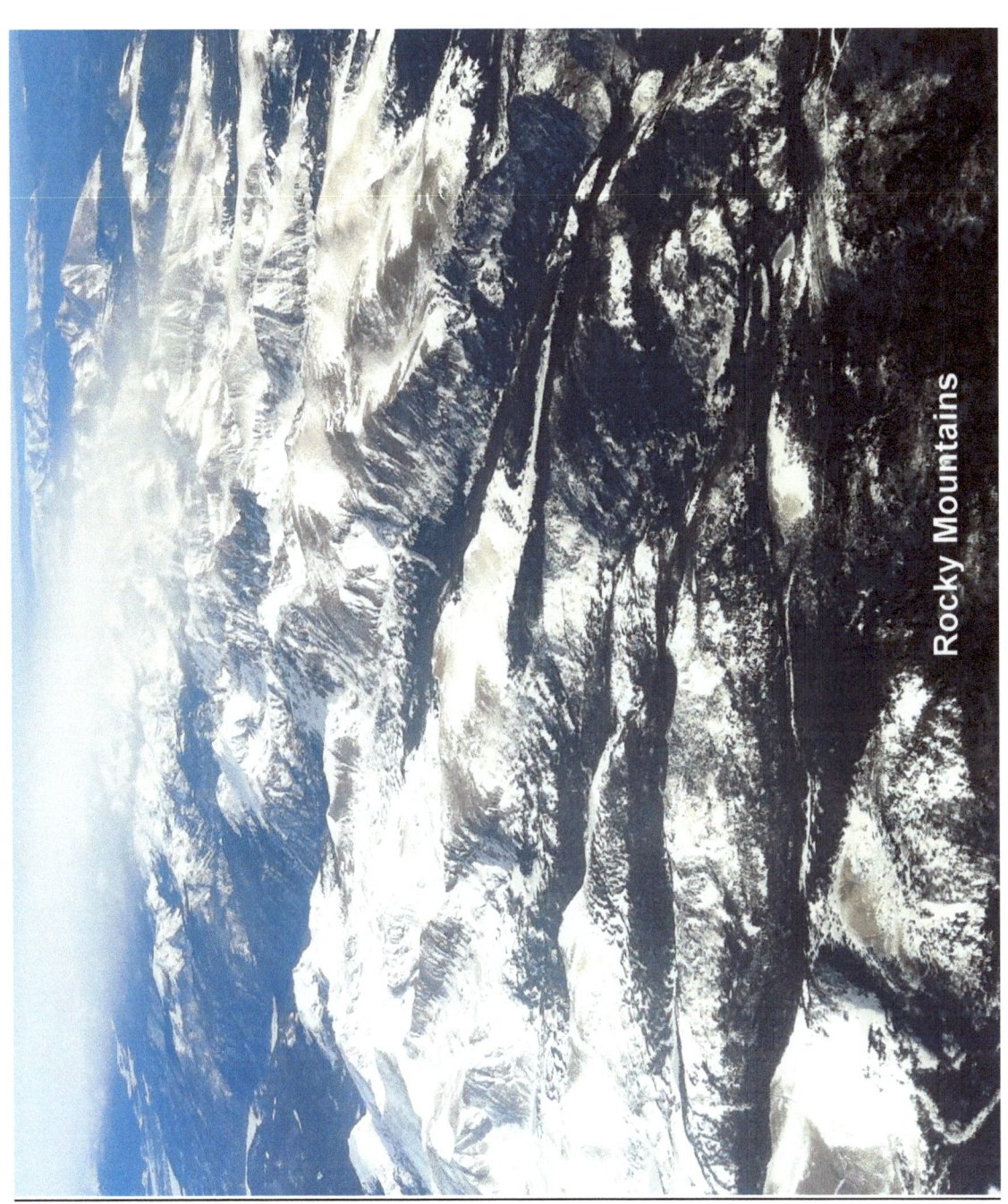

Rocky Mountains

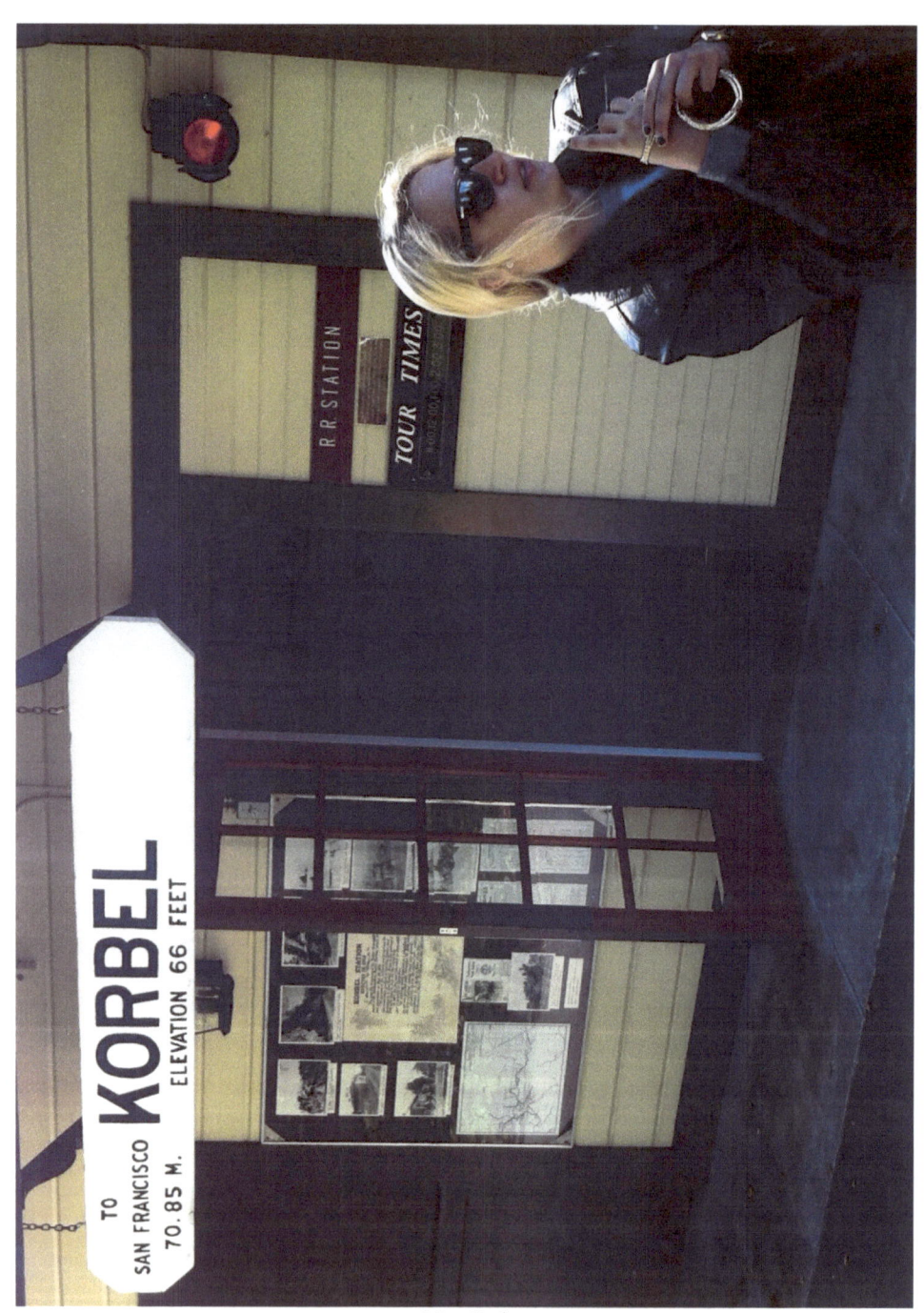

NorCal

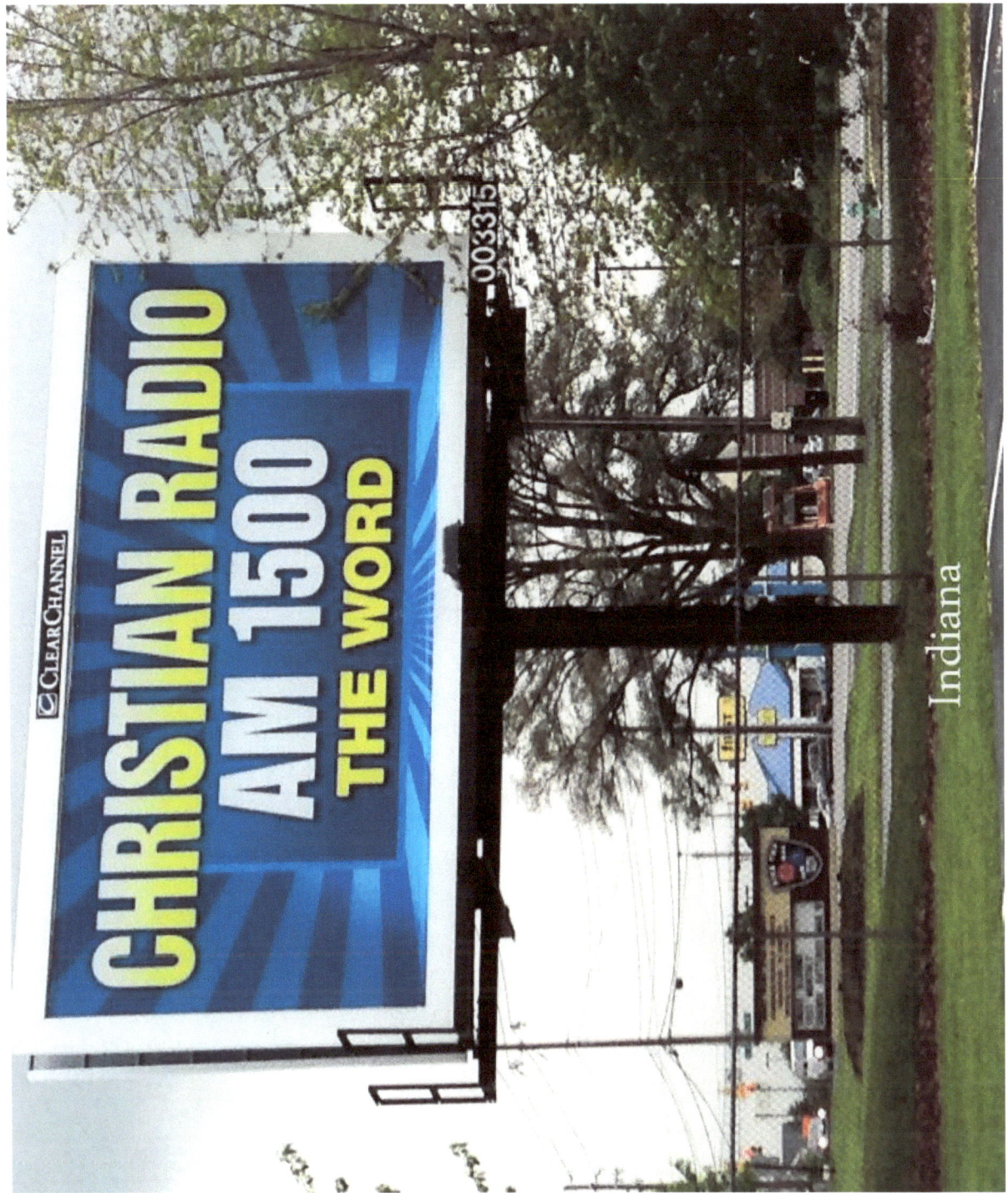

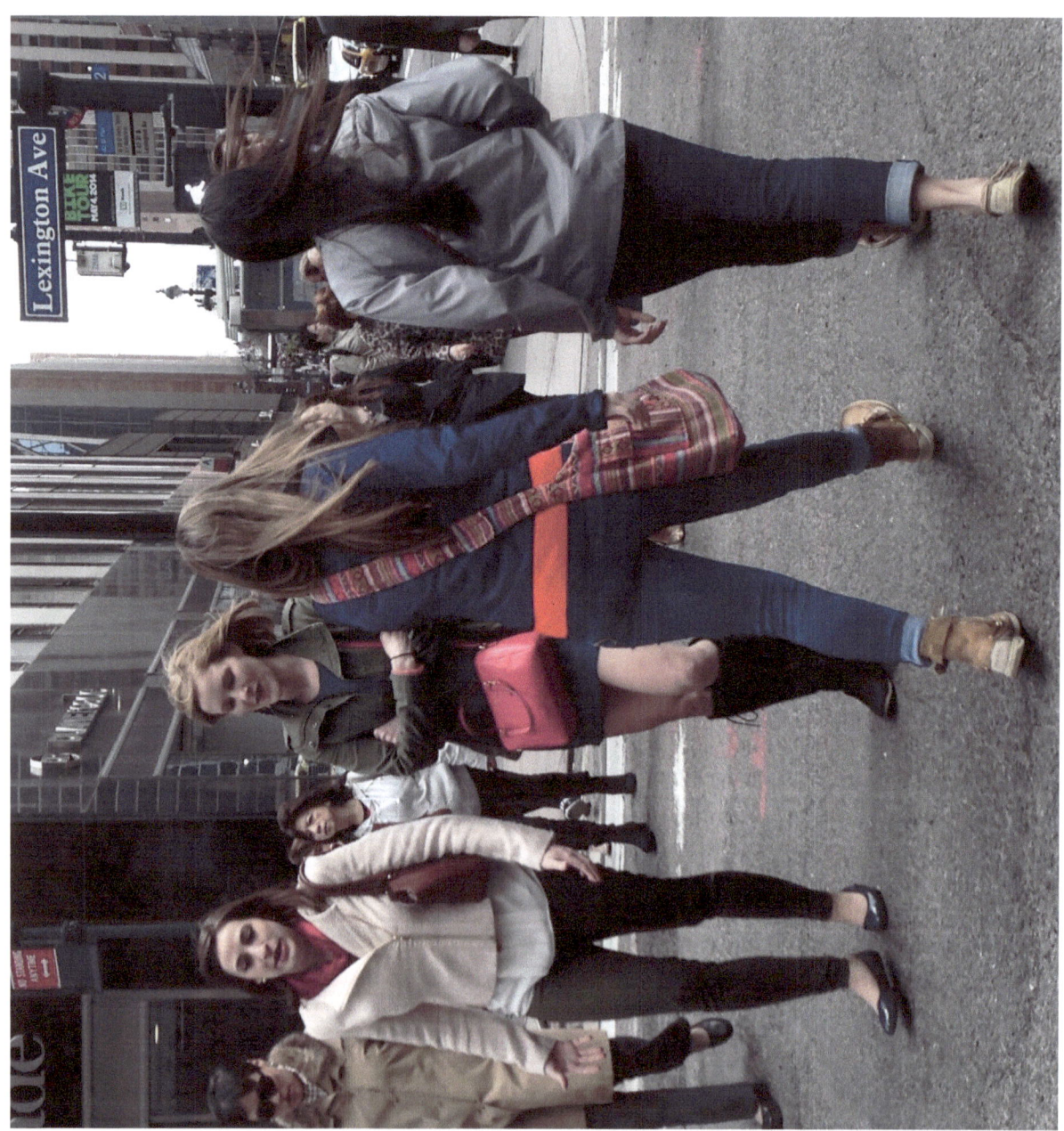

New York City

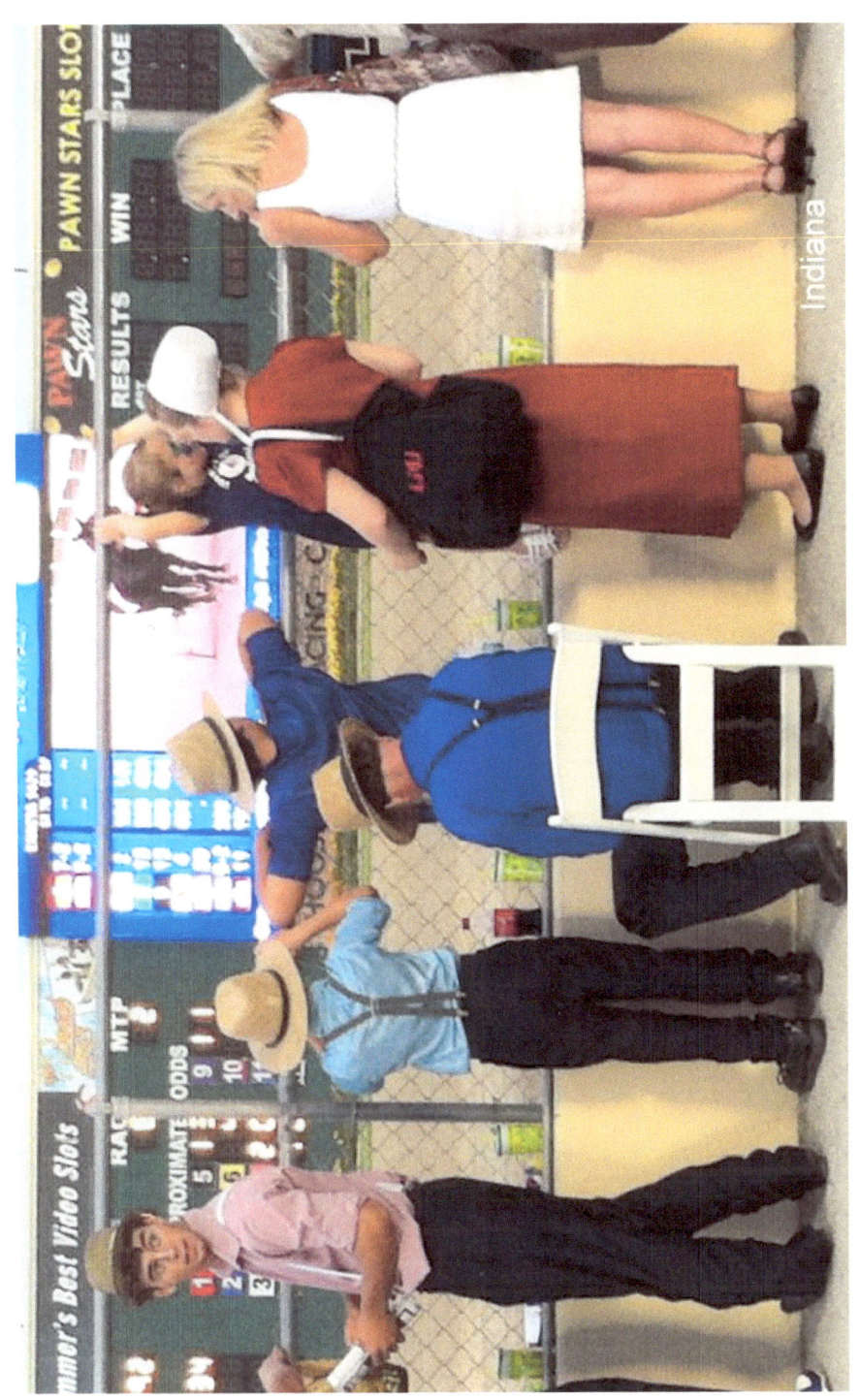

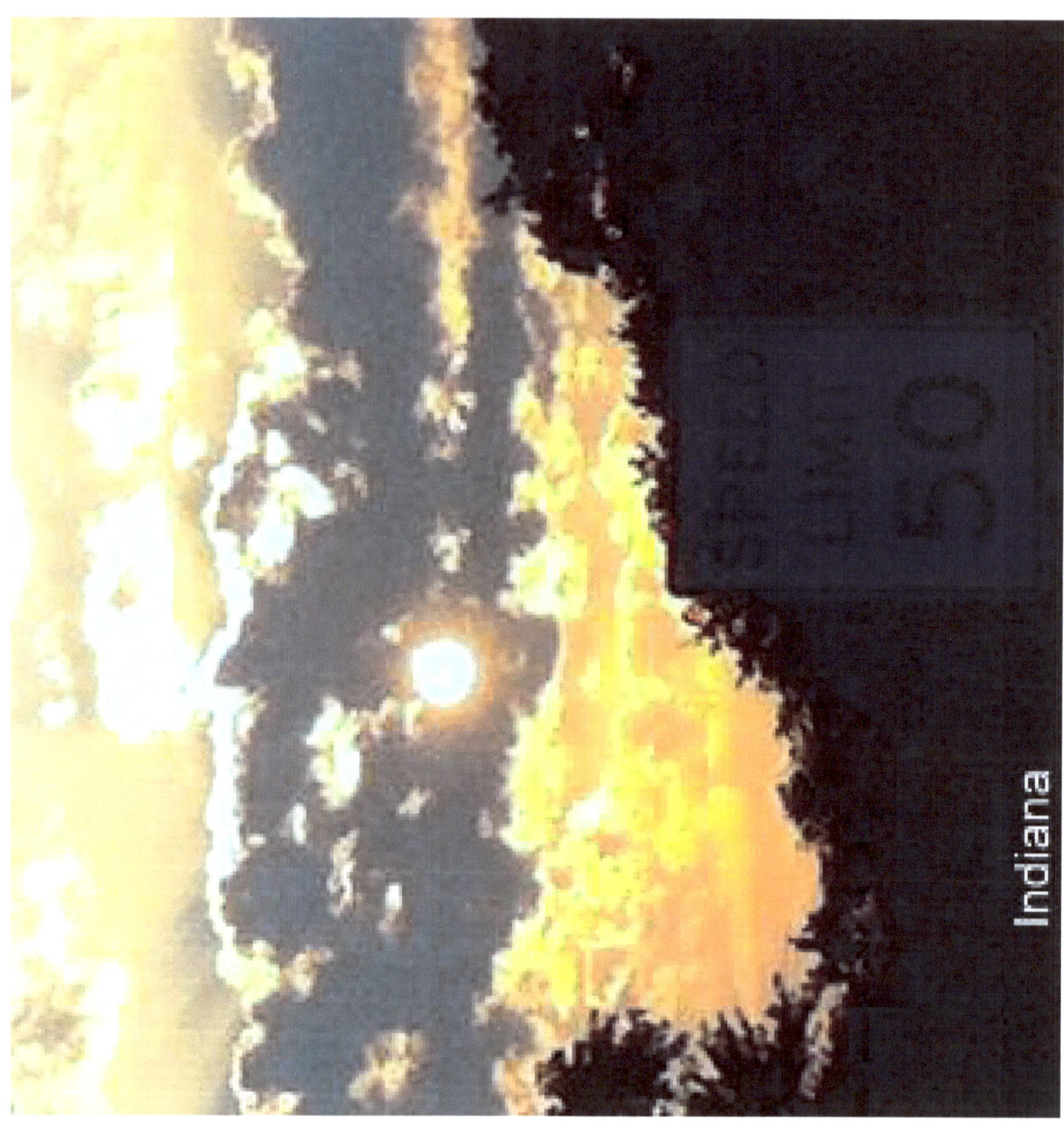

Indiana

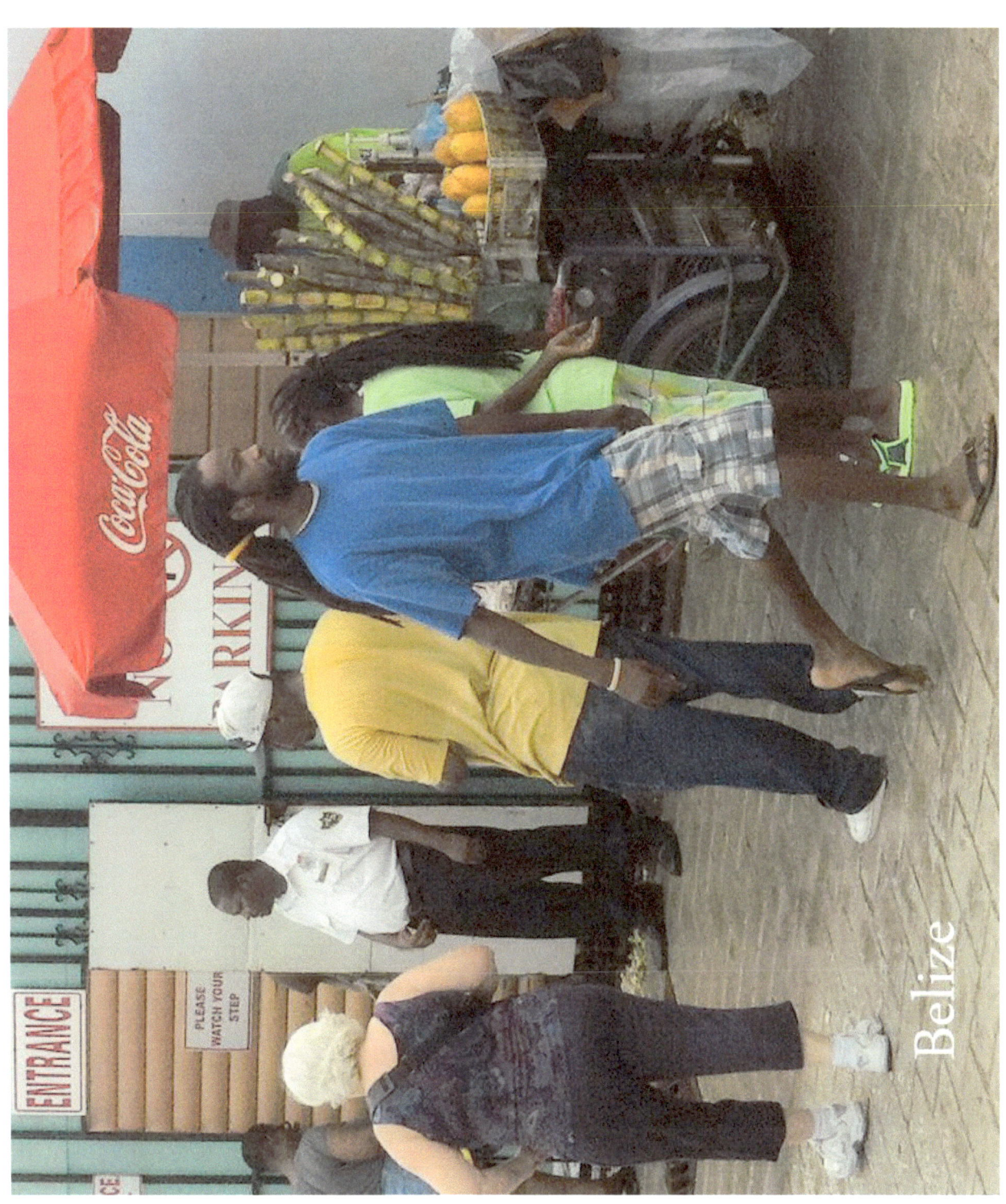

Belize

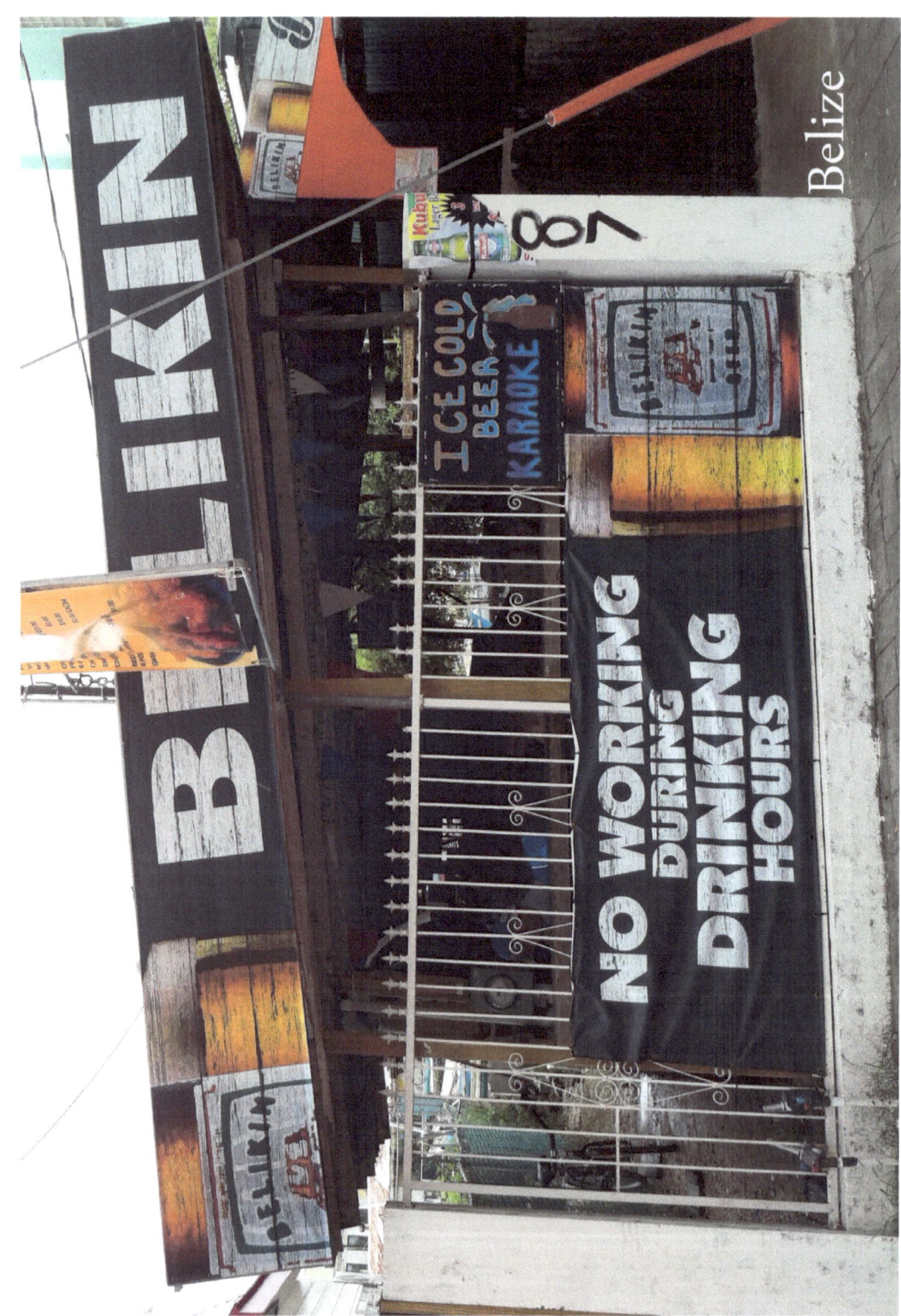

Belize

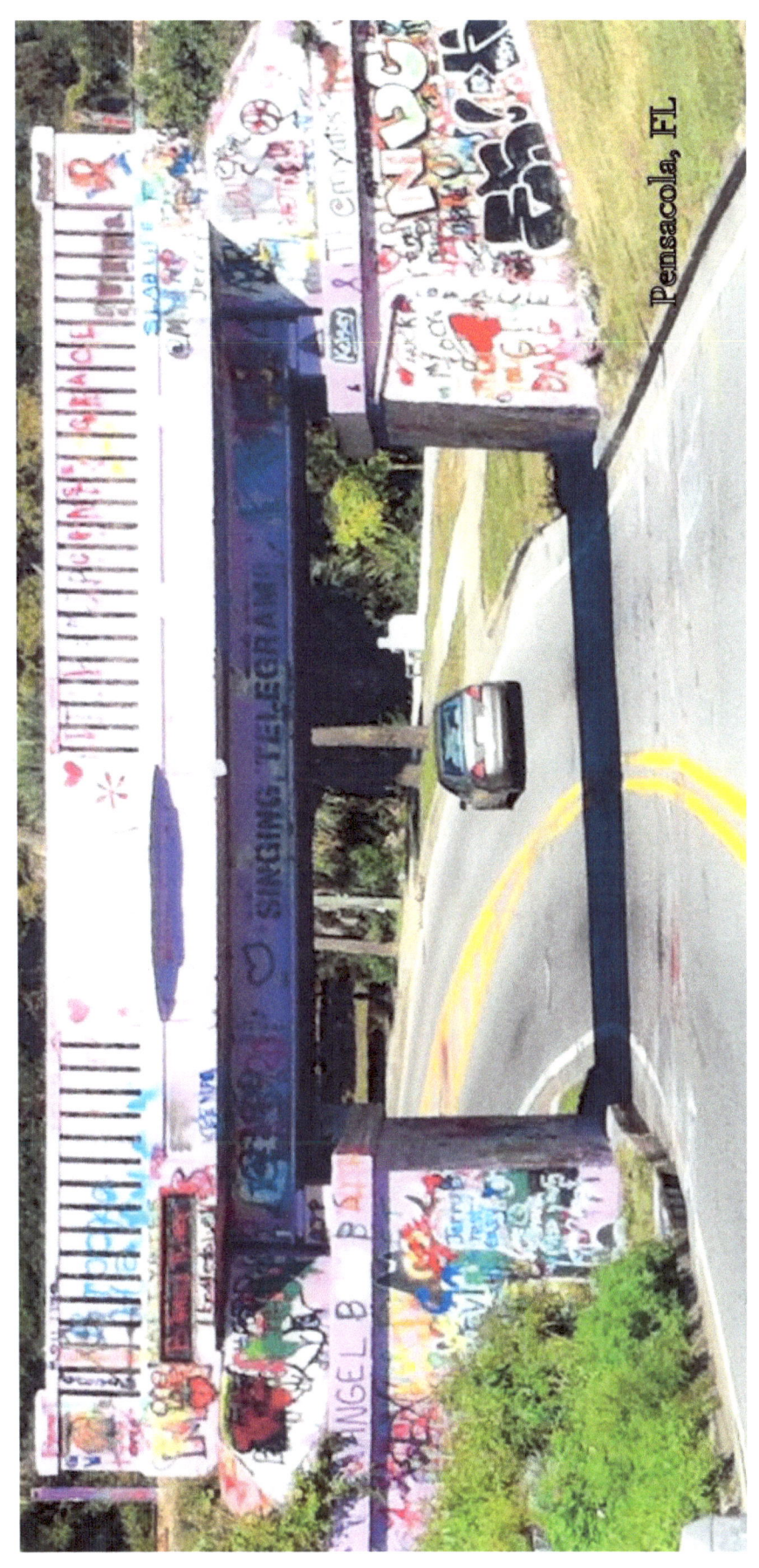

Pensacola, FL

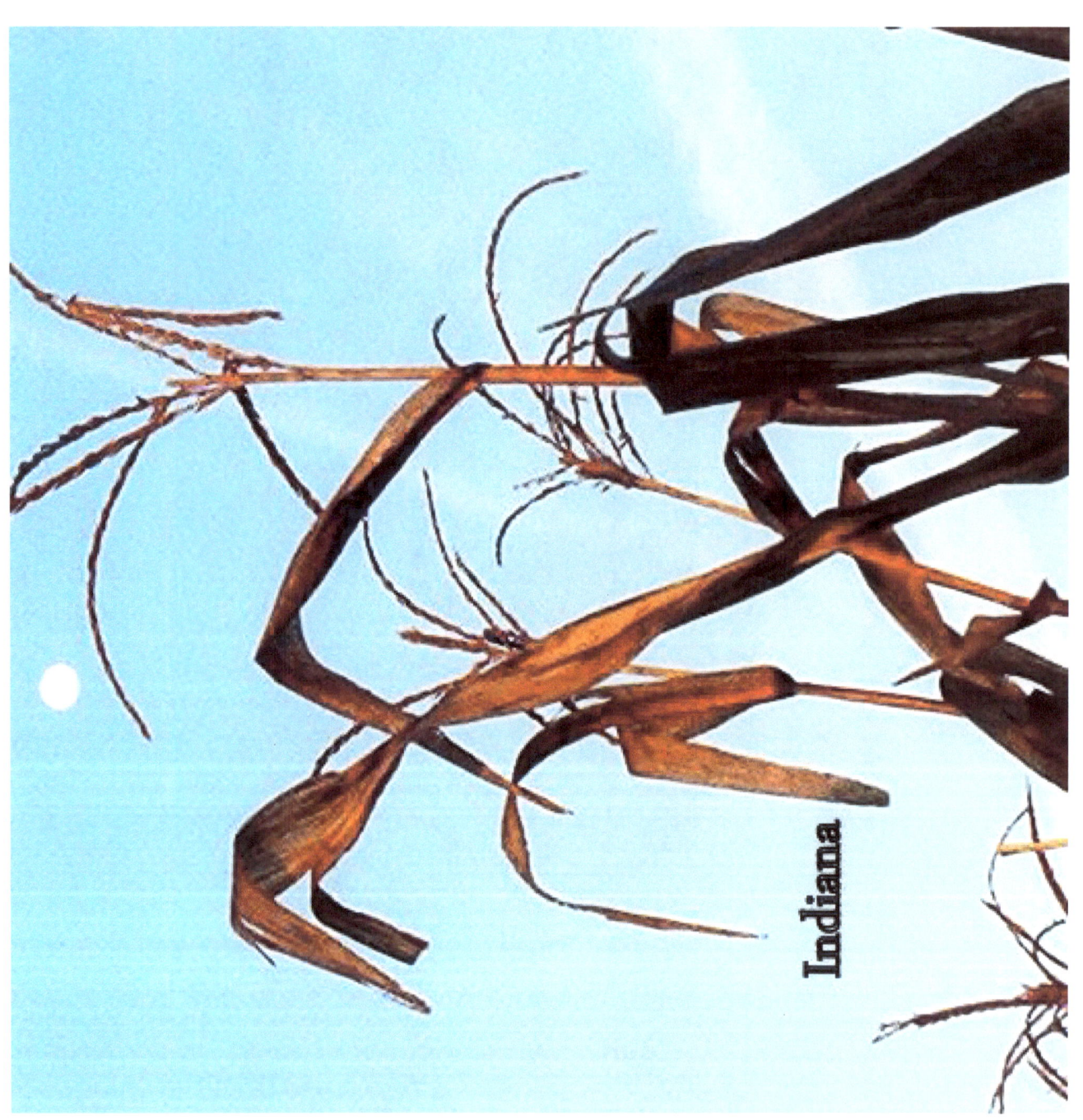

Indiana

SEEK FIRST THE KINGDOM OF GOD

BAPTIST CHURCH

Indiana

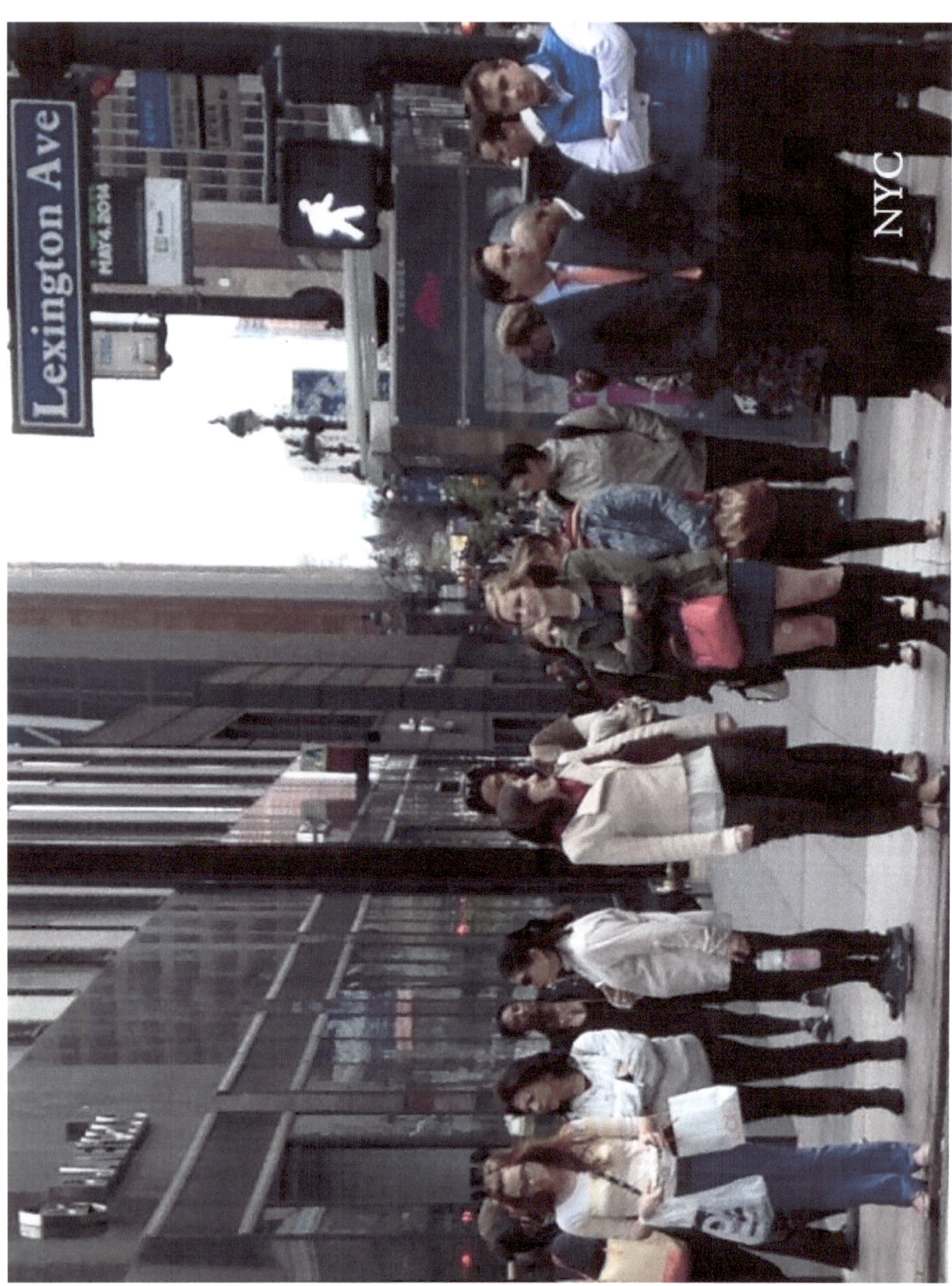

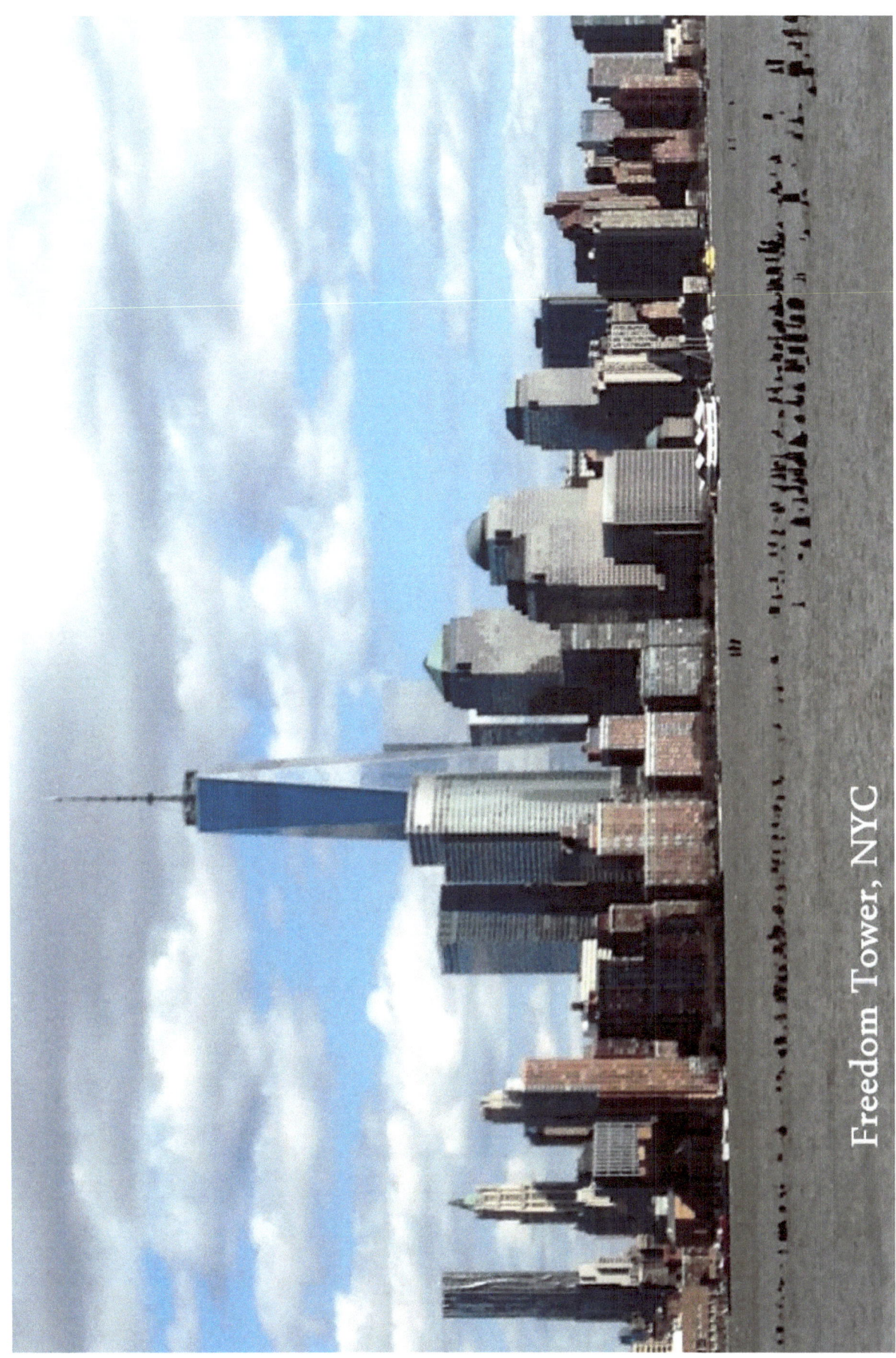

Freedom Tower, NYC

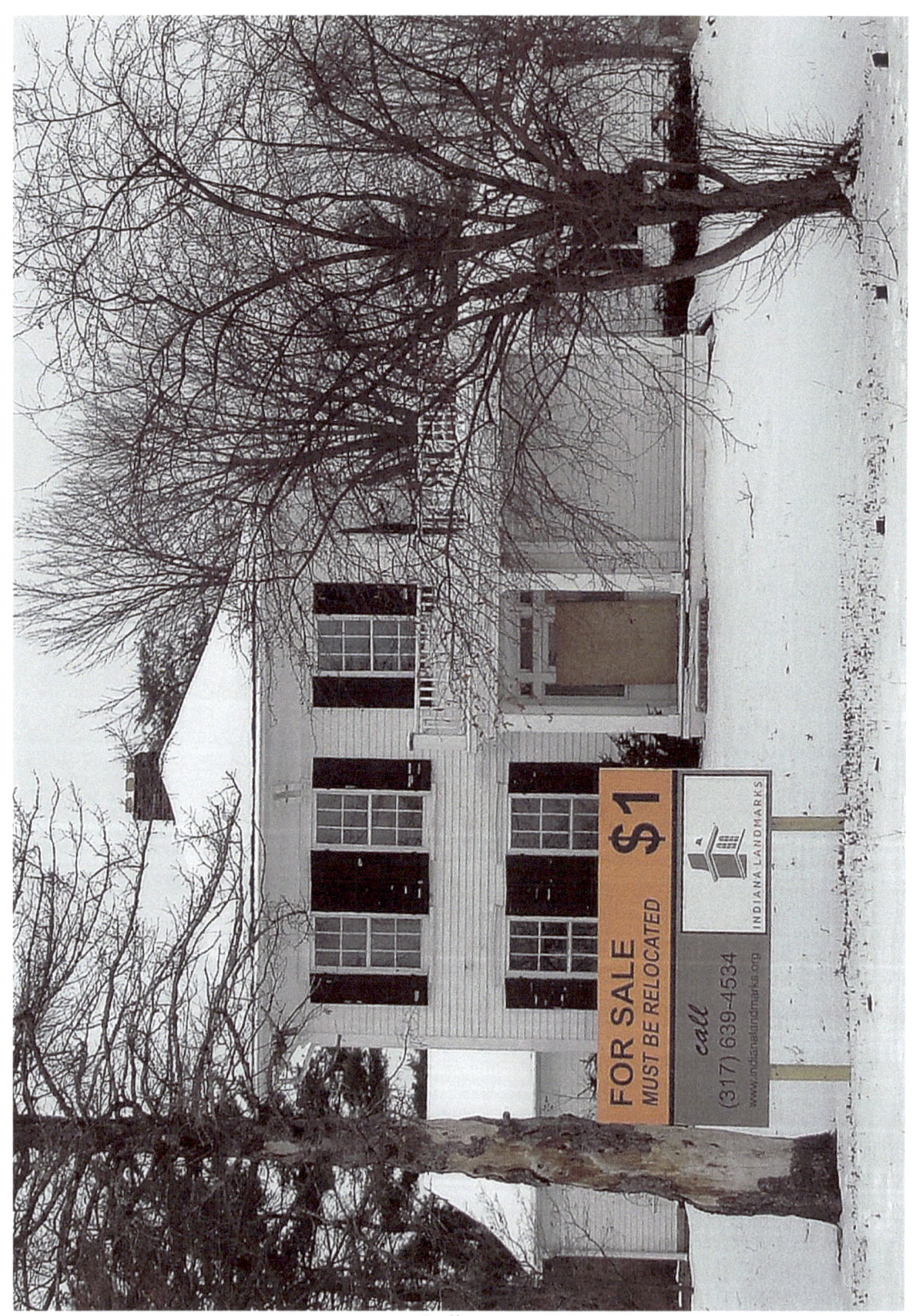

Indiana

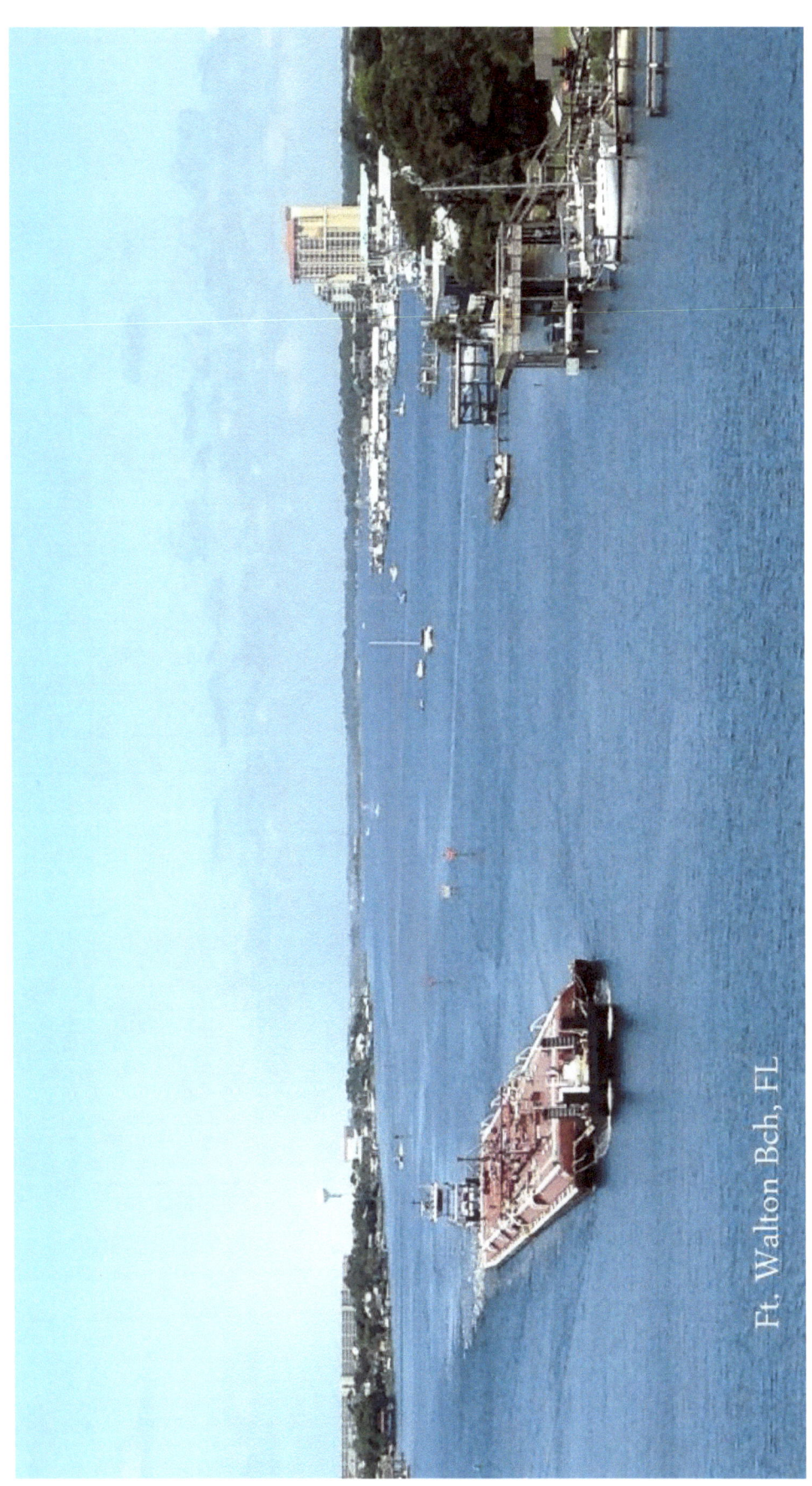

Ft. Walton Bch, FL

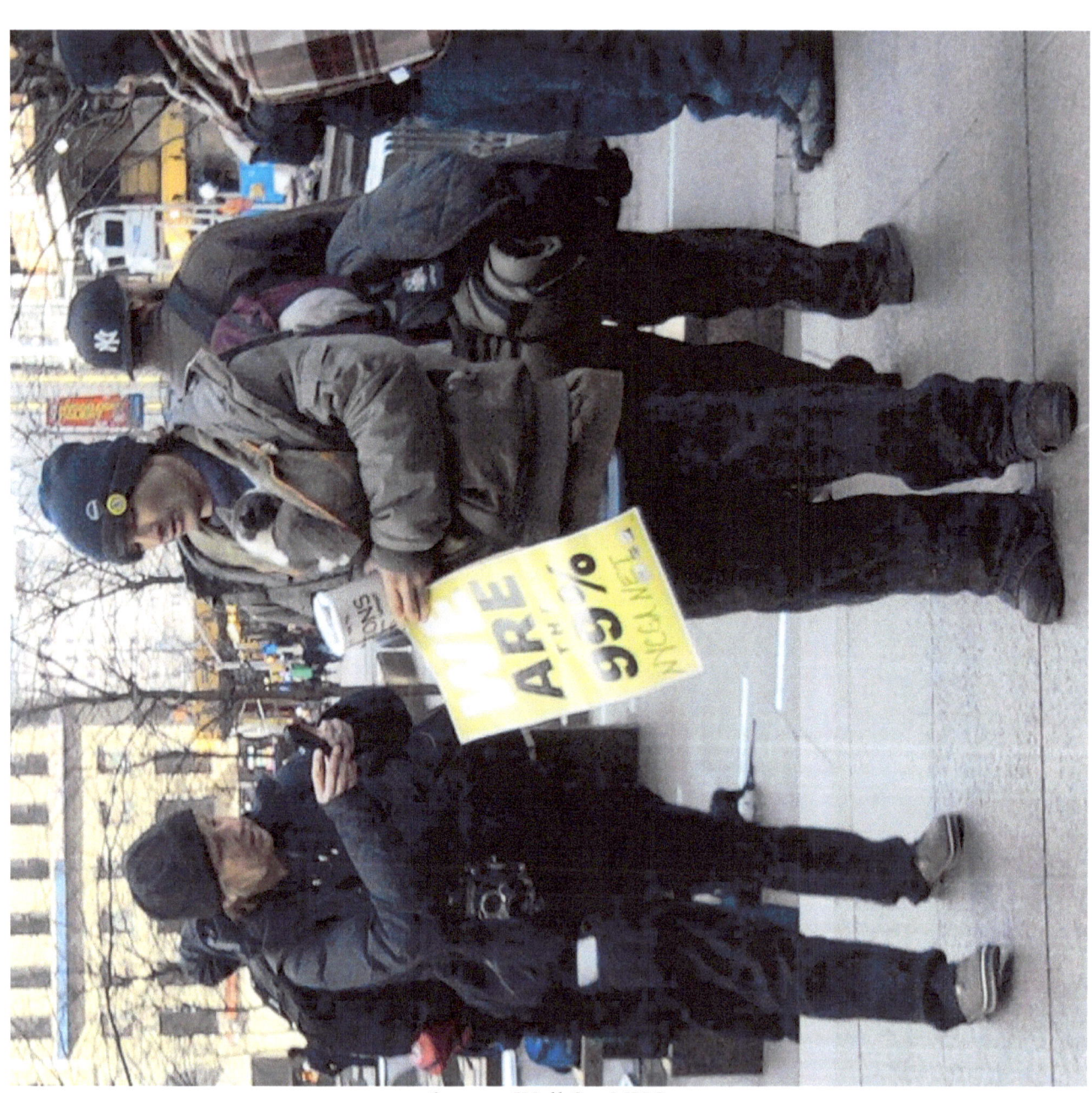

Occupy Wall St., NYC

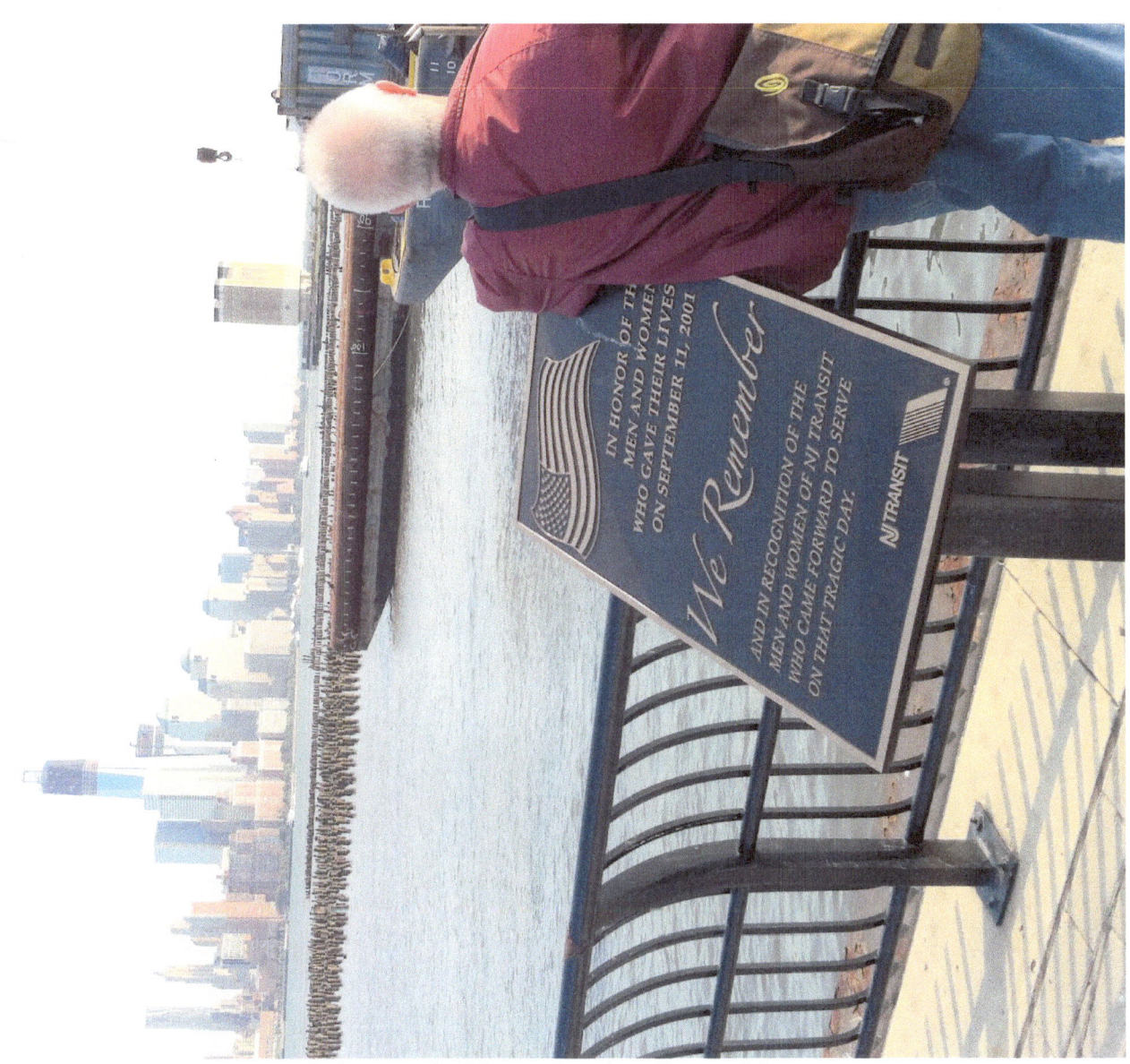

Hoboken, NJ looking at Freedom Tower rising

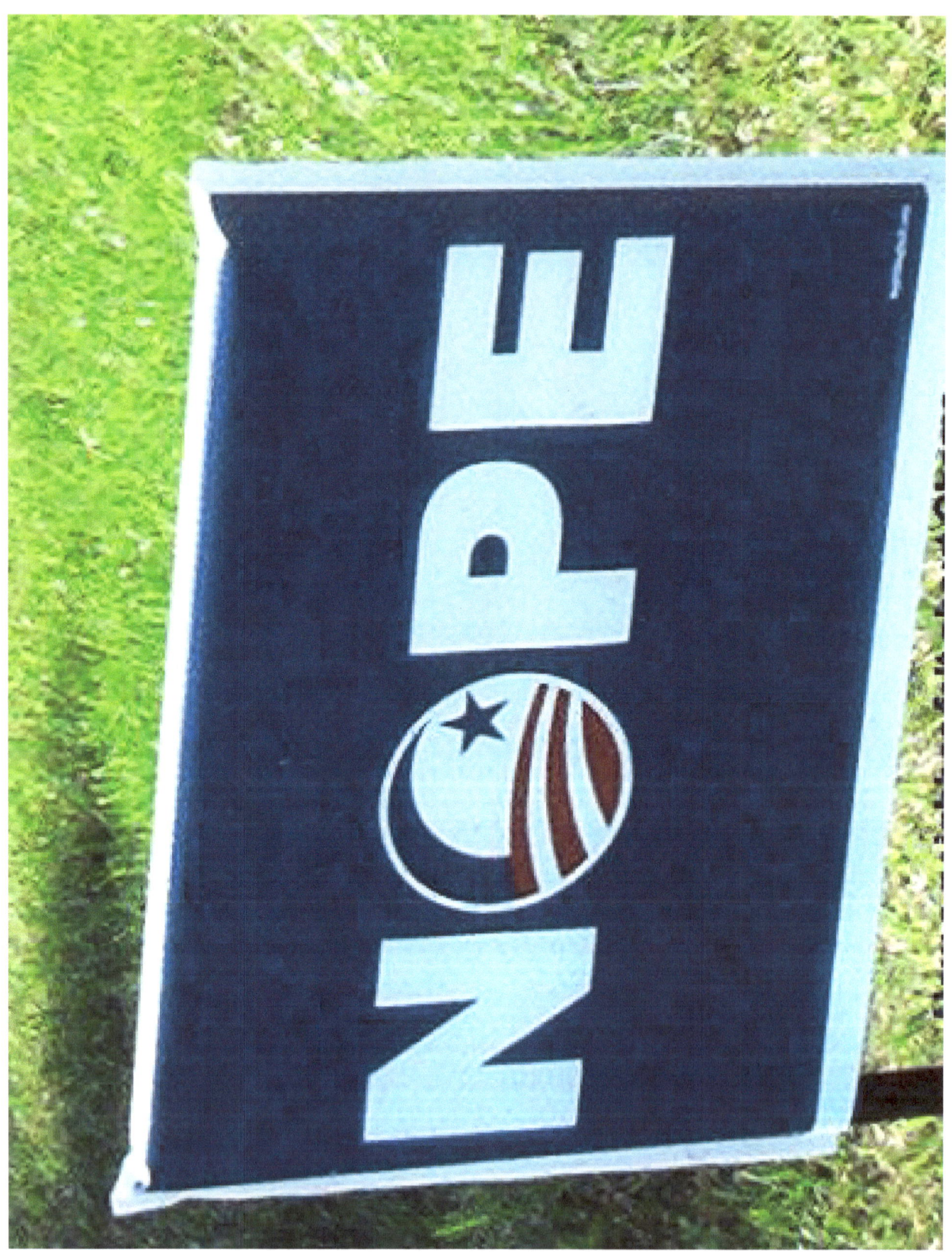

Indiana

www.ingramcontent.com/pod-product-compliance
Lightning Source LLC
Chambersburg PA
CBHW050712180526
45159CB00003B/1006
* 9 7 8 0 9 6 6 5 5 9 8 6 6 *